AMERICAN STUDIES – A MONOGRAPH SERIES
Volume 136

Edited on behalf
of the German Association
for American Studies by
REINHARD R. DOERRIES
GERHARD HOFFMANN
ALFRED HORNUNG

Transcultural Localisms

Responding to Ethnicity in a Globalized World

Edited by
YIORGOS KALOGERAS
ELEFTHERIA ARAPOGLOU
LINDA MANNEY

Universitätsverlag
WINTER
Heidelberg

Bibliografische Information Der Deutschen Bibliothek

Die Deutsche Bibliothek verzeichnet diese Publikation
in der Deutschen Nationalbibliografie;
detaillierte bibliografische Daten sind im Internet
über *http://dnb.ddb.de* abrufbar.

ISBN 3-8253-5226-9

© 2006 Universitätsverlag Winter GmbH Heidelberg
Imprimé en Allemagne · Printed in Germany
Druck: Memminger MedienCentrum, 87700 Memmingen

Gedruckt auf umweltfreundlichem, chlorfrei gebleichtem
und alterungsbeständigem Papier

Den Verlag erreichen Sie im Internet unter:
www.winter-verlag-hd.de

Table of Contents

III Auto-ethnography and Self-invention

IV Cultural Incommensurability and Hybridity

V The Challenges of Ethnic Incorporation

YIORGOS KALOGERAS, ELEFTHERIA ARAPOGLOU, LINDA MANNEY

Introduction

The present volume collects sixteen papers originally presented at the 4th MESEA conference sponsored and organized by the Department of American Literature and Culture, Aristotle University in Thessaloniki, Greece, in May 2004. The original title of the conference was "Ethnic Communities in Democratic Societies." The title was decided upon to emphasize MESEA's growing preoccupation with interdisciplinary studies; at the same time, however, it foregrounded the association's commitment not only to text, but also to context. MESEA's call for papers brought together approximately one hundred and thirty impressive presentations, all of which covered issues with a global relevance. Furthermore, the conference participants made reality the MESEA founders' original wish: namely, that the last letter of the association's acronym would refer to the Americas, Africa, as well as Asia. Ultimately, all of these continents were represented at the Thessaloniki conference.

Submissions for a collection of essays that would represent the spirit of the conference as well as MESEA's growing commitment to academic excellence were enthusiastic and generous. Subsequently, the editors felt responsible to create a scholarly volume that would not only reflect the essence of the conference's original title, but also venture into the socio-political and literary realities of the twenty-first century. Hence, our choice of a different title for the volume: "Transcultural Localisms." This alternative title occurred to the editors because, in collecting and editing the papers, Fredric Barth's pace-setting idea of the relevance of the boundary in discussions of ethnicity surfaced as a recurring motif among all contributions. Indeed, even if we accept that ethnicity and locality are especially beleaguered nowadays, this does not imply a cosmos in which all boundaries have dissolved. In today's increasingly globalized world, the cultural, economic and political hegemony of the West provides the veneer of common referents for diverse communities around the globe. At the same time, however, and notwithstanding globalization, boundaries remain distinct, or are constantly redrawn so that we can still talk vociferously of Greek, Jewish, Brazilian, Cambodian, or Indonesian ethnicities, albeit in a globalized world. Ultimately, as Saskia Sassen admits, globalization is a "contradictory space," characterized as it is by contestation, internal differentiation, and continuous border crossings (143).

In the twenty-first century, flows of culture, capital, and labor do not manage to curb the resurgence of local resistances that resist global dynamics. This is because today's global culture cannot integrate "everything," thus it remains a terrain open to contestation so that its edges are constantly in flux. If anything, these local resistances appropriate elements they find useful in that same global culture they are forced to accept, and, as a result, expedite their own projects of cultural, economic and political survival. Considering this realization, the word "localism" in the title does not allude to the established connotations of the word-that of the parochial, the provincial, the isolated. Rather, "localism" should be considered in conjunction with the adjective "transcultural," because, although it signifies the distinct, it also draws its distinction and asserts its difference in the context of a globalized world.

The essays collected in this volume approach critically the term "transcultural localism" as defined in the previous paragraph. In other words, they may foreground its liberating potential, but they also underline the problems it might engender. As the perceptive reader will understand, these problems are the result of reconfiguring the cross-fertilization of the local by the global, by introducing the local as part of the mainstream. More explicitly, the local figures both as acceptable and as accepted, an indispensable part of the multicultural nature of the global. Furthermore, the local becomes simply an exotic aspect of the global, soon to be sanitized of its uncompromising elements. Far from suggesting a depoliticization of the local, the essays collected in this volume emphasize the potential of the local to challenge-rather than to be appropriated by-a discourse that caters to the interests of institutional control.

The volume in hand is divided into five sections. The first one entitled "Anti-essentialist Configurations" begins with an essay on Maryse Condé. Pin-chia Feng maintains that Maryse Condé's Afro-Caribbean novels differ from conventional Third World allegorizations of the local in that their plots move towards a vision of "transcendental cosmopolitanism." This is a vision that significantly reconfigures the politics of home for the nomadic Afro-Caribbean peoples. More particularly, in The Last of the African Kings Condé deploys a meta-fictional perspective that re-examines the construction and writing of family romance. According to Feng, in this novel, Condé critically reviews what constitutes "family" and "home" in a post-colonial condition.

This anti-essentialist and relational reconfiguration is the focus of **Gary Okihiro's** article. Okihiro criticizes the concept of an Atlantic culture with its bias of valorizing its constituent parts; that is, the Blacks and the Whites. Such Eurocentric theorizations, although they zero in on racism and hybridity, exclude, nevertheless, Native Americans and Asians, while they embed the Africans within a European modernity. Okihiro foregrounds the issue of a Pacific Civilization that, like its Atlantic counterpart, has been and still is a system of flows of capital, labor, and culture that has produced transnational and hybrid identities and legitimized their counterclaims for homogeneity, nationalism, and racial purity.

On her part, **Elke Sturm Trigonakis** articulates her personal version of anti-essentialism, by grounding her discussion on Goethe's idea of *Weltliteratur* and re-evaluating it. Goethe's proposition, although Eurocentric in its conception, suggests a turning away from national canons and nationalisms and argues for a more inclusive, albeit infra-European, new approach to literary production. Stürm analyzes the contemporary relevance such a term has acquired and its unexpected extensions within a post-colonial and post-modern era. More specifically, she focuses on the poetry of the Chicano writer Juan Felipe Herrera and the Spanish German poet José F. A. Oliver, while the parameters she proposes suggest a literature that functions as a continuous performance of alterity. Furthermore, Stürm maintains that this present-day attempt at a world literature lays claims to a new radical poetic and transcultural subjectivity.

The second section is entitled "Western Political Unilateralism and Local Literary Responses." In it, **Chris LaLonde** discusses Blaesser's poetry, his own commentary on it, as well as Gerald Vizenor's and N. Scott Momaday's occasional poetic and political statements contrapuntally in a creative inter-text. According to LaLonde, Kimberly Blaesser produces a poetry that valorizes N. Scott Momaday's idea that words warrant survival-both individual and collective. LaLonde contends that the focus of Blaesser's poetry on place and displacement constitutes a creative answer and a critical intervention to U.S.A. politics that have misrepresented and overdetermined the existence and gradual extermination of Native American tribes.

The question of how language reflects institutional power is taken up by **Linda Manney**. Manney points out how everyday language can construct selfhood and identity. Critical feminists, educators, and linguists explain that language texts serve as vehicles for expressing structures of power and ideology and implicitly inform all levels of linguistic interaction. In her argument, she foregrounds the institutional basis of popular discourse which misrepresents the politically and socially disempowered. Concluding, Manney demonstrates how groups use language to resist and transform unjust representations of themselves, which are externally imposed by members of the power elite.

Kaeko Mochizuki's paper focuses on the work of Marguerite Duras, Masuji Ibuse, and Leslie Marmon Silko. Mochizuki's chosen texts allow us to hear the voices of the disempowered, those who do not face a local but a global disaster. In her unrelentingly politicized argument, Mochizuki maintains that the three authors bring together the local and the global. In other words, they demonstrate the familiar contours and local relevance of what appears to be happening "elsewhere." More particularly, Mochizuki argues convincingly that, in the nuclear age, obsolete nationalism and arrogant unilateralism, approving of and even producing wars, neither protect "home" nor control "the Other," but bring about the simultaneous destruction of both.

John Purdy provides further evidence on how the disempowered raise their voice against unjust representations. He begins by showing how the legal establishment of the border between Canada and the U.S.A. has complicated the relations between the two nation-states, but more importantly between these states and the Native Americans of the area. With time, the latter perceived this area as a field where they could challenge dominant forms and laws that circumscribed them within parameters familiar to the nation state. The indigenous response to this realization eventually led to a reversal: Native American writers used the border imaginatively as a correlative for the empowerment of indigenous nationhood and identity.

The third section is on "Auto-ethnography and Self-Invention." In it, **Mita Banerjee** critiques Denise Chong's work as that of an ethnic subject who employed auto-ethnography to confirm the allegations of the mainstream against the community out of which she (Denise Chong) came. Chong's work focuses on the fact that, early in the twentieth century, the San Francisco Chinese community had been accused of being a health menace to the mainstream. However, and employing the form of auto-ethnography, Chong internalizes the accusation and insists on a process which traces the "whitening" of her community from a health menace to model minority over the course of two generations. Inadvertently, Chong describes the rise of her family, but essentially of herself, from disempowered medicalized subjects to the position of power-brokers within Anglophone Canada, but without challenging the misrepresentations of the Chinese community by the power elite.

Sophia Emmanouilidou turns to a different type of self-invention: that of the self-conscious codification of popular mythology which goes beyond a useless "nativism" and becomes a political statement. According to the scholar, Rudolfo Anaya, the most popularly recognized Chicano writer of his generation, employs the myth of La Llorona in order to call into being a Chicano collective unconscious. Emmanouilidou illustrates how Anaya posits himself in the role of a writer who asserts his position as a social agent in order to expedite a collective mobilization.

In focusing her attention on self-invention, **Sidonie Smith** turns to a very popular children's book, *Zlata's Diary*, in order to analyze narratives of ethnic suffering and the violation of human rights. Smith draws our attention to the constructed nature of such narratives and their dependence on an interethnic appeal, most obviously in this case on *The Diary of Anne Frank*. For Smith, it is important to be aware, as middle-class readers in the West, of the dangers of "flattening history through an appeal to empathetic, de-politicized sentimentality." On another level, she also maintains that such narratives call into definition a dispersed ethnic audience, in the text before us-that of Bosnian Croat refugees-and she argues that *Zlata's Diary* could become "a story of the type that ethnic nationalism is both founded and sustained."

The fourth section entitled "Cultural Incommensurability and Hybridity" begins with **Pirjo Ahokas'** essay on Bharati Mukherjee and Monica Ali. Ahokas' discussion of Mukherjee's *Desirable Daughters* (2002) and Ali's *Brick Lane* (2003) probes into the processes through which transnational, post-modern female identities are constructed and enacted. Framing her essay within the recent theories of transnational feminism and performativity, Ahokas illustrates the ways in which Mukherjee's and Ali's female protagonists employ cultural hybridity to challenge gender as well as racial oppression. The author argues that the female transnational identities enacted in Mukherjee's and Ali's novels undermine the monolithic binary of "home" and "abroad" and prove conducive to the emergence of liberating post-modern subjectivities, characterized by fluidity, multiplicity, and heterogeneity.

The subject of the emergence of alternative subject positions within a global context is also raised by **Anjoom Mukadam** and **Sharmina Mawani**. The two authors present their current research into the identification processes of two contemporary groups of Nizari Ismailis: one which resides in Toronto, and another which resides in London. Mukadam and Mawani agree with Ahokas that, in today's multicultural societies, the process of self-definition is ongoing and associated with cultural hybridization-a historically open ended process shaped not only by diasporic experience, but also by the political mobilization of difference. Ultimately, the two authors conclude that second-generation Ismailis are nowadays asserting a positive ethnic identity by opting for an acculturative strategy which builds upon shared cultural preferences, while simultaneously maintaining integral aspects of Indian culture.

Similarly to Ahokas, and Mukadam / Mawani, **Ilana Xinos,** in her discussion of Christophorus Castanis' *The Greek Exile*, challenges the notion of a fixed identity construct and engages with recent critical approaches to identity politics and transnational identity formation. Xinos' reading is not only culturally but also historically informed. Therefore, the critic is careful not to build her discussion on the premise of hybridity, but to argue that Castanis' approach to identity construction does not suggest the formation of a new identity as hybridity does, but emphasizes similarities between nations. Xinos asserts that, by engaging in such an ambivalent process of identification, Castanis strives to create an imagined community between himself, Greece, and America-one that is not territorially grounded, but culturally induced and ideologically determined.

The three essays in the section entitled "The Challenges of Ethnic Incorporation" can all be considered case studies of public history, because they mainly focus on the ideological implications of historical analysis in view of the challenge of ethnic incorporation. On the one hand, **Stefano Luconi** outlines the history of the struggle on the part of Italian Americans for inclusion in affirmative action programs in the United States. Luconi reveals that such efforts have relied on a selective interpretation of the Italian-American experience as that of a minority group whose plight has been shaped by ethnic prejudice and discrimination on the part of the U.S. establishment. Luconi's criticism of those endeavors, while it acknowledges the development of Italian-American studies as an academic discipline, it, nonetheless, questions their validity, given the recent improvement in the social and economic standing of Italian Americans. Luconi concludes by stressing the serious socio-political implications of such a selective use of the past, and doubting whether such use can, in fact, contribute to the empowering of Italian Americans today.

On the other hand, the essay by **Stepanka Korytova-Magstadt** is a historical investigation into the struggle that led to independent Czechoslovakia. Magstadt contradicts historical accounts that credit Woodrow Wilson with the initiative behind uniting the Czechs and Slovaks. Instead, she offers an alternative interpretation, one that acknowledges the significant role played by the Czech and Slovak immigrants in the United States. The critic utilizes James Olson's study of the ethnic dimension in American history, only to expose its inadequacy to account for the role played by the Czech and Slovak elite in the development of a national conscience. Interestingly, Magstadt's investigation into the elite's involvement in the politics of Slovakia also raises questions as to the enactment of an American-Slovak identity, thus pointing to the problematics of ethnic incorporation.

Last, the essay by **Hale Yilmaz** discusses the Laz cultural movement in Turkey and in the diaspora community in Germany since the 1980s. Yilmaz provides a useful demographic and historical context to the analysis of the movement's emergence as a response to perceived threats against Laz language and culture. The critic problematizes the movement's function with respect to the preservation and revitalization of Laz culture, by revealing that the Laz movement has, essentially, been defining and re-defining Laz culture and identity by drawing on Laz language, history and folklore. Similarly to Luconi, Yilmaz is not blind to the socio-political implications of the movement and, therefore, questions its future within the broader context of nationalism, the democratization of Turkey, and its inclusion in the European Union.

As the brief discussion of the essays collected in this volume reveals, the overarching theme among all contributions is the complex, multi-layered and constantly evolving inter-relations between ethnic communities and the global context. The invention of a transnational global sphere has not made the concepts of ethnic communities and bounded localities obsolete; rather, it has necessitated a reconceptualization of the politics of community, identity, and cultural difference that sanctions new dynamics in a trans-local world. Hence, adopting a trans-ethnic and transnational perspective, the contributors to this volume offer keen insights into the processes of self- and community-transformation, processes that result not only from trans-national contacts, alliances, and influences, but also conflicts. Indeed, as Michael Watts has revealed, transnationalization has, on the one hand, contributed to local revitalization, while on the other it has triggered new modes of resistance. Echoing Watt's argument, all sixteen essays problematize the notion that every individual and, by extension, every community is a representative of a globalized totality; furthermore, these essays question whether such constituencies can, or need to, exist in the twenty-first century.

By attempting to contextualize this fluid concept of "transcultural localisms," the essays (by no means exhaustive in scope) examine historical encounters and clashes, political affiliations and cultural exchanges, as well as social and economic influences on a global scale. The volume's contributors acknowledge that, in a world of cultural and economic globalization and fast communication, ethnic communities are increasingly becoming trans-national, hence cutting across diverse boundaries: geographical, social, and political. Following the recent investigations of the constitution and politics of identity, the authors of these sixteen essays question the concept of static, originary, singular and authentic identities and communities. Nevertheless, they also recognize that the centrifugal force of globalization is counteracted by the centripetal pull to an ethnic identity that can be defined by either a common origin, or a common structure of experience, or both. Ultimately, to paraphrase bell hooks, the trans-national global spaces that emerge from this volume, on the one hand, offer a context in which ties are severed, while on the other they provide the occasion for new and varied forms of bonding (31).

In closing, the editors of this volume would like to acknowledge all those whose assistance made both the conference and the publication of this volume possible. In particular, we extend our thanks to the Greek Ministry of Education, Aristotle University of Thessaloniki, The Prefecture of Thessaloniki, The United States of America Embassy in Athens, and the Canadian Embassy in Athens. We would like also to express our gratitude to the anonymous reviewers in Greece and abroad who helped in the final selection of the sixteen essays of this volume.

Yiorgos Kalogeras, Eleftheria
Arapoglou, Linda Manney

Thessaloniki, November 2005

Works Cited

Barth, Fredric. "Ethnic Groups and their Boundaries." *Theories of Ethnicity*. Ed. Werner Sollors. New York: New York U P, 1996. 294-324.

hooks, bell. *Yearnings: Race, Gender and Cultural Politics*. Boston: South End P, 1990.

Sassen, Saskia. "Identity in the Global City: Economic and Cultural Encasements." *The Geography of Identity*. Ed. Patricia Yaeger. Ann Arbor: The U of Michigan P, 1996. 131-51.

Watts, Michael. "Mapping Identities: Place, Space, and Community in the African City." *The Geography of Identity*. 59-97.

PIN-CHIA FENG

Transcontinental Writing:
Reconfiguring the Politics of Home in Maryse Condé's *The Last of the African Kings*

> I think that for four centuries our people have been victims of political, cultural, and economic domination. Consequently, they are in the process of totally losing their voice. They are threatened. Artists and creators may have the duty to listen to our people before it's too late. In doing this, we may rekindle a pride that they are also about to lose. We may restore their power of speech and imagine what they can be tomorrow. This is the role of creators: not only to preserve the past but also to invent the future.
>
> Maryse Condé

As the most productive woman writer of the Francophone Caribbean, since the 1970s Maryse Condé's writing has been making a significant contribution to the creation of an Afro-Caribbean continuum that can effectively connect the past, present, and future of the Afro-Caribbean peoples. As a globe trotter, whose lived experience literally embodies different routings of the Afro-Caribbean diaspora, Condé, through her writing, also adds a spatial dimension to this continuum and maintains a cosmopolitan perspective in which she stresses the interconnectedness between the Americas, Africa, and Europe.[1] This interconnectedness, which is based upon a politics of relation, involves not simply physical and transnational migrations but also transcontinental connections in terms of sociopolitical history and memory. A re-examination of the concept of home is inevitable and indeed necessary within this transcontinental context. In this paper, therefore, the ways in which Maryse Condé reconfigures the politics of home for the Afro-Caribbean community based on her belief in transcontinental connectedness will be examined. The first

---

[1] In spite of the fact that Condé's texts are directly related to her cosmopolitan travels, Leah D. Hewitt rightly points out in the afterword to *The Last of the African Kings* that "Condé's ongoing interest in the intersections of cultures is also a reflection of, and on, what it means to be Antillean, a member of a crossroads culture that is constantly negotiating the links between tradition and postmodernity, realism and the supernatural, colonial and postcolonial, self and other. Before she even sets out, the Antillean novelist is already carrying multicultural baggage" (211).

part of the paper attempts to "place" Condé critically through a brief overview of her interactions with the Francophone Caribbean literary tradition and with other established critical schools such as feminism. By way of a brief comparison between Condé's cosmopolitan vision of Caribbean identity and those based on Afro-centrism and Creolist exclusiveness, it is argued that for Condé the site of home is necessarily a negotiation of different geopolitical locations for the nomadic Afro-Caribbean peoples. After locating Condé in her theoretical "home-base," this paper will engage in an investigation of Condé's practice of transcontinental writing and her politics of home through a close reading of her novel *The Last of the African Kings*.

Generally speaking, home for the descendents of the diasporic peoples has never been a simple term. It always involves complicated negotiations among multiple locations-different routes and roots-as well as interpenetrating temporalities. For the French-speaking Caribbean peoples, home can be "the ancestral land" in Africa, the former colonial "mother country" France, and other parts of the Americas besides the Caribbean. What complicates the issue further in the French Caribbean is the fact that the French overseas departments such as Guadeloupe and Martinique are yet to reach a post-colonial stage, politically speaking. Numerous writers and theorists have made attempts to determine the location of home for the French Caribbean by responding to this ambiguous state of belonging to neither entity. Condé is unique among the Francophone Caribbean writers in that she writes from the perspective of "transcendental cosmopolitanism" (Wyle 763).[2] And her cosmopolitan vision about Caribbean literature is markedly different from those of the followers of Négritude and Créolité in that Condé places more emphasis on transnational routes instead of place-specific roots.

Firstly, a brief introduction to Négritude and Créolité is in order here. As two of the major literary and theoretical movements in the Francophone Caribbean, Négritude and Créolité both attempt to claim to represent "authentic" discourses for the Caribbean people that are respectively based upon a filiative tie with Africa and an exclusive Caribbean interiority. Aimé Césaire, Léon-Gortran Damas and Lépold Sédar Senghor started to promote the concept of Négritude in the 1930s. Like the writers of the Harlem Renaissance, they stressed the importance of making connections with Africa, the original home of the Afrosporic peoples. There is no denial of the significant contribution of Négritude to Afro-Caribbean cultural

---

[2]   For Wyle, "Maryse Condé is a transcendental person and restless, but unlike many wanderers, she does not dissipate herself butterflying about. Instead, she is able to marshal her forces to draw upon the many places and episodes of her own Odyssey to forge a new unity by showing symbolist *correspondences* between the parts of the scrambled postmodern landscape" (763).

history. As Jean Bernabé, Patrick Chamoiseau and Raphäel Confiant, the editors of *In Praise of Creoleness*, comment: "To a totally racist world, self-mutilated by its own colonial surgeries, Aimé Césaire restored mother Africa, matrix Africa, the black civilization [. . .] Césaire's Negritude gave Creole society its African dimension, and put an end to the amputation which generated some of the superficiality of the so called doudouist writing" (79). And the creolists express their thankfulness to the master by claiming themselves "forever Césaire's sons." Yet, they also argue that Negritude cannot completely solve the aesthetic problems for Caribbean writers; instead, it only succeeds in replacing "the illusion of Europe by an African illusion" (82). What is lacking in Négritude, the editors contend, is an "interior vision" coming from "self-acceptance" (86). As the editors proclaim, "We cannot reach Caribbeanness without interior vision. And interior vision is nothing without the unconditional acceptance of our Creoleness" (87). Emphasizing orality, updating the collective memory of the history of colonization, examining the significance of daily existence in the Caribbean, bursting in modernity, and enforcing the use of the poetics of Creole language are listed as the ways to achieve this culture of Creoleness according to them.

Condé, on the other hand, argues for flexibility and freedom for Caribbean writers in this age of globalization and transnationality.[3] After her disappointing "return" to Africa in the late 1950s and in the early part of the 1960s, in fact, Condé became quite suspicious of the ideological stance of pan-African vision and spoke about any unconditional idealization of Africa with distrust:

> The people of the diaspora suffered a common estrangement from their motherland, but they remain as close to one another as orphans. For them it is essential to come to terms with the image of Africa. Too often they see Africa as a myth of beauty and lost grandeur but refuse to be concerned with the actual problems of the continent. ("The Role of the Writer 698)

For Condé, therefore, the unconditional mystification of a "mother Africa" inevitably leads to disaster and disillusionment. At the same time, she also criticizes the exclusive vision of Creoleness by the creolists as a flawed one in that it fails to acknowledge properly the African aspect of the Afro-Caribbean cultural heritage and this consequently creates another

---

[3] Condé always stresses the importance of cultivating a global vision. As she states, "We live in a world where, already, frontiers have ceased to exit" and "West Indies should be as changing and evolving as the islands themselves. Above all, creativity is a complex process which obeys no rule" ("Order, Disorder, Freedom, and the West Indian Writer" 130).

imbalance in the cultural and historical outlook of the Caribbean.[4] Instead
of an essentialist concept of Creoleness, she believes that the expression of
the Creole identity "is not restricted to the use of the Creole language,
which is part of a linguistic continuum"; furthermore, the word "Creole"
should be "reevaluated" since it "used to designate the population of the
islands at a time when migration and exile were unknown. Nowadays, it is
a fact that the majority of the West Indians are not Creole" ("The Role of
the Writer" 699). To her, moreover, the exclusive ideology of the creolists
comes close to a form of literary terrorism that one must strenuously battle
against.

Besides being against the exclusive practice of the creolists, Condé also
questions their neglect of gender practices inside the Caribbean society.
She points out that in African myth disorder appears in the image of a
woman, yet this feminine force is actually a source of creativity.[5] In the
male-dominated world of Caribbean society and literature, women are thus
cast in a transgressive role: "Whenever women speak out, they displease,
shock, or disturb. Their writings imply that before thinking of a political
revolution, West Indian society needs a psychological one" (131). Here
Condé acknowledges that indeed an "interior vision" is needed in the
Caribbean-yet one that is different from what the creolists have proposed-to
enable people to face the gender, class, and color prejudices in the region.
By commenting on the existing blindness to the "interior" problems of the
creolists, Condé demonstrates a sharp awareness of the difficult role of
Caribbean women in general and their women writers/creators in particular.

However, we must not hastily label Condé a feminist writer. In fact,
Condé always maintains an ironic distance from mainstream feminist
discourse. For instance, in the novel which attempts to reconstruct the
Salem witch hunt from the perspective of an Afro-Caribbean slave woman,
I Tituba, Black Witch of Salem, Condé's presentation of feminist lingo
through the conversations involving the West Indian protagonist Tituba
parody those of Hester Pryne from Hawthorne's *The Scarlet Letter*.[6]

---

[4]   Condé pointedly lays out the weakness in the concept of Creoleness, "it makes us
      forget the African origins of Caribbean culture. With its accent on the fusion of
      multiple cultural elements, African becomes just another constitutive culture. But
      this does not do it justice in terms of the role African has played in the Antillean
      history. It effaces the history of slavery, of the plantation culture, and the economic
      foundations of the island. The term *créolité* makes the cultural laboratory more
      important than the memory of a sugar-based economy" (Apter 94).

[5]   In "Order, Disorder, the West Indian Writer," Condé presents a gendered vision of
      creativity as disorder. She states, "In a Bambara myth of origin, after the creation of
      the earth, and the organization of everything on its surface, disorder was introduced
      by a woman. Disorder meant the power to create new objects and to modify the
      existing ones. In a word, disorder means creativity" (130).

[6]   Condé discusses the "ironic" nature of the novel, which to her is "a pastiche of the
      feminist heroic novel, a parody containing a lot of clichés about the grandmother,

Moreover, Condé often uses male protagonists as centers of reflection for her novels. A case in point is *The Last of the African Kings*, a novel in a large part about a failed marriage (Pfaff 91). In the textual exploration of the mystery of a failed relationship through the perspective of the male protagonist, Condé appears to be more sympathetic with the husband than with the wife. When asked to summarize the themes of the novel, Condé states that besides "the African-West Indian relationship," *The Last of the African Kings* "may also invite African-American women to undergo a sort of self-criticism" (93), a statement that clearly shows her sympathy for the failed artist husband and her criticism of the successful activist/professional wife.

One need not agree with Condé's perspective on African American womanhood; nevertheless, it is important to note that in resisting the hegemonic discourse of a universal feminism and the mandates of local literary movements, Condé always tries to maintain her independence by keeping a critical distance from established schools of criticism. What remains consistent throughout her writing is her deployment of experimental languages and narrative strategies as well as her engagement in a continuous dialogue with Caribbean critical discourses, feminist issues and the heritage of colonial history around the world and in the Caribbean. As a transcontinental writer, Condé works with both a sensitive awareness of Caribbean cultural specificities and a globalizing vision, and her writing thereby requires the reader to have a perspective that goes beyond geopolitical limits.

As a transcontinental writer, Condé has also made several changes in direction in terms of her career as a writer. When Condé started as a professional writer in 1970s, she worked mostly with African themes, such as the "back to Africa" narrative in *Hérémakhonon* and the history of African kingdoms in *Segu* and its sequel *The Children of the Segu*. Her creative project had a decided turn toward the Americas in the late 1980s, when she revisited her birthplace Guadeloupe after an extended absence. This homeward movement marks the beginning of a new dialogue with the history of colonization of the Afro-Caribbean peoples and significantly influences the temporal and spatial structure of her writing. More and more she engages in writing about transcontinental movements and the necessary revisions of the concept of home because of these migrations. For peoples of the African diaspora, Condé argues through her writing, it is necessary to reconstruct a transcontinental community that can account for different geopolitical locations because of the "originary" trauma of the Middle Passage. However, she also relentlessly deconstructs any romantic vision of

---

the sacrosanct grandmother, and about women in their relationship to the occult" (Pfaff 60).

a utopian return to the "roots" because this unchanging transcontinental family romance is already a story of absence and departure. For her, the site of home for the Afro-Caribbean community is neither Africa, the supposed *patrie* of the African diaspora, as idealized by believers in Négritude, nor the Caribbean islands only, as proclaimed by the disciples of Creolité. Race, skin color, and geographic locations, instead of being absolute deciding factors, are regarded by Condé as points of reference for the identification of nomadic Afro-Caribbean peoples.

Condé's familial conception is based upon a cosmopolitan nomadism that is closely connected with both Afrosporic history and her personal lived experience. As one consequence of their ancestors being forcefully transplanted from the African homeland, peoples of the African diaspora found themselves trying to make a home in different parts of the world, which results in a diasporic culture which Paul Gilroy terms "the Black Atlantic." Furthermore, Afrosporic peoples often travel to the European metropolitan centers of their former colonizers/slave masters and create routes of multiple migrations, some of which are delineated in Condé's works. As she is herself an errant middle-class writer who travels across the continents, Condé creates her fictional world with the privileged eye of an observer. And she manages to maintain a certain detachment so that her observation, although not uncritical, is devoid of the inevitable mystification of a place when one has set roots in it. Thus, the different geographical locales in her writing are presented non-hierarchically as points for emplotment that can exist independently yet at the same time are also closely linked. This nomadic aesthetic which deconstructs both the myth of an African homeland and that of a European mother country allows Condé to map out the lives of Afrosporic peoples materialistically, critically and unsentimentally. Nomadic yet relational, the characters in Condé's texts who shuttle among different locations embody the undeniable links between the colony and the colonizing country, the place of one's forced transplantation and the ancestral land of Africa. The location of home and the definition of family, within this context, are always multiple and de-centered. Thus the fixation on any "originary" home is replaced by an awareness of intercontinental connections among different locations which creates a writing strategy that can be termed "transcontinental writing."

The complicated familial story in *The Last of the African Kings* best illustrates Condé's transcontinental writing. The focus of the novel, as in Condé's previous work *The Tree of Life*, is about family history of Afrosporic peoples and the possibility of holding on to the present and carving out a future which is overshadowed by the crushing burden of the past. As a direct result of the dispersal of their ancestors because of the history of slavery, for Afrosporic peoples "family" is never simply a matter of bloodlines but instead a problematic and oblique construction.[7] And the story of *The Last of the African Kings* is meant to explore this construction. Spero's grandfather Djéré Jules-Juilette is the illegitimate son of an African king (a fictional representation of Béhanzin, the king of Abomey), "the ancestor" of the family who was exiled by the French government to Martinique. When the king returned to Africa, his Caribbean family is left behind to struggle on their own. "This abandonment would drastically affect Djéré's entire existence and that of his descendants" (5), the narrator informs us right at the beginning. Djéré and his son Justine who have spent their lives in poverty in the Caribbean have never forgotten about their royal lineage and their lives are wasted in this repeated ritual of remembering. Most of the novel is linked through Spero's stream of consciousness on October 10th, 1990, the day when he fails to remember the anniversary of the death of "the ancestor," a ritual that has been carried on in the family since 1906. On this particular day Spero thoroughly examines this family history of denied ancestry and suspended lives as well as his relationship with his African American wife, Debbie. After numerous affairs and failed attempts to make his name as an artist, Spero is now alienated from Debbie after twenty odd years of marital life. Their only daughter Anita also leaves home for the "ancestral land" of Benin and intentionally estranges herself from her parents. When Debbie goes to Charleston to collect oral history from the local black community, Spero goes through a re-collection of history on his own in which stories of his different families-African, Caribbean, and African American-are re-examined. It is through this journey that he is hoping to find a way to "start over again" with Debbie.

The psychology of a middle-age artist who suffers from the empty-nest syndrome and a failed marriage is not a new invention in terms of emplotment. *The Last of the African Kings*, however, is not an ordinary Third World *Künstlerroman* in its deployment of transcontinental chronotopes and the allegorical significance generated by the family romance. It is rather an exemplary text of a new conception of the politics of home in that Condé deploys the form of a family romance to engage in a redefinition of family and home in a (post)colonial diaspora. Here Spero's

---

[7]   Hortense Spillers in her seminal essay "Mama's Baby, Papa's Maybe" argues that because of the history of slavery, during which time slave men and women were sold at will by their masters, African American familial structure is permanently damaged. Spillers states at one point that "…'Family,' as we practice and understand it 'in the West,'—the *vertical* transfer of a bloodline, of a patronymic, of titles and entitlements, of real estate and the prerogatives of 'cold cash,' from *fathers* to *sons* and in the supposedly free exchange of affectional ties between a male and a female of *his* choice—become the mythically revered privileged of a free and freed community" (396).

status as an (unassimilated) émigré from the Caribbean and his physical
position on a remote island give a very good example of this new
configuration of geopolitical and familial relations. He is set on
contemplating people and events of other locations and temporal zones
while physically being situated on Crocker Island off the South Carolina
coast. Yet his isolated locale does not stop him from connecting with the
network of relationships created through transatlantic migrations. Through
his mental examination of the family's past both rooted in the Caribbean
and Africa and his own travel routes through Guadeloupe, France, and the
United States, Spero's stream-of-consciousness narrative materializes
Condé's transcontinental aesthetics.

Significantly, this transcontinental aesthetic is also theoretically rooted
in the Francophone Caribbean literary tradition. As Mildred Mortimer
argues, Aimé Césaire's *Return to My Native Land* has started an errant and
nomadic tradition in which there exists

> a tension between place and space, rootedness and freedom. As men and women
> often long for wider horizons from the security of home, the islanders' desire to
> claim as home the land their African ancestors cultivated in bondage is
> frequently challenged by the temptation of errancy. Nomadism appears in
> Antillean texts as a call to adventure (the lure of the sea and the open road) and
> also as a flight from the vestiges of colonialism. (757)

Despite being critical of the Afro-centric tenet of Négritude, Condé also
recognizes the tension between a longing for a homeland and a desire of
nomadic migrations. Many of her characters are globe trotters who are
always on the road. Spero's transatlantic travels, for instance, appear to
echo this errant desire. Condé's portrayal of Spero nevertheless takes away
the romantic implication of an escapist adventure. The novel shows that
although Spero's wanderings take him to different parts of the world, he
never feels completely at home anywhere. When he tries to claim his blood
connection with the African king and thereby to reconnect with his African
"roots," for instance, he is coldly rejected by a former colonial civil servant
in Paris and "left feeling like an impostor" (84). While the enforced
relocation of his royal ancestor from the Caribbean to a different part of
Africa by the colonial force creates the first break of the Caribbean family
line with the African one, this rejection once again cuts Spero off from his
African ancestry, which enacts an uncanny repetition of history that also
marks his moment of disillusionment about a definite "homeland." After
he himself is relocated in the United States, Spero dreams about a
homecoming in the Morne Verdol but he is unable to reverse his migratory
route to make this return to his native land and is thus left suspended in his
life's adventure. In this way the reader is guided to engage in an
examination of this suspended life along with Spero's self-contemplation,

which initiates the whole narrative of the novel, and rethinks the meaning
of this "Caribbean nomadism."

For Condé, the story is clearly "a symbol of the relationship that West
Indies always have with Africa" (Pfaff 92-93). This story of abandonment
is double-edged; it asserts filiative ties of Afro-Caribbean peoples with
Africa while it also questions the validity of retaining this umbilical cord.
Obsessions with the past will only lead to a hopeless entrapment and worse,
a loss of both the present and the future, just like the ancestor whose return
trip to Africa after his Caribbean sojourn is literally and symbolically a
journey of regression: "The more the journey advanced, the further back in
time he went, and when the ship docked in Marseilles he was nothing more
but a little child, scarcely out of Mehutu's womb" (88). This obsessive
desire to return to the womb/motherland embedded in the king's narrative
bespeaks the tenacity of the umbilical relation/condition and an
overdependence on the mother that has unfortunately become a family
heritage. Consequently, for three generations his Caribbean male
descendents have lived off their women. Thus Spero becomes enraged
when Anita insists on going to Africa:

> His blood burned. His body shook. Usually so sparing with words he was unable
> to control all those that were now jumbling out of his mouth. Can't we ever live
> our lives in the present? And, if need be, bear the ugliness of its wounds? The
> past must be condemned to death. Otherwise it will become the killer. Wasn't it
> all that nonsense about an ancestor and Africa that turned Djéré and Justin into
> what they were? Two Wise Men, two drunkards, the laughingstock of the Morne
> Verdol? Wasn't this the misfortune of too many blacks they knew who were so
> busy building imaginary family trees they had lost out on conquering their own
> America? (82)

Spero's outburst interestingly posits for the peoples of African descent in
the Americas an imaginary homeland which places both continents against
each other. At the same time, his statement underscores the point that an
obsession with the African dream will "murder" their chances of claiming
the Americas. So, the novel purposely begins with *forgetting* to highlight
the point that for the children of the "New World" it is necessary to walk
away from the influence of the African old world. And yet, Africa is not to
be simply forgotten either. In fact, through the narrative drive that
imaginatively tells a story of the Caribbean children of an African king, the
novel also effectively re-members the undeniable affiliation of both worlds.
Therefore, what Condé has presented is a narrative that is perched on
endless dialectics of forgetting and remembering, of African and American
homelands.

The use and transformation of African myths and belief systems exemplifies the way in which this dialectics work. The myth and belief systems in the novel are clearly of a hybrid nature, which reflects a state which seeks to address the results of the diaspora for the West Indian characters. Besides deploying a third-person omniscient narrative form in the western tradition to present Spero's family story, Condé also inserts three fragments about African myth and belief systems from Djéré's notebooks. This insertion of the twice-told stories-stories recorded from those told by Djéré's royal father-recognize the family's African heritage and an oral tradition. This recognition of African heritage and oral tradition reveals Condé's investment in "diasporic literacy."[8] It is a way to interpret the different heritages of the Afrosporic peoples from a local point of view. What further complicates the issue here is that this heritage of the diaspora nevertheless counts as a mixed blessing in that it can also create confusions in identification and overindulgence in ancestral worship when one fails to properly maintain the local perspective.[9]

In the novel, among the different references to African history and African American culture, the myth of Agasu the Leopard stands out as the most significant one originating from an African knowledge system. Presented as the first section of Djéré's notebooks, this is the story of the origins of the African ancestor as well as that of the Jules-Juliette family. Condé specifically highlights Djéré's somatic responses in retelling this story:

> I too lost my way in the labyrinth of the forest. I lay down between the roots of its trees and the powdery wings of the giant carnivorous bats brushed against my face. The darkness grew darker and darker and I could hear the commotion of the invisible monkeys from the forest canopy to the spongy soil. When at last I found my way back I snuggled up against my father's shoulder wishing this moment would never end, as if I felt I was soon going to lose it and that I would no longer be the son of the Leopard to anyone. (60)

---

[8] Although she emphasizes the importance of the present, Condé always advocates the importance of "diasporic literacy" suggested by Vèvè Clark, which "is the ability to read and comprehend the discourses of Africa, Afro-America and the Caribbean from an informed, indigenous perspective" (Clark 304).

[9] As Thomas Spear contends, Condé's characters are caught between the individualism of Western humanistic tradition and collective history. Spear discusses the exilic state of these characters: "While they seek to discover an irretrievable past, they are unable to define their fragmented present; their unsettled and unreconciled selves are torn from and attracted to tradition and are unsure of their place in modern community identities" (723). Ann Smock also argues that the novel "is a scathing satire of the religion of racial heritage whose inspiring aura is supposed to make the present bearable" (671).

The story ends on a note that emphasizes the slippage between the roles of
a storyteller and an audience: at this juncture Djéré the storyteller is turning
himself into the child audience of his father's storytelling and is fully
immersed in the mythical time and space. The act of storytelling becomes a
moment of narrative encounter with one's ancestry and paradoxically, its
negation. A sense of continuity is created through this relay of orature. At
the same time, in the notebook the pain of loss and discontinuity of a
damaged psyche is palpable. Abandoned by his African family at five,
Djéré, who has turned from a pampered prince into an illegitimate pauper,
tells a story that is not only about origins but also about the loss of origins.
Just as in the Christian story of the loss of Eden, the myth of creation and
the beginning of a family is juxtaposed with its irrecoverable loss: the
moment of connecting with one's origins is also the moment of losing it.

In fact, the myth of Agasu is already one step removed from the
"original" story from Africa because Condé rewrites the story in her own
way. For her, this kind of revision and transformation of myth is necessary.
As she asserts, "It means that you do what you want with the past. One uses
the text, or one does what one wants with it. It is not considered as a myth
that only has one meaning. It is considered as a story that can be interpreted
however you want it. It is, in fact, the proof that the past has to be
reinterpreted according to one's needs" (McCormick 527). In other words,
Condé stresses the importance of artistic independence in the act of
rewriting and cultural translation. If we carry the metaphor of translation
one step further, the African myth is like a "source text" that has been
translated into a Caribbean "version." And it is the task of the translator to
render the original story into one that is culturally and linguistically
compatible with the target text. As Benjamin famously theorizes in "The
Task of the Translator":

> Fidelity in the translation of individual words can almost never fully reproduce
> the meaning they have in the original…a translation, instead of resembling the
> meaning of the original, must lovingly and in detail incorporate the original's
> mode of signification, thus making both the original and the translation
> recognizable as fragments of a greater language, just as fragments are part of a
> vessel. (78)

Djéré's retelling of the father's story is very close to a practice of
translation. The story of "Origins" is therefore his own version of his
origins. Yet he misinterprets his role as a translator and becomes fixated
upon the "original text," and thereby forecloses the possibility of bringing
forth a new life through the "translated text."

Spero, on the other hand, as an artist, though an under-appreciated one,
sees through the enslavement of the Caribbean family by its "original"

African one and seeks to break new ground in the Americas.[10] After all, even the ancestor himself has started a new life again. In a short but fantastic episode near the end, the omniscient narrator travels to Africa and the spirit of the ancestor is seen to be wandering around discontented with the new way of life. He finally chooses to be reborn on the 6th of January 1980 and becomes the son of an Abomey princess and her soldier husband. This story of reincarnation ostensibly follows an African tradition and belief; nevertheless, what the author is truly concerned about, although it is only implicitly suggested in the narrative, is how the old spirit is going to respond to a life in the new world once he is reincarnated.[11] While Condé does not appear to deny the spiritual beliefs of the past, the ancestral culture has nevertheless also been subtly queried and re-evaluated in this seeming valorization. Both the ancestor, who for the obvious political reasons can never go back to his home country even after his return to Africa, and Spero, who is trapped in the United States, are destined to be exiles and expatriates. In the final analysis, nevertheless, it is Spero's courageous embracement of the new life that is endorsed by the author. Spero chooses life over easy death and dismisses the thought of committing suicide at the end of the novel: to "walk every step that remained to be walked on life's path" so that he may have the chance to meet with Debbie again (210). This open yet positive ending thus communicates a strong sense of hopefulness and opens up possibilities for the future. The last of the African Kings on this side of the Atlantic has finally seen a way through the impasse of history.

To conclude, in *The Last of the African Kings* Condé creates a (post)colonial family romance as a way to represent the interconnectedness of Africa, Europe and the Americas. This interconnectedness goes beyond superficial extension of the characters' travels to include a transcontinental connection based on the intricately related geopolitical history and memory of these different geographical locations. Hence, Condé's Caribbean writing differs from the usual Third World allegorization of the local in that it moves towards a vision of "transcendental cosmopolitanism," which

---

[10] I must pause here for a self-reflective/reflexive moment about my own role as a reader of a text that has been translated from French into English, which is Condé's rendition of a Caribbean family romance. With her privileged middle-class background and European education, can Condé be a good "translator" of this intricate familial relationship and its cultural milieu? And can I, an Asian reader who has spent years researching on Caribbean literature, be a good interpreter of this doubly translated text?

[11] Condé regards this story of reincarnation as "ironic and parodic"; in a mischievous spirit she imagines "the ancestor reincarnated in his own country at a time when things had completely changed, when there was no longer a traditional power structure but simply military power. You cannot but wonder how he will live his new existence" (Pfaff 96).

significantly reconfigures the politics of home for the Caribbean. Through a meta-fictional perspective that re-examines the construction and writing of family romance, Condé critically reviews what constitutes family and home in a (post)colonial condition. Finally, her anti-essentialist and relational reconfiguration of the Afro-Caribbean community as represented in *The Last of the African Kings* effectively exemplifies Condé's diasporic aesthetic that is rooted in, yet not limited to, the Caribbean.

Works Cited

Apter, Emily. "Crossover Texts/Creole Tongues: A Conversation with Maryse Condé." *Public Culture* 13.1 (2001): 89-96.

Benjamin, Walter. "The Task of the Translator." *Illuminations: Essays and Reflections.* Trans. Harry Zohn. New York: Schocken, 1985. 69-82.

Bernabé, Jean, Patrick Chamoiseau, Raphäel Confiant. *Éloge de la créolité/ In Praise of Creoleness.* Trans. M. B. Taleb-Khyar. Paris: Gallimard, 1990.

Clark, Vèvè. "Developing Diaspora Literacy: Allusion in Maryse Condé's Hérémakhonon." *Out of Kumbla: Caribbean Women and Literature.* Eds. Carol Boyce Davies and Elaine Savory Fido. Trenton, NJ: African World P, 1990. 303-19.

Condé, Maryse. The Children of Segu [Ségou: La terre en miettes]. 1985. Trans. Linda Coverdale. New York: Viking, 1989.

--Hérémakhonon. 1976. Trans. Richard Philcox. Washington, D.C.: Three Continents P, 1982.

---. I, Tituba, the Black Witch of Salem [Moi, Tituba, Sorcière...Noire de Salem]. Trans. Richard Philcox. New York: Ballantine, 1994.

---. The Last of the African Kings [Les derniers rois mages 1992]. Trans. Richard Philcox. Lincoln: U of Nebraska P, 1998.

---. "Order, Disorder, Freedom, and the West Indian Writer." *Yale French Studies* 83 (1993): 121-35.

--. "The Role of the Writer." *World Literature Today* 67.4 (Autumn 1993): 697-99. *Segu [Segou].* Trans. Barbara Bray. New York: Ballantine, 1988.

--. *Tree of Life [La vie scélérate 1987].* Trans.Victoria Reiter. New York: Ballantine, 1992.

Gilroy, Paul. The Black Atlantic: Modernity and Double Consciousness. Cambridge, Massachusetts: Harvard UP, 1993.

Hewitt, Leah D. "Afterword: The Critical F(r)iction of Maryse Condé." *The Last of the African Kings.* 211-16.

McCormick, Robert H., Jr. "A New Concept of Identity: An Interview with Maryse Condé." *World Literature Today* 74.3 (Summer 2000): 519-28.

Mortimer, Mildred. "A Sense of Place and Space in Maryse Condé's Les Derniers roismages." *World Literature Today* 67.4 (Autumn 1993): 757-62.

Pfaff, Françoise. Conversations with Maryse Condé. Lincoln: U of Nebraska P, 1996.

Smock, Ann. "Maryse Condé's Les Derniers Rois mages." *Callaloo* 18.3 (1995): 668-80.

Spear, Thomas C. "Individual Quests and Collective History." *World Literature Today* 67.4 (Autumn 1993): 723-30.

Spillers, Hortense. "Mama's Baby, Papa's Maybe." 1987. *Feminisms: An Anthology of Literary Theory and Criticism*. 2nd ed. Ed. Robyn R. Warhol and Diane Price Herndl. New Brunswick, NJ: Rutgers UP, 1997. 384-405.

Wyle, Hal. "The Cosmopolitan Condé, or Unscrambling the Worlds." *World Literature Today* 67.4 (Autumn 1993): 763-68.

GARY Y. OKIHIRO

Toward A Pacific Civilization

To find America, go to its heartland is the usual advice. America's great interiors–of purple mountains and fertile valleys, of expansive skies and rolling plains, of corn as high as an elephant's eye and amber waves of grain, of decent folk and honest talk and patriotism topped with a generous helping of cream. That's the American dream, its heartland.

Surely one of the earliest and most persistent American myths involves its origin story of how Americans became Americans. Europeans, the raced, gendered, and sexualized tale begins, crossed an ocean, staggered to shore, and sowed their seed. That implantation, that encounter between Europeans and America's wilderness (a tangle of plants, animals, natives) was the process of Americanization, the means by which the English, Scottish, Dutch, French became Americans.

Along the frontier, the divide between civilization and barbarism, light and darkness "the wilderness masters the colonist," in the words of historian Frederick Jackson Turner, giving him his coarseness and strength, acuteness and inventiveness, individualism and love of freedom. Those were among the core American virtues that were distilled within the crucible of the frontier (1,2,3).

That founding myth we know from Henry Nash Smith's classic study, *Virgin Land*, was part of an agrarian tradition that turned inward and found America's soul in the land, the unturned sod, the exceptional environment and encounter. According to this tradition, the ocean formed a protective moat, a barrier that allowed the American variety to develop and grow, shielded from foreign frosts and blights. American nationalism, Smith points out, was expressed in countless "rhapsodies on the West," and the agrarian tradition "made it difficult for Americans to think of themselves as members of a world community because it affirmed that the destiny of this country leads her away from Europe toward the agricultural interior of the continent" (4, 11, 260).

But there is a countervailing narrative, Smith informs us, of a maritime tradition that extends outward and connects America to its European forebears and its original stock (6-8, 12). Although apparently at odds one with the other as posed by Smith, the maritime tradition is, in my view, a complementary account of America's agrarian origins in that its peoples-as a raced collective-and their institutions and culture are derivatives of European antecedents. Whether arising from agrarian or maritime pasts, the

American species is essentially European, according to those accounts of
American history.

A version of that Eurocentrism holds that America was the western
terminus of an Atlantic civilization that embraced European "cultural
hearths" and their diasporas. Columbus' first landing in 1492 constitutes
the beginning of this Atlantic civilization as conceived. His "discovery,"
although unclear to him to his death (Columbus believed he had found Asia
and its outlying islands), fixed the America's onto European maps that
located islands and the eastern shores of the Americas by grids of longitude
and latitude. Eventually, with the global spread of Europeans, those
coordinates would delineate and encompass the entire world.

Europe is the genesis, the birth mother, the natal source in that rendition.
American peoples and their institutions and cultures were tributaries that
flowed and drew from European headwaters. Herbert Baxter Adams, a
mentor of Frederick Jackson Turner at Johns Hopkins University, was an
influential advocate of the "germ theory" that held that all American
institutions derived from medieval Germany and spread with European
migrants to the New World. Indeed, Turner's frontier hypothesis that
reversed the origin and direction of American institutions arose, he
confessed, as a reaction to Adams' germ theory "due to my
indignation"(38).

Turner's equally Eurocentric variant, however, simply stressed the
American side of Atlantic civilization, and the connection charted by
Columbus between the Americas and Europe remained the central feature
of a more global view of American history. As noted by the immigration
historian Marcus Lee Hansen, "the migration to America was one aspect of
the growth and spread of the population of Atlantic Europe," wherein
"Atlantic Europe" was conceived of the European peoples who bordered
the north Atlantic. Hansen, although framing the Atlantic migration from
America's shore (that is, from an American-centric point of view),
describes that movement of peoples as a reciprocal and complementary
process that was mediated by trans-Atlantic commercial networks. There
was, he writes, "despair in Europe" and "hope in America." Those
corresponding attitudes propelled the Atlantic migration, and in Ireland and
Germany, prosperity replaced grinding poverty, and in the U.S., pessimism
succumbed to boundless confidence and expectation (17, 286,305).

That perceived correspondence between Europe and the U.S. was
longstanding. Thomas Jefferson called it the "American system" because
America's founding inspired the eighteenth and nineteenth-century
revolutions in states bordering the north Atlantic, creating a republican
kinship that contrasted with the despotisms of central and eastern Europe.
And in 1906, Henry Adams more generously proposed the "Atlantic
system," which was a "community of interest" among the nations of the
north Atlantic basin. Forrest Davis, writing on the eve of America's entry

into World War II, argued that the Atlantic system was "old, rational, and pragmatic," that its roots ran "deep and strong into the American tradition," and that it had emerged from "strategic and political realities" (xi, xii). The Atlantic Charter, signed by Churchill and Roosevelt in 1941, exemplified that common interest in defending the ties of blood and tradition.

The ocean and its shores, to some advocates of the Atlantic world, hold much virtue as a unit of analysis. Devoid of national boundaries, the ocean-unit foregrounds transnationalisms that fracture the binary of the "old" and "new" world, the distinction between metropole and colony, and insular nationalisms like American exceptionalism. The Atlantic world, they maintain, was a system of "cultural hearths" in Europe, Africa, and the Americas that spread and interacted in complex ways, and that therefore requires comparative and cross-cultural studies (Karras, McNeill 4-6). Despite that postmodernist gesture toward multiculturalism, this version of the Atlantic world still centers Europe and the expansion of its peoples and their deeds upon indigenous Africa and the Americas. Herein, whites act upon non-whites.[1]

Paul Gilroy takes on that Eurocentrism in his *The Black Atlantic*. In truth, Gilroy tells us, the book arose from his experience trying to persuade students that history and the life of the mind held significance for their circumscribed interests and pursuits. "*The Black Atlantic* developed from my uneven attempts to show these students that the experiences of black people were part of the abstract modernity they found so puzzling and to produce as evidence some of the things that black intellectuals had said-sometimes as defenders of the West, sometimes as its sharpest critics-about their sense of embeddedness in the modern world" (ix). In his influential intervention, Gilroy describes a black Atlantic that was not specifically African, American, Caribbean, or British, but one that was all of those simultaneously transcendent of nation, race, and ethnicity and emphatically and mutably mixed and hybrid.

Although unacknowledged, Gilroy's unit of study is the old Atlantic world and its pedigree of the American system, Atlantic civilization, and Eurocentrism. Africans within that universe become "embedded" within European modernity, and racialization is more complicated by hybridity but its constituent parts remain in essence black and white. Slighted are Native Americans who preceded and were overwritten by Atlantic civilization and Asians who, like Africans, were transported to the Americas and became thereby "embedded" in the "black Atlantic."

What I would like to propose in this brief study is that the Americas are surely parts of the north Atlantic world and the black Atlantic, but they are also "cultural hearths" of a Pacific civilization that, like its Atlantic

---

[1]   A similar critique has been leveled at Orientalism. See, e.g., A. L. Macfie (ed.), *Orientalism: A Reader* (New York: New York U P, 2000).

counterpart, was a system of flows of capital, labor, and culture that produced transnational and hybrid identities as well as their counterclaims for homogeneity, nationalism, and racial purity. In that sense, I'd like to suggest that the U.S. is an island surrounded by lands north and south, but also oceans, east and west. And as an island, unlike the imagined insularity of the agrarian tradition and frontier hypothesis, the U.S. must be viewed properly as a center with its own integrity but also as a periphery and a fluid space of movements and engagements that resist closure and inevitable or final outcomes.

Indeed, as figured in Atlantic civilization, America's very "discovery" resulted from a transnational project—Europe's ancient and persistent search for a passage to Asia. As noted by Christopher Columbus in his ship's daily log, his expedition's purpose was to go "to the regions of India, to see the Princes there and the peoples and the lands, and to learn of their disposition, and of everything, and the measures which could be taken for their conversion to our Holy Faith" (51). In 1513, Spain's Vasco Nunez de Balboa traversed Panama's isthmus, waded into the Gulf of San Miguel after waiting for hours for the tide to come in for a photogenic moment, gazed across the Mar del Sur toward Asia, and issued the absurdly grandiose claim of "real and corporeal and actual possession of these seas and lands and coasts and ports and islands of the south, and all their annexures and kingdoms and provinces to them pertaining . . . in the name of the Kings of Castile present or to come . . . both now and in all times, as long as the world endures until the final day of judgement of mortal man"(Spate 1, 32, 33).

A consequence of American and European mappings of the Pacific was the outflow of Asia's peoples, mainly laborers, to the Americas. The peripheries were thereby drawn toward the core along the Pacific's rim. Apt is the metaphor of a ship, as pointed out by Paul Gilroy, "a living, micro-cultural, micro-political system in motion. . . ." Ships, Gilroy explained, shift attention from the shore to the middle passage and the circulation of people, ideas, and culture.[2]

Images come to mind of Filipino and Chinese seamen on board Spanish galleons beginning in 1565, and Hawaiian sailors who, during the 1830s, comprised the majority of the crews on American ships that carried animal furs from America's Pacific Northwest to Canton, China.[3] Those were the

---

[2]   Gilroy, *Black Atlantic*, 4. On traveling cultures, encounters, and translations, see James Clifford, *Routes: Travel and Translation in the Late Twentieth Century* (Cambridge, Massachusetts: Harvard U P, 1997).

[3]   On Pacific islanders on European ships, see David A. Chappell, *Double Ghosts: Oceanian Voyagers on Euroamerican Ships* (Armonk, New York: M. E. Sharpe, 1997); Richard H. Dillon, "Kanaka Colonies in California," *Pacific Historical Review* 24 (February 1955): 17-23; Janice K. Duncan, "Kanaka World Travelers and Fur Company Employees, 1785-1860," *Hawaiian Journal of History* 7 (1973): 93-

forerunners of Asian migrants today, called "trapeze artists" in Chinese because they hang suspended over the Pacific between the U.S. and Asia.

With the focus on the crossing, their frequency and multiple directions, the parents are called "astronauts" and their children, "parachute kids" who land in America to attend school. And culture, like people, dart across the Pacific's expanses and defy easy capture and labels. Can the Hong Kong, Jackie Chan movies so popular in America be classed as Asian cinema, and is Taiwan-born director Ang Lee's filming of Jane Austen's *Sense and Sensibility* (1995) a translation? When Japanese capital in the form of Sony and Nissan locate their plants in the U.S. their products bear the label "Made in America," and Sony's Akio Morita told *Newsweek*'s readers, when his company bought Columbia Pictures in 1989, "We are still expanding our facilities in this country [the U.S.]. I don't like the word 'multinational.' I don't know what it means. I created a new term: 'global localization.' That's our new slogan."[4]

Those new natives, like the old imperialists and expatriates, assume the names of the indigenous peoples, allowing them to make claims upon the land as if it were their own. Thus Europeans become *native* Americans and Asian capital make *American* products. The Native Sons (and Daughters) of the Golden West—white American and European immigrants to California following the gold rush–designated themselves as natives, and then sought to expel aliens and foreigners–Chinese who were like them migrants, but also Mexicans and Californios who had preceded them in Mexico's far north and who, in turn, had staked claims in disregard of the original caretakers of the land, America's Indians.

And seen from Asia's shore, Asian migration to the Americas constituted an Asian diaspora from the Asian core to American peripheries, from Asian cultural hearths to American cultural hearths. Indeed, this paper's archaeology, Andre Gunder Frank has argued, is Eurocentric and ahistorical. In his remapping of the world economy, Frank proposes that Asia, including China, India, Persia, and Turkey, were the major centers of a global system that long predated Europe's rise. "Europe," Frank notes, "climbed up on the back of Asia, then stood on Asian shoulders–temporarily."[5] Its search for Asia was as a supplicant, not a master, and

---

111; and Tom Koppel, *Kanaka: The Untold Story of Hawaiian Pioneers in British Columbia and the Pacific Northwest* (Vancouver: Whitecap Books, 1995).

[4] *Newsweek*, October 9, 1989, 66. See, Sau-Ling C. Wong, "Denationalization Reconsidered: Asian American Cultural Criticism at a Theoretical Crossroads," *Amerasia Journal* 21:1/2 (1995): 6-7.

[5] Andre Gunder Frank, *ReOrient: Global Economy in the Asian Age* (Berkeley: U of California P, 1998), 5. For a review of books that counter the idea of European initiatives, see John E. Wills, Jr., "Maritime Asia, 1500-1800: The Interactive Emergence of European Domination," *American Historical Review* 98:1 (February 1993): 83-105.

Europe was dependent upon silver drawn mainly from Mexico and Peru to initiate trade with Asia, cover its perennial deficits, and rectify its Asian trade imbalance. Europeans served as brokers between Asia and the Americas, Africa, and Europe in an expanded world-system that centered on China and India. In the eighteenth century, Frank reminds us, the well-known Atlantic trade triangle was in fact an adjunct of the Afro-Eurasian trade in which Europeans exchanged Indian textiles and European manufactures for African slaves who produced America's sugar, tobacco, and other goods exported to Europe. Economic decline, political instability, and European conquest and colonialism in Asia and the labor of slaves in and silver and gold from the Americas led to Europe's preeminence that lasted for less than two centuries, a brief interlude in Asia's dominance from 1500 to 1800 and again in our time.

Frank poses in this study a provocative challenge to Eurocentrism in the works of Fernand Braudel and Immanuel Wallerstein,[6] but Asia-centrism, like Eurocentrism, disallows other centers and slights the margins that pose resistances to the more glaring hegemonies. Similarly, in this study's bid for a Pacific civilization and its absorption with the crossing, it loses sight of those who have made the ocean their home, the place of their nativity.

The Pacific is not a negative space between continents or the hole in a doughnut, the breakfast food of champions and a tasty trope for the Pacific's rim. Niuean poet John Pahiatua Pule reflected upon that absence and Henry Kissinger's comment when asked about U.S. nuclear tests on the Marshall Islands, "There are only 90,000 people out there, who gives a damn?"

> I look at the map of the Pacific.
> The American navy calls the Pacific the American Lake.
> They have ships in Samoa
> Hawaii, Taiwan, Philippines,
> Belau, Kwajalein, Truk
> the Mariannas, the Carolines.
> In Micronesia there are only 90,000 people,
> who gives a damn?
> The dead are louder in protest than the living.
> The living are silent.
> Everything is silent (73-75)

Samoan novelist and university professor Albert Wendt rejected the "fatal impact theory" of colonial literature that pronounced the death of native cultures with the arrival of the Europeans. "We and our cultures

---

[6]   For example, Fernand Braudel's three volume, *Civilization and Capitalism, 15th-18th Century,* and Immanuel Wallerstein's three volume, *The Modern World System.*

have survived and adapted when we were expected to die, vanish, under the influence of supposedly stronger superior cultures and their technologies," he wrote. "Our story of the Pacific is that of marvelous endurance, survival and dynamic adaptation, despite enormous suffering under colonialism in some of our countries. We have survived through our own efforts and ingenuity. We have indigenised much that was colonial or foreign to suit ourselves, creating new blends and forms" (3).

Instead of conceiving the Pacific as "the last and greatest unknown quantity" from the drawing tables of European map makers (Spate 24) we might conceive of Pacific civilization as "Oceania" as appropriated and reconceived by the Tongan writer Epeli Hau`ofa who distinguishes between "Pacific islands" and "Oceania."[7] The former, he observes, denotes tiny bits of land and reefs surrounded by a vast and empty ocean, whereas the latter conjures a "sea of islands" and their inhabitants. "Theirs was a large world in which peoples and cultures moved and mingled, unhindered by boundaries of the kind erected much later by imperial powers," wrote Hau`ofa of Oceania's peoples. "From one island to another they sailed to trade and to marry, thereby expanding social networks for greater flows of wealth. They traveled to visit relatives in a wide variety of natural and cultural surroundings, to quench their thirst for adventure, and even to fight and dominate." The sea, before Europeans, had no exclusionary laws, fences, or border patrols or imaginary cartographic lines, "but rather points of entry that were constantly negotiated and even contested. The sea was open to anyone who could navigate a way through." It was imperialism that erected boundaries, created island states and territories, and confined people to restricted spaces isolated from each other (153-4, 155).

The efficacy of an Oceania identity, Hau`ofa tells his readers, rests in its ability to steer clear of the "reef of our diversity" and the imposed alienations of nation states and to promote a consciousness "that would help free us from the prevailing, externally generated definitions of our past, present, and future." (Hau`ofa, "The Ocean in Us" 113). That capacious apprehension, Hau`ofa cautions, is not in place of but in addition to Oceania's diverse ethnicities that counter the homogenizing forces of global culture. A regional identity offers a powerful antidote to the caricatures of noble savage, lost and debased souls, and helpless pawns in the conflicts between civil and savage, Christianity and barbarism, and West and East. With the advent of the Pacific century, Hau`ofa points out, "our erstwhile suitors are now creating with others along the rim of our

---

[7] Hau`ofa cites as a landmark in this new idea of Oceania the pioneering essay by Albert Wendt, "Towards a New Oceania," first published in *Mana* 1:1 (January 1976): 49-60.

ocean a new set of relationships that excludes us totally"(119)[8] That
exclusion has relevance to Oceania's very survival, including nuclear tests
that poison both land and sea, depletions of fisheries and the ocean's
resources, and erasures of cultural identities.

The assertion of Oceania, thus, is in resistance to the blank space created
by Euro- and Asia-centrisms and evokes the solidity of the boundless,
fecund sea. "Oceania is vast, Oceania is expanding, Oceania is hospitable
and generous, Oceania is humanity rising from the depths of brine and
regions of fire deeper still, Oceania is us," Hau`ofa exhorts. "We are the
sea, we are the ocean, we must wake up to this ancient truth and together
use it to overturn all hegemonic views that aim ultimately to confine us
again, physically and psychologically, in the tiny spaces that we have
resisted accepting as our sole appointed places, and from which we have
recently liberated ourselves. We must not allow anyone to belittle us again,
and take away our freedom" (Hau`ofa, "Our Sea," 160).

In truth, whether conceiving of Pacific civilization as an overarching
hegemony of Europe and the U.S. or Asia or as a resistance to colonialism
through an Oceania identity, there is no Pacific region as an "objective"
given, as pointed out by historian and cultural critic Arif Dirlik, only "a
competing set of ideational constructs that project upon a certain location
on the globe the imperatives of interest, power, or vision of these
historically produced relationships" (56). And those discourses are not
simply plural but are oppositional in relations of power, one seeking
dominion and the other resisting that imposition. Within the idea of the
Pacific, hegemony is commonly rendered as global while resistance, local.[9]
There is much virtue to the construct, especially because it positions
Oceania's peoples against the activities over, through, and upon the Pacific
by peoples along the rim–Europeans, Americans, and Asians. But there are
multiple meanings to "local," as when some Hawaiian nationalists
distinguish "indigenous" from "local" and therewith rights and privileges,
or when multinationals like Sony assimilate and assume the name and form
of natives through "global localization." Dirlik thus urges a "critical

---

[8] For an exposition on Pacific rim discourse as an American construct during late
     capitalism and the late cold war years, see Christopher L. Connery, "Pacific Rim
     Discourse: The U.S. Global Imaginary in the Late Cold War Years," in *Asia/Pacific
     as Space of Cultural Production*, edited by Rob Wilson and Arif Dirlik (Durham,
     North Carolina: Duke U P, 1995), 30-56.

[9] See e.g., Peter Hempenstall and Noel Rutherford, *Protest and Dissent in the Colonial
     Pacific* (Suva, Fiji: Institute of Pacific Studies of the University of the South Pacific,
     1984); and Rob Wilson, *Reimagining the American Pacific: From South Pacific to
     Bamboo Ridge and Beyond* (Durham, North Carolina: Duke U P, 2000). For a more
     sophisticated account of the engagement, see Martha Kaplan, *Neither Cargo Nor
     Cult: Ritual Politics and the Colonial Imagination in Fiji* (Durham, North Carolina:
     Duke U P, 1995).

localism" that simultaneously rejects essentialist notions of indigenous cultures and the glossings of globalism.[10]

Pacific civilization is both global and local, a crossing and a home. It is multiply positioned and occupied. Sighted from the U.S. shore, the Pacific marks the continent's edge and the ocean's uncharted expanses. It is the vast unknown. It is the other ocean. The Atlantic is the self—familiar and raced European, whereas the Pacific is the other—alien and raced Asian. And yet Asia has weighed on the minds of Europeans as part of their patrimony and destiny, as an opportunity and "open door." But Asia also poses a threat to white supremacy. The Atlantic alliance confronts the Pacific menace. In the nineteenth-century European imaginary, the "yellow peril" threatened to swamp European civilization and Christianity, and in the late twentieth century it strived to usurp capitalism and Western civilization and complete the unfinished business that began with Pearl Harbor.[11]

Atlantic civilization, whether white or black, creates binaries that have been integral to the U.S. social and racial formations. The white Atlantic features a Eurocentrism that positions the U.S. as a correlate of European civilization, while the African diaspora (or the black Atlantic) mitigates Eurocentrism but also reinscribes the racial dualism of black and white. This chapter proposes a Pacific civilization not to displace Atlantic civilization, but to intervene in the binaries of Eurocentrism and race. America has, since its "discovery," found its manifest destiny in westering, in its thrust toward Asia, and Asians have, like their African diasporic counterparts, been captured and recruited for the plantations of the "new world." The U.S. is equally an Atlantic as well as a Pacific civilization. That recognition allows for multiplicities within the U.S. social and racial formations that contradict the Republic's foundational binaries. (It also releases Africa from the Atlantic to an embrace of its Indian Ocean civilization and ties with Asia.)

Yet that notion of a Pacific civilization, if centered around the "self" of the U.S., establishes another binary of the U.S. and "others" that reduces as local global social relations while privileging the "self" (the U.S.). It might

---

[10] Arif Dirlik, "The Global in the Local," in *Global/Local: Cultural Production and the Transnational Imaginary*, edited by Rob Wilson and Wimal Dissanayake (Durham, North Carolina: Duke U P, 1996), 21-45. See also, Wilson, *Reimagining*, 11, 22, 148-49.

[11] See e.g., Pierton W. Dooner, *The Last Days of the Republic* (San Francisco: Alta California, 1880); Homer Lea, *The Valor of Ignorance* (New York: Harper & Brothers, 1909); George Friedman and Meredith Lebard, *The Coming War With Japan* (New York: St. Martin's Press, 1991); Samuel P. Huntington, *The Clash of Civilizations and the Remaking of World Order* (New York: Simon & Schuster, 1996); and Richard Bernstein and Ross H. Munro, *The Coming Conflict With China* (New York: Alfred A. Knopf, 1997).

also inspire a white and yellow racial binary (white North America and yellow East Asia) and a rim-centered American and Asian binary that slights the transnational ocean and the peoples of Oceania (and non-East Asian Asians). And why add Pacific civilization to Atlantic civilization when the very idea of "civilization" is bloated with Eurocentric and hegemonic meanings? The "burden" (and challenge), thus, of constructing a Pacific civilization is simultaneously to disrupt the hegemonies of Atlantic civilization and describe alternatives that don't replicate old or conjure new hierarchies.

Works Cited

Bernstein, Richard, and Ross H. Munro. *The Coming Conflict with China.* New York: Alfred A. Knopf, 1997.

Braudel, Fernand. *Civilization and Capitalism, 15th-18th Century.* Berkeley: U of California P, 1992.

Chappell, David A. *Double Ghosts: Oceanian Voyagers on Euroamerican Ships.* Armonk, New York: M. E. Sharpe, 1997.

Clifford, James. *Routes: Travel and Translation in the Late Twentieth Century.* Cambridge, MA: Harvard U P, 1997.

Columbus, Christopher. *The Log of Christopher Columbus.* Trans. Robert H. Fuson. Camden, Maine: International Marine, 1987.

Connery, Christopher. "Pacific Rim Discourse: The U.S. Global Imaginary in the Late Cold War Years" in *Asia/Pacific as Space of Cultural Production.* Eds. Rob Wilson and Arif Dirlik. Durham, North Carolina: Duke U P, 1995.

Davis, Forrest. *The Atlantic System: The Story of Anglo-American Control of the Seas.* New York: Reynal & Hitchcock, 1941.

Dillon, Richard. "Kanaka Colonies in California." *Pacific Historical Review* 24 (February 1955): 17-23.

Dirlik, Arif. "The Asia-Pacific Idea: Reality and Representation in the Invention of a Regional Structure." *Journal of World History* 3:1 (Spring 1992): 56.

---. "The Global in the Local" in *Global/Local: Cultural Production and the Transnational Imaginary.* Eds. Rob Wilson and Wimal Dissanayake. Durham, North Carolina: Duke U P, 1996.

Dooner, Pierton W. *The Last Days of the Republic.* San Francisco: Alta California, 1880

Duncan, Janice. "Kanaka World Travelers and Fur Company Employees, 1785-1860." *Hawaiian Journal of History* 7 (1973): 93-111.

Frank, Andre Gunder. *ReOrient: Global Economy in the Asian Age.* Berkeley: U of California P, 1998.

Friedman, George, and Meredith Lebard. *The Coming War with Japan.* New York: St. Martin's Press, 1991.

Gilroy, Paul. *The Black Atlantic: Modernity and Double Consciousness*. Cambridge, MA: Harvard U P, 1993.

Hansen, Marcus Lee. *The American Migration, 1607-1860*. Cambridge, MA: Harvard U P, 1945.

Hau`ofa, Epeli. "Our Sea of Islands." *Contemporary Pacific* 6:1 (Spring 1994): 153-54, 155.

---. "The Ocean in Us" in *Voyaging Through the Contemporary Pacific*. Eds. David Hanlon and Geoffrey M. White. Lanham, Maryland: Rowman & Littlefield, 2000.

Hempenstall, Peter, and Noel Rutherford. *Protest and Dissent in the Colonial Pacific*. Suva, Fiji: Institute of Pacific Studies of the University of the South Pacific, 1984.

Huntington, Samuel P. *The Clash of Civilizations and the Remaking of World Order*. New York: Simon & Schuster, 1996.

Kaplan, Martha. *Neither Cargo Nor Cult: Ritual Politics and the Colonial Imagination in Fiji*. Durham, North Carolina: Duke U P, 1995.

Karras, Alan L., and J. R. McNeill, eds. *Atlantic American Societies: From Columbus Through Abolition, 1492-1888*. London: Routledge, 1992.

Koppel, Tom. *Kanaka: The Untold Story of Hawaiian Pioneers in British Columbia and the Pacific Northwest*. Vancouver: Whitecap Books, 1995.

Lea, Homer. *The Valor of Ignorance*. New York: Harper & Brothers, 1909.

Macfie, A. L., ed. *Orientalism: A Reader*. New York: New York University Press, 2000.

Pule, John Pahiatua. *The Shark that Ate the Sun*. Auckland: Penguin New Zealand, 1992.

Smith, Henry Nash. *Virgin Land: The American West as Symbol and Myth*. Cambridge, MA: Harvard U P, 1950.

Spate, O. H. K. *The Spanish Lake*. Minneapolis: U of Minnesota P, 1979.

Turner, Frederick Jackson. *The Frontier in American History*. New York: Henry Holt, 1920.

Wallerstein, Immanuel. *The Modern World System*. New York: Academic Press, 1974.

Wendt, Albert, ed. *Nuanua: Pacific Writing in English since 1980*. Honolulu: U of Hawai`i P, 1995.

---. "Towards a New Oceania." *Mana* 1:1 (January 1976): 49-60.

Wills, John E. Jr. "Maritime Asia, 1500-1800: The Interactive Emergence of European Domination." *American Historical Review* 98:1 (February 1993): 83-105.

Wilson, Rob. *Reimagining the American Pacific: From South Pacific to Bamboo Ridge and Beyond*. Durham, North Carolina: Duke U P, 2000.

Wong, Sau-Ling C. "Denationalization Reconsidered: Asian American Cultural Criticism at a Theoretical Crossroads." *Amerasia Journal* 21:1/2 (1995): 6-7.

ELKE STURM TRIGONAKIS

Global Playing in Poetry: The Texts of Juan Felipe Herrera and José F. A.
Oliver as a New *Weltliteratur*

"Ich sehe mich daher gern bei fremden Nationen um und rate jedem, es
auch seinerseits zu tun. Nationalliteratur will jetzt nicht viel sagen, die
Epoche der Weltliteratur ist an der Zeit, und jeder muß jetzt dazu wirken,
diese Epoche zu beschleunigen," Johann Wolfgang von Goethe said to
Eckermann, on January 31, 1827 (Eckermann174) urging him to have a
look at the literature of other nations because the era of national literature
had come to an end and that of world literature was beginning. With these
words the German poet, scientist and cosmopolitan introduced the idea of a
world literature, a concept destined to be discussed for many decades and
in different contexts. Although the expression *Weltliteratur* was used in the
1800s by other intellectuals, such as the brothers Schlegel and Wieland, the
word is inseparably associated with the name of Goethe, because it was he
who launched it into the realm of ideas and concepts. As we can deduce
from the contexts of Goethe's allusions to *Weltliteratur* within his vast
work, for Goethe, this concept was propagated by three factors: first, by
the modifications and developments Goethe observed everywhere during
his time in the realms of economy and technology –changes that allowed
people, goods and information to come together to a greater degree and in
far less time than ever before;[1] second, it reflected Goethe's personal
resistance to the increasing tendency towards nationalist isolation in the
German-speaking countries of his time; and third, it was a project for the
future, because Goethe seemed to be very conscious of the fact that
international cooperation was beginning to emerge. In summary,
Weltliteratur was far from being a concept or a theoretical method, but due
to its vagueness and openness, the term became a challenge first to
scholars in Comparative Literature and then to those in Cultural Studies
who attempted to surpass national borders. Hence, Goethe's idea has
undergone many interpretions and definitions, emphasizing either the
quantity (world literature as the sum of all national literatures) or the

---

[1]　In a similar way, Karl Marx subsequently observed the parallels between industrial
development and intellectual teamwork throughout Europe that led to a world
literature composed of national and local literatures; he wrote in his *Manifest der
Kommunistischen Partei* of 1848: "Die geistigen Erzeugnisse der einzelnen
Nationen werden Allgemeingut. Die nationale Einseitigkeit und Beschränktheit
werden mehr und mehr unmöglich, und aus den vielen nationalen und lokalen
Literaturen bildet sich eine Weltliteratur" (Marx/Engels 23-24).

quality (the best works of every national literature). However, the starting point has been traditional national literature, written in a national standard language, belonging to the artistic production of a certain national state and investigated by a national philology.

Under conditions of globalization, the established criteria for a national literary canon and a selective or summarizing approach to *Weltliteratur* will no longer work, because we observe a worldwide increase of hybrid texts that do not fit in any national literature and therefore, cannot be analyzed properly by nationally-based description and evaluation methods. Neither Cultural Studies, with its marked orientation to the anglophone world ("Anglo-Globalism"), nor linguistic constructions like *francophonie* or *lusofonia* are able to offer methodical solutions beyond an asymmetrical and hegemonic discourse as much as this type of discourse might present itself as a postcolonial one.

With this lack of an independent system for describing and evaluating hybrid literature in mind, this paper intends to create a new system that adequately approaches mixed forms of literary production. The first step consists in the establishment of differentiating criteria for the new system that I would like to denominate "new world literature" or *Neue Weltliteratur*; these criteria are empirically based and result from extensive reading in order to build up a global corpus of literary texts which fulfills the following requirements:

1. Multilingualism: there must be more than one language prevalent in the text, if not evident, at least in form of a structure, a topic of the plot or as intertextuality;

2. Transnationalism: there should be movements in space or time, for instance from one country to another, or from one historical space to another, or some kind of literal or metaphorical border-crossing;

3. Localism: there should be an obvious affiliation to one or more particular region or to urban agglomerations that can function as a (lost or found) homeland, one of the stages of a life in permanent movement or generally as a reservoir for universal affairs

The new *Weltliteratur* should be seen as a complementary concept to Goethe's, it represents the dialectics between the global and the regional or the universal and the particular by negotiating between different cultures. In other words, it can be described as a continuous process of cultural translation. "*Translatio imperii et studii,*" that means translation of empires and cultures, as Utz Riese puts it in referring to the contact zones of America (9), is far more than just mediation between different cultures, empires and products that has been going on for centuries in both Americas, Europe and Africa. Nowadays, it means the negotiation of fluent identities, historical epochs and geographical spaces, a never ending border-crossing in the literal and metaphorical sense.

In literature, this negotiation of borders is realized through the performance of alterities. Thus, an aesthetics of otherness is the common attribute in every utterance of the new *Weltliteratur*. As soon as all these "Migrantenliteratur," Chicano literature, Afro-American literature or whatever are classified as a subcategory or a "minority literature" in relation to an established national literature, it is difficult to avoid the trap of a hegemonic discourse and an asymmetrical center-periphery value system. This is what I would like to overcome by creating the new category "world literature;" by grouping together all these hybrid, heterogeneous, patchwork literatures, some independent hermeneutic instruments to an approach to this kind of literary production can be introduced. The national literary canons no longer serve as the point of reference; thus, it would be possible to study this category as a group of its own, with an independent system of standards, values, methods, strategies, and, last but not least, aesthetics. This paper attempts to demonstrate the usefulness of new world literature by comparing the poetic work of two authors without a homeland in the traditional sense of the word and whose work is representative of the global tendency to create hybrid forms in literature. The texts comply to the three requirements multilingualism, transnationalism and localism and reveal by their poetic strategy the will to function as a continuous performance of alterity as a cultural practice. Therefore, they are appropriate to a typological comparison as I would like to undertake here in order to authorize us to establish a new literary system "world literature" by the similarities in their poetic discourses.

Juan Felipe Herrera is an outstanding representative of the generation of younger Chicano writers, publishing poetry and dramas since the seventies. Salvador Rodriguez del Pino counts him among the "poetas de influencia claramente americana," which means "incluyendo la poesia 'Beat'" (in Jiménez 80). Alfred Arteaga characterizes Herrera as "an amazing poet whose recognition does not correlate with his talent" because he "is a difficult poet" for the average monolingual Anglo reader adding that "Herrera is the poet of the hybrid subject. For him, each poem is a site of play and conflict, an unfinalized process where the reader must participate." (153)

José F. A. Oliver made his first appearance in 1987, publishing his poems in the genre of the then so-called "Gastarbeiterliteratur", a fairly derogoatory term that is applied to the circle of foreign workers in Germany who explore crisis-of-identity themes; although Oliver's first books can be characterized as a personal search for identies between Spain and Germany, very soon his interest encompassed far more universal themes. As in the case of Herrera, literary critics emphasize the quality of Oliver's poems, while also describing them as "schwierig, dunkel und vielfach hermetisch" ("difficult, dark and very hermetic") because they confront the reader with an "Entautomatisierungsprozess"["process of de-automatization"] on a literal as well as a metaphorical level. (Ruiz in Chiellino 94)

The texts of both authors have several characteristics in common: although they are written in a standard language – English in the case of Herrera, German in that of Oliver–there are entries from other languages and varieties such as Mexican vernaculars, Mexican Spanish as well as European Spanish, the Andalusian dialect and the Alemannic dialect; both authors have translated themselves into one or more secondary languages. This allows us to consider a multilingual poetic discourse that begins with one-word entries and reaches a wide range of intertextual references in the secondary languages. A further common feature is the fact that this kind of literature is "glocalized," so that we can find transnationalism as an typical utterance of globalization in its widest sense as well as a deep rootedness in certain regions or in local features, i.e. megalopolis like Mexico City-Los Angeles or Berlin-Istanbul, whereas the national level has become more or less irrelevant. Thus, we are confronted with a unique literary genre that obviously does not belong to a clearly-shaped national literature, a hybrid literature which is nevertheless influenced by various national canons. In the following discussion then, I will examine this literature as New World Literature as it is evidenced in the work of Herrera and Oliver.

Multilingualism[2]

Here, I will look at different forms of multilingualism and its function within the textual construction in the work of both writers. The starting-point for this kind of literary production is (to a greater or lesser extent) the bi- or multilingual individual author. It is not by chance that Gloria Anzaldua claims: "I am my language" (59). Language is, or better yet, languages are the strongest identity factor in multicultural literature, since they are the element which describes and defines the multifaceted identity of individuals in the contact situation between different cultures (Ikas 203). This is the reason one can find deviations from standard forms of national languages in all those cases where a bi- or multicultural environment is to be transformed into literary texts. For Gary D. Keller, the fact that Chicano literature is characterized by code-switching [...] constitutes a radical way for artistic language to draw attention to itself, to foreground, in the parlance of the Prague school. Moreover, because code-switching is a

---

[2]   Although in Chicano literary criticism the term "interlingualism" is more usual I prefer "multilingualism" for my purposes because I intent to stress the fact as such that there are many languages existing at the same time in the same text entity.

radical, overt stylistic occurrence, it requires adequate literary justification in order to be deemed valid or successful (311).

As far as Germany is concerned, scholars have not reached yet the epistemically high-levelled discussion we find in Chicano literature. Only in the nineties, has a younger generation of scholars begun to deal with bi- or multilingual strategies in German multicultural literature, and it is noteworthy that a plethora of fundamental studies foregrounding bilingualism are written by people who are themselves bilingual as is the case of Carmine Chiellino, Immacolata Amodeo, Aglaia Blioumi or Gürsel Aytaç for example. Attention to German Multicultural Literature can, however, gain a lot by comparative "excursions" to the United Kingdom, the U.S.A., Canada or the Caribbean with their well-established so-called minority discourses.

Both authors, Herrera as well as Oliver, use different linguistic techniques to create a multilingual poetic universe. One of them, for example, is self-translation in order to create–in the framework of one book–texts in different languages. Actually, this is not extraordinary. Everyone with a good grounding in more than one language can do the same. What makes it a poetic strategy is the decision about what is translated and what is not translated on the one hand, and how it is translated, that is, literally or quite freely.

In the case of Juan Felipe Herrera, he starts his book *Giraffe on Fire* (2001) with a Spanish "Tabla de materias" without any explanation, announcing five long poems: two of them, "Bull and Octopus/ Pulpo y Toro (Adios, querido PRI)" and "Beneath Your Skin/ Bajo tu piel" seem to lead the reader to a translated version of the same poem but this is an error: the fact that "Pulpo y Toro" contains an explicative or ironical addition referring to the Mexican ruling party PRI, excludes everyone unfamiliar with Mexican history or its political scene. Thus, from the beginning the text creates a disadvantage for monolingual English recipients by denying them information, turning upside down the real hegemonical situation between white US citizens and the Mexican population by elevating the Mexican position. Of course, this poetic counter-world aims at an utopic future, but exactly here lies an obvious political statement in favour of the immigrants. In general, the main topic of the seven English poems of "Bull and Octopus" is to discuss the relationship between the Anglos, i.e., the white, US Americans, and the Mexican immigrants using numerous images and names grounded in the Hispanic and pre-Columbian universe. The first poem ends with an outcry of protest:

> Amerinothing of your great lobster hands like this
> You want us (*Giraffe* 17)
> In Spanish:

> Amerinada de tus grandes manos langostinos as-
> Nos quieres (*Giraffe* 27)

The neologism, "amerinothing," from "Amerindian" and "nothing" appears in the Spanish version in a literal translation as "amerinada", but things are not always that simple. The English texts are characterized by a good number of non-English references, for instance to painters like the Spaniard Goya or the Mexican Frida Kahlo (*Giraffe* 22), to Mayan tribes as in "with my Huichol women [...]" or Aztec localities like Tlatelolco[3] (*Giraffe* 20), which, of course, remain like that in the Spanish version. But whereas the Spanish entries are reduced to these few references to names plus the Catholic ritual, in the Spanish poems we can find far more English entries, as for instance in the poem with the title "Lunes: (avion PRI)" in the Spanish version:

> (avion PRI) *This is the string – this is the noose –*
> *this is the Brown slashed head*, el nudo perdido, la piola sagrada
> [...]
> coco y alfombras de barata y pepitas y reiletes
> *in the stone rubble volcanic ash* (*Giraffe* 29)
> The English version is
> Monday: (PRI jet)

> (PRI jet) This is the string – this is the noose
> this is the brown slashed head, the lost knot, the holy twine
> [...]
> coconut and carpets on sale and pumpkin seeds and confetti
> in the stone rubble volcanic ash (*Giraffe* 19)

At first sight, the English parts of the Spanish text draw the reader's attention to themselves by the italics, that is, by an optical method that generally is not used in Herrera's English texts with Spanish entries. Whereas "Brown" begins with a capital in the Spanish version, it appears in the usual orthography "brown" in the English poem – thus, this expression sets off the linguistic environment and seems to allude to the pride of the fact of being brown or Indian. The fact that there are more English entries in the Spanish versions than vice versa transforms the Spanish poems to an optically and linguistically uneven, heterogenous construction alluding, in this way, to the difficult living conditions of the Mexican (or Indian) part of the US-population, always invaded by the

---

[3]   A central part of Mexico City. In 1968, under the rule of President Diaz Ordaz, there was a massacre of demonstrating students on the square of Three Cultures, so that Tlatelolco became a symbol of state repression by the ruling party PRI.

English major culture. As a sort of counter-strike, the texts of *Giraffe on Fire* do not make the slightest attempt to explain the foreign language entry. The result is that the "ideal" reader should be linguistically equipped with a knowledge of English, Spanish and some vernacular languages like Mayan dialects to be able to follow the texts not only in their code-switching, but also in their cultural-switching between US-American, Mexican and pre-Columbian allusions, images and metaphors–this obviously provides the readers of Latin American origin with a great advantage and inverts the real conditions of economic and political power.

After self-translation, a subsequent consideration would be longer entries such as sentences or whole paragraphs in the primary language. This option is seldom used in Herrera's poems. Only in the drama "Jaguar Hotel," included in the *Mayan Drifter*, are there longer passages in Spanish (222 and 228) or even a prayer of the Lacandón Indians in their own language (185). In this context, the function of code-switching is obviously the imitation of colloquial speech, whereas in the poems the reasons for the foreign language entries can be the rhythm of a verse as well as the synecdochic representation of a second or third cultural background, in short, *poeisis* instead of *mimesis*.

José F. A. Oliver goes in his texts far beyond Herrera's in the quantity as much as in the quality of longer passages in languages other than German. Consequently, he begins the poem "Poem eines mir anvertrauten Gastlings" with twelve lines in Spanish followed by German, thus, precisely thematizing the point of code-switching:

> Despierto.
> De madrugada despierto.
> [...]
> Las aguas.
> Su memoria.
> Oh, pardon...
> Ich vergaß,
> dass ich in Deutschland bin.
>
> Ich wache auf.
> Es scheint Nacht zu sein. (*Gastling* 10)[4]

This poem is written by a lyrical "I" that is fighting against the identities forced upon him, the Andalusian, the Spanish, the German.

---

[4]   In English it would be approximately: I wake up./ I wake up in the early twilight./ [...] The waters./ Their memory./ Oh, I am sorry.../ I forgot,/ that I am in Germnay. / / I wake up./ It seems to be night,

Living through the events of autumn 1992, when neo-nazi groups attacked the homes of Turkish and other foreigners in Germany, the protagonist of the poem searches for another homeland but discovers that Spain also smells of fire. The murders of Germany remind him of other murders, so he associates them with Fuentevaqueros, the birth place of Federico Garcia Lorca (by the way, a standard motif in all of Oliver's books), who was shot by the fascist *Falange Española* in 1936. Thus, there is no place for this protagonist, because he is confronted with the same violence everywhere; consequently, the text comes to the following conclusion: "Die Fremde hat also ihren Geruch./ Straßenzüge./ Überall Buenos Aires./ fadengehaltenes Buenos Aires" (*Gastling* 14), that is, "The foreign has its smell (odour?)./ Avenues./ Everywhere Buenos Aires./ Buenos Aires, hold by a threat". This passage is quite characteristic for Oliver's poetry which does not care much about the question if the reader is able to follow the associative chains exposed in the text: Here, for instance, it is an ironical play upon words with the capital of Argentina, Buenos Aires, that means "good winds"; it refers to the "Holy Virgin of the Good Winds" in Sevilla, where the sailors of the 16th used to ask for a last blessing before they started their transatlantic voyages. In this contex here, it emphasizes the fact that nor the air of the Spanish bonfires neither the burning houses in Germany produce "buenos aires".

Irony plays a decisive role in another poem entitled "dorfidylle heimattduft" ("village idyll homeland's fragrance") with a wrongly spelt word "Heimat", where the text juxtaposes a "dialogue" between a saleswoman at a butcher's shop somewhere in the Black Forest region and the famous monologue of Goethe's Faust in the first act of *Faust I*, which, however, is slightly contorted: it sounds like the original, it rhymes like the original, it has the same theme as the original – but it is not:

(original text)
Derf's susch no ebbis si??
Ha jo! E bißle Goethe, bittschee!
Habe nun Philosophie Juristerei und   Habe nun, ach!
Philosophie,
De Doktor mocht'r, ei, ei   Juristerei und Medizin,
Wie schee, wie schee, lideradur
Derf's sunsch no ebbis si usserem Schinke pur
Medizin und leider auch Theologie Und leider auch Theologie!
s'Feschd isch gruusig gsi, vergeß i ni
selle bleede Kapell, Gott weiß worum
die Wurscht isch krumm, des isch saudumm
durchaus studiert mit heißem Bemühn Durchaus studiert, mit heißem Bemühn.
[...] [...]

so ziehe ich schon Jahr um Jahr Und ziehe schon an die zehen
Jahr
herauf herab und kreuz und krumm Herauf, herab und quer und
krumm
mich selber an der Nase rum Meine Schüler an der Nase herum.
Und sehe, daß wir nichts wissen können.
deutsch-sein, meinte ein freund, heißt,
goethe in sich zu spüren. (*HEIMATT* 15)[5]

Surely, there are only a few more elegant methods to undermine a
canonized national poet such as Johann Wolfgang von Goethe. The fact
that this happens through a dialect makes things even "worse," because the
discourse destroys the usual asymmetrical relationship between high
Standard German and low dialect variety, which reflects the center-
periphery hegemony and expresses a clear statement in favour of the
dialect and the periphery. In other poems, Andalusian dialect or Spanish
plays this role. Besides the decontextualization of Faust's famous
monologue, it is mocked at by the changes it undergoes: The punctuation is
neglected, the verse order has become different, the main topic has
changed the involved persons, for in Goethe' s version Faust is frustrated
about the impossibility to teach any useful knowledge to his pupils –
always in consciousnenss of not knowing anything at all – whereas in
Oliver's poem the lyrical I in vain aims at teaching himself. At the end of
the poem, irony reaches a peak through the assertion that to be German
means automatically to feel Goethe (written without capital!) deep inside, a
sentence that has been undermined by the poem as a whole. Of course, it is
obvious that Oliver's kind of multilingualism presupposes a great deal of
intertextual background knowledge for the recipient to understand the
texts. In many cases, the poems become quite hermetic, drawing attention
to the materiality of the poetic language, its rhythms and sounds and
refusing communication.

As far as one-word entries are concerned, it would be easy to show
through a plethora of examples that this is the most frequent form of
multilingualism in the texts of both poets. And in the case of Herrera, I
would not completely agree with Alfred Arteaga's statement that "for the

---

[5]   *May I help you with anything else??/ Oh yes, a littlebit of Goethe, please!/* I have
studied philosophy jurisprudence and/ *he writing his Ph. Dissertation, really fine/
how wonderful, how wonderful, literature/ would you like anything else except the
raw ham/* medicine and theology, too, unfortunately/ *the party was awful, I will
never forget it/ such a bad music band, god knows why/ the sausage is crooked
(curved?), that is so stupid (silly?)* / I have tried really hard/ [...]/ that is how I lead
myself by the nose, year after year, up and down, criss-cross/ to be German, said a
friend to me/ that is to feel goethe inside.

poet Juan Felipe Herrera, the monolingual unit tends to be the book. *Rebozos of Love* and *Akrilica* are primarily Spanish books, while *Exiles of Desire* and *Facegames* are English" (69). At least for the books considered here, the reader is confronted with multilingualism to an extent that makes them a blend of the American-way-of-life, *mexicanidad* and *chicanidad*.

In Oliver's texts, the reader also encounters several one-word entries, but in different forms. In the first half of his work, the entries are nearly always Spanish or Alemannic in German, but from 1997 on, Alemannic disappears completely, whereas Spanish mainly refers to concrete, geographical places and is enriched by French, English, Serbian or Turkish. Very often the secondary language entries are part of the title or the title itself, which means they have a highly appellative function.[6] Like the longer entries, they are not usually explained: The fact is that titles such as "Beyoglu, istiklâl cad." refers to the main road of Istanbul or "D. F. surreal, »circunvalacion«" to Mexico City (*fernlautmetz 70/ 102*) do not even become clear after reading the rest of the poem, what means that from the beginning with the titles, the texts refuse to communicate.

To sum up, multilingualism plays a significant role and has different functions. The least important among them is the mimetic function. Neither Oliver's texts nor Herrera's tend to reproduce colloquial language, and when they do so, this usually furthers an ironic or parodistic purpose. A far more interesting function here is the representative function: every strange word stands for a geographically strange world; every code-switching marks a border on the one hand, but produces contact-zones on the other hand. All this translates into borderlands, where identities, spaces and localizations are negotiated again and again without being finally fixed. Furthermore, the secondary language represents–beneath the spatial dimension – an historical dimension, pointing at different times, for example through references to the Spain of Franco or the Aztec civilization in Mexico. Another function is the loss of common language habits; in confrontation with the strange word or sentence the reader loses his or her normal context of the words, which leads to a de-automatization of language and emphasizes the material character of language, as well as the complete arbitrariness of the relationship between things and words–de Saussure's concepts in poetry. Precisely here lie the poeticity of the multilingual text[7] and the specific aesthetics by which these hybrid texts differ from monolingual texts allowing us to consider them as an

---

[6]   Having treated multilingualism in Oliver's poetry quite extensively in my study "Formen und Funktionen des Multilingualismus im poetischen Werk von José F. A. Oliver", in *Festschrift für K. Karpusa-Dorfmüller* 2005, I will not go into details here.

[7]   For the history of multilingualism in literature, cf. Forster, Leonard (1970).

independent literary system of their own – *Neue Weltliteratur* or New
World Literature.

Transnationalism

   Until now, the paper has treated formal criteria whereas in the following
pages, thematic aspects will be in the center of interest and I will
concentrate on transnationalism as a poetic strategy. First of all,
transnationalism is expressed by the plethora of movements of every kind,
from one country to another, from one region to another, contact with other
cultural spaces and so on. For good reason, the German poet Durs
Grünbein talks about the transitory as a typical attribute of contemporary
art, and in fact, polyvalence – the avoidance of stable positions, the
absence of frontiers, programs or canons – is the outstanding property of
the so-called "Transit-Poesie" of the nineties, and not only in German–
speaking countries (Elm 21).
   The texts of both poets present numerous references to traveling: one of
Oliver's books, the *Vater unser in Lima,* contains almost exclusively
poems that describe a journey to Peru, offering a sometimes cynical
confrontation (beginning with the title of the book, which refers to the
Decalogue) with the desolating living conditions of the greatest part of the
population in this South American country. Although there are subjective
experiences and individual feelings, the main purpose of poems like "und
die sonne weinte tränen" ("and the sun sheded tears"), "campesina" or
"abendessen/ cena" ("diner/cena") is a sharp political statement against the
exploitation of the (neo)colonized parts of the world. Other poems narrate
the traversing of large territories or staying in different places. So for
example, stream of consciousness, while sitting in an aircraft, often
appears in Oliver's texts; and especially the last two books *fernlautmetz*
("stone-mason of distant sounds") and *nachtrandspuren* ("traces of the
nocturnal edge or the edge of the night' tracks?), lead the recipient from
one point of the world to another: titles of poems are "Kufstein" (a city in
the north of Austria), "Beyo-lu, istiklâl cad." (the main road of the center
of Istanbul) or "Madrid, Parque de Berlin" (a park in Madrid with a piece
of the former Berlin wall). According to the poetic strategy of
multilingualism, these names are referred to in the original, leaving the text
open to many different readings or even becoming quite hermetic in some
cases. A reader who is familiar with the fact mentioned previously that
"Beyoglu, istiklâl cad." is the name of the central shopping street in
Istanbul will have another approach to the text than someone who does not
know about this road.

As for Herrera, more or less the same thematic phenomena can be found but in other poetic forms. For example, his book *Mayan Drifter* is a description of a journey to Chiapas in Mexico. It is a journey that not only provides the recipient with a great deal of information about this region, but, also attempts to "reimagine America" (*Drifter* 3). It is equivalent to a "double quest, a journey into indigenous territories and a slippery trek into myself" (5), as the narrator states, conceiving himself as deficient, someone who wants to get rid of his "Americanness" without having gained "Indianness" (86). He refuses to belong to the "In-Between People," meaning the Indians of Chiapas, who sell their culture to tourists, or the chicanos in the USA, who dream of a utopian Aztlan-homeland: "I was split," he concludes about his situation (69). As the only solution, "my language, then, emerges as a possible re-cognition" (4), as a space of expression and identification. For this reason, perhaps, Herrera expresses an impressive mental independence in his texts by numerous references to other countries or cultural territories. He mention Rome and Italy – among other places – throughout the poems in *Love after the Riots*; he refers to; Spain and Catalonia and makes many allusions to Central America in *Giraffe on Fire*, whose title, by the way, is taken from a picture by the Catalan painter Salvador Dali (who is only mentioned occasionally in the book); in the *Border-Crosser with a Lamborghini Dream*, the poems jump from the USA to Tijuana, from Mexico to Rwanda, and from the Chinatown of Los Angeles to Bulgaria.

These sudden and superficially unmotivated changes demonstrate that displacement is a decisive element of this literature. Obviously, the narrators or lyrical protagonists have different identities, dependent on particular cultural contexts. Every time someone trespasses national borders, the "I" in these texts becomes another and the result is very often a feeling of repression, as when Oliver writes about waking up in Germany "wie man gezwungen wird,/ in Deutschland aufzuwachen,/ wenn man in diesem Land geboren wurde,/ aber nie dazu gehören durfte" (*Gastling* 11) (how you are forced/ to wake up in Germany/ when you were born in this country/ but never allowed to belong to it"), but there are no alternatives and Andalusia has the same smell of fire as Germany: "wie man gezwungen war,/ Andalusien zu riechen,/ wenn man dort nicht geboren wurde/ und dazu gehören mußte"(13) ("as one was forced/ to smell Andalusia,/ when one was not born there/ but had to belong there"). Similar to Herrera, Oliver in his earlier books displays as intense feeling of belonging nowhere. In his later work, this feeling is replaced by a very self-conscious belonging to everywhere and by the creation of a real "third space" in Homi K. Bhabha's sense, especially in his last two books, which focus on places in the whole of Europe and America. The lyrical "I" undergoes a change of perspective, which sometimes leads to a diametrically opposite positioning in new circumstances. In this way, the

Spanish immigrant, the "Gastarbeiter" of the first trilogy, turns into the
rich "gringo" or "gringuito" throughout the poems in *Vater unser in Lima*.
Another aspect of transnationalism, besides the crossing of spatial
borders, is the mixing up of temporal spaces. When the texts of Herrera
incorporate US-American and ancient Mexican narrations or when Oliver
draws Columbus into the administration in the former German capital
Bonn (*Land* 100) and juxtaposes the murder of Federico Garcia Lorca by
the fascist *Falange* in 1936 with the German contemporary neo-nazi
attacks on foreigners, we face a hybridization of different narrations, that,
in consequence, undermines the dominant discourses by other, peripheral
ones.

According to Utz Riese, the transnational element in this kind of
literature discussed here makes it possible to perceive these texts as contact
zones, where–using different languages or dialects-an updating of very
different cultural dates happens, where heterotopian spaces confuse times
and territories (Herlinghaus and Riese 9, 102) The continuous border-
crossing in a concrete and a metaphorical sense deprives the traditional
national discourses of their importance, thus, the hierarchical relationship
center-periphery becomes obsolete. In the next section I will attempt to
demonstrate that localism or regionalism does the same, only on another
level.

3. Localism

The fact that globalism is more than just "McDonaldization," but is
accompanied by a strong revalorization of the local, has become
commonplace among the theorists of globalism, such as Anthony Giddens
or Ulrich Beck. As for culture, Richard Münch notes: "Eine reichhaltige
lokale Kultur ist das Arsenal, aus dem die globale Kultur unablässig
schöpfen muss" (229)[8], in other words, globalism without localism is
inconceivable. Paola Mildonian maintains a critical attitude towards
globalism when she writes that it "peut comporter une réévaluation de ce
qui est précisément pluriel, périphérique, différent, de ce qui se constitue
dans la différence et qui est porteur de différence,"[9] but on the other hand,
she warns that globalism "pourrait aussi mettre fin, satisfaite de ses
définitions, à toute dialectique et, en dernière instance, cacher la substance
la plus dangereuse de la globalisation moderne occidentale, qui consiste à

---

[8] "A rich local culture is the reservoir out of which the global culture always draws"
[9] Globalism can "re-evaluate everything that is polymorphic, peripherical, different,
     that constitutes itself by difference and carries difference"

construire des systèmes locaux à partir de son propre centre"[10] (167), because this could lead every local centre to a new centre-periphery-hierarchization in the face of other local centres.

In 1979, in his paper "Identifying Chicano Literature," Luis Leal stresses the fact that, "Chicano literature by lifting the regional to a universal level has emerged from the barrio to take its place alongside the literatures of the world" (5). This is a different point of view from those previously held, explicable by the longing of Chicano literature for recognition as a literary discourse that is equivalent to the traditional ones. Nowadays, the question is not so much if Chicano literature can be considered "high culture" in terms of contents and forms; it is much more interesting to analyze which way local or regional elements are made to differ from the mainstream ones, not to compete with established national literatures. Globalism's most important attribute is that it offers a new space of experiences that consists in global, individual and local aspects and, thus, develops new contexts of meaning and acting (Beck 38).

At least in Herrera's texts, neither the USA nor Mexico as national states play important roles. "El México contemporaneo no les ofrece [a los chicanos] una alternativa con fuerza suficiente para contrarestar la cultura de masas de Estados Unidos. Asi las cosas, los chicanos buscan 'reindianizarse', establecer un contacto con el pasado que México subyugy en cierta forma canceló," emphasizes Juan Villoro (7, 161), pointing at the actual tendency among chicanos to re-design their Indian past because contemporary México has nothing to offer as an alterantive to the US-mass culture. Instead of Mexico as a national state and point of reference, Chiapas as a concrete region – especially in *The Mayan Drifter* (1996) -and pre-Columbian symbolism as a metaphorical region gain an impressive presence in Herrera's work. In our context, the journey itself through Chiapas is of less importance than the intensity of the Aztec and Mayan background in Herrera' s poetic texts, interweaving the English poems with an explicit other cultural discourse. This happens, for example, in many poems in the *Border-Crosser*, beginning with the first poem "punk half panther," the title of which refers to one of the animals worshipped by the Aztecs:

> i stand in pure light, a blaze of eyes & arms,
> volcanic & solar, autistic, anti-written,
> burned by mad friars & clerics, uptown
> octopi readers, my long hair falls as reddish honey,

---

[10] She warns, that globalism "end up with any dialectic relationship, satisfied by its definitions, and could, at the end, hide the most dangerous substance (or topic, issue) of modern western globalization that consists in the construction of local centers starting from exactly these centers themselves"

on a naked supple back,
on breasts small and secretive. (6)

The lyric "I" adopts the guise of a female Aztec on fire, with positive and
negative connotations: on the one hand, there is the fire of the sun as a
symbol for the hero Huitzilopochtli, the war god of the Aztecs, son of the
earth goddess Coatlicue, on the other hand, the fire refers to the Spanish
conquest of Mexico when whole libraries of Aztec books and parchments
were burnt by the Spanish clerics. Further, these lines build up a conscious
antithesis between the "autistic, anti-written" Indian population of Mexico,
or an oral literary tradition, and the "uptown octopi readers," an expression
that could refer to any white reader. Nevertheless, the vernacular cultural
baggage is anything but homogenous; to no extent does it offer a
dimension of a holistic identity. This is the reason I would agree with
Rafael Pérez-Torres in his critical attitude against Cordelia Candelaria's
rather idealistic idea of the pre-Columbian symbology's function as "a
mythic 'memory' that implies an unproblematic and uninterrupted
recuperation and 'remembering' of devalued knowledge manifested
through myths and legends," establishing "connections between the
troubled and unfulfilling present of Chicano disempowerment and a richer
fuller, more holistic but lost past," as he points out paraphrasing
Candelaria's perspective (173 and 175). More than a possibility of evasion
of the unsatisfying actuality, the Indian universe becomes part of this
shattered and split everyday situation, just another example of the
discontinuities of human life. In the same way, Herrera uses Aztec and
Mayan images against the dominant Mexican discourse in the poems in
The Book of Lives, the revival version of the Mexican *loteria*. Generally,
the literary discourse of localism is subversive in relation to the US-
American hegemony as much as the Mexican one, because it enriches the
official center-discourses with so-called peripherial ones. Thus, the center
of gravity changes in favor of the periphery, which becomes a center of its
own. At the same time, the texts provoke comparison between similar
mechanisms of repression and exploitation: by showing the miserable
living conditions in one region – for example, Chiapas–the equally poor
conditions in the US-American Southwest become obvious. Therefore,
localism functions as a poetic strategy as much as internationalism, just on
another hierarchical level, not beyond, but under the nation as an
"imagined community" (Benedict Anderson).
    In José F.A. Oliver's poems the reader is confronted with the same
functionalization of localism as a counterpoint to the dominating German
and, to a lesser degree, Spanish discourse. What Herrera's texts express by
the Pre-Colombian symbology, in Oliver's becomes manifest by using the
Alemannic dialect or typical Andalusian expressions, or by references to

the German Black Forest region: "Folklore ist eine subkulturelle, regional spezifische Formation, die sich ebenso zur dominierenden Kultur verhält wie eine mundartliche Umgangssprache zur Hochsprache. [...] In der Situation kultureller Unterdrückung, Überfremdung und Marginalisierung [...] verfestigt sich solches Brauchtum zur symbolischen Ausdrucksform einer Gegenidentität"[11] (Assmann 155). With the lyric book *Duende* (1997), written in German, Spanish and Alemannic, a certain point of equilibrium is reached, because it demonstrates the equality of the dialect as a poetic language-equality with German and Spanish standards. Consequently, it is interesting to note that the dialect language disappears and is replaced by a highly artistic deconstruction of German by Spanish and many neologisms. This does not mean that localism plays a less important role; on the contrary, although internationalism predominates as a poetic strategy in the last three books, there are a numerous references to specific towns like Amsterdam, Berlin or Bogota, and again to Andalusia, the sea and Garcia Lorca as a *leitmotiv* of the whole work. The only dimension not mentioned is that of the national state.

4. Conclusion

The material presented here has demonstrated the existence of so many similarities between the texts written by José F. A. Oliver and Juan Felipe Herrera that we can refer to a typological relationship. Against the monolingual, hegemonic discourse of Germany and the United States, Oliver and Herrera establish a multilingual poetic strategy of an impressive variety that diametrically changes the center-periphery-relationship by putting the monolingual recipient in the position of alterity. The hybridizised language results in the decontextualization of the standard utterances in the standard poetic language, the destabilization of the national literary canon, and, finally, the establishment of a new poetic discourse whose aesthetic qualities can be evaluated only with difficulty in comparison with the national literature; a better and more fruitful starting point is a reciprocal comparison of these texts. As a result, I have introduced two further categories in order to assure a well-defined, convenient classification: beyond multilingualism, these texts must express transnationalism as well as localism–these two categories being a *conditio sine qua non* of the literature of globalization.

---

[11] "Folklore is a subcultural, regionally specific formation with the same relationship to the dominating culture as a dialect to a standard language. [...] In conditions of cultural repression , massive foreign influence and discrimation these traditions become a fixed symbolic expression of a counter-identity.

Conforming   to   these   three   parameters–multilingualism, transnationalism, localism–this kind of literature functions as a continuous performance of alterity as a cultural practice. It presents a platform where cultural translation is realized or is rejected, claiming a new radical poetic subjectivity. The striking fact, in my opinion, is the noteworthy quantity of these texts that allow us to draw a line from the literary production of Salman Rushdie and Assia Djebar to that of Chinua Achebe and Derek Walcott, to refer only to a few representative, famous authors. This line unifies the literature of these and other authors by its similar poetic discourse creating a category of its own, New World Literature. Of course, this term no longer evokes anything more than echoes of the earlier concept proposed by Johann Wolfgang von Goethe. I think, however, the time has come to establish this new literary genre, a genre that is increasing in quantity and quality worldwide.

Works Cited

Primary Sources

Herrera, Juan Felipe. *Border-Crosser with a Lamborghini Dream.* Tucson: U of Arizona P. 1999.

---. *Giraffe on Fire.* Tucson: U of Arizona P, 2001.

---. *Loteria Cards and Fortune Poems: A Book of Lives.* San Francisco: City Light, 1999.

---. *Love After the Riots.* Willimantic: Curbstone, 1996.

---. *Mayan Drifter: Chicano Poet in the Lowlands of America.* Philadelphia: Temple U P, 1996.

Oliver, José F. A. *Auf-Bruch.* 1987. Berlin: Das Arabische Buch, 1997.

---. *Austernfischer Marinero Vogelfrau.* Berlin: Das Arabische Buch, 1997.

---. *Duende. Meine Ballade in drei Versionen.* Gutach: Drey-Verlag, 1997.

---. *Fernlautmetz.* Frankfurt/Main: Suhrkamp, 2000.

---. *Gastling.* Berlin: Das Arabische Buch, 1993.

---. *HEIMATT und andere FOSSILE TRÄUME.* 1989. Berlin: Das Arabische Buch. 1993.

---. *Nachtrandspuren.* Frankfurt/Main: Suhrkamp, 2001.

---. *Vater unser in Lima.* Tübingen: Heliopolis. 1991.

---. *Weil ich dieses Land liebe.* Berlin: Das Arabische Buch. 1991.

Secondary Sources

Ambrosioni, Maria Gabriella. "Global Exile." *Literatur im Zeitalter der Globalisierung*. Eds. Manfred Schmeling, Monika Schmitz-Emans, and Kerst Walstra. Würzburg: Königshausen & Neumann, 2000. 261-270.

Amodeo, Immacolata. *Die Heimat heißt Babylon: Zur Literatur ausländischer Autoren in der Bundesrepublik*. Opladen: Westdeutscher Verlag, 1996.

Anzaldua, Gloria. *Borderlands – La Frontera: The New Mestiza*. San Francisco: Aunt Lute, 1987.

Arteaga, Alfred. *Chicano Poetics: Heterotexts and Hybridities*. Cambridge: Cambridge U P, 1997.

Assmann, Jan. *Das kulturelle Gedächtnis: Schrift, Erinnerung und politische Identität in den frühen Hochkulturen*. München: C.H. Beck, 2002.

Aytaç, Gürsel. "Sprache als Spiegel der Kultur. Zu Emine Sevgi Özdamars Roman 'Das Leben ist eine Karawanserei.'" *Interkulturelle Figurationen: Zur deutschsprachigen Erzählliteratur von Autoren nichtdeutscher Herkunft*. Ed. Mary Howard. München: Iudicium, 1997. 171-178.

Beck, Ulrich. *Macht und Gegenmacht im globalen Zeitalter: Neue weltpolitische Ökonomie*. Frankfurt am Main: Suhrkamp, 2002.

Blioumi, Aglaia. *Interkulturalität als Dynamik: Ein Beitrag zur deutsch griechischen Migrationsliteratur seit den siebziger Jahren*. Tübingen: Stauffenburg, 2001.

Calderon, Héctor and José David Saldivar, eds. *Criticism in the Borderlands: Studies in Chicano Literature, Culture and Ideology*. Durham, NC: Duke U P, 1994.

Candelaria, Cordelia. *Chicano Poetry*. Westport, Connecticut: Greenwood,1986.

Chiellino, Carmine, ed. *Interkulturelle Literatur in Deutschland: Ein Handbuch*. Stuttgart and Weimar: J.B. Metzler, 2000.

Donghi, Tulio Halperin.*Geschichte Lateinamerikas von der Unabhängigkeit bis zur Gegenwart*. Frankfurt am Main: Suhrkamp, 1994.

Eckermann, Johann Peter. *Gespräche mit Goethe in den letzten Jahren seines Lebens*. Wiesbaden: Brockhaus, 1975.

Elm, Theo, ed. *Lyrik der neunziger Jahre*. Stuttgart: Reclam, 2000.

Forster, Leonard. *The Poet's Tongues: Multilingualism in Literature*. London: Cambridge U P, 1970.

Giddens, Anthony. *Entfesselte Wel:. Wie die Globalisierung unser Leben verändert*. Frankfurt am Main: Suhrkamp, 1999.

Görling, Reinhold. "'Stubborn chunks in the menudo chowder': Sprachliche Hybridisierung und 'grotesker Leib' am Beispiel der Literatur und Kunst der

Chicana/ os." *Multilinguale Literatur im 20 Jahrhundert*. Eds. Manfred Schmeling and Monika Schmitz-Emans. Würzburg: Königshausen & Neumann, 2002. 273-282.

Herlinghaus, Hermann and Utz Riese (Eds.). *Heterotopien der Identität: Literaturin interamerikanischen Kontaktzonen*. Heidelberg: C. Winter, 1999.

Howard, Mary, ed. *Interkulturelle Figurationen: Zur deutschsprachigen Erzählliteratur von Autoren nichtdeutscher Herkunft*. München: Iudicium, 1997.

Ikas, Karin. *Die zeitgenössische Chicana-Literatur: Eine interkulturelle Untersuchung*. Heidelberg: C. Winter, 1999.

Jiménez, Francisco, ed. *The Identification and Analysis of Chicano Literature*. New York: Bilingual Press/ Editorial Bilingüe, 1979.

Keller, Gary D. "The Literary Strategems Available to the Bilingual Chicano Writer." *The Identification and Analysis of Chicano Literature*. Ed. Francisco Jiménez. New York: Bilingual Press/ Editorial Bilingüe, 1979. 263-316.

Koch, Manfred. *Weimaraner Weltbewohner: Zur Genese von Goethes Begriff "Weltliteratur."* Tübingen: Niemeyer, 2002.

Krysinski, Wladimir. "La fin du siècle: systèmes littéraires et "régimes globalitaires." *Literatur im Zeitalter der Globalisierung*. Eds. Manfred Schmeling, Monika Schmitz-Emans, and Kerst Walstra. Würzburg: Königshausen & Neumann, 2000. 147-158.

Luis Leal. "The Problem of Identifying Chicano Literature." *The Identification and Analysis of Chicano Literature*. Ed. Francisco Jiménez. New York: Bilingual Press/ Editorial Bilingüe, 1979. 2-5.

Marx, Karl and Friedrich Engels. *Manifest der Kommunistischen Partei*. Stuttgart: Reclam, 2002.

Mildonian, Paola. "La dialectique du global et du local au seuil de l'âge moderne et les perspectives inter-disciplinaires de la thématologie." *Literatur im Zeitalter der Globalisierung*. Eds. Manfred Schmeling, Monika Schmitz-Emans, and Kerst Walstra. Würzburg: Königshausen & Neumann, 2000.159-180.

Münch, Richard: "Europäische Identitätsbildung. Zwischen globaler Dynamik, nationaler und regionaler Gegenbewegung." *Kultur – Identität – Europa: Über die Schwierigkeiten und Möglichkeiten einer Konstruktion*. Eds. Reinhold Viehoff and Rien T. Segers. Frankfurt am Main: Suhrkamp, 1999. 223-252.

Pérez-Torres, Rafael. *Movements in Chicano Poetry: Against Myths, Against Margins*. Cambridge: Cambridge U P, 1995.

Riese, Utz, ed. *Kontaktzone Amerika: Literarischer Verkehrsformen kultureller Übersetzung*. Heidelberg: C. Winter, 2000.

Rodriguez del Pino, Salvador. "La poesia chicana: una nueva trayectoria." *The Identification and Analysis of Chicano Literature*. Ed. Francisco Jiménez. New York: Bilingual Press/ Editorial Bilingüe, 1979. 68-89.

Rudin, Ernst. *Tender Accents of Sound. Spanish in the Chicano Novel in English*. Tempe, Arizona: Bilingual Press/Editorial Bilingüe, 1996.

Ruiz, Ana. "Literatur der spanischen Minderheit." *Interkulturelle Literatur in Deutschland: Ein Handbuch*. Ed. Carmine Chiellino. Stuttgart; Weimar: J.B. Metzler, 2000. 84-95.

Schmeling, Manfred, Monika Schmitz-Emans, and Kerst Walstra. *Literatur im Zeitalter der Globalisierung*. Würzburg: Königshausen & Neumann, 2000.

Schmeling, Manfred and Monika Schmitz-Emans. *Multilinguale Literatur im 20 Jahrhundert*. Würzburg: Königshausen & Neumann, 2002.

Schmitz-Emans, Monika. "Globalisierung im Spiegel literarischer Reaktionen und Prozesse." *Literatur im Zeitalter der Globalisierung*. Eds. Manfred Schmeling, Monika Schmitz-Emans, and Kerst Walstra. Würzburg: Königshausen & Neumann, 2000. 285-315.

Spitta, Silvia. *Between two Waters: Narratives of Transculturation in Latin America*. Houston, Texas: Rice U P, 1995.

Steinmetz, Horst. "Globalisierung und Literatur(geschichte)." *Literatur im Zeitalter der Globalisierung*. Eds. Manfred Schmeling, Monika Schmitz-Emans, and Kerst Walstra. Würzburg: Königshausen & Neumann, 2000. 189-201.

Viehoff, Reinhold and Rien T. Segers, eds. *Kultur – Identität – Europa: Über die Schwierigkeiten und Möglichkeiten einer Konstruktion*. Frankfurt am Main: Suhrkamp, 1999.

Villoro, Juan. "El juego de identidades cruzadas." *Iberoamericana* 7 (2001): 159-166.

CHRIS LALONDE

Place, Displacement, and a Pathway Home in Kimberly Blaeser's Poetry

Place matters: White Earth Anishinaabe Kimberly Blaeser makes that clear in the Preface to her 1994 award-winning volume of poetry, *Trailing You*, when she says "I know that I write out of a place, a center, that is greater than what I alone am or could be" (*Trailing You* xi).[1] The importance of the particular place that is the White Earth Reservation in north central Minnesota is articulated at the close of the Preface when, before naming other people, Blaeser lists a half-dozen locations in White Earth that the Twin Lakers, for whom the poems are written, will remember. She also offers the names of plants, foods, and activities that are fundamental elements of the fabric that is White Earth. She does not end her list of names of places, people, and activities, really, opting to close the Preface with an ellipsis rather than with a period, because, I think, she wants and needs to do everything she can to keep the lines connecting her to White Earth, and White Earth to her, open and alive even as she lives her day-to-day life at a physical remove from that place.[2] The distance weighs heavily on Blaeser, as both the titles of her two volumes of poetry and a number of the poems in them suggest, but she is able to bear it thanks to acts of writing that articulate connections and community. In the process, *Trailing You* and 2002 *Absentee Indians and Other Poems* reaffirm the centrality of place even in the face of displacement.

Sustaining place can be difficult: broadly speaking, the place of the Native American has always been under threat by the dominant culture.

---

[1] *Trailing You* won the Diane Decorah first book award for poetry from the North American Native Authors Association. The Anishinaabe are known and identified as the Chippewa by the United States Government and the Ojibway, or Ojibwa, by the Canadian Government. Their traditional homeland extends westward from what is today northern Michigan and southern Ontario in the east to Turtle Mountain in North Dakota. Minnesota was and is home to both Lake Superior and Mississippi bands of the Anishinaabe. In addition to White Earth, the Anishinaabe reservations in the state are Bois Fort, Leech Lake, Red Lake, Fond du Lac, Grand Portage, and Mille Lacs. A large number of Anishinaabeg live in the Minneapolis-St. Paul metropolitan area, as well.

[2] Blaeser, an associate professor of English at the University of Wisconsin, Milwaukee, presently lives in southeastern Wisconsin, some six hundred miles southeast of White Earth.

Blaeser's poetry does not shy from this fact. In "Rewriting Your Life" from *Trailing You* and again in "Twelve Steps to Ward Off Homesickness" from *Absentee Indians and Other Poems*, Blaeser offers her reader painful reminders of what it means to be positioned as *indian*, in White Earth Anishinaabe Gerald Vizenor's sense of that term, in the "democratic society" of the United States. Vizenor has long forcefully argued that the *indian*, rendered in italics, signifies an invention of the dominant culture, a simulation that, in giving voice and form to the dominant culture's desires and anxieties, dooms the Native American to absence.[3] The narrator of "Rewriting Your Life" describes "a people born poor / studying in school to be ashamed" (*Trailing You* 70); we know, of course, of the ways in which the educational system in America, public and private, worked and works to position Natives as *indians* so that they might suffer shame.

Vizenor, for instance, has stressed how, in the early 1970s, White Earth children were subjected to the "colonial pedagogics, and the dominant social unions" (*Interior Landscapes* 210) found just off the reservation. Those children had done well while enrolled in the Pine Point school on reservation, many outperforming the national average on standardized tests in fact, but suffered when they made the move to high school in Park Rapids. Hired to direct a federally-funded project entitled "Cultural Understanding Through Education," Vizenor recognized that education was the culprit here, the instrument with which the White Earth Anishinaabeg children were positioned to fail. He saw that too many of the Park Rapids teachers were unable to move beyond their feeling that the White Earth youth were incapable "of abstract thought or reason because they were culturally deprived *indians*" (*Postindian Conversations* 176). It is that sort of mindset that schools the White Earth Anishinaabeg to be ashamed of who they are and where they come from.[4]

Blaeser's "Downwinders," from *Trailing You*, makes clear that what was true of Park Rapids schools is also true of schools to the west of White Earth. In that poem we read of the memory of "being called from classes in high school / going to the little trailer in the parking lot -- / the dentist office for all the Indian kids" (*Trailing You* 54). The summons sends a simple, damning message to the "Indian kids" and the Euroamerican students, faculty, and staff: *indians* are different, they are too impoverished intellectually and economically to take care of themselves. Made to weather the pain of electric shock rather than novocain because they are the unwilling subjects of someone's experiment, an experiment that echoes Dr.

---

[3] Vizenor's formulation can be found, for instance, in *Fugitive Poses: Native American Indian Scenes of Absence and Presence*. Throughout this essay I follow Vizenor's lead and use italics when I wish to signal the dominant culture's construction of the *indian*.

[4] Anishinaabeg is the plural form of the singular Anishinaabe.

Ales Hrdlicka's work in 1916 to determine the blood quantum of White Earth residents, the Native students then have to suffer the humiliation of returning to the classroom marked in yet another way as Other.

"Twelve Steps to Ward Off Homesickness" indicates that the work of the schools to define and position the White Earth Anishinaabe is re-enforced by the repressive state apparatus of law enforcement. Step four dictates that one "Look in the mirror and say 'Damn Indian' until you get it right. Stop only when you remember the voice of every law officer that ever chanted those words" (*Absentee Indians* 5). This is the danger of mimicry, of course, as the repeated words threaten to lead the Native to see her or himself as they are seen by the dominant culture. "Damn Indian" can become precisely that: the phrasing of an identity, a subject position, that at once does violence to the Native and prohibits the articulation of Native identity.

In "Twelve Steps to Ward Off Homesickness" the Native is silenced by an officer of the State. The Law appears in "Recite the Names of all the Suicided Indians," the poem that follows "Twelve Steps to Ward Off Homesickness," and there too it stands as that which silences the People. The poem's second stanza opens on the image of a young Anishinaabe boy

> handcuffed
> roughed up.
> Hard set chin
> quivering
> beneath cakes of blood. (*Absentee Indians* 7)

Here, the violence committed against the boy leads to both the silence of those who end up committing suicide and the silence of those, like the man being described by the narrator, who at one time "stood by. / Without the words" (*Absentee Indians* 8) as the violence occurred.

To be silenced by the State is to run the risk of remaining subject to a placement that is nothing less than literal and figurative displacement. Small wonder then that "Recite the Names of all the Suicided Indians" makes clear that one must find one's voice and sing one's name, for in doing so one is singing one's life. Blaeser has indicated the connection between haiku and traditional Anishinaabe dream songs as both relate to Vizenor's art and aesthetic, and in doing so she reveals the relationship between song and identity for the Anishinaabe. Dream songs "stem from a moment of intense personal awareness" (*Gerald Vizenor* 110) and, because such moments are articulated in songs that are then sung, "seek . . . to assist the reader or listener in the attainment of a similar moment of spiritual awareness or illumination" (116). Singing, then, helps one see oneself even as it links past experiences to the present. Because names for the

Anishinaabe are traditionally connected to both dreams and stories,
moreover, to sing one's name is to connect oneself to the name-giver, to the
power that comes with a dream name, and to the stories that come with the
nicknames one comes to carry (Vizenor *The People Named the Chippewa*
13-14).

An intertextual connection between "Twelve Steps to Ward Off
Homesickness" and Kiowa writer and artist N. Scott Momaday's *The Way
to Rainy Mountain* reveals another reason why finding one's voice and
singing or speaking out is critical.[5] Language can protect you. In
Momaday's memoir, we learn that his grandmother turned to a particular
word when "she confronted evil and the incomprehensible" (33). Momaday
recognizes that the uttered word is "a warding off . . . [of] ignorance and
disorder" (33). Indeed, it is language well and appropriately used that
enables Blaeser to "ward off" both the damning identity conferred by the
dominant culture and homesickness. The law's chant of "Damn Indian"
must be countered with chants that, as the "guy back home" (*Absentee
Indians* 7) makes clear in "Recite the Names of All the Suicided Indians,"
can heal instead of wound.

Like songs, the language and rhythm of poems can counter both the
ignorance that keeps the figure of the *indian* in place and the disorder and
dis-ease that comes of that representation. Consider Blaeser's "Road Show"
from *Trailing You*. The poem's narrator recounts her experiences on a trip
to the Franklin Avenue area of Minneapolis. She is apprehensive, and the
poem makes clear that her anxiety centers on questions of identity. She
knows her "edges will not match the master template" because she is "too
much or too little" of what is desired by those interested in getting a fix on
the *indian* (*Trailing You* 62). The consequences of those definitions are
phrased in the poem's third stanza with the lines "Wonder if this is some
kind of omen: / To be taken for a regular at a bar on Franklin Avenue. /
Worse, to be abandoned at a bar on Franklin Avenue" (*Trailing You* 62).
Yoking the verb for ontology with the past participles "taken" and
"abandoned" indicates the ways the Anishinaabe, and indeed all Natives,
have been identified and treated: they are imagined and positioned as
passive objects to be taken by whites, made into *indians*, and then
abandoned. Such an act of definition leaves the People with no place save
the anachronistic "wild west show" that Blaeser's narrator fears could be
one way to read the road show she is part of in support of the White Earth
Land Recovery Project.

Countering that reading, and in the process affirming the political and

---

[5]   Blaeser is very familiar with Momaday's work, having published an essay on *The
Way to Rainy Mountain* that stresses the open form of Momaday's text and the
necessity that the reader participate in performing the text. See "The Way to Rainy
Mountain: Momaday's Work in Motion."

recuperative powers of poetry for the Anishinaabeg, depends upon acts of revision that begin with the language of the poem itself. Throughout her criticism, Blaeser has called attention to and asks us to pay attention to the language in and of Native texts. In "'Like Reeds Through the Ribs of a Basket': Native Women Weaving Stories" she reminds us that "Indian people 'speak' themselves" so it behooves us to pay attention to "words for speaking, not for print" (275). The second line of "Road Show" offers us words for speaking: "takin' a bunch of Shinabes on the road" includes both non-poetic and idiomatic discourse to effectively mark the distance between Blaeser's poetic utterance and that of the dominant culture. Moreover, the revision of "taking" to "takin'" gives the reader a counterpoint from which to read the damning "taken," and the slang of the reservation, "Shinabes," lets us know that this counterpoint is rooted in a contemporary Anishinaabe perspective that is itself grounded in tradition.

The second line's inclusion of the title of one of the Beat Generation's seminal texts, *On the Road*, helps to reiterate the political import of the poem announced with the opening line: "White Earth Land Recovery Project" (*Trailing You* 62). Both project and poem are committed to the recovery of that which is critical to the White Earth Anishinaabe: land and identity. In the words of White Earth Anishinaabe Winona LaDuke, who founded the White Earth Land Recovery Project in 1989, "We, the Anishinaabeg, are a forest culture. Our creation stories, culture, and way of life are entirely based on the forest . . . [Therefore] the White Earth Land Recovery Project works to restore the forests, recover the land, and restore our traditional forest culture" (*All Our Relations* 4-5). Recovering the land is necessary because it was taken by federal and state governments, companies, and individuals, a sad and chilling testament to the legacy of the Dawes Allotment Act of 1887, the Nelson Act of 1889, and the Clapp Rider of 1906 that Melissa Meyer chronicles in *The White Earth Tragedy: Ethnicity and Dispossession at a Minnesota Anishinaabe Reservation*.

Given both the history of relations between Euroamericans and Anishinaabeg and its contemporary tenor, Blaeser is well aware of the potential for anxiety to surface. Freud links anxiety to danger, separation, and object-loss, and considering the forced separations and losses the People have suffered it makes sense that Blaeser's narrator would worry. In addition to fearing that she will not "match the master template," she worries that others will. For instance, she responds with worry when the clerks at an "Indian store" on Franklin say that her destination has pull tabs and that "maybe we'll close up and come with you" (*Trailing You* 62) because doing that could be read as fitting the image of the irresponsible, frivolous *indian* given to gambling. Blaeser uses anxiety to her advantage, however, by having the repetition of "I worry," or a variation on it, unite the first three stanzas of the poem. Worry over being subject to a damning

misreading is assuaged with a return to orality, stories, and the storytelling
tradition that is prefigured with the repeated phrase and articulated most
fully in the poem's fourth stanza when Blaeser's narrator describes listening
to fellow White Earth band member Gordon Henry Jr.'s reading after the
meeting. In *Absentee Indians and Other Poems*, Blaeser notes that poems
"seek shape from an aesthetic older than our remembrance of it" (*Absentee
Indians* 127), and the repetition and stress on the spoken word in "Road
Show" helps us see that it is shaped by an oral aesthetic, one held by the
Anishinaabe, that emphasizes the importance of stories and storytelling.

Tellingly, the passage from Henry Jr.'s *The Light People* invoked in
"Road Show" concerns how the protagonist Oskinaway talks to a wounded
bird in order that he might be able to see what is wrong with it. His first
attempt to examine the crow, one made without words, brings only a quick
strike that rips open the back of his hand. After recalling lessons from his
veterinary courses and stories his elders told him about "approaching and
speaking to animals" (185), Oskinaway opts to follow the latter and speaks
to the bird with "song-whisperings" (186) that connect them and lead the
bird to trust him. Spoken words, song-whisperings, connect characters;
they also connect teller, audience, and story. We strain with Blaeser's
narrator, not to hear what the dominant culture would like to have happen
to the Native, a desire humorously phrased in the name of Henry Jr.'s
character, but to catch the words that will ensure survival and
understanding. Oskinaway may well phrase the dominant culture's desire to
be rid of the Native, O-skin-away, but the skin will not go away. She and
he remain before us in and with written texts that give the lie to the White
Man's *indian*, and in the process reveal the Mastering template for precisely
what it is.

Blaeser's narrator feels okay when she is listening to the story being
offered by Gordon Henry Jr. because the storytelling event enables her to
know that she and her fellow shinabes are not the *indians* of the dominant
culture's wild west show. She also feels okay thanks to the tear in Henry's
jacket: this too helps her be "not so worried about what people thought / we
were supposed to be" (63). "Tear" signifies something in addition,
however, thanks to its placement at the end of a line. In connecting a line
with the one that follows it, "tear" makes meaning manifest; prior to the
union, the signifier could just as easily be the noun signifying the liquid
secreted by glands in the eye as it could the noun signifying that which
results when something is torn or ripped or pulled forcibly apart. The
written sign, then, is the space where meaning arises, but that meaning is
contingent, always born of the play of difference and metonymy.

Tear creates a space, a gap, that we can read as analogous to the space of
the written poem, or story or drama. For some time now we have been
encouraged to pay attention to the betwixt-and-between, interstices,
borderlines, borderlands. At such sites, such contact zones, presence

becomes possible, can be realized, especially with regard to people of color. Following and expanding Derrida's observation that a nation "is rooted first of all in the memory or anxiety of a displaced--or displaceable--population" (*Specters* 83), Homi Bhabha sees a link between the borderline and a culture's anxiety. He suggests that anxiety "provides a space of representation" ("Irremovable Strangeness" 35) in which to articulate difference. For Blaeser, anxiety over being displaced, physically and figuratively, is answered in and with the space of poetic discourse. The tear, and the poem, let in "fresh air" (63), let in, that is, the touch of language and story that help to ensure survival.

Interstices, contingency, indeterminacy, hybridity: these terms are something more than simply the recognizable signifiers of poststructuralism. Rather, they phrase crucial elements of the Anishinaabe worldview and the nature of White Earth. The Anishinaabe's cosmos is layered, with the earth occupying a position suspended between realms. The borders between layers or realms are neither hard nor fast. Thus, as White Earth Anishinaabe Winona LaDuke notes, "The Anishinaabeg world undulated between material and spiritual shadows, never clear which was more prominent at any time. It was as if the world rested in those periods rather than in the light of day. Dawn and dusk, *biidaabin* and *oshkidibikad*" (*All Our Relations* 115). Situated within this liminal space and time, the People need always to recognize the indeterminacy and mutability of their world and therefore the critical role context, contingency, and experience play in knowing and living with it.

White Earth is itself a borderlands: indeed, it is the betwixt-and-between nature of the place that led to its selection as the site for a reservation that would bring the Anishinaabeg of Minnesota together. White Earth is characterized by a diversity of ecosystems: prairie, deciduous forest, wetlands, and coniferous forest meet within the borders of the reserve. The group of Tribal leaders and Federal and State officials who determined the exact location of White Earth following the 1867 treaty that called for its creation noted the diversity of habitat and flora in the area (Peterson 161). Some thirty-five years later the Reservation newspaper, *The Tomahawk*, applauded the choice of location, remarking in its history of the events that led to the White Earth's creation that "the reservation is now considered the garden spot of Minnesota" (1). More recently, in emphasizing place in her chapter on White Earth in *All Our Relations*, LaDuke notes that the diversity "has been called the Medicine Chest" of the Anishinaabe, "it is the wellspring of a traditional way of life, one that has nurtured biodiversity for thousands of years" (115). Government officials thought that this diversity would help the Minnesota Anishinaabeg to make the transition from a forest-based culture and economy to an agrarian one. Anishinaabeg more comfortable practicing the traditional seasonal round of the People could find what they needed in the eastern part of the reservation: lakes and streams with fish and wild rice beds, larger game in the woodlands, stands of maple for sugarbushing, white birch for canoes, containers, and Mide scrolls. Anishinaabeg ready to embrace the Jeffersonian ideal would find more arable land in the western part of White Earth.

As is true of LaDuke's work, Blaeser's poetry touches the nature of White Earth and the Anishinaabe worldview. Poems like "Where I was that Day" voice a recognition of the indeterminacy and transformation that are hallmarks of the world: butterflies "materialize / out of the flower blossoms," "rocks crack open into grasshoppers" and "snakes became branches" (*Trailing You* 19-21). The poem "Lines from an Autumn Litany" reminds us that "patterns form / and disintegrate with autumn's breath" (*Absentee Indians* 32) and "we are more truly ourselves" (33) when we recognize both the possibility of transformation and the reality of the connections between things. The poem's first stanza emphasizes the reality of connections when the sheep, hay bales, and field stone together in the field before the observer

> merge in their reality,
> flock one into another
> until sight can no longer distinguish
> sheephayorstone (32)

Just as objects and moments in the natural world are "on the verge of transformation" (32), so are we, provided we pay attention, remain aware that things can change in an instant, and bear in mind that transformation is the order of the day everyday. This is not easy, to be sure, as Blaeser's narrator in "Where I was that Day" reminds us when she speaks of learning to hold the spell of awareness and understanding "a little longer each time" (*Trailing You* 20).

In the Preface to *Absentee Indians*, Blaeser imagines herself as an absentee Indian, home with a child, who "names the markers, like she was writing a pathway" (xi) back to White Earth. Words lead one home. The poem "zen for traveling bards" phrases both that simple, important truth and, subtly, how words connect one to people and place. Driving through a fog that obscures everything, the narrator recalls the voice of another advising her how to make her way when the pathway is shrouded. The voice and what it says serve as the "point of reference" (*Absentee Indians* 41) she needs to stay on course. Moreover, one needs to "learn to wait for poems this way // fill words with small sure lights / and follow them home" (41). The image of light-filled words that illuminate the way home calls to mind the grandfathers' winter fires that shimmer across the night sky as the *aurora borealis*. The lights remind the People of their ancestors and what they taught them about life and living. They also help to light the path to the next world. Words filled with connection to others, to kin, and to Anishinaabe ways of seeing and knowing, then, are what enable the poems to help one stay connected to home even when not there.[6] Vizenor emphasizes the connection between words and place for the Anishinaabe, noting that traditionally words had power because they "were connected to the place the words were spoken" (*People* 24). Blaeser extends this connection to encompass that which is built with and in words: stories. "Studies in Migration" makes clear that the storied landscape of White Earth is both waiting for the People to return and contributes to the homecoming. The first phrase of the poem, "Pulled into Joe Olson's landing" (*Absentee Indians* 30), indicates the dual action of pulling in and being pulled in to place. One sees there "Patterns of the past" (30); one comes to recognize "each space held for years in stories. Waiting. Now reclaimed. *Your name was never empty*" (30). "Clouded titles fill courthouse files" (30) to be sure, a reminder of the theft and fraud that reduced Anishinaabe holdings in White Earth to less than ten percent of the original 800,000-plus acres, but so long as "spring sap spills out" (30) and there are stories connected to it the People will be able to come home and be home.

Over and over, Blaeser's poetry explicitly and implicitly indicates that words and voices connect Native people to place and to each other. In "On the Way to the Chicago Pow-wow," again from *Trailing You*, Blaeser's narrator is comforted by the words of a friend, remembering that "Sometimes you have to go in the wrong direction / to get where you're heading" (13). Wanting to go to White Earth, to place and community and connection, Blaeser turns to writing, for written words are the right way to go in the wrong direction and get where you want and need to go.

Moreover, by quoting Oneida writer Roberta Hill and invoking Chickasaw Linda Hogan's poem "The Truth Is," "On the Way to the Chicago Pow-wow" also indicates that words can connect Native writers with each other. Poems like "Road Show" and *Absentee Indians and Other Poems*' "Where Vizenor Soaked His Feet" celebrate the influence Anishinaabe writers have had on Blaeser's work and life. The former ends with the narrator remarking that she'll "try sometime to wear one [a tear] for" Henry (*Trailing You* 63). The latter opens with "White Earth," closes on an image of place, and in between offers up with thanks words, phrases, and titles from Vizenor's work which have helped Blaeser along her pathway. "*Survivance* your legacy" (*Absentee Indians* 92), she writes, and

---

[6] See Basil Johnston, *Ojibway Heritage*, 27. The northern lights also dance across the night sky in *Last Standing Woman*, by Winona LaDuke, as part of that text's concern with place, kinship, and tradition.

in writing stresses the connection and the medium that help her to survive so that she might offer words to help others do the same. Vizenor's neologism speaks volumes here, for survival is connected to resistance and resistance is best accomplished by using language to articulate Native identity.

"American Indian Voices: I Wonder if this is an Indian Poem" from *Trailing You* stresses that "even though us Indians have never been experts on ourselves / we've done pretty good in finding one another . . . / --even if we're all far from home" (*Trailing You* 57) thanks to poems and stories that offer and are infused with Native voices. For Blaeser, then, anxiety over displacement and absence is answered with connections to others that are made manifest throughout her work. Indeed, we might go so far as to say that those connections frame her two volumes of poetry. Her Preface to *Trailing You* begins by stating that the poems in the book are offered as "a celebration of influence" (n.p.) that stands as a counter to the anxiety of influence. *Absentee Indians and Other Poems* closes with "Y2K Indian," a poem that gives thanks to and pays tribute to the Native voices that Blaeser has found and that have found her. The poem is connected to an experience Blaeser had while reading her poetry abroad several years ago and to a story told to her by a colleague. In France, Blaeser looked up as she read the end of a poem and saw a man in the audience mouthing the words with her. The story is of a colleague learning a lesson about honoring the work of others and the spirit of community while teaching writing to Lakota grade schoolers: the students would use in their poems lines written by their peers. Together, the spirit at the heart of these two events motivates the creation of Blaeser's poem.

"Y2K Indian" celebrates, in Blaeser's words, "the woven story path of Indian nations by building itself partly from the words of other Native authors" (128). What is phrased, as a result, is nothing less than the articulation of a transnational Native community of writers that, as we have seen, is prefigured in "On the Way to the Chicago Pow-Wow." "Y2K Indian" brings together Blaeser's words and those from writers such as Leslie Marmon Silko, Joy Harjo, Vizenor, Hogan, Henry Jr., and others, along with the titles of Native American literature anthologies. The story woven by the poem tells of how its narrator discovers the images of her ancestors around and with her and thus "become[s] comfortable / with the story of doubleness" thanks to "Finding their reflections / harbor mine" (131). The "story of doubleness" is that of making it in two worlds, that of the dominant culture and of particular Native cultures. It is, as well, the double meaning of reflections here, both the images and the thoughts of her ancestors and the thoughts of other Native writers, that "harbor" her reflections. At the end of *Trailing You*, Blaeser writes in "Certificate of Live Birth: Escape From the Third Dimension" that her poem enables her and her mother to escape the prison constructed by the dominant culture.

That prison, "'stands in ruins' within the circle of our lives" (86), a circle that provides her safe haven. Returning to the image and the cyclical thinking it highlights at the end of *Absentee Indians and Other Poems*, Blaeser gives us the reflections of "Another Y 2 K Indian / *writing the circle* / of return" (131) and returning in and with the writing of that circle.

Works Cited

Bhabha, Homi. "On the Irremovable Strangeness of Being Different." *PMLA* 113 (1998): 34-39.

Blaeser, Kimberly. *Absentee Indians and Other Poems*. East Lansing, MI: Michigan State U P, 2002.

---. *Gerald Vizenor: Writing in the Oral Tradition*. Norman: U of Oklahoma P, 1996.

---. "Like Reeds Through the Ribs of a Basket: Native Women Weaving Stories." *OtherSisterhoods: Literary Theory and U.S. Women of Color*. Ed. Sandra Kumamoto Stanley. Urbana: U of Illinois P, 1998. 265-76.

---. *Trailing You*. Greenfield Center, NY: Greenfield Review P, 1994.

---. "*The Way to Rainy Mountain*: Momaday's Work in Motion." *Narrative Chance: Postmodern Discourse on Native American Indian Literatures*. Ed. Gerald Vizenor. Norman: U of Oklahoma P, 1993. 39-54.

Derrida, Jacques. *Specters of Marx*. Trans. Peggy Kamuf. New York: Routledge, 1994.

Henry, Jr. Gordon. *The Light People*. Norman: U of Oklahoma P, 1994.

Johnston, Basil. *Ojibway Heritage*. Lincoln: U of Nebraska P, 1976.

LaDuke, Winona. *All Our Relations*. Boston: South End , 1999.

---. *Last Standing Woman*. Stillwater, MN: Voyageur, 1997.

Meyer, Melissa. *The White Earth Tragedy: Ethnicity and Dispossession at a Minnesota Anishinaabe Reservation*. Lincoln: U of Nebraska P, 1994.

Momaday, N. Scott. *The Way to Rainy Mountain*. Albuquerque: U of New Mexico P, 1969.

Peterson, Jr., Edward. "That So-Called Warranty Deed: Clouded Land Titles on the White Earth Indian Reservation in Minnesota." *North Dakota Law Review* 59 (1983): 159-181.

Vizenor, Gerald. *Fugitive Poses: Native American Indian Scenes of Absence and Presence*. Lincoln: U of Nebraska P, 1998.

---. *Interior Landscapes*. Minneapolis: U of Minnesota P, 1990.

---. *The People Named the Chippewa*. Minneapolis: U of Minnesota P, 1984.

--- and A. Robert Lee. *Postindian Conversations*. Lincoln: U of Nebraska P, 1999.

"The White Earth Reservation: Brief History of Events Which Lead to its Establishment." *The Tomahawk* [White Earth Reservation] 15 June 1903: 1.

LINDA J. MANNEY

Soliloquy, Story, and Song:
Language as Social Practice and Social Change

> The ability of story, prose and poetry to transform the storyteller and the listener into something or someone else is shamanistic. The writer, as a shape-changer, is a *nahual*, a shaman.
>
> Gloria Anzaldua

Introduction

Poets, teachers, and politicians have long understood the potential of language to represent as well as to shape human experience and understanding, each group characteristically utilizing this potential for their own purposes. Career politicians, for example, use language strategically to construct scenarios for public consumption, to negotiate compromises, to project a particular self-image, and to win support for personal and professional objectives. The work of experienced teachers relies on the mediating role of language, since it is primarily through language that teachers interact with students to build or discourage meaningful relationships, to establish varying degrees of rapport or distance, to both maintain and relinquish control, to involve or alienate students as active learners. As visionaries, poets more often than not use language experimentally, giving expression to a wide range of subterranean images, associations, and emotions, and thereby extending our conscious awareness of who we are and what it is to be human. The function of language to simultaneously shape as well as reflect the emergent reality as we experience and create it in our routine daily interactions has been explored in depth in recent scholarship in a number of disciplinary fields, beginning with post-structuralist literary theory and extending across the social sciences.

In the present paper, I consider critical approaches from a number of disciplinary perspectives as I explore the role of everyday language to convey, perpetuate as well as dismantle unjust representations of entire classes of people as they are constructed by members of a more powerful social group (Ashcroft, Griffiths, and Tiffin; Fairclough; Luke; McLaren and Giroux; van Dijk 1987; 1993b). Through the human capacity for agency and change (cf. Freire; de Certeau; Mc Laren and Giroux), people use familiar language forms in new ways to resist oppressive patterns of representation, as well as to construct alternative models of self-definition and self-representation. In the discussion below, I focus on the social construction of selfhood and identity through the medium of everyday language texts. In part one, I review related scholarship from the social sciences; these studies, drawn primarily from psychology, anthropology, and sociology, provide a framework for conceptualizing the ongoing construction of self, identity, and the worlds in which they find expression. In part two, I summarize views of language developed by critical feminists, linguists, and educators to explain how language texts are instruments for expressing and creating structures of power and ideology which implicitly inform all levels of linguistic interaction. Thus, language both represents and constructs self and identity institutionally, interpersonally and individually. Finally in part three, I look at linguistic strategies used to challenge and change patterns of thinking that have disempowered marginalized communities. Through recognizing and deconstructing 'commonsense' ideological conceptualizations that misrepresent the experience of less powerful people (cf. Fairclough; van Dijk 1995, 1998) members of particular minority groups have resisted and transformed unjust representations of themselves as they redefine their experience through speaking out and writing back (cf. Ashcroft, Griffiths, and Tiffin).

The role of language in constructing identity

A major segment of social science research explores the reciprocal relationship between human knowledge, on the one hand, and culturally defined symbolic systems, particularly language, on the other hand. Constructivist models foreground the context-dependency of all human knowledge, and thus challenge essentializing frameworks which argue for a prior descriptions of self and identity and a conception of reality as unitary, absolute, and objectively determined. Although it is difficult to determine precisely where and when a constructivist approach first emerged, it is clear that original research by Soviet psychologist Lev Vygotsky provides a strong empirical and theoretical foundation from which future constructivist work in the social sciences would evolve. Drawing on empirical data from studies of children acquiring language, Vygotsky challenged materialist paradigms of his time by emphasizing the role of language and thought in both defining and describing reality. While it is not possible to explore the fine details of Vygotsky's thinking in the present paper, I believe that the following passage from his seminal book

Language and Thought is representative of his view on the mutual shaping of language and thought.[1]

> "The relation of thought to word is not a thing but a process, a continual movement back and forth from thought to word and from word to thought. In that process the relation of thought to word undergoes changes which themselves may be regarded as development in the functional sense. Thought is not merely expressed in words; it comes into existence through them." (Vygotsky 1934 / 1961: 125)

More recently, social science research has focused on the central role of narrative structure in both representing and organizing our understanding of human events and interactions. A pre-eminent scholar of human cognition and learning, Jerome Bruner maintains that "we organize our experience and our memory of human happenings mainly in the form of narratives – stories, excuses, myths, reasons for doing and not doing, and so on." (1991:4). Research in narrative psychology (Sarbin; Bruner) as well as cultural anthropology (Rosaldo) has examined both the form and the function of culturally-defined narratives which individuals use in typical social exchange. People draw on a repertoire of narrative forms to experience and label their ongoing interaction and reflection in culturally specific ways. Through a set of narrative templates common to a community, members of the community conceptualize their own and others' actions, observations, desires, intentions and goals; they discuss these with others; and they define the range of future possibilities for themselves and others. Therefore, the idea that human knowledge and understanding are universal, unitary and disinterested is called into question. Parallel developments have emerged in sociology and education, especially in micro-studies of face-to-face interaction. Recent research in ethnomethodology (Antaki and Widdicombe) and classroom discourse analysis (Sfard and Prusak) has shown through careful analysis of spontaneous conversation that individuals present and revise their sense of self and identity through narrative constructions which they jointly create with co-participants in routine social interactions.

Guided by compatible research goals to explain the construction and reconstruction of knowledge, self, and identity, critical feminists, educators, and linguists have emphasized the political nature of identity construction, seeking to clarify the complex dialectic relationship between the range of identities that any one person can assume, on the one hand, and the types of resources, both material and symbolic, which are within or

---

[1] Vygotsky's elaboration on the nature of this relationship is set forth as a fully elaborated learning theory. For the complete collection of Vygotsky's scholarly work translated into English, see Vygotsky, 1987.

outside of her reach, on the other hand (cf. Bourdieu). And it is precisely through one's access to culturally valued resources (i.e., formal education, financial assets, political status, etc.) that s/he gains entrance to channels of public discourse, where the ideological representations of elite social groups are created and disseminated through language and other symbolic systems (van Dijk 1993a; Crawford; Fairclough; Luke).

Discourse, power and ideology

Discourse, as the term is used by critical feminists, linguists and educators, refers to specific instances of language use as well as the general institutionalized social practice which calls forth and gives meaning to a particular sample of language. Building on Foucault's original three-tiered system, Fairclough (1995) develops a model of discourse comprising three interconnected levels of structure; these are (1) the local level of actual linguistic texts, (2) the intermediate level of general discourse practice, and (3) the global level of sociocultural structure. The critical study of discourse involves carefully examining all three of levels of overlapping structure, while at the same time clarifying the interconnections and influences across the three levels.

At the local level, linguistic texts are the written or spoken stretches of language, interconnected both thematically and structurally, that people produce to communicate. An authentic language text can range from the highly stylized and pre-planned speeches delivered publicly in ritualized ceremonies, to informal and spontaneous conversations in everyday encounters between acquaintances, to a one-word caption on a billboard. The second level of discourse focuses on particular functional domains of language use, defined in part according to particular subject areas or themes which connect a group of texts, such as the discourse of parliamentary debate or the discourse of urban youth culture. Also included at this intermediate level are the actual practices that people follow to produce, distribute, and interpret particular texts within a given functional domain. Institutionalized discourse practice authorizes certain options while ruling out others, typically resolving questions such as: (a) what to include and what to exclude in a given text; (b) how to represent particular groups of people and the issues that concern them; (c) how, when and to whom texts should be available; (d) which interpretations of a given text should be privileged and promoted, and which ones should be discouraged or suppressed. The third level of discourse, the most global and abstract, comprises sociopolitically defined beliefs and attitudes which determine how communities of people are positioned with respect to each other, and which therefore influence all aspects of text creation. In other words, the entire range of historically situated sociocultural practice within a community is invoked when people of the community produce and interpret discourse (Fairclough). Through carefully scrutinizing all three levels of discourse as defined above, critical linguists aim to uncover the interconnections of discourse, power, and ideology. Power is defined as an ability, negotiated in particular interactional circumstances, to exert control over the creation, distribution and / or interpretation of linguistic texts for social consumption (Crawford; Fairclough). Among other things, control over linguistic texts allows people to determine how a particular group is defined, positioned, or constructed in a text with respect to other groups (Crawford; Fairclough; van Dijk 1993a, Luke). Displays of power presuppose having the resources needed to control actual textual practice, and often occur in local institutional exchanges where some texts and textual practices are elevated to the so-called "official" status, while other kinds of texts and textual practices are either completely silenced, or else they are trivialized or disparaged (Luke). In the text-based framework of critical linguistics, ideology is defined as a biased view of the world which is constructed and perpetuated through public discourse by a particular group of people in order to further their own interests (van Dijk 1995, 1998). While every social group is shaped in part by defining ideologies which specify their core values and beliefs about themselves and others, obviously not every social group wields the degree of power needed to promote their own views in public discourse. Typically it is the members of the power elite, i.e., the wealthy and the politically well connected, who use their control over text production, dissemination, and interpretation to present their own ideological views as the implicit norm or the "common sense" view, while at the same time suppressing or distorting the perspectives of other people who challenge their world view.

An intersection of language, power, and ideology: The Ebonics controversy of 1997-98

There are many documented cases of public discourse where members of a more powerful majority culture control the representation of a less powerful minority culture, using their control over representation to present themselves positively and/or to present the minority group negatively (i.e. van Dijk 1987; Smitherman-Donaldson and van Dijk 1988; van Dijk 1993b). One widely discussed instance of control over representation occurred in the U.S.A. during 1997-1998, when the local Board of Education in Oakland, California, tried officially to recognize Ebonics, and not Standard American English, as the native speech of the Oakland

Unified School District's 28,000 African American students, most of whom were and still are at risk for massive educational failure (Rickford 1999a, Baugh 2000). Although the school board proposed concrete educational interventions designed to increase the students' fluency in standard English, their proposal aroused public outrage and strong political criticism when they categorized the speech of the African American students as a language in its own right, and then, based on this categorization, requested federal funding for educational support earmarked for language minority students.

Because I was working as an educational linguist in southern California at the time of the Ebonics controversy, I am familiar with both the local sociocultural setting and the particular linguistic and educational issues involved. In my view, the 1997 – 1998 controversy over Ebonics in Oakland, California clearly illustrates the overlapping relationships among power, discourse, and ideology in a local setting: an ongoing power imbalance and unjust treatment of one group by another group, enhanced by the use of public discourse to misrepresent the issues, affected official policy and practice in and beyond the Oakland Unified School District. From the perspective of critical linguistics, the Ebonics controversy of 1997-1998 revealed a network of ideological structure in North American mainstream culture which limits personal freedoms of African Americans as expressed through language codes, language practice, and sociopolitical policy.

Ebonics and language code

A wealth of scholarly research has explored numerous facets of African American Vernacular English, the native speech of most African Americans. (See Rickford, Sweetland, and Rickford 1998 for a nonexhaustive bibliography of nearly 700 citations of scholarly work on African American Vernacular English.) The North American linguistic community has produced several scientific analyses of the structure of the language, beginning with William Labov's seminal studies (Labov 1969, 1972), and presently includes detailed descriptions by linguists, accessible to the non-specialist, on both the structure (Rickford and Rickford 2000) and the lexicon (Smitherman 2000) of African American Vernacular English. Among other things, this research demonstrates clearly that African American Vernacular English is a systematic and rule-governed linguistic system which is capable of expressing logic and other forms of abstract thought.

Although linguists agree that it is a dialect of English, African American Vernacular English differs substantially from Standard English, much more so than any other dialect of American English spoken in continental North America, both linguistically and sociohistorically (Labov 1997, as cited in Baugh 2000: pg.59). African American Vernacular English is the linguistic consequence of the African slave trade conducted in North America; unlike all other immigrant groups to the U.S.A., black Africans were brought in against their will as slaves, they had no legal rights or protections under American law, and they were legally denied access to literacy and schooling (Baugh 2000: 31 – 33). They were completely isolated, both geographically and linguistically, and even today African American slave descendants often live in segregated communities and experience the negative effects of a racially segregated education. Yet as Baugh (2000) points out, these issues have not been dealt with adequately or even acknowledged by policy makers and political leaders in the U.S.A., and equal educational opportunities have not been provided to the African American community.

Ebonics and language practice

In recognition of these facts, the local board of education in Oakland, California attempted to meet the unique educational needs of its 28,000 African American students. Confronting the documented failure of more traditional methods used to develop literacy skills with African American students in Oakland and across the U.S.A. (Rickford 1999a), board members drafted a federal grant proposal to use the students' native speech, referred to as *Ebonics*, as a bridge to developing proficiency in standard American English. Although the board's proposal did not cite the relevant research, their reasoning reflects current scholarship in educational linguistics which suggests that African American students develop literacy skills in standard English most effectively when their native vernacular is included in the learning process (Rickford and Rickford 1996; Rickford 1999b). This position is further supported by parallel research in second language acquisition which suggests that language minority language students acquire English language literacy most effectively when given the opportunity first to develop basic literacy in their native language (See *Languages in America: A Pluralist View,* Chapter 4, "Language in the Schools," by Susan Dicker 1996, for a summary of this research).

Against the backdrop of racially polarized North American mainstream ideology, local educators in Oakland, California recognized African American speech as a legitimate linguistic system in its own right. Furthermore, they requested that their proposed educational interventions for African American students be funded by federal grant money earmarked for minority students whose native language is other than

English. It was precisely these two aspects of their proposal that sparked a national controversy and provoked a prolonged media blitz which was misinformed at best and overtly racist at worst (Perry and Delpit; Baugh 2000). Stanford University sociolinguist John Rickford, a well-known scholar of African American Vernacular English, reports his own experience of the Ebonics controversy:

> In the case at hand, the mainstream view was the Ebonics itself was street slang, and that Oakland teachers were going to teach in it, or allow students to talk or write in it instead of in English. It was in response to *this* misrepresentation (emphasis in the original) of Ebonics and the Oakland resolutions that editorials, Op-Ed pieces (texts submitted to newspapers by the public), letters to the editor, cartoons, and agitated calls to radio talk shows were directed, and attempts to get alternative viewpoints aired were often very difficult, especially in the most prestigious media. For instance, although the *New York Times* published several editorials and Op-Ed pieces critical either of Ebonics or the Oakland resolutions, linguists' attempts to get them to present a different viewpoint were all unsuccessful. I know of at least four Op-Ed submissions which they summarily rejected (by Salikoko Mufwene, by Geoffrey Pullum, by Gene Searchinger, and by myself), and there were undoubtedly others. (Rickford 1999c: 270 – 271).

Both John Rickford and fellow Stanford University linguist John Baugh cite anonymous hate mail which they each personally received in response to their publicly circulated statements about the Ebonics issue, and further report the particulars of several blatantly racist jokes and parodies, directed against all African Americans, which appeared on various web sites during the Ebonics media blitz. As Rickford points out, the strongly negative attitude expressed by the mainstream media toward a minority vernacular is essentially an implicit expression of a more deeply rooted and widespread fear and prejudice about the speakers of the vernacular. (Rickford 1999c: 272). When such irrational fear and prejudice is given expression through so many public channels, as was the case during the Ebonics controversy, a destructive chain reaction is set off, with extremely detrimental effects on the misrepresented minority community.

Ebonics and sociopolitical policy

There were a number of immediate sociopolitical repercussions to the Ebonics controversy of 1997 – 1998. After Ebonics had been the focus of so much negative media coverage, several Anti-Ebonics bills were introduced at the state and national level. Although differing slightly in specific recommendations according to local conditions, all of the proposals shared the same explicit goal of forbidding U.S. federal funds for any educational program based on the premise that Ebonics was a legitimate language. (See Richardson 1998 for a summary and discussion of the various legislative proposals submitted.) The media continued to condemn the use of African American vernacular speech for educational purposes in public schools with large numbers of African-American students, and the practice was forbidden even before it could be tried and tested empirically (Baugh 2000). However, neither the Anti-Ebonics legislation nor the journalists who criticized the Oakland Ebonics proposal provided any further suggestions or remedies to address the massive language-related educational failure of African American students attending public schools in Oakland, California, Philadelphia, Pennsylvania, and many other American cities (Rickford 1999a).

Alternative expressions of language, power, and ideology

The Ebonics controversy of 1997-98 brings into clear view the ideological construction of public discourse by powerful groups who protect their interests at the expense of other less powerful groups. However, while the negative media coverage of the Oakland Ebonics proposal was indeed harmful to the African American community, it also prompted a strong countermovement, in both popular and academic circles, to defend the language rights and human rights of African Americans and other minority groups. Drawing on her extensive experience in the language education of African American Vernacular English speakers, Geneva Smitherman, critical linguist, advocate of African American language rights, and native speaker of African American Vernacular English, has spoken out for years as a knowledgeable expert on behalf of both circles. Well known for her resolve and stamina to get the job done, Smitherman suggests a strategy for resisting the hegemonic structure of public discourse as she sketches an insider's view of African American Vernacular English.

> Large and in charge, we should bum rush the media with our own Master Narrative. In doing so, we need to reconceptualize and broaden our notion of African American Language. We need to stress the generational, class, and gender similarities in Black Language use. For African American Language is not only language structure, it is also language use and discourse practices. It is not just the language of Black children and youth in the public schools, but also the language of the Black Church, of everyday folk, of seniors, of the working class, of preachers, of Nobel and Pulitzer Prize winners, of a long line of "race" women and men. And it is long past time for us to produce a film / video on African American Language, one that would speak both to the Academy and the Street (Smitherman 2004: 194).

Clearly, African American Vernacular English is not street slang or lazy speech, as it was erroniously depicted in the mainstream North American media during the late 1990's. Misrepresented by the power elite through major channels of public discourse, native speakers of African American Vernacular English such as linguists John Baugh and Geneva Smitherman use their own alternative language resources which display the potential to challenge and transform mainstream racist discourse.

Language as a resource for challenge and change

Current scholarship in the social sciences supports the view expressed by Smitherman (2004) above that alternative visions of less powerful groups can find expression through public discourse controlled in large part by the mainstream power elite. While recognizing the depth of entrenchment of power structures already in place, many scholars also recognize the dynamicity of sociocultural structure which allows for some degree of innovation and change. Social anthropologist Renato Rosaldo proposes that human cultural communities are porous and dynamic, so that people constantly move across and negotiate within diverse cultural spaces, even when they all occupy a more inclusive cultural unit.

In Rosaldo's view, a human culture comprises a crossroads of people in constant motion, rather than a static set of norms that members of a community consistently follow. Furthermore, as Rosaldo points out, there is a strong force of unpredictability which typifies actual human interaction (112). Novelty and innovation are the rule, rather than the exception, and people who respond well to the unexpected are often admired and rewarded by fellows and peers. Microsociologist Frederick Erickson makes similar claims. Acknowledging that human actors are both limited and enabled by social structure, Erickson argues that unpredictable moments of opportunity arise in all human communities, giving human actors a chance to improvise and adapt existing structure to new situations, which, in turn, transforms existing social relations (2004).

In the area of critical pedagogy, research documents how minority culture students respond with a language of resistance when confronted with the exclusionary views of majority culture staff and administration in public school settings (cf. Gutierrez, Larson, and Kreuter). Building on insights from this research, Allan Luke illustrates through careful ethnographic description how local tensions arise across different language texts and discourse traditions when minority students challenge existing power relations to present their own world view, in counter-position to the world view being promoted by majority culture school personnel (Luke). In this way, diverse views of the world occasionally find expression at the community level, and chance local innovations as well as systematic concerted action can influence community discourse practice. The possibility of expressing a minority viewpoint through everyday language has led critical theorists to view language texts as "contested sites" where conflicting voices struggle to be heard and acknowledged within a larger discourse community. In such "contested sites," members of less powerful groups use their linguistic resources as both a means and a site of struggle. Drawing on and mobilizing their own cultural understandings of everyday experience, members of disempowered groups find opportunities to create new categories of knowing and to put forward new interpretations of familiar texts (cf. Pennycook). According to the model of critical discourse analysis depicted above (cf. Fairclough), an empowered minority community, deconstructing a world view which marginalizes or excludes them, use their own resources effectively to speak out and write back to the power elite, thus gaining visibility in areas of public discourse practice.

Speaking out and writing back: a challenge to mainstream authority

Scholars from a number of disciplines have examined the processes of speaking out and writing back as effective strategies of resistance. Particular studies which elaborate on these or similar strategies have come from the fields of post-colonial literary studies (Ashcroft, et. al.), critical pedagogy (Freire; Luke; McLaren and Giroux), critical linguistics (Fairclough; van Dijk 1995, 1998), popular culture (Rose; Dawson), and feminist discourse (Crawford, hooks). In this section, I look at two instances of minority discourse, one from popular culture, and one from radical feminism, both of which utilize a language of resistance to question unjust mainstream sociopolitical practice. Critical linguistics (Fairclough; van Dijk 1995, 1998) offers models for examining the ideological basis of all discourse practice and for clarifying the relationship between sociopolitical power and language usage; post-colonial studies (Ashcroft, Griffiths, and Tiffin) provide a definition of "writing back" as a process of taking on the standard language and discourse practice and repositioning them within a local or minority cultural framework (38). Crucially, "writing back" involves two key strategies, which are **abrogation**, a denial and refusal of the colonial categories and fixed meanings already in place, and **appropriation,** a process whereby the language is seized and re-placed in a specific cultural location.

DATA SET ONE: ""The Message"

In her compelling sociohistorical study of African American rap music, *Black Noise: Rap Music and Black Culture in Contemporary America,* Tricia Rose demonstrates how black rap music is deeply embedded in a history of economic and racial discrimination which people of color have endured in the United States (1994). African American rap music, which emerged from the hip-hop Black nationalism of the 1960's, reflects the harsh realities of inner-city economic depression and substandard housing which African Americans experience in large urban centers of the United States. Historically, the genre of rap music developed in the 1970's among Puerto Rican and African American young men whose families had been relocated to the South Bronx borough of New York City. Clearly a form of social protest, early rap music confronted unequal relations of power directly and chronicled the experiences of the disenfranchised black community, experiences which the white power elite would have preferred to ignore or dismiss, since they themselves are sustained by the system of institutionalized racism and economic inequality which disenfranchised the black community in the first place. (Since its early inception as a vibrant form of community art, rap music has appealed to the social consciousness of a number of minority groups outside of the U.S.A. Dawson 2002 shows how the genre of rap has been adapted to express the experience of the South Asian minority community in London, England, while Fernandes 2003 analyzes the emergence of rap music as a form of protest among the Afro-Cuban community in contemporary Cuban society.)

In one of their many well-known rap songs, "The Message," Grandmaster Flash and the Furious Five, an early rap group from South Bronx, New York City, spell out the harsh facts of urban poverty and offer an insider's perspective on the tragically destructive effects of institutional racism which the African American community historically has endured. In the first stanza of the song, the narrator speaks out about despair and frustration which life in the ghetto engender.

Text 1.1

It's like a jungle sometimes, it makes me wonder
How I keep from going under.
It's like a jungle sometimes, it makes me wonder
How I keep from going under.

Broken glass everywhere
People pissing on the stairs
You know they just don't care
I can't take the smell, can't take the noise

> Got no money to move out, I guess I got no choice
> Rats in the front room, roaches in the back
> Junkies in the alley with a baseball bat
> I tried to get away but I couldn't get far
> 'Cause the man with the tow truck repossessed my car

In a later stanza of the song, the rapper describes the conditions of ghetto life through which African American youth are drawn into the tragic web of crime that ultimately destroys them. Challenging the mainstream racist ideology which labels African American men as natural born criminals, the narrator demonstrates that African American inner city youth are not inherently predisposed toward a life of crime; rather, urban poverty, unequal educational opportunities, and the harsh realities of ghetto street life conspire to diminish other more promising possibilities for African American young men. As the speaker in "The Message" explains,

Text 1.2

> A child is born with no state of mind
> Blind to the ways of mankind
> God is smiling on you but he's frowning too,
> Because only God knows what you go through
> You grow in the ghetto, living second rate
> And your eyes will sing a song of deep hate
> The place that you play and where you stay
> Looks like one great big alleyway
> You'll admire all the number book-takers
> Thugs, pimps, and pushers and the big money makers

In Text 1.2 above, there is a decentering of the mainstream deterministic view of urban crime in African American communities, and another perspective is positioned in the textual space created. The speaker shows how residents of economically depressed African American communities are limited by conditions of extreme poverty which preclude any opportunities for advancement or change. Discouraged and disillusioned by the absence of reasons to hope for anything better, some turn to crime as a way out of the ghetto. Consider Text 1.3 below.

Text 1.3

> You say, "I'm cool, huh, I'm no fool"
> But then you wind up dropping out of high school
> Now you're unemployed, all nonvoid

Walking 'round like you're Pretty Boy Floyd
Turned stick-up kid but look what you done did
Got sent up for a eight-year bid

In Text 1.3, the speaker shows the results of the vicious cycle of poverty and deprivation which runs full circle in the ghetto. Although a young person may try to resist the strong social currents leading to self-destruction that are set in place by socioeconomic oppression and institutionalized racism ("You say, 'I'm cool, huh, I'm no fool' "), the wider sociopolitical structure of a highly racialized society frustrates any efforts to move beyond the ghetto. As a result, "you wind up dropping out of high school," and "Now you're unemployed." Recall the discussion of the 1996-97 Ebonics initiative in section 2.1 above, where it was shown that African Americans were and are systematically oppressed by unequal educational opportunities, resulting in documented widespread educational failure. Proposed innovations in the public educational system to remedy this situation have been ridiculed and misrepresented in the mainstream American press and rejected outright by mainstream American policy makers, while efforts by educational linguists to present an alternative perspective based on research results were largely unsuccessful. Within this sociopolitical context, perhaps it is more obvious why some African American students in North American urban centers might be led to drop out of school and resist the mainstream culture and power elite through street crime.

Unfortunately, the tragic cycle often runs full course, with no intervention, and young lives are sacrificed to a racialized sociopolitical system which oppresses its African American citizens at many levels of institutional structure. In fact, the speech which the speaker in Text 1.4 below directs to his peer could be addressed to any number of nameless African American males who find themselves disproportionately represented in North American prisons.

Text 1.4

Being used and abused to serve like hell
'Til one day you was found hung dead in the cell
It was plain to see that your life was lost
You was cold and your body swung back and forth
But now your eyes sing the sad sad song
Of how ya lived so fast and died so young.

"The Message" presents an uncompromising picture of African American urban ghetto life which denies the young, especially young men, of their futures and even their lives. In terms of Ashcroft et. al. (1989), Texts 1.1.-

1.4. above abrogate the mainstream racist ideology which blames the victims of oppression for the tragedies of their lived experience, and offer an alternative explanation that traces the origins of urban crime to unequal opportunities and socioeconomic oppression.

DATA SET 2: *Borderlands: The New Mestiza*
Radical feminist and visionary Gloria Anzaldua, on the other hand, uses the more intimate form of autoethnography as a way to recall, confront and reconceptualize the pain and deprivation she has experienced first-hand in her native South Texas homeland. In her intensely personal narrative, *Borderlands: The New Mestiza,* Anzaldua uses her skill with language to rename and restructure her experience as she explores her identity as a Mexican-American lesbian woman from rural South Texas. In Text 2.1 below, she reveals a segment from the psychological remnants of her life as a child.

Text 2.1

> I still feel the old despair when I look at the unpainted, dilapidated, scrap lumber houses consisting mostly of corrugated aluminum. Some of the poorest people in the U.S. live in the Lower Rio Grande Valley, an arid and semi-arid land of irrigated farming, intense sunlight and heat, citrus groves next to chaparral and cactus. I walk through the elementary school I attended so long ago, that remained segregated until recently. I remember how the white teachers used to punish us for being Mexican (89).

Anzaldua often recalls her painful childhood experience as a member of a racial minority, but also pinpoints the mainstream Anglo-American cultural hegemony as the perpetuator of oppression against people of color in the U.S.A.

Text 2.2a

> The dominant white culture is killing us slowly with its ignorance. By taking away our self determination, it has made us weak and empty. As a people we have resisted and we have taken expedient positions, but we have never been allowed to develop unencumbered – we have never been allowed to be fully ourselves. (86)

In Text 2.2a above, the speaker confronts the monopoly held by mainstream Anglo culture over representation and control. As noted by van

Dijk (1993a), power over representation is based on privileged access to highly valued resources, including such things as wealth, social position and status, ability to use means of force and coercion, membership in elite groups, formal education, and / or easy access to forms of public discourse and communication. Such privileged access to key resources explains why, in spite of resistance, "we have never been allowed to develop unencumbered" and why "we have never been allowed to be fully ourselves." Power over representation allows one group to control the thinking of others through texts and talk, and is often subtle and indirect. The speaker is acutely aware of this subtle but potent force, as illustrated in Text 2.2b below.

Text 2.2b

> The whites in power want us people of color to barricade ourselves behind our separate tribal walls so they can pick us off one at a time with their hidden weapons; so they can whitewash and distort history. Ignorance splits people, creates prejudices. A misinformed people is a subjugated people. (86)

Once people recognize the ideological basis of mainstream discourse which shapes public opinion, they have moved one step closer to self-determination and liberation. Furthermore, as a woman of color who grew up in poverty and segregation, Anzaldua knows that in order to resist those in power and check their ability to "whitewash and distort history," people like her whose histories have been misrepresented must relearn and rewrite their own history, since "A misinformed people is a subjugated people."

Yet the speaker also confronts oppressive elements of the minority culture as well, speaking out against misogynist acts committed by Mexican males, and refusing to accept, for any reason the use of violence by Mexican men against Mexican women. Consider Text 2.3 below.

Text 2.3

> Though we "understand" the root causes of male hatred and fear, and the subsequent wounding of women, we do not excuse, we do not condone, and we will no longer put up with it. From the men of our race, we demand the admission / acknowledgement / disclosure / testimony that they wound us, violate us, are afraid of us and of our power. We need them to say they will begin to eliminate their hurtful put-down ways. But more than the words, we demand acts. We must say to them: We will develop equal power with you and those who have shamed us (83 – 84).

Through identifying and confronting oppression from multiple sources, including her own culture, the speaker in Text 2.3 actively develops her own style of empowerment. This hard-earned personal power, paid for dearly with sweat, pain, and tears, leads her to question accepted ways of thinking and subsequently to restructure her own system of meanings.

The speaker in *Borderlands: The New Mestiza* rejects a cultural model which allows for violence against women. She consciously strives to understand, respond to, and shape the world around her on her own terms, as affirmed in Text 2.4 below.

Text 2.4

> The struggle is inner: Chicano, *indio,* American Indian, *mojado, mexicano,* immigrant Latino, Anglo in power, working class Anglo, Black, Asian – our psyches resemble the bordertowns and are populated by the same people. The struggle has always been inner, and is played out in the outer terrains. Awareness of our situation must come before inner changes, which in turn come before changes in society. Nothing happens in the "real" world unless it first happens in the images in our heads (87).

Rather than rely on the meanings imposed on her by members of both the dominant white and the dominated Chicano cultures, the speaker above has begun to step outside of conceptual categories created for her by others, and draws on a new set of images to create her own meanings. In terms of critical linguistics (van Dijk 1995, 1998), the speaker in Text 2.4 above recognizes the ideological structuring which permeates all instances of text and talk, and actively analyzes and questions the world view which such texts present as normal or commonplace. In terms of constructivist psychotherapy (cf. Neimeyer and Mahoney), the speaker recognizes that change is equivalent to creating a new story, and that she is crucially both the narrator and the key actor in her new life story.

Consider Text 2.5 below.

Text 2.5

> As a mestiza I have no country, my homeland cast me out; yet all countries are mine because I am every woman's sister or potential lover. As a lesbian I have no race, my own people disclaim me; but I am all races because there is the queer of me in all races. I am cultureless because, as a feminist, I challenge the collective cultural / religious male-derived beliefs of Indo-Hispanics and Anglos; yet I am cultured because I am participating in the creation of yet another culture, a new story to explain the world and our participation in it, a new value system with images and symbols that connect us to each other and to the planet.

Soy un amasamiento, I am an act of kneading, of uniting and joining that not only has produced both creature of darkness and a creature of light, but also a creature that questions the definitions of light and dark and gives them new meanings (80 – 81).

While Anzaldua speaks from the perspective of a Chicana radical feminist, her work as a visionary and a creator includes all people who have ever known the feeling of being silenced, trivialized, or ridiculed by a member of a dominating culture. As she questions the existing definitions and orders of things in her own world, and gives them new meanings which more adequately reflects her own experience, Anzaldua inspires other groups similarly silenced or trivialized to reclaim their rights to name and label their experience on their own terms.

Having appropriated language for her own purposes to forge new meanings out of old definitions, and having paid the price for having done so, Gloria Anzaldua is now fully empowered to create and recreate herself anew in her own version of her life narrative.

Text 2.6

I write the myths in me, the myths I am, the myths I want to become. The word, the image and the feeling have a palatable energy, a kind of power. *Con imagenes domo my miedo, cruzo los abismos, que tengo dor dentro. Con palabras me hago piedra, pajaro, puente de serpientes arrastrando a ras del suelo todo lo que soy, todo lo que algun dia sere* (70 – 71).

Conclusion

In this paper, I have used insights from critical discourse analysis to show how everyday language is used to create, maintain, and challenge representations of entire classes of people. In the first section, I reviewed recent scholarship in the social sciences which focuses on the role of narrative in representing as well as creating self concepts and cultural meanings. Next, I considered the work of critical theorists from a number of disciplines which examines the intersection of language, power, and ideology, and I showed how a model of critical discourse analysis could be usefully applied to characterize particular instances of misrepresentation carried out through various channels of public discourse. Finally, in the third section, I looked at two particular instances of language use which challenge the ideology of the dominant culture and offer an alternative world view of a less powerful group. Because people can become agents of their own life stories, they may use familiar language forms in novel ways to resist oppressive patterns of representation, as well as to create new meanings and self-definitions.

Works Cited

Antaki, Charles, and Sue Widdicombe, eds. *Identities in Talk.* Thousand Oaks, CA. / London, UK.: Sage Publications, 1998.

Anzaldua, Gloria. *Borderlands / La Frontera: The New Mestiza.* Spinsters / Aunt Lute: San Francisco, 1987.

Ashcroft, Bill, Gareth Griffiths, and Helen Tiffin. *The Empire Writes Back: Theory and Practice in Post-Colonial Literatures.* London, U.K. / New York: Routledge.

Baugh, John. *Beyond Ebonics: Linguistic Pride and Racial Prejudice.* Oxford, U.K. / New York: Oxford U P, 2000.

Bourdieu, P. *Language and Symbolic Power.* Transl.G. Raymond and M. Adamson. Cambridge, U.K.: Polity Press, 1991.

Bruner, Jerome. *Actual Minds, Possible Worlds.* Cambridge, Mass.: Harvard UP, 1986.

--- .*Acts of Meaning.* Cambridge, Mass: Harvard UP, 1990.

---. "The Narrative Construction of Reality." *Critical Inquiry* 18.1 (1991): 1-21.

Crawford, Mary. *Talking Difference: On Gender and Language.* Thousand Oaks, CA / London, U.K.: Sage Publications, 1995.

Dawson, Ashley. ' "This is the Digital Underclass': Asian Dub Foundation and Hip-Hop Cosmopolitanism." *Social Semiotics* 12:1 (2002), 27-48.

De Certeau, M. *The Practice of Everyday Life.* Berkeley: U of California P, 1984.

Dicker, Susan J. *Languages in America: A Pluralist View.* Clevedon, U.K.: Multilingual Matters Ltd., 1996.

Fairclough, Norman. *Critical Discourse Analysis: The Critical Study of Language.* London, New York: Longman, 1995.

Fernandes, Sujatha. "Island Paradise, Revolutionary Utopia or Hustler's Haven? Consumerism and Socialism in Contemporary Cuban Rap." *Journal of Latin American Cultural Studies* 12:3 (2003), 359-375.

Foucault, M. *The Archaeology of Knowledge and the Discourse on Language.* Transl. A.M. Sheridan Smith. New York: Pantheon Books, 1972.

Freire, Paolo. *Pedagogy of the Oppressed.* New York: Continuum, 1993 (Originally published in 1970).

Goncalves, Oscar. "Hermeneutics, Constructivism, and Cognitive-Behavioral Therapies: From the Object to the Project," in Neimeyer and Mahoney, eds. *Constructivism in Psychotherapy.* Washington, D.C.: American Psychological Association, 1995. 195-230.

Grandmaster Flash and the Furious Five. (19XX). "The Message."

Gutierrez, Kris D., Joanne Larson, and Betsy Kreuter. "Cultural Tensions in the Scripted

Classroom: The Value of the Subjugated Perspective." *Urban Education* 29.4 (1995): 410-442.

Labov, William. "The Logic of Nonstandard English." *Georgetown Monograph Series on*

Languages and Linguistics 22 Ed. James Alatis. Washington, D.C.: Georgetown U P, 1969. 1-44.

---. *Language in the Inner City: Studies in the Black English Vernacular.* Philadelphia: U of Pennsylvania P, 1972.

Luke, Allen. "Text and Discourse in Education: An Introduction to Critical Discourse Analysis." *Review of Research in Education 1995 - 1996.* Ed. Michael W. Apple.

Washington, D.C.: American Educational Research Association, 1996.

Mc Laren, Peter, ed. *Revolutionary Multiculturalism: Pedagogies of Dissent for the New Millenium.* Boulder, CO.: Westview Press, 1997.

--- and Henry Giroux. "Writing from the Margins: Geographies of Identity, Pedagogy, and Power" in McLaren, ed., 1997.

Mc Laren, Peter. *Life in schools* (4th Edition). New York: Allyn and Bacon, 2003.

Pennycock, Alastair. *The Cultural Politics of English as an International Language.* London / New York: Longman, 1994.

Perry, Theresa, and Lisa Delpit. *The Real Ebonics Debate: Power, Language, and the Education of African American Children.* Boston: Beacon Press, 1998.

Rickford, John. *African American Vernacular English: Features, Evolution, Educational Implications.* Oxford, U.K.: Blackwell, 1999 a.

---. (1999b). "Using the Vernacular to teach the Standard." in Rickford (1999a).

---. "The Ebonics Controversy in my Backyard: A Sociolinguist's Experiences and Reflections." *Journal of Sociolinguistics* 3.2 (1999c): 267-275.

Rickford, John, and Angela Rickford. "Dialect Readers Revisited." *Linguistics and Education* 7 (1996): 107 – 128.

Rickford, John, and Russell Rickford. *Spoken Soul: The Story of Black English.* New York: John Wiley, 2000.

Rosaldo, Renato. *Culture and Truth: The Remaking of Social Analysis.* Boston, Mass.: Beacon Press, 1989.

Rose, Tricia. *Black Noise: Rap Music and Black Culture in Contemporary America.* Middletown: Wesleyan U P,1994.

Sarbin, Theodore. *Narrative Psychology: The Storied Nature of Human Conduct.* New York: Praeger Publishers, 1986.

Sfard, Anna, and Anna Prusak. "Talking Identities: In Search of an Analytical Tool for Investigating Learning as a Culturally Shaped Activity." *Educational Researcher* 34.4 (2005): 14-22.

Smitherman, Geneva. *Black Talk: Words and Phrases from the Hood to the Amen Corner.* (2nd Edition). Boston: Houghton Mifflin, 2000.

---. "Language and African Americans: Movin On up a Lil Higher." *Journal of English Linguistics* 32.3 (2004): 186-196.

Smitherman-Donaldson, Geneva, and Teun van Dijk, eds. *Discourse and Discrimination.* Detroit: Wayne State U P, 1988.

Van Dijk, Teun. *Communicating Racism: Ethnic Prejudice in Thought and Talk.* Newbury Park, CA. / London: Sage Publications, 1987.

---. "Principles of Critical Discourse Analysis." *Discourse and Society* 4.2 (1993a): 249-283

---. *Elite Discourse and Racism.* (Sage Series on Race and Ethnic Relations). Newbury Park, CA. / London: Sage Publications, 1993b.

---. "Discourse Semantics and Ideology." *Discourse and Society* 6.2 (1995): 243-289.

---. *Ideology: A Multidisciplinary Approach.* Thousand Oaks / London: Sage Publications, 1998.

---. "Multidisciplinary CDA: a plea for diversity." *Methods of Critical Discourse Analysis.*

Eds. Ruth Wodak and Michael Meyer. London, U.K. / Thousand Oaks, CA. U.S.A.: Sage Publications, 2001.

Vygotsky, L. S. *Thought and Language.* 1934. Transl. Eugenia Hanfmann and Gertrude

Vakar. Cambridge, Mass.: MIT Press, 1961.

---. *The Collected Works of L.S. Vygotsky,* including the volume *Thinking and Speech,* ed. by R.W. Rieber and A.S. Carton, New York: Plenum Press, 1987.

Wodak, Ruth, and Michael Meyer, eds. *Methods of Critical Discourse Analysis.* Thousand Oaks / London: Sage Publications, 2001.

KAEKO MOCHIZUKI

Duras, Ibuse and Silko:
Narrating Nuclear Destruction in Atomic Societies

Introduction

High-technological weapons were used in 1954, half a century ago, when the USA tested the hydrogen bomb, "Bravo," on Bikini Island, a part of the present Republic of Marshall Islands in the Pacific Ocean. The hydrogen bomb then was 1000 times as powerful as the atomic bomb that had been dropped in Hiroshima nine years before. It was tested six times from March to May of that year. At that time, near Bikini, there were more than 10 Japanese boats fishing tuna, all of them showered in radioactive "ashes" or fallout after the bombing. One engineer aboard *Daigo-Fukuryu-maru*, or the fifth "Happy Dragon-boat," died of leukemia in half a year. He was the first peacetime nuclear victim. Also in 1954, 28 American soldiers, mostly meteorologists, working on Eniwetok Island, 250 kilometers east of Bikini, were exposed to "the dazzling light," "roaring sound" and "the falling gray snow."[1] They, too, later suffered from leukemia upon return to the USA.

Both the atomic bomb and hydrogen bomb tests had begun much earlier than 1954 on Bikini and on a few other islands selected as nuclear testing grounds. These tests were carried out 67 times from 1946 to 1958, contaminating about 7000 native islanders with radioactive fallout. 840 of them died of leukemia and other kinds of cancer by 2004. All sicknesses are grouped and called "atomic-bomb illnesses" in my literal translation of the Japanese words *genbaku-byo* or "radiation sickness" in John Bester's translation of the same words in Ibuse's *Black Rain*. In those twelve years, 992 Japanese fishing boats and several fishing boats from Korea and Taiwan were contaminated by radioactive fallout.[2] Similarly, Britain,

---

[1] *Asahi Shinbun (Asahi Newspaper)*, February 29, 2004. (tr. Mochizuki) They likened radioactive fallout from the hydrogen bomb explosion to "gray snow" in the tropical area, and it corresponds to the "black rain" the atomic bomb scattered on Hiroshima. The column *"Tensei-Jingo"* (*Celestial Voice -Terrestrial Words*) in *Asahi Newspaper*, February 29, 2004 features Aikichi Kuboyama, the engineer aboard the fifth "Happy Dragon-maru" who was the first victim of fallout after the war. He wrote in his memoir on the moment of the hydrogen bomb explosion that " ... at about 3:50 [AM] the round cabin window shone like the time of the sunrise ... but the light was seen in the west." (tr. Mochizuki)

[2] *The Nishinippon Shinbun (Western Japan Newspaper)*, January 14, 2004.

supporting and following the nuclear defense plans of the USA, tested the hydrogen bomb on nearby Christmas Island nine times from 1957 to 1958. The result of the tests was that approximately 270 soldiers from New Zealand and 300 Fijian soldiers were exposed to radioactive ashes.[3] All of these incidences, in addition to the dismal aftermath of the bombing of Hiroshima in the South Pacific, warns against the proliferation of nuclear weapons, which have claimed many victims since World War II.

   Hiroshima Mon Amour by Marguerite Duras (1915–1996), *Black Rain* by Masuji Ibuse (1898–1993) and *Ceremony* by Leslie Marmon Silko (1948) narrate nuclear destruction and violence, respectively, in a French woman's love affair in Hiroshima of the 1950s, in a Japanese family's *hibakusha*, or atom-bombed experience, of the 1940s, and in a Native American man's experience of World War II post-traumatic stress disorder in the 1950's, upon return to his home reservation, a site of numerous uranium mines. Explicitly, *Hiroshima Mon Amour* (1966), *Black Rain* (1969) and *Ceremony* (1977) elaborate on the fact that conventional low-technological weapons of destruction were used at many sites of combat during World War II. Implicitly, they reflect upon and critique the contemporary low-technological violence that transpired during the Vietnam War in the 1960's and 1970's. Finally, all three works focus on the emergence of unprecedented high-technological weapons that have been mass-produced and tested since the beginning of the Cold War and which are being produced and tested even today. A comparative reading of these narratives of nuclear destruction reveals a common history of racism, fascism and colonialism, the multiethnic features of atomized people, and the ruin of life, spirit and land caused by high and low technological wars.

   In the first part of this essay, I examine ways in which Duras, Ibuse, and Silko, through their stories, merge discrete sites of home and Other as simultaneous locations of annihilation as demonstrated in the collapsing of Nevers and Hiroshima in Duras' screenplay, Hiroshima and Singapore in Ibuse's novel, and Laguna Pueblo and a Philippine jungle in Silko's story. It seems that the three authors had to merge home and Other to reveal that in the nuclear age obsolete nationalism and arrogant unilateralism, approving and even producing wars, neither protect home nor control Other but bring about simultaneous destruction of both home and Other. In the second part of the essay, I discuss the significance of curing, healing and remembering ceremonies amidst and against these histories of nuclear destruction.[4]

---

[3]   *Asahi Shinbun* (*Asahi Newspaper*), March 1, 2004.
[4]   Along with those discussions I will point out a few problems of English translations, such as objectionable emissions of original French sentences and inexact renditions of original Japanese key words. I will then offer my version of an English translation to convey, though only to some extent, the original idea of the non-English texts.

The Art of Uniting Home and Other

Duras, Ibuse and Silko all explore how their homelands have been devastated by wars. They also imagine the conditions of other peoples' homelands similarly destroyed. Duras, in fact, refers to the Bikini Island hydrogen bomb test in her original text of *Hiroshima mon amour* as follows: "The film starts with the development of the famous 'mushroom' in Bikini ..."[5] She brackets the part in which this sentence is included to note that Allain Resnais abandoned this scene in his film production of *Hiroshima mon amour*. Regardless of Resnais' artistic choices in producing the film version of *Hiroshima mon amour*, the current translation in English of Duras' text omits her bracketed text, negating the extent of her concern, a concern clearly reflected in the other portions of her non-bracketed text concerning the development and proliferation of nuclear weapons.

In her original text, Duras succeeds in combining separate locations, Nevers in the 1940's, Hiroshima in the 1940's - 50's, and Bikini in the 1950's, as collective sites of destruction. Duras' interest in juxtaposing Nevers and Hiroshima throughout her screenplay is to emphasize the importance of World War II, singling out Bikini as a starting point in a post-war atomic society and continuing with her merging of Nevers and Hiroshima when she locates her French and Japanese protagonists in Hiroshima in the summer of 1957. 1957 marked a time when many Japanese people had begun to forget the Hiroshima of twelve years before. Of course, some attempted to remember the cataclysm for posterity by recording survivors' narratives, collecting victims' memoirs and diaries, as well as organizing demonstrations against nuclear testing.

In *Hiroshima Mon Amour* the Japanese protagonist, who is the French woman's temporary lover in Hiroshima, cynically comments that she, an outsider and an actress, cannot imagine the disaster of Hiroshima, saying, "You saw nothing in Hiroshima. Nothing." (15) She, then, starts to talk about her affair with a German soldier, remembering that she "was eighteen and he was twenty-three." (48) She discovers that the killing she has witnessed at home and the holocaust in Hiroshima are similarly violent acts of war. She reveals that after her German lover was killed in Nevers in 1944, she slept holding his body, and was later made to live in a basement with her hair shorn as punishment for 'sleeping with the enemy.' The next year, she fled to Paris with the help of her mother, and read about the

---

[5]   Richard Seaver did not translate this sentence into English. It is my translation of the original French text. Duras, Marguerite. *Hiroshima mon amour*. Paris: Gallimard, 1960, 15.

atomic bombing of Hiroshima. Her narrative sounds like an incantation, simple, repetitive, almost infantile:

> Not long after that my mother tells me I have to leave for Paris, by night. She gives me some money. I leave for Paris, on bicycle, at night. It's summer. The nights are warm. When I reach Paris two days later the name of Hiroshima is in all the newspapers. My hair is now a decent length. I am in the street with the people. (67)

Twelve years following this incident, in 1957, the French woman is in Hiroshima surrounded by Japanese people, one of whom is the man she loves. In the monument to the dead of the city she acknowledges that to talk of love and to make love with her Japanese lover is to talk of death and to confront the trauma of necrophilia, lynching and confinement simultaneously. She dares to recall and reexamine her experience of love and death in Nevers, learning to philosophize the horror of Hiroshima in order to acquire the wisdom and strength to live again.

In response, the Japanese lover repeats his cynical comment on her ignorance of the nuclear holocaust in Hiroshima in order to hide his inability to cope with his own feelings, saying, "*Nothing*. You know *nothing*." (21) The French woman responds, "Listen to me. Like you I know what it is to forget," and goes on to tell him the contemporary story of Bikini:

> People are afraid of the rain.
> The rain of ashes on the waters of the Pacific.
> The waters of the Pacific kill.
> Fishermen of the Pacific are dead.
> People are afraid of the food.
> The food of the entire cities is buried.
> An entire city rises up in anger.
> Entire cities rise up in anger. (22-23)

The woman's monologue, in verse form, sounds all the more like an incantation of a sorceress who predicts: "Women risk giving birth to malformed children, [...] Men risk becoming sterile" (22). She warns about the radiation of food, foretells of human lives in danger, and mediates between the people of Hiroshima and people from other "cities in anger. "

Duras, in the narrative that precedes the verses above, juxtaposes two contrasting but analogous images. One is the deadly "spiraling atomic cloud" (21) which hovers over Bikini Island, and the other, which the English translator mysteriously overlooks from the original French text, is the sculpture of "the spinning Atomium"[6] in Brussels. The Atomium is a huge monument, in the shape of the molecular structure of iron, built to

---

6   My translation of *Hiroshima mon amour*, 41.

commemorate the 1958 World Fair whose theme was "scientific technology and humanism." Duras must have been skeptical of such a highbrow theme and therefore placed the two images next to each other to highlight her cynicism. It seems likely that Duras knew that the uranium for the atomic bomb unleashed on Hiroshima had come from a mine in Congo, Belgium's ex-colony. Whether or not hers is a conscious choice, she here calls attention to the monument to question whether Brussels will acknowledge the other "cities ... in anger" or will remain one of the cities ever merry and prosperous in the atomic age. By introducing the Atomium into the text, Duras emphasizes the responsibility of the international community for nuclear destruction. She thus connects the French woman born in Europe, the home ground of "scientific technology and humanism," to the people of Bikini, Hiroshima, Tokyo, Kochi, and other "angry" places where they cannot choose but live on fish polluted by radioactive fallout.[7]

It is interesting to note that Duras, a politically progressive and concerned outsider, wrote about Hiroshima three years earlier than Ibuse. Born in the city of Fukuyama, 100 kilometers east of Hiroshima, Ibuse, who barely escaped atomic bombing in his native village, saw and heard about the most painful reality of *hibakusha*, or the atom-bombed, crying and dying everyday and every year around him. Understandably, he could not write about such a shattering experience until the late 1960's. While Duras unites Europe, Asia and the South Pacific in *Hiroshima Mon Amour*, Ibuse, in *Black Rain*, brings together two Asian cities destroyed in World War II. The first, Singapore, is attacked by old-fashioned Japanese bombing squads, while Hiroshima, the second, is devastated by a modern high-technological bomb. A middle-aged man, Shigematsu, a steady, diligent engineer, with a subtle sense of humor, supervising a textile mill narrates in the novel from the day of Hiroshima's bombing in 1945 to its aftermath in the mid 1950s. Ibuse, however, chooses to shift the narrative voice to that of a young woman, Yasuko, Shigematsu's niece and his foster child, to relate the intense scene in which "umbrella-shaped mass" smoke covered Hiroshima and killed 140,000 people in one moment. Ibuse must have believed that he should articulate her voice to give attention to how a woman with the capacity to reproduce life, among the then meek, silenced half of the population, perceived the scene of mass killing.[8]

---

[7] In 1955 my mother decided to quit using "Bikini tuna" or "A-bombed tuna" to cook sushi. Her decision lasted for one year.

[8] Original Japanese text of "a small white flower" is one word, *Foo-ran*, which means "wind orchid" or "noble orchid." This Finetia falcate, less than 10 cm high, is native in Japan, and its cultivation used to be one of the status symbols of feudal landlords in the Edo period. Many people still like it because of its fragrance and elegant shape.

Yasuko, urged by her uncle, fled to a village about four kilometers northwest of Hiroshima on the morning of August 6. Given shelter at a wealthy landowner's residence, she is invited to a morning tea ceremony with several other evacuees. In a cool, calm room she suddenly sees "a terrible flash ... outside ... like a shooting star the size of hundreds of suns" (21). One of the children playing in the garden falls down:

> In the direction of the city, smoke was rising high up into the sky. We could see it above the white clay wall of the garden. It was like the smoke from a volcano, or a column of cloud with sharply etched outlines; one certain thing was that it was no ordinary smoke. My knees as I squatted there shook so uncontrollably that I pressed them against a rock, heedless of *a small white flower* clinging to it.
> "They must have dropped some new weapon," said Mr. Nojima from behind the rocks.... The smoke had climbed high into the sky, spreading out wider the higher it went. I remembered a photograph of oil tanks burning in Singapore that I had once seen. It had been taken just after the Japanese army had brought about the fall of the city, and the scene was so horrifying that I wondered at the time whether such things were really justified. The smoke climbed ... umbrella-shaped mass that loomed over everything like some top-heavy monster. (22) [emphasis mine]

Ibuse thus juxtaposes the bombing of Singapore in 1942 and bombing of Hiroshima in 1945 to reveal the cause and effect of Japan's wartime aggression. In this passage, Ibuse expresses both Yasuko's intellectual and emotional strength to imagine and deplore the horror that the Japanese military men, as a new, late group of colonizers, have caused to the Singaporeans and clearly discerns the grave injustice committed against them. In so doing, Ibuse reflects a belief in women's ability to acutely perceive the violence of war, allowing a female protagonist to imagine and connect two discrete locales, instead of utilizing male characters to reflect male intelligentsia of the period typically better informed of wars in Indo-China than women were.

Yasuko naively suspects that similar, powerful conventional weapons have bombed both Singapore and Hiroshima. In time, she watches and learns the thoroughly lethal effects of the atomic bomb. She then notices the slow, painful symptoms of leukemia that begin to appear in her own decaying body and mind. Ibuse later depicts Yasuko, showered in the radioactive "black rain," as a helpless victim of leukemia, stressing the irony that she immediately leaves the safe suburban shelter and returns to the center of Hiroshima in the rain "fall[ing] in streaks the thickness of a fountain pen" to make sure that her foster parents are safe. (34) Ibuse then sensitively abstains from the atrocity of retaining Yasuko as the narrator of her own illnesses and returns the narrative stream to Shigematsu and, occasionally, to his wife, Shigeko.

Since *Black Rain was* published in 1968 it has been the object of severe criticism in Japan, especially from right-wing critics.[9] Such critics consider Ibuse's narratives too quiet yet also too political. Some of them argue that the narratives on the whole are too soft and flat because the author, Ibuse, had not been at the site to witness the horror himself. Yet, their argument does not address Ibuse's skill in weaving into the text quoted above a more subtle site of destruction besides Hiroshima and Singapore, that of a fragile plant's biosphere. Careful readers will notice that Yasuko, terrified by the "top-heavy monster," carelessly crushes and destroys a dainty "Foo-ran" or wind orchid. She knows what she has done to the flower. She is hurt by her own "heedless[ness]" though she is unable to articulate her dismay over her unintentionally destructive act as a contemporary ecologist might do. I therefore contend that Yasuko's soft "undertones" and also the quiet understatement of the whole novel better convey "the grimmest of subjects" and the complex relation between the destroyers and the destroyed than the loud voices of protest and lamentation. (Bester 14) I assert that they also surpass the louder voices of the right-wing critics who still falsely insist that the Japanese imperialist army tried to liberate Korea, China, Indo-China and the Pacific islands. In other words, Ibuse juxtaposes the large urban center of Hiroshima and the wind orchid's delicate biosphere in an artfully designed Japanese garden to suggest that both places are of equal value and that both are destroyed at the same moment

---

[9]   Two representatives among the right wing critics are (1) Naose Inoki and (2) Kenichi Takemura. (1) Inoki even now attacks Ibuse on his homepage, claiming that Ibuse copied and "stole" the whole contents of a diary written by Shizuma Shigematsu (1903-1977), a witness of the atomic bombing of Hiroshima and a person from the same province as Ibuse. Inoki's accusation was proved to be false when the diary was published by Chikuma-Shobo Publishing Company in Tokyo in 2001 as *Shigematsu Diary* to which are attached the letters from Ibuse to Shigematsu. The letters tell that Ibuse obtained full permission to use and quote from the diary. Ibuse also in his letters implored Shigematsu to become the co-author of *Black Rain.* Shigematsu, knowing that Ibuse had been an established writer with his own style, declined Ibuse's offer with courtesy and respect. *Shigematsu Diary,* Ibuse's letters and the testimony by Shizuma Shigematsu's son, Fumihiro Shigematsu, confirm that Ibuse's *Black Rain* is a creative novel based on Shigematsu's diary and the diary itself is another piece of literature. Fumihiro Shigematsu, a fine keeper of the Shigematsu archives in the city of Fukuyama, offers on his homepage the record of his lectures on the friendship between his father and Ibuse, the diary and the letters. http://www.fuhc.fukuyama-u.ac.jp/human/hc/jpn/sigematuniki/sigematuniki.htm (2) Takemura invented the expression "nuclear allergy" meaning allergic reaction or opposition against nuclear energy in the 1960's and has preached to the Japanese people who are against any form of nuclear development that they should "overcome such allergy or disease" and support the construction of nuclear plants and Japan's future nuclear armament. He is a strong advocate of the plutonium-thermal-use plans now. See *Fukui Shinbun (Fukui Newspaper)* March 3, 2003.

by the carelessness of human beings. He implies that Yasuko, a victim of the atomic bomb, has victimized Foo-Ran's life and habitat. Ibuse, in so doing, questions a harsh view of the world in which the military elite rule other people, other creatures and other places. He presents another softer, less aggressive view of the world in which a tiny orchid exists in its own place and a human being exists in her own place to share equal ground.

Similarly to Ibuse in *Black Rain*, Leslie Marmon Silko connects an island in the South Pacific with her native land of Laguna Pueblo, providing a thread between two remote places, home and Other, through grim images of killing. Toward the end of the World War II, many of the Pacific islands like Iwo Jima, Wake, Saipan, Tinian and the Philippines, all close to Bikini, were the most dreadful sites of destruction where Japanese soldiers and American soldiers fought bloody low-technology wars. In *Ceremony*, Silko connects the killing "in the jungle of some nameless Pacific island" with the post-war killing on a Native American reservation in New Mexico. (7) She describes how Tayo, a young Laguna Pueblo war veteran, suffers from post-traumatic stress disorder, experiencing hallucinations of having killed his favorite uncle Josiah, who is peacefully alive and settled on the reservation:

> Rocky made him look at the corpse and said, "Tayo, this is *Jap*! This is a *Jap* uniform!" And then he rolled the body over with his boot and said, "Look, Tayo, look at the face," and that was when Tayo started screaming because it wasn't a Jap, it was Josiah, eyes shrinking back into the skull and their shining black light glazed over by death. (8)

Because of their similar skin color and complexion, the Native American soldiers and the Japanese soldiers look so much alike that Tayo, unable to shoot the latter, mistakes an enemy for his uncle. I do not think, however, that Silko describes Tayo's mistake in order to emphasize the ethnic bond between the two races. Rather, she points out the absurdity of human beings killing other human beings, any one of whom could be a remote uncle or aunt in a genealogical tree of one species. She concludes that Tayo's inability to kill becomes the key to his survival and healing.

Ironically it is not "battle-fatigue[d]" Tayo but Rocky, Tayo's brave, manly cousin that is actually killed in "The Bataan Death March" in the Philippine jungle in 1942.[10] Silko, like Ibuse, carefully and quietly records the cruelty of the aggressors to depict the least heroic reality of death and the sense of loss of a Laguna Pueblo young man. Then, she meticulously describes the rest of Tayo's fellow soldiers, the young war veterans, back

---

[10] Silko here refers to the Bataan Death March in 1942. Approximately 12,000 American prisoners and 64,000 Filipino prisoners were moved by the Japanese soldiers from Bataan to San Fernando which was 60 kilometers away. 1,200 Americans and 16,000 Filipinos died or were declared missing during the march.

on the reservation. They are absorbed in alcohol, sex and the wartime habit of killing, but now killing amongst themselves:

> They found Harley and Leroy together in the big boulders below the road of Paguate Hill. The old GMC pickup was crushed around them like the shiny metal coffin the Veterans Office bought for each of them. In that way it was not much different than if they had died at Wake Island or Iwo Jima: the bodies were dismembered beyond recognition and the coffins were sealed. The morning of the funeral an honor guard from Albuquerque fired the salute; two big flags covered the coffins completely, and it looked as if the people from the village had gathered only to bury the flags (258-259).

Silko, with her dry narrative style, conveys the meaningless death of Laguna Pueblo young men, back home, inside their own country. Focusing on the gathering of the villagers who mourn for them, she exposes the emptiness of an army-sponsored ceremony whose gaudy adornments like "the shiny metal coffin," "an honor guard," and "the flags" confirm that Harley and Leroy have been killed by the USA.

Tayo narrowly escapes being killed or killing others because he learns the life-oriented arts, one of which is the art of storytelling in healing ceremonies, ceremonies that have survived the systematic genocide of the Pueblo peoples in New Mexico. Before he learns to speak of what he has seen in the Philippine jungle and on the Laguna Pueblo reservation, Tayo listens to his grandmother's storytelling of the world's first atomic bomb test at nearby Trinity Site on July 16, 1945, one month before the bombing of the two Japanese cities, Hiroshima on August 6 and Nagasaki on August 9, the former of which attacked with the atomic bomb and the latter with the hydrogen bomb. Old Grandma narrates, "a flash of light through the window. So big, so bright ... I thought I was seeing the sun rise again, but it faded away ..." (245) Tayo spends six years thinking of the meaning of her story and finds "a circle of death" that connects the Pacific islands, Laguna Pueblo with uranium mines, and "cities twelve thousand miles away." (246) The grandmother does not articulate their names but directs Tayo's attention to other places across the Pacific Ocean, to Hiroshima and Nagasaki in Japan, so that he may realize the cause and effect of the war in a broader scope.

Curing, Healing and Re-membering Ceremonies

At the end of Duras' *Hiroshima Mon Amour*, Duras portrays her French protagonist as follows: "[she] gives this Japanese – *at Hiroshima* – her most precious possession: herself as she now is, her *survival* after the death of her love at *Nevers*." (112) The French woman confides to her Japanese lover that she has been completely mute about the 1944 incident in Nevers even to her French husband and children. In Hiroshima she gains courage to tell her story for the first time in her life to her Japanese lover. He is also married but yet unable to talk fully of Hiroshima and of his experience in the army with his wife. By talking about "the grimmest subject" she and he share the horror of wartime violence, in order to be cured of its trauma. Duras' scenario ends with the now famous dialogue: "Hi-ro-shi-ma. ... That's your name. ... Yes. Your name is Nevers." (83) Duras explains the dialogue as follows in the original text of *Hiroshima mon amour*: "They have the names of the place, the names that are not theirs. It is, as if the disaster of a woman shorn in Nevers and the disaster of Hiroshima respond to each other *exactly*.[11] After this storytelling ceremony they are ready to tell others their own stories, represent what has happened at home, and take responsibility for what they have loved and killed.

Duras seems to insist that this talk-sharing ceremony should be continued in the present world because she is aware of the covert tactics of post-war fascism, set in people's daily personal events and affairs. The post-war smiling fascism prevents people from talking freely and seriously of such vital and politically significant subjects as nuclear violence, racism and holocausts.[12] Duras herself writes about the possibility of interracial but apolitical co-ownership of Hiroshima as follows: "One can talk about Hiroshima anywhere even in [an] [...] adulterous love affair. The bodies of both protagonists, who are really in love with each other, will remind us of this. What is really sacrilegious, if anything is, is Hiroshima itself" (9).

Duras here applies her usual materialist irony to imply that the "bodies" that remind her of silent corpses of passionate lovers can indeed "talk" of the atomic bombing of Hiroshima. She seems to suggest that those human bodies engaged in sexual intercourse can tell the story of the ultimate site of violence and destruction they have survived. They recognize in the Eros/Thanatos fusion of lovemaking the ruin of Hiroshima and reveal their understanding of life emerging from death in the revival of Hiroshima and their own discrete resurrections.

---

[11] The English translator should not have omitted these sentences, either. They are my translation of *Hiroshima mon amour*, 9 -10.

[12] Duras tells Xavière Gauthier in *Woman to Woman* that many readers of her *Hiroshima mon amour* say, " It didn't happen during the war, but it's my story." (117) Duras, embarrassed a little by the readers' lack of war consciousness, complains that "the war is crucial" but soon concedes that "people still found their own story, outside of all contexts." (117) Hiroshima is thus shared among the witnesses of violence in France and its ex-colonies and in any other places where fascism, whether it controls people in times of war or peace, has prohibited them to tell their own stories.

While Duras discovers the way to heal from war trauma through interracial ceremonies of talk-sharing in *Hiroshima Mon Amour*, Ibuse introduces in *Black Rain* two kinds of ceremonies that cure the atom-bombed. One depicts women bathing in a river while the other depicts Shigematsu's conversion from a lay Buddhist priest to a pantheist farmer who worships all life in nature. In the former, Shigematsu writes in his diary of August 9, 1945 about his wife and niece, who have returned from bathing and washing their clothes in the river for the first time in four days after the bombing. With his practical sense of humor, he urges them to wash their clothes in the river first and then to go on "swimming." He advises them to stay in the water until their only clothes "they [have] stood up in" get dry on the shore. (147) As the two women come back from the river much later than Shigematsu expects, he learns that bathing has cleansed and refreshed them. He, however, notices that Shigeko, older and more tired than Yasuko, is suffering from a stomachache caused by staying in the water too long: "Shigeko, who had griping pains in the stomach as a result of over-immersion in the river, said very little. Both of them had had nothing but towels around their waists as they squatted in the shallow part of the river while their underwear dried" (158).

Here Ibuse hints that Shigeko and Yasuko have gone through a cleansing ceremony. It is not so solemn as it is funny and imperfect, unlike the ceremonies performed by the clergy of institutionalized religions. It offers, however, a possibility of contrasting and uniting a living middle-aged woman suffering from pains "as a result of over-immersion" with tens of thousands of citizens from Hiroshima dying at the time whose last words are recorded unanimously as: "Give me water." In Hiroshima, known as "city of many rivers," there was no water to drink after August 6 because the rivers were jammed with rotting bodies.

The cleansing ceremony cures not only Shigeko and Yasuko but also Shigematsu, the narrator, who has witnessed the devastation of Hiroshima more deeply than his wife or niece. Shigematsu, who has gallantly given up the opportunity to bathe in the river so that his wife and niece may go, listens carefully to their story of "squatting" in the cool water for too long, smiles quietly, and recovers from the horror of having seen a deserted body with "swarms of maggots tumbling from the mouth and nose and crowding in the eye sockets ..." (161). As a good listener, he partakes of the cleansing ceremony and obtains in his imagination sufficient water with which to cleanse the desecrated body and the scars on his face.

Ibuse, therefore, successfully employs the irony of life-giving water in this depiction of a healing ceremony; the dead are recorded in the readers' memory, and the two women to some extent are restored to the dignity of life. A critic, Tetsutaro Kawakami, notices the element of a purifying ceremony in the narrative above, writing that "there is something holy like religious performance ... more than something smile-provoking and touching." (401) I agree with Kawakami, on the condition that the holiness of this cleansing ceremony is related to the absence of authoritarianism or statements of physical need.

In the second healing ceremony in *Black Rain*, Shigematsu quits his job as a textile engineer as well as his job as a lay Buddhist priest and becomes a farmer who nurses his sick niece, grows closer to living things in nature, and acquires energy to foretell the future of his niece and, eventually, of his country. He leaves Hiroshima several years after 1945 and returns to his native village, Kobatake. Yasuko's illness is getting worse in the village in spite of her parents' tender, loving care. Shigematsu's whole lifestyle gradually becomes a ceremony of quietism to pray for the dead, dying and alive. His one wish as a pantheist farmer is to hold a ceremony to ask heaven to send a beautiful rainbow. The rainbow is to become a miraculous sign that brings about good rain, the antidote to black rain, and good luck for ailing Yasuko.

The one he hopes to see is the antithesis of the two phantasmagoric "white rainbows," which he insists have appeared at the crucial moments of Japanese history. On August 14, 1945, one day before Japan's unconditional surrender due to the atomic bombing of Hiroshima eight days before, Shigematsu sees a "white rainbow, stretching across the morning sun that gleamed dully in the thinly clouded sky." (288) His supervisor at the textile factory tells Shigematsu that a strange white rainbow is a bad omen. The former remembers the years between World War I and World War II, warning "I saw one too when I was in Tokyo, on the day before the February [2] 6 Incident. ... A 'white rainbow that pierces the sun – it was a sign from heaven that armed disturbance was imminent ..." (292-293)[13] February 26, 1936 was the starting point of military fascism in Japan. Ibuse, by presenting the ominous, surrealistic sign of "a white rainbow," expresses his doubt that Japan, after being occupied and "democratized" by the American army in 1945, will be free from "armed disturbance" in the future. Ibuse's concern is prophetic as, writing these words, I witness in Japan the emergence of a cunning, smiling fascism in "a Disney-ish world." (Rose 410) It is manipulating the great majority of people with such propagandistic phrases as the "peaceful use of clean nuclear energy" and "clever reuse of radioactive waste matter" while carrying out the unconstitutional buildup of Japan's military forces. The memories and experiences of respectable older citizens like Shigematsu and the textile factory manager, most of whom are dead now, are still being respected and handed down to the next generations, but the successors to or storytellers of their legacy are in the minority.

---

[13] English translator's error for February 26.

Ibuse's concern to preserve the healing arts may explain why he, in designating Shigematsu as a performer of a ceremony, presents an ordinary, colorful rainbow as an antidote to an ominous white rainbow that has produced toxic black rain. By the time he holds a rainbow inviting ceremony, however, Shigematsu has become more sensitive to the lives of all creatures in nature. He realizes that the life of baby fish and small flowers and the life of human beings are of equal importance. He, of course, wishes for Yasuko's recovery from "radiation sickness" but he hopes also for the revival of all that has been destroyed. Meanwhile, the villagers spread rumors that Yasuko's illness is terminal, and therefore "her marriage so remote." (9) They also label Shigematsu a lazy, shameful *hibakusha*. A social outcast, he performs the ceremony at the very end of the novel, looking over the mountain, looking through the world beyond it:

> Shigematsu looked up. "If a rainbow appears over *those hills*, a miracle will happen," he prophesied to himself. "Let a rainbow appear – not a white one, but one of many hues – and Yasuko will be cured." So he told himself, with his eyes on *the nearby hills*, though he knew all the while it could never come true. (300) [emphasis mine][14]

Shunning "a white one," Shigematsu longs to see a multi-colored rainbow so that it may bring soothing rain and allow Yasuko to recover from leukemia. His heart is heavy, however, since he senses the impossibility of his wish. The ending is gloomy and unsentimental but full of love. Ibuse implies that Shigematsu, not accepted fully as a member of his small native village, fails to connect to his ancestral home. He also suggests that Shigematsu, as the performer of the rainbow ceremony, still remembers the particular kind of violence that has atomized not only human lives in Hiroshima but also the traditional bond or solidarity of a village only "one hundred miles to the east of Hiroshima." (9) Ibuse, however, does not allow Shigematsu to despise or bear a grudge against his village kin but keeps him aware that they cruelly ostracize him and "a dozen or more" *hibakushas* back home like him only because they sense and feel the horror of the sickness that makes "their limbs start to rot on them." (27)

---

[14] For this crucial last scene Ibuse mechanically repeats the same words meaning "the mountain beyond" or "the mountain farther away" both in the former sentence and the latter. I, therefore, prefer the literal translation of "the mountain farther away" to the plural "those hills" and "the nearby hills" because Japanese people, of natural piety, have worshipped a mountain in each village, not hills.

Eight years later, in 1977, Silko, in *Ceremony,* introduces Tayo, who has an even harder time in his home village, suffering from the effects of severe post-traumatic stress disorder, one of which is the uncontrollable urge to attack and kill others and even himself. Despite this, Silko presents the possibility of recovery from his illness. Violence in Laguna Pueblo, however, continued unabated until the 1970's, when on-site uranium mining had been stopped. Silko records in her book of collected essays, *Yellow Woman and a Beauty of the Spirit,* about the "suicide club" on Native reservations, drawing the seemingly normal, smart teenagers to death and the "motiveless murder[s]" prevailing among Native adults (131). Laguna Pueblo elders have attributed such killing to the angry revenge of the desecrated earth around the old mines. A more prosaic explanation would single out the results of centuries of colonialism, which brought about, as Brill de Ramirez points out, "Euroamerican genocide, deicide, and [...] the devaluation and destruction of their culture, traditions, and beliefs" (104). The uranium boom gone, strange illnesses and the cult of money remaining, and the usual rate of fifty percent unemployment, people might well have indulged themselves in despair and nihilism. Silko thus narrates how the nuclear experience can affect such a small society as Laguna Pueblo, revealing as she does so, according to the local people, the "witchery" of the nuclear industry.

Tayo in *Ceremony* is one of a few young people who escape this witchery. By means of the healing arts, preserved by the people of Laguna Pueblo, Tayo understands where he is and in what age he lives. He realizes that "Trinity Site, where they exploded the first atomic bomb, was only three hundred miles to the southeast ...[and] the top-secret laboratories where the bomb had been created were deep in the Jemez Mountains, on land the Government took from Cochiti Pueblo." (245-246) He also learns that "Los Alamos, only a hundred miles northeast of him ... still surrounded by high electric fences" has been the sanctity for Jemez Pueblo. (246) He decides to stay in his atomic society to take care of plants that "would grow there like story, strong and translucent as the stars" as he is initiated into traditional thinking, which regards the lives of plants as valuable as human lives. (254)

Combining all the stories his Native American mentors have told him and connecting to them what he has seen in the war and back on the reservation, Tayo at last acquires his own stories to share with other members of his community. Now he can tell the villagers that the people of Laguna Pueblo are not isolated but are related to the peoples on the continent of Americas, the Pacific Islands and Japan: "From that time on, human beings were one clan again, united by the fate the destroyers planned for all of them, for all living things; united by a circle of death that devoured people in cities twelve thousand miles away [...]" (246).

Silko suggests that Tayo's recognition of "a circle of death" will lead him to acknowledge the propagation of nuclear violence, prophetically labeled as "Whirling darkness/ started its journey/ with its witchery/ and/ its witchery/ has returned upon it." (260 -261) Tayo's recognition of and escape from the witchery is the starting point for a journey to search for alternative ways to a circle of life. Interestingly, Paula Gunn Allen, the Laguna Pueblo scholar and writer, discussing the themes of *Ceremony*, insists that Silko "writes ... all about the feminization of a male. ... And the ideal for a Laguna or an Acoma male is that he learn how to be a woman. ... to nurture and to think more about peace ... " (Allen 30-31)

Silko as well as Duras and Ibuse, each present in their narratives an exemplary, decent and humane being and perhaps a model of a feminized man as well who tries to cure, heal and remember others. The Japanese man in *Hiroshima Mon Amour* is a good listener to the French woman's story as well as a gentle lover and a good storyteller. Shigematsu in *Black Rain* becomes adept at nursing the small, ill and wounded. Tayo in *Ceremony* learns how to tend to plants, honor women and preserve traditional stories in New Mexico. All three of them, the witnesses and survivors of World War II, confront nuclear violence, speak intelligently and listen carefully, as they learn to respect women and women's comparatively less aggressive, more peacefully oriented ways of life.

Conclusion

Through their narratives, Duras, Ibuse and Silko invite us, the scholars in the humanities, to reexamine the signs of nuclear violence and find ways to surpass them. They remind us that we are reading their narratives from the vantage point of half a century following the emergence of atomic societies. They warn us against international amnesia regarding nuclear violence in the 20th century. Each encourages us to confront the numerous accidents at nuclear power plants, the increasing number of *hibakusha*, or atom-bombed victims, due to the nuclear tests conducted in the USA and on Marshall Islands, including Bikini, the 2000 tons of depleted uranium bombs dropped on the people of Iraq, and other continuing examples of the many by-products of atomic societies. They persuade us to consider seriously the possibility of a multi-ethnic communality which resists the push toward collective extinction through nuclear violence, offering visions of our reunion and collaboration to achieve, in Silko's words, "one clan again."

Works Cited

Allen, Paula Gunn, and Laura Coltelli. "Paula Gunn Allen," *Winged Words: American Indian Writers Speak*. Ed. Laura Coltelli. Lincoln: U of Nebraska P, 1990.

Brill de Ramirez, Susan Berry. *Contemporary American Indian Literature & the Oral Tradition*. Tucson: U of Arizona P, 1999.

Duras, Marguerite. *Hioshima Mon Amour*. Tr. Richard Seaver. New York: Grove Press, 1961.

---. *Hiroshima mon amour*. Paris: Gallimard, 1960.

Duras, Marguerite, et Xavière Gauthier. *Les Parleuses*. Paris: Les Èdition Minuit, 1974.

---. *Woman to Woman*. Trans. Katharine A. Jensen. Lincoln & London: U of Nebraska P, 1987.

Ibuse, Masuji. *Black Rain* (1969). Tr. John Bester. Tokyo: Kodansha International, 1979.

---. *Kuroi Ame (Black Rain)* (1968). Tokyo: Shincho-sha, 2003.

Kawakami, Tetsutaro. "On *Black Rain*." *Kuroi Ame (Black Rain)* (1968). Trans. Kaeko Mochizuki. Tokyo: Shincho-sha, 2003. 396-403.

Rose, Wendy. "The Great Pretenders: Further Reflection on White Shamanism." Ed. Annette Jaimes. *The State of Native America: Genocide, Colonization, and Resistance*. Boston: South End, 1992. 403-421.

Silko, Leslie Marmon. *Ceremony* (1977). New York: Viking, 1986.

---. *Yellow Woman and a Beauty of the Spirit: Essays on Native American Life Today*. New York: Simon, 1996.

JOHN PURDY

Drawing the Line: Native American
Fiction and National Identities

In 1846 under The Treaty of Oregon between the U.S. and Britain, the
U.S.-Canada border was established, thus resolving-ostensibly-the
ownership of the contested landscapes between the two countries. While it
is true that the United States and Canada are both democratic societies, it is
equally true that they enact different models of that political system, and
that each responds differently to international events based, in part, upon a
difference in conceptualization of the role of democracies internally and
globally. However, despite these differences, they *both* share a checkered
history in the ways their governments have interacted with ethnic
communities within their borders, including the indigenous peoples of the
continent. Each nation has a colonial history that reflects the violent
appropriation of lands belonging to indigenous people and the subsuming
of their nations within the boundaries of each new nation state. Moreover,
despite the treaty and the clarification of the boundary of the two countries,
there has been an ongoing rivalry between them that often reveals their
nationalistic egos, with a particular emphasis on which nation feels it holds
the higher moral ground on issues of democracy and international policy.
Given their checkered colonial histories, however, neither nation can claim
a prize in the area of ethnic ethics.

Interestingly enough, at the border crossing between Blaine,
Washington and Vancouver, British Columbia, one will find a monument
commemorating the countries' shared colonial history, at least from an
Anglocentric point of view. Built in 1914, the Peace Arch and its park
celebrated the one hundredth anniversary of the signing of the Treaty of
Ghent, which ended the War of 1812 between the United States and Great
Britain. On the U.S. side of the monument, one will find an inscription that
reads, "Children of a Common Mother" (i.e. England), and on the Canadian
side, "Brethren Dwelling together in Unity." Also, on the east side one will
find a very interesting idealism uttered: "May These Gates Never Be
Closed." While the Arch may chronicle the end of a war and thus justify its
name, it does not, however, commemorate the end of international
hostilities in North America, either between the two nation states or
between their federal governments and those indigenous nations now
located within their borders.

In 1952, Paul Robeson, the African-American singer, actor and activist-who fell into disfavor with the U.S. government for his views on human rights and democratic realities-appeared at the Peace Arch. Intending to cross the border for a concert appearance, he was stopped by U.S. border guards and not allowed back in the country of his birth, so thousands of his fans came to the Peace Arch to hear him sing across this interesting, political line. For some people and ideologies, the gates have, indeed, been closed at times.

Of course, Robeson was learning a lesson learned long ago by Native American nations, and the specific site of the lesson-this arbitrary, invisible line created through language-is of particular, ironic significance. The national histories, taken separately, do not reveal the curious predicament of the peoples whose cultures cut across the line of demarcation the two countries created to solidify their individual sense of nationhood: the paradoxical existence of cultures whose nations were, in effect, partitioned in 1846.[1] For them, the continued rivalry and contentiousness between the two countries gives the border an odd and interesting character, at once a barrier to freedom and a symbol of it. For these nations, however, it is always an example of absurdity.

Less than a mile to the west of the Peace Arch, there is the site of Semiahmah, where an ancient coastal Salish village once stood. For thousands of years, it welcomed travelers from the inland waterways of what is now called the Puget Sound, and from the north and the British Columbia coast. Related by language and lifeways, the people's canoes found a ready haven here, as did those travelers who came from the south or by land from a thousand miles inland. The trading network was extensive, as the Lummi Nation, descendants of the original inhabitants, are currently finding with recently recovered artifacts.[2] In any event, travel north and south along the coast was a common occurrence, because families and clans were often widely dispersed over this landscape.

With the advent of the European and subsequent definition of the two nation states, this all changed. The ritual of border crossing now complicates the visits, and this ritual changes as the relationship between the U.S. and Canada changes. When tensions between the two countries are high, the border is quite dense; when relations are friendly, the border is very permeable. In any event, for those nations straddling the border the

---

[1] The history of nations partitioned by other countries or international organizations such as the United Nations needs little recounting. In almost every instance, it has been a disaster: Palestine, Korea, Vietnam.

[2] These artifacts are the result of an effort to reclaim the skeletal remains and funeral objects of Lummi ancestors, whose graves were destroyed when the local city of Blaine, Washington started construction of a new sewage treatment plant. In all, sixty thousand cubic meters of soil and bones and artifacts were hauled away as "fill dirt" for local landowners.

old routes and the freedom of movement along them became quite complicated as border guards and customs inspections imposed themselves upon those wishing to "cross the line."

There are times, however, in the course of human affairs-often at moments of perceived or real threat to a sense of national selfhood-that the professed ideals of democratic societies are set aside for politically expedient reasons: the internment of Japanese-Americans during World War II, for example, or, more recently, the "war on terror" and U.S. Patriot Act. During another turbulent time-during the Vietnam Conflict-the Canadian border became a haven for 50,000 U.S. citizens, some of whom crossed the border through the Peace Arch on the 20th Century's "Underground Railroad." At these times, the border can provide a haven for those escaping the oppressive moments of national ideology, and this has been the case for quite some time. For Sitting Bull after the battle of the Little Big Horn, or when the Nez Perce with Chief Joseph made their famous run for freedom, the border represented safety and peace and a future. This relatively new phenomenon in the indigenous world can be used to benefit, at times, depending upon who is crossing it, and when.

And, this works both ways. In 1885, Isidore Plante Parenteau crossed the border with his family going south. Although there is some debate about the degree of his participation in what Canadian history calls "The Northwest Rebellion," and others the Riel Rebellion, there is no doubt that he left behind a lucrative ranch to avoid the repercussions of the conflict; Louis Riel and some of his warriors were executed. Of Cree and French descent, Parenteau, like other Métis, objected to the sale of ancestral lands in what is now called Saskatchewan to nonnative settlers. It is an old story, with a familiar ending, but in this instance-ironically, much like Sitting Bull but in the opposite direction-Parenteau found a safe haven by crossing the line and taking up residence on the Flathead (Montana Salish) Reservation near St. Ignatius, Montana. Subsequently, the Salish adopted his daughter and grandchildren. These included his grandson, D'Arcy McNickle. Ironically, again in the sense of the odd history of the border, late in his life McNickle returned northward across the line his family had crossed eighty years previously; he had been hired to head the anthropology department at the University of Saskatchewan, Regina. [3]

Throughout his career McNickle was also a writer. His published books include three novels, none of which deals with his Métis/Cree heritage directly, opting instead for the Native peoples of his youth, his adopted people and homeland.[4] I would argue that the plight and flight of his family

---

[3] For a full history of his life, see Dorothy Parker's *Singing an Indian Song*.

[4] Interestingly, though, his 1954 novel for young people, *Runner in the Sun*, recounts the story of a young Anasazi boy in an era before European colonization. To save his

provided him with a moral, historical and literary lesson: democratic societies are an imaginative construct, a thing made of words and images that often conflict with the lived experience of individuals, particularly individuals of color, or who possess a sense of identity that does not reflect the Eurocentric standard of the time. Also, fiction can help change the social situation of indigenous peoples, by bringing audiences into a more comprehensive understanding of Native cultures, and of colonial history. He became an avid political activist, a founder of the Congress of American Indians, and a force that worked to help the U.S. democracy realize its promised potential by recognizing the conflict between its professed ideals and its history.[5]

There are other Native American authors whose works reflect the same ideological goals and who often make overt fictional use of this international line to deconstruct the national binary of the border itself, and thus promote a recognition of indigenous sovereignty. Through their efforts, the border reveals the long colonial history of the two nations, but also the survival of indigenous people, who long understood the line as a new site of power in an ancient landscape, either as barrier or gateway to freedom.[6] For instance, in the Blackfoot/Gros Ventre writer James Welch's first novel, *Winter in the Blood* (1974), one finds a very subtle exploration of the importance of the border in the lives of contemporary Native people.

Historically, the Blackfoot nation's borders were primarily east and west, since they often traveled (north and south) along the eastern slopes of the Rocky Mountains in an area extending far to the east. However, with the advent of the American, and the border, the topography of the movements altered. The nation was partitioned, and thus north-south travel became more difficult, at best, and at worst it was sometimes impossible. Thus, an east-west pattern became very prominent, and this replicates the movement of Manifest Destiny across the continent, a pattern made concrete in the national railroads, but also-for Welch's works-by Montana's "Highline," Highway 2. The movements of the protagonist in

---

people, Salt journeys south from an area of current-day New Mexico, crossing the line that is currently the U.S.-Mexico border. His story, though, charts the older types of borders on the continent, those that denote differences in culture.

[5] In fact, during World War II when McNickle was on the staff of John Collier, Commissioner of the Bureau for Indian Affairs, he was involved in the internment of Japanese Americans, trying to employ cultural anthropology to soften the effects of the camps.

[6] One could learn a great deal by looking at the older stories of the cultures along the border, to see how places of power—particularly places of perceived threat or evil—are deployed as narrative devices. In monster stories, for example, these evil beings often inhabit places along the traditional routes of the people, thus acting to restrict free, safe movements. Killing them becomes an act of liberation for the people.

Winter mostly parallel the border, running east and west along this black
ribbon through "the tan land."
     As I argue elsewhere, however, at moments of reconnection with his
family's Blackfeet history and heritage, he is found on a north-south axis,
away from the highway and thus the sign of Manifest Destiny and all that it
brought.[7] I would argue that the border operates as another, parallel sign of
colonial constriction that highlights the protagonist's identity as surely as
the "tan land," one ironically deployed in the novel. One of the narrative
strands, that of the enigmatic character scholars simply refer to as "The
Airplane Man," is given depth by the mystery of his desire to escape the
east-west axis and to go north, across the border into Canada, and it is this
unrealized goal that provides an interesting look at the border from an
indigenous point of view in the early and mid -1970s.
     The novel was published in 1974, so it was written just as the war in
Vietnam was coming to an end for the U.S. As the stream of expatriates
across the border to escape the draft signifies, the two nations had different
ideas about the war, and these differences had an effect upon the border
itself. Welch's idea of Canada as safe haven is given through the story of
the Airplane Man, who has disguised himself as a tourist from the East but
who is actually on the run from the federal government. While he is not a
Native American, he is an "outlaw" moving alone on the fringes of society,
and his desire to escape northward to avoid capture by the Federal Bureau
of Investigation certainly resonates with the desire of other individuals of
the era, in particular those members of the American Indian Movement
who dispersed after the occupation of Wounded Knee a few years before
the novel was published. In an era of heightened discourse about
nationhood/citizenship, and resultant attempts to restrict freedoms and
ensure conformity, the border in the earlier part of the 1970s offered an
escape for Indian and non-Indian alike, so it is quite revealing that the
Airplane Man wants the protagonist to drive him across, thus forming a
cross-cultural alliance.

     "And you just want me to drive you across the border and that's
all?"
     "That's it."
     "Those border guards get pretty cranky sometimes."
                              . . .
     "I can't figure out why you picked me—maybe I should tell
you, those guards like to harass Indians. They can never figure out
why an Indian would want to go to Canada."

---

[7]   See "'He Was Going Along': Motion in the Novels of James Welch." *American
Indian Quarterly.*

"Man, you don't know anything about intrigue. . . . Now listen:
there are two of us in the car, right? One of us gets harassed; you said
it, right? In fact the harassed one is going to keep those guards so
busy harassing him that they aren't going to pay any attention to the
other one. I'm going to drive across, see—I'll say I just picked you
up. Now who do you suppose is going to question me?" (94)

Given the weighted political binaries of the time, resurrected from a long
colonial history and intensified by A.I.M.'s radical and highly publicized
activities-citizen/militant Indian, white/red-the answer is obvious. The
Airplane Man will exploit the border to aid in his escape. However, he
never gets to use the racial myopia of the border guards to gain his freedom
since he is arrested by the authorities, in a town on the Highline, before he
can escape its east/west trap by going north. Nonetheless, his plan and
presence in Welch's narrative speak for both the political and ethnic
identity of the protagonist; soon after the Airplane Man's capture, the
unnamed protagonist discovers his true Blackfoot heritage by riding into
the tan land to visit his grandfather. His identity is established by colonial
history-his grandparents coming to this place to escape the U.S. Army—
and thus it is constructed in opposition to and free from the political
binaries and legal definitions the border represents.

The influence of the border on those whose traditional lands have been
partitioned by it, however, is given further handling a decade later, after the
northward flow of expatriates avoiding the war had ceased. In Louise
Erdrich's first published novel, *Love Medicine* (1984), we find Gerry
Nanapush, one of the characters whose story weaves through several of her
later novels as well. It is he, and his identification as an "outlaw," that
reflect the border's prominence for the indigenous nations that reside in
proximity to it, including the Anishinaabe (or the "Chippewa"), Erdrich's
Native people. Gerry's character is a blend of ancient literary motifs and
modern political realities. Louis Owens, in his ground-breaking book on
Indian fiction *Other Destinies*, calls him "the most unmistakable trickster
of the novel, bearing the traditional name of the Chippewa trickster,
nanapush or *nanabozhu*" (199). However, as one character, Lipsha,
describes him, he is also a "famous politicking hero . . . charismatic
member of the American Indian Movement" (248). Thus, Nanapush
provides the ethnic and political counterpoint to the national ideology the
border represents.

He is convicted of assault after winning a fight with a "cowboy" who
called him a name. The relatively minor infraction gets him a long,
unwarranted prison sentence, and thus the democratic ideal of justice for all
is once more in conflict with lived experience, and in this case it is revealed
as racist illusion. Fortunately, for Nanapush, his trickster character allows
him to escape seemingly inescapable situations, so, once more free from

prison and "on the run," he meets and connects with his son, Lipsha. As they drive west along the northern plains after narrowly escaping capture by the authorities, father and son touch and the younger man is changed forever. (For one thing, he suddenly receives a heart murmur that will keep him out of the Army, so he can stay home rather than make a run for the border as so many others had in the recent past.) Then, the axis of movement shifts:

> It was miles and miles before [Nanapush] roused himself to ask if I [Lipsha] would take the next right-hand turn I came to and drive until I hit Canada. He said he'd be obliged if I could let him out near the border.
> "I got a wife and little girl up there," he said. "I'm going to visit them."
> "You're going to make it this time," I said. "Home free." (267)

Like McNickle's grandfather and his family, Nanapush is able to exploit the national boundary to escape the repercussions of an attempt to exert his rights as an indigenous person: to find the freedom he should never have been denied in the first place, to find justice. The ironic phrasing, resonating with "Home [of the] Free," is revealing.

The next decade finds a similar motif in Louis Owen's first novel, *Wolfsong* (1991). Set in northern Washington, it explores the identity issues faced by an Indian protagonist, Tom Joseph, who returns home from a university in California due to the death of his uncle. As he struggles through subsequent events, he inadvertently drowns the town's most prominent citizen, one who is planning to destroy the surrounding wilderness with a mine in the Cascade Mountains. Owens once called this "accident" a trickster twist, so it very clearly aligns Tom with Gerry Nanapush, but in a different cultural landscape along the border.[8] Hounded by a posse of local loggers, Tom escapes northward towards Canada and an enclave of mixedblood characters; wounded, he transforms and becomes free for the first time in his life. Here, in the middle of the mountains and wilderness where there are no guards to intervene, the crossing of the border signifies both a return to the movement patterns of the pre-colonial past, but also to a belief system that predates the imposition of the border and its Eurocentric ideology on the landscape and lives of indigenous

---

[8] "The story of trickster causing a great destructive flood is important in the novel, as of course is the seal from the opening passage and the presence of Raven." The tribal affiliation of the characters is somewhat vague, but Owens based them upon the Suiattle and Upper Skagit people-the coastal Salish-of the area. This is from a personal communication with the author.

people. It celebrates the survivance of that belief system in contemporary times, despite all attempts to partition, repress and eradicate it.[9]

I would argue that the fictional movements in these three novels and their referential alignment with the Canada- U.S. border are more than the simple convention of the "run for the border" of Hollywood fame wherein the Mexican border in Westerns is the goal of all fleeing desperadoes. Much as Leslie Marmon Silko problemitizes the southern U.S. boundary with Yaqui history and north-south movement patterns, but also with prophetic forward thinking, in her incredibly powerful novel *Almanac of the Dead*, the authors I have mentioned all use the Canadian border as a correlative for identity, one that places a sense of tribal self in sharp and conflicting relief *over* one of a merely national binary: "American," or "Canadian." Instead, the line becomes a liminal space, perhaps, one that ironically offers the potential of self-identification and survival beyond the reach of U.S. or Canadian law and colonial repression. This is not to imply that Canada (or the U.S.) becomes a utopian haven; instead, in these works of fiction the line between the two countries becomes an oppositional binary prime for deconstruction: a place where the social ills the characters encounter are fictionally foregrounded as they slip into the interstices between two national identities and ideologies. It is flight, a very old convention of stories from first contact, but flight that exploits the colonizer's own rules and identity formulations for survival.

However, the border as sign also possesses the potential for ironic humor. Cherokee writer Thomas King brings this forward in his tremendously humorous short story "Borders." Published in 1993, two years after *Wolfsong*, the story is a first-person narrative of a twelve-year-old Blackfoot boy who travels by automobile with his mother to visit his older sister who lives in Utah. The travel narrative is quickly, and dramatically in a comic sense, complicated by the border crossing between Coutts, Alberta and Sweetgrass, Montana on the eastern slopes of the Rocky Mountains, in other words on an ancient route for the various clans and tribes of the Blackfeet Nation. (It is also directly south of Lethbridge, where King has taught for many years.)

Here, at the U.S. border station, his mother is asked the simple, ritualistic questions, which are simple from only one point of view, and ironic from another:

> "Morning, ma'am."
> "Good morning."
> "Where are you heading?"
> "Salt Lake City."

---

[9] This resistance to confinement resonates, in the novel, with the plight and survival of the indigenous wolf; interestingly, wolf populations in the area are being rebuilt with the "importation" of wolfs from Canada.

"Purpose of your visit?"
"Visit my daughter."
"Citizenship?"
"Blackfoot," my mother told him.
"Ma'am?"
"Blackfoot," my mother repeated.
"Canadian?"
"Blackfoot."
The guard is disoriented. He smiles, looks back to his post and
colleagues for support.
Then he turned back and nodded.
"Morning ma'am."

"Good morning."
"Any firearms or tobacco?"
"No."
"Citizenship?"
"Blackfoot." (291)

The results are as expected: they are detained and then told to turn around
and go "home." The word resonates with Lipsha's utterance in *Love
Medicine* yet it also symbolizes the ironic situation of the Blackfeet after
two centuries of colonial history in both countries. No matter which way
one goes, is one ever really free from colonial restrictions and impositions,
and since tribes and sometimes families are found on both sides of the line,
which actually constitutes home? In this instance, the old phrase from the
children's game of "tag" (i.e. "home free") with its implication of a
freedom from harassment on home base is immediately problematized.

At the Canadian guard station, which is a very short distance away, the
pilgrims, who have been barred from entering the U.S., find their trip even
more complicated.

"Hi," she [the border guard] said. "You folks sure have a great day
for a trip. Where are you coming from?"
"Standoff." [At once the town they live near in Alberta, but also,
of course, descriptive of their recent experience at the U.S. border.]
"Is that in Montana?"
"No."
"Where are you going?"
"Standoff."
. . . "Wow. Are you both Canadians?"
"Blackfoot."
Alarmed by the complication of the simple national binary, the guard gets
down to the business of borders and laws:
"You're not bringing any liquor back, are you?"
"No."
"Cigarettes?"

"No."
"Citizenship?"
"Blackfoot." (293)

As can be expected, the outcome is the same as at the U.S. border. Each
border patrol staff reflects the same inflexible, bureaucratic prejudice the
binaried national identities embody. Also, customs officers are to control
the transport of liquor, firearms, and tobacco (and thus the taxation of these
commodities) across the national boundary, but these commodities have
also come to signify with the history of Native peoples and the colonial
influence of the European. They have, as well, a special cultural
significance for the Blackfoot Nation. Thus, the irony compounds as the
physical border highlights an ideological, historical and cultural crossing.

Although our narrator and his mother are ultimately allowed to make
their trip, it is only after the media intervene to report their story. They
spend days trapped in the "no-man's-land" between the borders, in that
liminal space, sleeping in their car and eating the food she had packed for
their trip. The arbitrariness and thus the absurdity of the border are thus
revealed, but it is also ironically shown as a means of resistance and self-
identification. For the young narrator, it ultimately teaches him a valuable
lesson about who he is and what he should value: at once an unjust and
subjective barrier, but also a site of empowerment, self-realization and
ethnic connection.

And then, published the same year as Owens' novel, we find *The Heirs
of Columbus* (1991) by Gerald Vizenor, the Anishinaabe author. The novel
chronicles the exploits of Stone Columbus, the Anishinaabe trickster
descendant of Christopher Columbus. Stone's ironic sense of the colonial
history Columbus embodies empowers him and thus his relatives: the heirs
to the colonial story. In brief, Stone builds the *Santa Maria Casino*:

> the decorated bingo flagship, [which] was anchored on the
> international border near Big Island in Lake of the Woods. The
> casino was an enormous barge that had been decked for games of
> chance on the ocean seas of the woodland. The *Nina*, a restaurant,
> and the *Pinta*, a tax free market, were situated caravels anchored and
> moored on the border near the casino. (6)

In characteristic Vizenor fashion, the border, the sign of colonial power and
nationalistic separatist philosophy, is co-opted and made to serve for the
empowerment of the local indigenous people. Both Canada and the U.S.
see the lucrative nature of Stone's enterprise, and, since taxing it is not an
option given its location, the U.S. acts by boarding the casino and
confiscating it. However, since it is anchored straddling the border-the
same "no-man's-land" King describes in his short story-neither nation has

jurisdiction. The International Court at The Hague decides the case, beyond the influence and self-interests of either colonial nation state: an inherent conflict of interest to be sure. The laws of the colonizer, once again, open a space within which Native sovereignty is realized.

Later, Stone moves the concept westward, to Point Roberts, Washington, that odd little peninsula and symbol of the absurdity of borders across from Semiahmah and within sight of the Peace Arch. Extending down into the Puget Sound from Canadian territory, it is a small patch of the U.S.[10] It falls below the 49th parallel, true, and is thus a part of the U.S. by treaty. Ironically, it is also the site on which Governor Issacs signed treaties with many of the Northwest tribes, and thus a fit historical/political location for Vizenor's humor. Here, much as on the Lake of the Woods earlier in the novel, he constructs a floating, sovereign nation, straddling the U.S. and Canada border but belonging to neither. Its inhabitants move freely either way, north or south, and thus the patterns that existed before 1846 are reestablished, at least fictionally.[11]

These are but a few examples of the how the change in the topography of the landscape of some indigenous peoples has resulted in the imaginative use of the border as a correlative for the empowerment of indigenous nationhood and thus identity. At once a boundary and a refuge, its character is fluid, changing with the times and the national imperatives of the two countries it both separates and unites. Since September 11, 2001, it has changed once again as border inspections and patrols intensified, and the so-called War on Terror resulted in the politically expedient diminishment of civil rights, particularly for people of color. In times of such tension and repression in the past-particularly in times of war-the border has become a character in the works of artists attuned to its imaginative potential. I look forward to the literary production that will come in the near future and, once more, redefine the U.S.-Canada border in a world where borders are, ostensibly, becoming a thing of the past.

* Note: throughout this essay I have alternated between the terms "Blackfoot" and "Blackfeet" to denote the indigenous nation under discussion, and various tribes that comprise that nation. However, often the usage of the terms is determined by which side of "the line" they inhabit, so

---

[10] In fact, every morning during the school year, young people there of high school age must cross the border into Canada, travel to the Peace Arch crossing, and re-enter the U.S., to get to school.

[11] Interestingly, this is where the characters undertake the curing of all the children of the world who have become ill or disfigured by modern societies; it is also the place where anyone can become an "Indian," simply by having his/her DNA altered. Vizenor's humor is telling.

this is just another example, a linguistic one, of the influence of the border to consider.

Works Cited

Erdrich, Louise. *Love Medicine*. New York: Holt, Rinehart and Winston, 1984.

King, Thomas. "Borders," in *One Good Story, That One*. Toronto: HarperCollins, 1993; Reprinted in *Nothing But the Truth: An Anthology of Native American Literature*. Eds. John L. Purdy and James Ruppert. Saddle River, NJ: Prentice Hall, 2001.

Owens, Louis. *Other Destinies: Reading the American Indian Novel*. Norman: U of Oklahoma P, 1992.

---. 2001. Personal Correspondence, May 2001.

---. *Wolfsong*. Albuquerque: West End P, 1991; U of Oklahoma P, 1993.

Parker, Dorothy R. *Singing and Indian Song: A Biography of D'Arcy McNickle*. Lincoln: U of Nebraska P, 1992.

Purdy, John Lloyd. "'He Was Going Along': Motion in the Novels of James Welch." *American Indian Quarterly* 14.2 (Spring 1990): 133-47.

Silko, Leslie Marmon. *Almanac of the Dead*. New York: Simon & Schuster, 1991.

Vizenor, Gerald. *The Heirs of Columbus*. Hanover, N.H.: Wesleyan U P, 1991.

Welch, James. *Winter in the Blood*. New York: Harper & Row, 1974.

MITA BANERJEE

Skunk's Gall Bladders in Gin: Normalizing Chinatown in Denise Chong's *The Concubine's Children*

How does it feel to be a medical menace? This paper will juxtapose historical accounts of Vancouver Chinatown as a haven not only of vice, but also of viruses and bacteria, with a fictional account of Chinatown as an ethnic space. Where historical analyses must necessarily be confined to historical accounts of ethnic communities as the carriers of contagion, fictional narratives by these presumably contagious subjects themselves can shed light on the other side of this equation. Even as it is not the virus itself which is speaking, it is the subject of contagion who is now doomed to a practice of medical autoethnography: an ethnography of the self where the ethnic subject constantly has to inspect itself for signs of being diseased. The point of this paper is thus not only that the history of Western Civilization, as Rothman, Marcus and Kiceluk have argued, is also the history of medical exclusion, the exclusion of subjects deemed medically deviant and therefore dangerous, but that it is also the history of an ethnic self-sanitation. This paper will thus also be concerned with the interplay between medicine and culture as it has historically affected Chinese diasporic communities in North America. As Rothman et al. suggest,

> Medicine is itself a culture and a world of its own, with institutions and subinstitutions peculiar to it, and with rites of passage, forms of education, standards of behaviour, and sets of norms that have their own history and development and semi-autonomous life . . . . Over time, medicine has acquired the power to demarcate the line between the normal and the abnormal, the biologically innate and culturally determined . . . . In a more intimate sense, medicine affects what people will - or will not-eat, drink, touch, or embrace. It separates the clean from the dirty, the wholesome from the noxious. (1)

In the following, I will map these considerations onto an ethnic plane to examine how the ethnic subject sets out to cleanse herself of an ethnicity which is deemed by the dominant culture to be unsanitary.

In the context of this paper, I am using the term "autoethnography" as the ethnic subject's consciousness of being looked at. As Eleanor Ty has proposed, referring to Rey Chow's notion of autoethnography, "for those who have been 'formerly ethnographized, . . . what are 'subjective' origins now include a memory of past *objecthood* - the experience of being looked at - which lives on in the subjective act of ethnographizing like an other, an optical unconscious'" (Ty 270). In Denise Chong's *The Concubine's Children*, I will suggest, the consciousness of being looked at as "ethnic" and hence potentially unsanitary entails a portrayal of the self as observing the *norms* of cleanliness and ultimately, of whiteness.[1]

By reading contrapuntally a historical account (Nayan Shah's history of Chinatown as a presumed site of contagion) and a fictional narrative (Denise Chong's autobiographical narrative *The Concubine's Children*), I will attempt to complicate the line of demarcation between assimilationism and resistance. The choice between remaining a walking virus and becoming a sanitary subject may not be such an easy one. Internalizing racialist ideas, in the 19th century, thus meant internalizing the idea of one's own ethnicity as unsanitary. The history of access to Western democratic societies, this paper will propose, can be re-read through the practice of self-sanitation. While Shah's historical account has to leave blank the feelings of the medical menaces themselves, Chong's fictional narrative restores precisely this blind spot. The flesh Chong's narrative restores to Shah's historical account is the point of view of the (presumably) unsanitary subject itself. The fictional protagonist's internalization of the racialist idea of cultural difference as unsanitary sets off a desperate attempt at self-cleansing.

Conversely, however, while the fictional narrative revolves around a clear-cut picture between unsanitary ethnicity and the mainstreaming of ethnicity, Shah's observations complicate such a facile distinction. Shah's account, I suggest throughout this paper, can help us resist a judgment at the core of Chong's fictional narrative: the dismissal of Chinatown as unsanitary. Where Chong's narrative judges Chinatown and sides with the normal, then, Shah contextualizes precisely this normalcy. Not only is Chong's a narrative about the mainstreaming of ethnicity, then, but it could be said to adopt a strikingly mainstream perspective: a perspective which this paper seeks to explore in its medical assumptions. What is so disturbing is that Chong's narrative not only provides an answer to the question of how it feels to be a health menace, but that she also answers in the affirmative the mainstream inquiry whether to be truly ethnic is really

---

[1] While Ty reads Chong's account as a resistance to exoticist images of the Chinese concubine, especially in Chong's portrayal of her grandmother, I am interested in the assimilationist undercurrent which, I believe, can nevertheless be seen to run through *The Concubine's Children*. As Ty proposes, "Throughout her biography, Chong carefully avoids referring to May-ying in terms of the criminal or the lurid. She calls her a 'waitress,' a 'kay-toi-neu,' . . . which, though 'considered to be almost one and the same as a prostitute,' has a different connotation. Instead of focusing on her grandmother's work as prostitute, she stresses themes of maternal duty, necessity, and sacrifice. These motifs work to counter the vision of the wanton and servile Oriental woman" (271).

to be potentially unsanitary. Far from defying the medical assumptions chronicled by Shah, Chong's novel goes on to confirm them.

Denise Chong's life, which she chronicles in her autobiographical novel, *The Concubine's Children*, seems a perfect tale not only of success, but also of access. Chong, whose grandmother had been a concubine raising her daughter on her own in Vancouver Chinatown became an economic adviser to Prime Minister Trudeau in the 1970s. *The Concubine's Children* retraces the story of a Chinese immigrant's second family. Having left his wife in mainland China, Chong's grandfather sent for a concubine - Chong's grandmother, May-ying - to join him in Vancouver. May-ying, however, never fully adapts to her life as a concubine, a rebellion from which her daughter Hing will suffer all her life. The story is told from the perspective of Hing's daughter, the narrative persona of Denise Chong herself. Yet, there is often a superimposition of the mother's on the daughter's voice. Hing's strong feelings against her mother blur with the narrator's memory of her own grandmother, May-ying.

My claim in this paper is that Chong's journey into Canadianness–from Chinatown to the nation's capital, is predicated on the practice of *normalizing* Chinatown. There is a place for Chinatown within the Canadian nation only as long as it conforms to the medical standards which are beginning to emerge in the 19th century. To make Chinatown amenable to the standard of the "normal," then, is at once to "sanitize" it of its ethnicity. There can be no self-sanitation, however, without an unlearning of the very ethnicity which is deemed unsanitary in the first place. The history of medical civilization, from this perspective, would also be a cultural history; medicine seeks to universalize, as both historical and fictional accounts remind us, cultural assumptions which may be far from universal. What is at stake is thus a racializing of medical knowledge itself -a racializing, I will argue in the following, which Chong's account inscribes, but ultimately fails to resist.

Perfectible Citizens

The move from the periphery to the center is thus accompanied by a shedding of ethnic markers. This transcendence of ethnicity, in turn, mirrors a key shift which has historically taken place in the norm culture's perception of Chinatown. As Nayan Shah has observed in his account of San Francisco Chinatown, the Chinese section of the city was transformed, under or for white society's watchful gaze, from an unsanitary ghetto imperiling the health of the nation in the 19th century to a space of perfectibility in the 20th century. In the equation of Chineseness with medical contagion, then, the terms of social access changed significantly over time. Where in the 19th century, your ethnicity condemned you to being a health menace and there was nothing you could do about it, the 20th century gave you an option: by unlearning ethnic cultural practices and hence embracing the sanitary norm of the dominant culture, you could "perfect" yourself as a Canadian citizen. Ethnicity and exclusion were no longer mutually constitutive. What today is termed cultural citizenship could be achieved through an act of self-sanitation. As Shah notes, "[f]or Chinese Americans, the journey from menace to model minority followed a deep undercurrent of ideas about citizenship, conduct, and health" (3). *The Concubine's Children*, I will propose in the following, charts this very development from Chineseness as health hazard to model minority, a model of which Chong's own access to the political and economic mainstream of the Canadian nation seems a salient example. The perspective which the narrative adopts is thus strikingly in keeping with dominant discourses denouncing Chinatown and Chineseness as unsanitary.

Paradoxically, Chong's journey into success and Chinatown's strife for perfectibility end in a void. Not only does the ethnic subject have to leave Chinatown behind, both physically and epistemologically, but she has to agree as to its undesirability for both the city and the nation-space itself. Crucially, this is a practice of self-sanitation which has to be performed not only by the ethnic subject, but Chinatown itself. If Chinatown is to escape being erased from the map of the city itself, it similarly has to perfect itself. By discontinuing the practices deemed unsanitary by the dominant culture, it is allowed to retain only a hint of exoticism. Significantly, in Chong's narrative, Chinatown's move into Canadianness is predicated on the autoethnography of its inhabitants. It is by surveying, in the service of the local health board, their own cultural (and, implicitly, their medical practices), that Chinese subjects strive to prove their fitness to be Canadian citizens. Citizenship, medical knowledge, and cultural practice are hence mutually constitutive. Chong's autobiography, which, I suggest, is also an account of the Chinese community's autoethnography, can thus serve as the missing link between history and fiction. Chong's narrative restores the biographical flesh to Shah's historical account of Chinatown at the turn of the 20th century. Where Shah points to the choices made by Chinese immigrants in their attempt to negotiate between the medical ethnography of the Board of Health and the auto-ethnography of proving to the authorities that a Chinese life could be moral as well as sanitary, Chong fleshes out the motivations for these choices. Yet, it is significant that the text can also be seen as curiously self-normalizing. Where Shah's historical records point to the existence of alternatives, Chong's narrative rules out such alternatives as potentially abnormal.

In this sense, *The Concubine's Children* inscribes a tension between the genre of autobiography and its content. If, as Alfred Hornung has argued, autobiography can be considered a form of "outlandish writing" given its juxtaposition of "generic" with "geographical" transgressions, Chong's novel turns this juxtaposition on its head. *The Concubine's Children* is a containment of transgression through a transgressional form. Chong inscribes, through the very form of autobiography considered transgressional by Hornung, the *normalizing* of an ethnic subject. The correlation between narrative content and narrative genre is suspended. In Chong's novel, the "outlandishness" of both Chinatown and Chinese Canadian subjectivity is transcended through an attempt to become part of the medical mainstream. Not only does Chong describe the "mainstreaming" of a Chinese subject, but in so doing, she implicitly normalizes the genre of autobiography itself.

Chong's account of her own access to and participation in Canadian civic life takes the form of perfectibility: the potential of the ethnic subject to 'perfect' itself by becoming mainstream, a mainstream which is at the same time deemed medically safe. Chinatown is "perfectible" to the extent that it can shed its Chineseness, to the extent that the very practices deemed "unsanitary" by white society can be replaced by the much "healthier" habits of Canadianness. The autobiographical journey which Chong's novel chronicles, a journey from exclusion to access, is complete only once her own gaze on Chinatown has become that of a tourist, when auto-ethnography has turned into just ethnography. The journey into Canadianness is complete only once Chinese cultural practices have come to seem as outlandish as the author's grandmother's collection of skunk's gall bladders preserved in bottles of gin. In this sense, Chong's autobiographical account participates in a number of discourses which culminate in the normalizing of Chinatown.

Life writing, in *The Concubine's Children*, implies a twofold move. First, it chronicles the trajectory from practicing culture to autoethnography. Second, it traces the shift from autoethnography to ethnography: from an ethnography of the self to an ethnography of the Chinese community by a hyphenated Chinese subject who no longer feels part of this community. It is from this latter perspective that Chinatown is seen as ultimately foreign. What is striking, then, is that this shift is implied by the narrative to be a positive one. The narrative moves from the meaningfulness of Chinese traditional medicine - skunk's gall bladder used to alleviate back pains-to the grossness of animal intestines in bottles of booze. The first shift-from lived cultural practices to autoethnography - has been described by Nayan Shah as a key moment of resistance by the Chinese immigrant community to authorities demonizing of their living conditions. While Chong's narrative suggests that this dismissal of Chinese medical "superstition" is a mere yielding to the dominant culture's superior reason, Shah demonstrates that succumbing to autoethnography was a historically occasioned choice: "In the arduous struggle to be perceived as "normal" in their social habits and living styles, Chinese American activists in the 1930s and 1940s proceeded upon a strategy of highlighting those Chinese persons who had adapted to middle-class norms in consumer tastes, hygiene, and respectable domesticity" (15).

It is here that the shift from autoethnography to an ethnography of the community one no longer feels a part of is most pronounced. Self-hatred and paranoia are mutually constitutive. If one is deemed by the board of health to be a medical menace, the first reaction is to survey one's own habits as to their presumed unsanitariness. Once these unsanitary cultural practices have been unlearned, the next step is to induce one's community to embark on a similar journey out of Chineseness. It is in this sense that the activists described by Shah report to the city authorities the extent of their own communities mainstreaming: the "middle-class norms" are clearly that of the dominant culture; becoming mainstream here is synonymous with becoming normal. What is key, of course, is the generalization of white middle-class cultural practices as the sanitary norm which would then seek to impose its mould on an entire nation. Chong's fictional narrative, on the other hand, renders invisible precisely the *constructedness* of these norms, a constructedness which Shah emphasizes. Chong's account seems to confirm, from the point of view of an ethnic subject, the mainstream suspicion that to be truly Chinese is really to be unsanitary.

Chong's autobiographical account, I propose, can be read as an auto-ethnography in terms of cultural hygiene, a hygiene which presupposes the expunging of Chinatown's practices which are allegedly abnormal in both health and moral terms. In the official discourse at the turn toward the 20th century, Chineseness as such was collapsed into a health risk. As Shah observes, "[t]hese investigations produced a 'knowledge' of Chinese women and men's seeming unhygienic habits, the unsanitary conditions in which they lived, and the dangerous diseases they carried" (17). Significantly, this practice of the surveillance of Chinatown by city authorities took the form of ethnography, of recording, in presumably "objective" terms, the cultural practices of the Chinese community. According to Shah, "[t]he collection and interpretation of knowledge about the incidence of epidemic disease, mortality, and morbidity produced an ethnography of different groups and locations in the city, of their habits, and of their conditions" (4). This health risk, in turn, was synonymous with a depravity, which was not only of a spatial but also of a moral nature. Shah notes, "the vivid and visceral narration of the midnight journey through Chinatown became one of the standard forms of knowledge used in both medical and popular accounts to establish the truth of Chinatown as the preeminent site of vice, immorality, degradation, crime, and disease" (29).

It is in this image that the abnormality of Chinatown, and the life of her own grandmother in it, is contained by Chong's narrative. Chong's normalizing gaze mirrors that of her own mother, Hing, as she recollects the vices of May-ying, her own mother and Chong's grandmother. Significantly, the vices of alcoholism and sexual promiscuity intersect in the eyes of second- and third-generation Chinese-Canadians yearning for cultural assimilation: the outlandishness of Chinese medicine parallels, in its incompatibility with the norm culture's idea of "sanitary" behaviour, the moral depravity of Chinatown's citizens. Chong's autobiographical account is thus also a purging, a normalizing of Chinatown; she becomes a "normal" Canadian citizen to the extent that she can exteriorize her own vision of Chinatown. Not only does Chong's text attempt to answer the well-meant inquiry about how it feels to be a health menace, but it fails to register that the racism is in the question. By linking the "mainstreaming" of the Chinese community to a self-sanitation in medical terms, *The Concubine's Children* can also be said to "whitewash" highly problematic medical practices of racial and cultural exclusion.

I would argue, then, that the perceptions of Chinatown which Shah traces at the turn from the 19th to the 20th century - the shift from health risk to model minority-are simultaneously present in Chong's novel. By invoking her grandmother's Chinatown as a haven of vice and unsanitary living conditions and by stressing her own mother's belief in the perfectibility of Chinese culture through assimilation, Chong's narrative traces the shift from the ethnic alien to the Canadian subject, from a Chinatown inhabited by inassimilable aliens to the normalizing behavior of good citizens like herself.

Interestingly enough, Canadian public authorities denouncing the unsanitary living conditions of Chinatown were by no means unsympathetic to the inhabitants of the Chinese section of the city. In fact, they were aware that these living conditions were historically occasioned and were an outcome of segregation. In this sense, the surveillance by city authorities of Chinese cultural practices was seen to be in the best interest of the inhabitants of Chinatown themselves. Nevertheless, they failed to distinguish between the historical circumstances themselves and the demonization of Chinese "habits" which ensued from the medical surveillance of the Chinese community in Chinatown. Similarly, Chong's own account of her grandmother's life - an account based above all on her mother's perception of May-ying-is colored by sympathy, by an attempt to understand how the historical intersected with the personal in May-ying's life. Yet, just as city authorities could ultimately not abstain from pronouncing moral judgments on Chinatown's inhabitants, Chong's narrative ultimately dismisses the historical circumstances which occasioned May-ying's life style. In both instances - the authorities' treatment of Chinatown and Chong's depiction of her grandmother -, there is a sense that a strife to adhere to the practices of the medical norm (which was in turn synonymous with the mainstream) would be in the ethnic community's best interest. Yet, historically, the (well-meant) surveillance of this community led to a voyeuristic obsession with Chinatown as a health menace. It is striking, then, that such an obsession should surface also in the pages of Chong's own text.

For city authorities at the end of the 19th century, the professionalization of science went hand in hand with excluding Chinatown from the city and hence, by extension, also from the space of the nation. Shah's historical account of Chinatown, then, is crucial in its intersection of a growing body of work in the humanities which, like the volume *Medicine and Western Civilization* edited by Rothman, Marcus, and Stephanie Kiceluk referred to above, traces the Othering of certain bodies by Western medical discourse. Those bodies which diverged, in appearance or cultural practices, from the "medical norm" (a norm increasingly synonymous with a middle-class mainstream) were marked as sites of contagion, a medical threat to the nation itself. According to Rothman et al., "Disease is associated with that which is taboo, contaminated, and filthy, particularly when it is supposed that disease poses as danger to public health" (5). Medical surveillance was hence inextricably connected with a form of medical ethnography because this surveillance meant the recording of such practices which were deemed unsanitary to begin with. Medical discourse, in its disavowal of its own subject position and the normative white gaze on which it was predicated, was thus instrumental for the racialization of immigrant communities. Yet, Chong's autobiographical account *The Concubine's Children* emphasizes not the destructive potential of the medical surveillance, but its benefits. As a medical autoethnography, it supplies the flesh to the bone of the success stories which city authorities could only have imagined.

For medical and city authorities, the living conditions of the Chinese in Chinatown were synonymous with an alleged "Chinese" disregard for the residents' own living conditions. Because the Chinese survived what no white person could have survived, it was reasoned, they had to have the sturdiness of the very creatures with whom they shared their close quarters, rats. It was only a small step, Shah notes, from the argument of Chinese 'resilience' to filth to the claim that they in fact wallowed and rejoiced in the mud. Shah notes that city authorities reasoned that if it were not for their own "sanitary surveillance" (19) of the Chinese community, "[t]he Chinese were expected to 'relapse' into a 'more dense condition of nastiness, in which they apparently delight to exist'" (42). For the authorities, then, the inhabitants of Chinatowns were what Chong's grandmother pickled, animals.

There is an interesting link here, of course, between the city authority's "sanitary surveillance" of ethnic communities and the practice of voyeurism. Precisely because Chinatown's "filth" was correlated, through the authorities' white gaze, with moral depravity, the dominant culture's watchful gaze did not only hope to find sanitary transgressions. The unsanitariness of the cultural practices imagined by the dominant culture, above all, was linked to unspeakable sexual acts. What is the link, then, between autoethnography and mainstream voyeurism, a voyeurism which associates ethnic difference with transgressive sexuality? Perhaps unwittingly, the ethnic citizen-subject's autoethnography was bound to give city authorities an inside view of what they were expecting to find. In this sense, Chong's narrative becomes what Sau-ling Wong, in another context, has called a "guided tour" into the Other space within a nation that strove to define itself as white. Chong's is a guided tour into the haven of filth that is both moral and cultural. Historically, as Shah demonstrates, creating an ethnography of a sanitary self was the only way for Chinese Canadians to limit government interference into their lives, an interference justified by medical intervention. Moreover, the idea of voyeurism adds an interesting facet to Shah's image of ethnicity as contagion: if Chinatown was demonized as a contagious health risk, the voyeuristic interest by the dominant society in the moral depravity which this social space was seen to be synonymous with, may lead us to a different conclusion. It may point to the ways in which, for the dominant society, the idea of ethnicity as contagion may in fact have been a form of wishful thinking. Even or especially in its most demonized form, ethnicity is always both fascinating and repulsive. In this respect, the medical gaze may be far from disinterested, and its owner may be far from detached.

The strife to become what Shah, in his own historical account of Chinatown, has called becoming a "citizen-subject" is inseparable from a rejection of Chinatown. Shah describes Chinese immigrants' self-transformation into "citizen-subjects," a transformation which is achieved by jettisoning what is perceived by the immigrants themselves as the "filth" of Chinatown. This practice of self-transformation parallels Chong's own story of access to Canadian civic life. The tragedy of such a remaking of the ethnic self, of course, was twofold. First, the narrowness of Chinatown's space and the ensuing problems of hygiene were by no means self-chosen. Secondly, the demonization of Chinatown was based on reversing cause and effect, and of reading unsanitariness both as a real and a moral issue. Moral depravity and personal filth were said to precede rather than result from inadequate living conditions. What is more, the allegation of immorality was itself predicated on the dominant culture's ignorance of Chinese social patterns. This ignorance, in turn, can be seen as the starting point for Chong's own narrative. Her grandmother was her husband's concubine, a family situation unknown to the emerging Canadian middle class with its emphasis on nuclear families. What is significant, however, is that Chong's novel can be said to erase the line between the accident of personal history and a normalizing gaze that indicts any social structure incompatible with Western social norms.

Unspeakable Acts

The Concubine's Children parallels the dominant discourse in its coupling of disgusting medical practices with more unspeakable sexual acts. Given the synonymy, in official discourse, of Chinatown with filth and the health risk it entailed, it seems an irony of family history that Chong's mother would become a trained nurse: a young woman on the verge of becoming a citizen-subject by exchanging her own mother's atavistic Chinese medical practices for the scientific discourse of Western medical knowledge. It was this knowledge, of course, that enabled a demonizing of Chinatown in the first place. What is crucial, moreover, is that Chong's narrative parallels the historical development of Chinatown in the absence of *bicultural* alternatives. Similarly, the historical requirements for becoming what Shah calls a "citizen-subject" (7) were such that they ruled out cultural fusions, which, as Shah highlights, Chinese immigrants did in fact create. Shah notes,

> Although the authors and editors of local medical journals expressed a lively fascination with Chinese techniques and treatments, writers of articles for medical journals regarded Chinese medicine as ruled by "superstition," "tradition," and an incomplete, "unscientific" understanding of the human body and the nature of disease. Health officials mobilized these perceptions in their attempts to eliminate the potential competition of Chinese physicians. (55)

In its emphasis on the outlandishness of May-ying's Chinese remedies, then, Chong's text dismisses these alternatives underscored by Shah. Not only does the text chronicle the shift from alien to citizen, then, but it sets out to confirm the very parameters which this shift was predicated upon.

Ironically, of course, it could be argued that the very image of the outlandishness of Chinese tradition - skunk's gall bladder pickled in gin - is already a hybrid one. The container belies its content; the remedy indicates less that Chinese medical practices are beyond cure in their exoticism than the fact that the remedies, like the containers which hold them, are adapted to their new context. May-ying has already adapted to New World circumstances by pickling the skunk's intestines in whatever became handy, such as a bottle of gin. This hybridity, the mutability of Chinese tradition, however, is never taken into account by Chong's narrative. In Hing's memory, her mother's medicine cabinet is the epitome of Chinese tradition, and its hideousness. May-ying's strict discipline of her daughter, the feeling of being yoked to Chineseness, is intricately interwoven with the mother's medical knowledge:

> For Hing, the first lessons of serving her mother involved having to tend to May-ying's aches and pains. . . . A line of pickle jars on her dresser was her medicine cabinet. To treat various ailments were rarities such as deer's tail, deer tendon, bear claw, sometimes skull's gall bladder and lady slipper bulbs. These were preserved in spirits, supplied from the bottles of gin and whiskey standing alongside. (94)

For Hing, then, the grossness of her mother's traditional medicine is synonymous with Chinatown's squalor. This squalor, in turn, indexes a depravity which was not only a sanitary but a moral one. In this collapsing of actual filth with moral transgressions, *The Concubine's Children* once again mirrors historical observations. Not only does the text provide a guided tour to the unsanitariness of Chinese living conditions, but it confirms the dominant culture's voyeuristic speculation that in their practices, the Chinese take their cue from the animals they pickle.

Hing's decision to become a nurse is a move into Western medical knowledge, the very knowledge which historically led to the demonization of Chinatown in the first place. Significantly, Hing's determination to take up nursing is preceded by an attack on her mother's medicine cabinet - a grossness of Chinese tradition associated, in Hing's mind, with her mother's immoral lifestyle. Hing's self-sanitation, then, is both of a hygienic and a moral nature:

> After the man left and May-ying passed out asleep, Hing was wider awake than ever. The things she hated most about her mother's life - the gambling, the men, the drinking, her frail health - had that evening come rolled into one. Before she knew it, she was out of bed and around the partition, and she had both hands on the heavy pickle jar. (162-63)

Chong's account, then, restores the flesh to Shah's account in a very problematic sense: it confirms what even city authorities shuddered to think about. That her mother's plight of having to witness May-ying's sexual encounters was occasioned not by May-ying's immorality but simply by the squalor of living conditions is dismissed in Chong's account, just as city authorities were aware of these conditions but nevertheless suspected the Chinese of not minding them.

What disturbs me, then, is that the genre of life-writing may render impossible the claim that Chong's narrative is in fact strikingly assimilationist in its overlaps with dominant discourses of an unsanitary ethnicity. From this perspective, it would seem that Chong's account cannot be blamed for its assimilationism because it emerges from her own mother's childhood trauma, a trauma occasioned by her mother's strict discipline of her daughter. This discipline, in turn, was caused by May-ying's helplessness to control her own life's circumstances:

> But Hing, like any child, looked for guidance in growing up. As a child does of a parent, she looked for consistency. She was to find it only in the knowledge that she would be disciplined, with or without provocation. . . . In the new world, where there were few children and their absence was sadly missed, the attitude of many parents had softened. May-ying's had not. She was determined to prove that she was not afraid to stand by the traditional values of what made a good parent and what produced an obedient child. (105-106)

Yet, even as life-writing is more than fiction, it is also fiction. Just as Shah's account exposes the constructedness of both medical history and historical records themselves, Chong's narrative in its turn fictionalizes historical events. It is as fiction that it can be critiqued for retracing the narrative of Chinese Canadian access to mainstream society as a narrative of self-sanitation. By personalizing history, by portraying these incidents in her family's life not as accidental, but as representative of different ways of being "ethnic" in Canada, Chong's narrative can itself be said to perpetuate normalizing practices.

From Hing's perspective, May-ying's immorality is indistinguishable from the squalor of her living conditions. The city authorities portrayed by Shah collapsed Chinese living conditions in Chinatown with their reaction to these conditions - making them not victims, but agents of their own conditions. Similarly, Hing's vision associates the poverty of her mother's and her own living conditions with her mother's promiscuity:

> Hing made sure she was absolutely still. But the next thing she knew they had climbed into bed beside her, and he was on top of her mother. Hing's arm was pinned under them. "I wish they'd hurry up," she kept thinking to herself, so that the weight would be gone from her arm. . . . If Hing didn't know right from wrong of what she saw of her mother's encounters with men, her gambling and her drinking ways, she did now she didn't like it. (108-109)

Hing is unable to see her mother's conduct as a rebellion against the role which Chinese society has assigned to her, that of a concubine whose husband's unemployment forces her to earn her family's living. Crucially, the complimentarity between historical accounts and autobiographical writing which this paper seeks to explore implies not only that Shah's findings are fleshed out through Chong's literary narrative, but also the ways in which *The Concubine's Children* may yield different conclusions when seen through the historical background provided by Shah's *Contagious Divides*. What Hing's vision of her own mother is incapable of providing, even in her daughter's fictional account, is the historical *context* for May-ying's decisions, the choices she made or the ones she was unable to make.

Inserted into a paradigm of racialization, in which mainland Chinese living patterns intersected with a Canadian society which partialled out social and urban space for its immigrants, May-ying's agency in her own life's poverty and moral conditions may be more difficult to judge than Chong's account would have it. Reading autobiography through history writing, then, may also cause us to resist the narrative itself.

Queer Domesticity

Interestingly, this self-normalization, in keeping with the dominant culture's collapsing of material filth with moral depravity, also took the form of a "normalizing" of social patterns. Shah notes that in the Chinese community's struggle for self-sanitization, the bachelors were soon marginalized. Shah uses the idea of "queer domesticity" to account for the "abnormality" of bachelors in a Chinese community which sought to transform itself after the Western model of the nuclear family, and the deviance of women's behavior which did not correspond to this newly adapted model. Interestingly, Hing's disgust at her mother's behavior converges with her desire to erase her father from her own genealogy, the man who resumed the life of a bachelor. As in the dismissal of May-ying's lifestyle as promiscuous and not as historically occasioned, however, Chong's narrative does not contextualize her grandfather's choice, nor does she contextualize the dominant community's targeting of certain lifestyles as abnormal.

As Shah notes, what is at stake in the "normalizing" of Chinese cultural practices is also the narrowing down of masculinity to fit the mould of the dominant culture. Deviant ways of life, Shah points out, were considered abnormal, "queer":

> [t]he prevailing social arrangements of Chinese bachelor society produced several types of queer domesticity, such as multiple women and children living in a female-dominated household, the affiliation of vast communities of men in bunkhouses and opium dens, and common law marriages of Chinese men and fallen white women. . . . I use [the term "queer"] to question the formation of exclusionary norms of respectable middle-class, heterosexual marriage. (13)

The connection which had been drawn by city authorities between the morality - and indispensability - of the nuclear family and the sanitariness of living conditions, left no place for the "bachelors" who, due to racist immigration restrictions, had been forced to leave their families in China. It is striking that the undesirability of these men whose social status did not match the requirements of the dominant culture in North America is also reflected in Chong's novel. In the very attempt at self-normalization observed by Shah, Chong's mother cuts out her father from the family photographs - a father who, after his concubine had left him, resumed the life of a bachelor:

> A day or two later, Mother went to the cedar chest, opened the bottom drawer and took out the pile of black-and-white photographs of her family. Whenever she went through them, the one portrait of her father, the eight-by-ten in the cardboard frame, always made her weep, and she never knew why. This time was no different; it was that one, not the ones of her mother, that bothered her the most. Mother removed the offending photograph from the pile; she never wanted to look at it again. (229)

Hing thus blames her father for inflicting on her mother the life of a concubine. At the same time, however, her own attempt to become a normal citizen-subject is tied to the necessity of establishing a nuclear family. There is in this family structure, in keeping with Shah's historical observation about Chinatown's social structure, no place for a man like Chan Sam.

Moreover, as Shah underscores and as Chong's narrative confirms, "marshalling" the dominant discourse rules out from the outset the possibility of cultural fusion. There can be no access to civic life from a Chinatown vantage point; participation is based on acculturation. Shah observes,

> The rhetoric about the degraded and regressive space of Chinatown and the recalcitrant Chinese was so strident and deafening that it was difficult for Chinese Americans and their supporters to address this white American audience. Chinese Americans had to marshal the dominant discourse in order to intervene effectively in politics and participate in society. From the nineteenth to the twentieth century the terms and tactics of effective participation in the public sphere changed dramatically. (9)

Sanitizing the Self

Hing's decision to move into nursing, then, can be seen as the ultimate instance of "marshalling the dominant discourse." The discourse of racialization, as Shah underscores, is an inextricable part of sanitary policing. What is crucial, however, is that *The Concubine's Children* renders invisible the constructed nature of normativity. Moving into the mainstream is not seen as a matter of choice, but an act occasioned by the superior logic of the mainstream.

As in the city authorities' depiction of Chinatown, moreover, there is, in Hing's account, a jumbling of cause and effect. Her mother's ill health may be an outcome of her living and working conditions, not a self-inflicted ailment exacerbated by her drinking. Similarly, May-ying's alcoholism may be an attempt to cope with circumstances beyond her control. It is these historical circumstances which Chong's narrative dismisses only to embrace the idea that to become a sanitary subject is at once to become white. Hing, having renamed herself Winnie Chin, moves into a world in which whiteness and sanitation are mutually constitutive: "A nervous Hing walked across the extensive manicured grounds to the hospital's Main Building, and presented herself as Miss Winnie Chin. . . . Never was Winnie so proud as when she walked through the grounds in her uniform and cap and was addressed by the doctors as "Miss Chin" (166-67).

Hing's decision to become a nurse, then, can be seen in terms of this self-introspection and perfection of conduct. Adopting Western medical knowledge - a knowledge which led to the demonization of Chinatown as 'unsanitary' in the first place, Hing once and for all transcends what the novel portrays as the superstitious squalor of her mother's medicine cabinet. By the same token, it is in this moving into Western medical science that Hing leaves Chinatown behind as well. Hing's decision to be a nurse is significant in a twofold sense. For it is at once a way of leaving Chinatown, her mother's medical "superstition," and a giving in to the requirements of a racially biased society. Hing's longing for a university degree is sabotaged by her Chinatown origins as much as by a racialized labor market. Having grown up in Chinatown, she hardly fits the pattern of those destined for university careers. At the same time, however, due to racialized hiring practices, even these university graduates may end up in Chinatown. Either way, Hing is determined to escape the narrow confines of Chinatown, and the Chineseness from which it seems inextricable:

> The few who went to university came mostly from middle-class families living *outside* Chinatown, families that had taken one step up the social ladder. Living among white neighbours, some of whom were professionals, encouraged their own children's ambitions. There were virtually no professionals among the generation of Hing's immigrant parents, most of whom were rural-born and poorly educated. (160)

By the same token, incidentally, the narrator's own success as well as Chong's working for Prime Minister Trudeau as an economic adviser, seems to be made possible only with Hing's decision to leave the confines of Chinatown.

Paradoxically enough, Chinatown has been normalized, in the logic of Chong's novel, only once the 'ethnic' subject has acquired an outsider's, a tourist's perspective. Looking back, the narrator notes: "One by one, the children left home for university and after that, jobs. There were family gatherings in Vancouver, but our lives bypassed Chinatown. On rare occasions, we tried a new restaurant there" (234). As she visits her grandchildren, May-ying remains the inassimilable Chinese subject. This inassimilability is reflected as much by her bringing of vegetables from Chinatown as by her inability to quit drinking. Hing, on the other hand, has made possible her own children's success by letting go of her "Chinese" habits:

> Mother felt that her children ought to eat as robust as their playmates. So she cooked Chinese-style only infrequently and instead put roasts on the table, enriched the milk in our glasses with extra cream and introduced cheese into her cooking - in Mother's childhood cheese was what was used to bait mousetraps. Lasagna, along with cinnamon buns, pound cake and apple pie, became one of her specialties. (224)

What is so striking is that from this outsider's perspective, the twin discourses of epidemology and Chineseness are implicitly confirmed. Self-sanitation can be achieved only by a move outside Chinatown. In this sense, Chong's is clearly an assimilationist narrative. Chong's narrative demonstrates that the marginalized subject may be doomed by choosing to express resistance in the language of normalizing discourses. For it is in this resistance that the ethnic subjects moves into the parameters of the norm. A normalizing of the self, in Chong's novel, confirms the abnormality of Chinatown. Strikingly, however, the novel implicitly criticizes the authorities' *sanitization* of Vancouver Chinatown in the 1960s whereas the narrative itself enacts this same sanitization of the self in the success story of the narrator's nuclear family:

> Derelict buildings were condemned. Vancouver's city council enacted bylaws to sanitize the squalor and ordered commerce off the sidewalk - gone were the squawking chickens in cages, the barbecued pork and duck that once hung for the customer's perusal. The gambling dens that used to be my grandmother's livelihood and entertainment had disappeared; the last one had been padlocked by city police. Now when we went to Chinatown, I couldn't help but feel, as its walls seemed to close in, that we were walking through the debris of my mother's past. (228)

When read in line with the narrative's own logic, and its rehearsal of the success story of de-ethnicization as sanitization of the self, however, this disappearance of Chinatown from the dominant culture's landscape and city space comes to seem inevitable. For Hing, the walls of Chinatown were closing in long before the city authorities decided to demolish them. On her own family's menu, there is no longer any use for barbecued pork. It is at this point only that the project of self-normalization is complete. It is here that autoethnography - the narrative of one's own perfectibility, the journey into Americanness - has turned into mere ethnography. As Shah points out, in 1939, city health officer Dr. Jacob Casson Geiger pronounced the following hope for a future in which the Chinese would be neither a cultural nor a health menace. According to Shah, "Geiger saw hope for improvement in the commitment of 'younger' Chinese families to transform their habits and adapt 'Oriental customs to Occidental living,' as well as in their eagerness 'to participate in city-wide activities'-which evidenced 'desire to be good citizens' (2).

By turning autoethnography into an ethnographic gaze on a Chinatown to which she no longer feels connected, Chong's narrative persona proves her desire to be a good citizen.

Chinatown Rediscovered

The end of Chong's narrative clashes, however, with contemporary visions of Chinatown as a *desirable* ethnic space par excellence. This renewed desirability of ethnicity, then, is inseparable from the idea of the model minority. From a monstrous enclave at the close of the 19th century, the Chinese community has suddenly become a paragon to be emulated by white society - an irony which Dr. Jacob Geiger could never have foreseen. Today's sitcoms inevitably feature the Asian doctor as a nerd, as the ultimate embodiment of the model minority. The model minority, in turn, seems the contemporary terminology for Hing's attempt at self-sanitation. Even though she only succeeded in becoming a nurse with mid-century racism barring her from medical school,[2] Hing precedes the contemporary

---

2   Chong's narrative itself points to this dilemma: "Enfranchisement - a requirement for practicing a profession - would come only after exclusion was lifted. However, the reality was that other barriers would have to fall before there were more Chinese engineers, lawyers, accountants, pharmacists, doctors or dentists. Most parents in Chinatown, even if they could afford it, saw little practicality in paying for a university degree only to have their children end up no further ahead than they were - waiting tables, driving taxis, working in laundries, mills or wholesale houses - in

Asian stereotype of the model minority precisely through the idea of the perfectibility of the self. The model minority myth, then, erases the struggle by ethnic subjects to climb the social ladder by postulating an inherent "Asian" talent for discipline. As such, the model minority myth is profoundly ahistorical, and it leaves little room for insights into the heterogeneity of ethnic communities. The myth of the model minority is thus also a form of re-ethnicization: "Asian" success in a white world, paradoxically, is seen not as the ability to pass as "citizen-subject" but as being itself an outcome of "Asianness." This Asianness, in turn, is inseparable from the dominant culture's understanding of Confucian "work ethics." According to David Palumbo-Liu,

> nearly everyone seems to be an expert on "Confucianism," a key signifier in this social and racial discourse. Throughout its evocations, "Confucianism" is simultaneously envisioned as a particular product of the ancient "Orient" and a social form eerily like "our own." This produces the notion of Asians "outwhiting the whites," since "Confucianism" seems a primordial genetic disposition, passed on from generation to generation and only strengthened by its transplantation in the free soil of American capitalism. (197)

Ironically, the "Asian" subject cannot win. Even as she succeeds in "outwhiting the whites" (becoming whiter than the whites themselves) in terms of economic success, she can do so only with the help of a work ethic informed by "Confucianism." Thus, she is simultaneously re-racialized as Other.

Yet, there is another twist to the contemporary rediscovery of ethnicity which Chong's narrative, whose focus is on Hing's "arrival" in mainstream society in the 1940s, cannot take into account. With Chinatown as one of the major attractions of North American cities such as Toronto, New York, or San Francisco, we seem to have come full circle from a demonizing to a fetishizing of "Chinese" cultural difference. As Trinh Minh-ha puts it,

> Chinatown, which until recently was "the wickedest thoroughfare in the States," the taint of "America's dream town" [San Francisco], a vice-ridden and overcrowded ghetto where tourists hardly venture, is now *the* not-to-be-missed tourist attraction, an exotica famed for its packed restaurants, its Oriental delicacies, its glittering souvenir-crammed shops . . . . (102)

As the most desirable subject of the nation, the model minority has paradoxically been brought back to Chinatown. Ironically, the "tightly knit" Chinatown community which was once denounced as breeding immorality is now rediscovered by the mainstream as the basis for Chinese family

---

other words, either working in Chinatown or where whites allowed Chinese to work" (160).

values. Even as this family structure with its premise of heteronormativity could have been attained only after the disappearance of bachelor communities, the historical irony remains. Close living quarters have now miraculously been metaphorized into Chinese families' inane cohesiveness. As Samuel Huntington's contrasting of Western "decay" with non-Western "stability" implies, this cohesiveness has now become a key value in saving the West. According to Huntington,

> The future health of the West and its influence on other societies depends in considerable measure on its success in coping with those trends [2. family decay, including increased rates of divorce, illegitimacy, teen-age pregnancy, and single-parent families, . . . 4. general weakening of the 'work ethic' and rise of a cult of personal indulgence] which, of course, give rise to the assertions of moral superiority by Muslims and Asians. (304)[3]

Huntington's thesis of Western decay and its lacking work ethics, of course, clearly support Palumbo-Liu's reading of the deployment of "Confucianism" by the dominant culture.

The historical irony could hardly be more complete. As Trinh underscores, the "crammed" nature of Chinatown's spatiality which was once denounced as a health hazard is now the very sign of its authenticity, an authenticity which has once again become desirable. Today's Chinatown craze, then, is the other side to Chong's belief in perfectibility. For the criteria of good citizenship are themselves subject to historical transformations as the dominant culture changes its idea of what is desirable in an ethnic subject. It is in this sense that, against the clash of today's discourse on Chinatown, Chong's narrative reminds us not only of the timebound nature of autobiographies, but also the fickleness of calls for normalization. At the beginning of the 21st century with its increasing interest in alternative medical knowledge, members of the Canadian mainstream would hunt high and low for the miracle drug of skunk's gall bladders pickled in gin. What in Chong's narrative seems the pitiable past of recalcitrant grandmothers has been turned, a century later, into the medical future of Western civilization. Ironically, it is thus that history seems to catch up with *The Concubine's Children* and its dismissal of the constructedness of normative assumptions. At the turn of the twenty-first century, to become a good citizen, the ethnic subject has to raid her grandmother's medicine cabinet, and to learn that skunk's gall bladders in gin are more than disgusting: they may cure an entire nation of its back pain. Not only is the ethnic not abnormal, but it may ironically have

---

[3] The "symptoms" of Western decay I have inserted are Huntington's; in his own text, they precede the phrase I have quoted.

become the new norm. In this sense, *The Concubine's Children* may have sanitized a Chinatown which was only biding its time.

Works Cited

Chong, Denise. *The Concubine's Children*. New York: Penguin, 1994.

Hornung, Alfred. "Out of Place: Extraterritorial Existence and Autobiography." *ZAA* 52.4 (2004): 367-77.

Huntington, Samuel. *The Clash of Civilizations and the Remaking of World Order*. New York: Touchstone, 1998.

Palumbo-Liu, David. *Asian/American: Historical Crossings of a Racial Frontier*. Stanford: Stanford UP, 1999.

Rothman, David, Steven Marcus, and Stephanie Kiceluk, eds. *Medicine and Western Civilization*. New Brunswick: Rutgers UP, 1995.

Shah, Nayan. *Contagious Divides: Epidemics and Race in San Francisco's Chinatown*. Berkeley: U of California P, 2001.

Trinh, Minh-ha. *Woman Native Other: Writing Postcoloniality and Feminism*. Bloomington: Indiana UP, 1989.

Ty, Eleanor. "Writing Historiographic Autoethnography: Denise Chong's *The Concubine's Children.*" *English Studies in Canada*. 28.2 (June 2002): 269-292.

SOPHIA EMMANOUILIDOU

Mythography and the Reconstitution of Chicano Identity in Rudolfo Alfonso Anaya's *The Legend of La Llorona* (1984)

> Myth, as a statement of primeval reality which still lives in present-day life and as a justification by precedent, supplies a retrospective pattern of moral values, sociological order, and magical belief. It is, therefore, neither a mere narrative, nor a form of science, nor a branch of art or history, nor an explanatory tale. It fulfills a function, *sui generis* closely connected with the nature of tradition, and the continuity of culture, with the relation between age and youth, and with the human attitude towards the past. The function of myth, briefly, is to strengthen tradition and endow it with a greater value and prestige by tracing it back to a higher, better, more supernatural reality of initial events. (Malinowski 146)

Introduction: Myth, Culture and Social Representation

The Mexican-American response to a long history of discrimination and geocultural displacement, roughly dating back to 1848 with the Treaty of Guadalupe Hidalgo, was most resonantly expressed in the mobilizations of the Chicano Movement. As part of the broader Civil Rights Movement within the US since World War II, *el movimiento* is primarily a political movement against Anglo society, but also a means to reassess and fortify Chicano cultural identity. The resistance politics of *el movimiento* has been recorded as a revolt against Anglo institutional power, but at the same time it has given rise to a cultural (re)affirmation of Chicanismo. Concerning the world of arts, the Mexican-American resistance to US dominance influenced the vast majority of Chicano artists, who drew their inspiration from the real life experiences of *campesinos* (farmworkers) and urban *barrio* (neighborhood or section of US city) dwellers. Chicano artists conceived of their works as political "positionings," composed at the height of the Mexican-American socio-political unrest and motivated by a combination of political, historiographic and aesthetic goals (Hall 223). By and large, Chicano literature of the late 1960s and through the 1970s sustained the political aims of the era, mainly by writing what could be labelled as Marxist literature or "*littérature engagée*" (Adereth 445).[1]

Along such general lines for the purposes of economy of space, a substantial league of the Chicano intelligentsia was propelled by a folk and historical interest in the Southwest, while a more specifically activist body of artists promoted a politically motivated didacticism in Chicano literature. Rudolfo Alfonso Anaya introduced a third current into Chicano *belles lettres* with his extensive use of folk motifs and folklore mysticism. Anaya's first novel *Bless Me, Ultima* (1972) received the Second Annual Premio Quinto Sol in 1971 and brought its writer wide critical acclaim and public recognition. Along with the subsequent publications of *Heart of Aztlan* (1976), *Tortuga* (1979) and the collection of short stories entitled *The Silence of the Llano* (1983), Anaya's novels are superb examples of philosophical and social skepticism, supported by the rich mythic stores of *mexicanos* from both the north and the south side of the Rio Grande border. Born, raised and educated in New Mexico, Anaya never really departs from the cultural richness of his native soil. Instead, he draws from the cultural heritage of his ethnic kin to form his artistic vision. Moreover, the fascination he maintains for the myths and *cuentos* (tales) recited to him by his parents and other local *ancianos* (the old ones) is proof of a keen cultural consciousness. Anaya seems to regard this rich store of myths, which is deeply rooted in the Southwest, as his primary source of inspiration. Thus, his unique literary idiom becomes an interpretive technique for contemporary social issues while it is persistently woven with the mytho-cultural reserves of Mexican-Americans.

Anaya started his writing career at the peak of Chicano activism in the early 1960s. This suggests that his contribution to the Mexican-American literary canon may have been realized through the unique magic realism and local color of his novels, but the complexities of politics have certainly influenced his work. If we accept Joseph Sommers's and Ramon Saldivar's separate and yet similar critical assumptions that history sustains and often sparks off most Chicano literary production,[2] then the resistance to the hegemonic group and the political struggles for self-affirmation constitute

---

[1] According to Max Adereth, the concept of "*littérature engagée*" applies to those literary works which express a political commitment to the realities of the world and which also make a contribution to the requirements of society. For Adereth, the role of the writer is "to commit himself. This simply means that he becomes aware that the real nature of his art is to focus attention on an aspect of reality and thus, inevitably, to pass judgement on it. [...] His success in this respect is determined by the fact that he himself is no mere spectator in the drama that he depicts, he is also an actor. What is required of him is that he should be a conscious actor" ("What is *littérature engagée?*" 445).

[2] See Joseph Sommers's "historical-dialectical" preferred form of literary analysis and Ramon Saldivar's notion of "the dialectics of difference" in Chicano literature.

the driving force for most early Chicano artists. This sustains the ongoing paper's critical belief that Anaya's narratives do not in fact breach the highly political trend of the 1960s and 1970s. More to the point, his narratives comprise an intriguing variation of the community's literary idiom, promote the cultural facet of Chicanismo, and function as a means of interpreting socio-political life. Far from deteriorating into a useless "nativism,"[3] Anaya's deployment of indigenous cultural elements and primeval realities is a powerful reclamation of Chicano heritage and a viable call for collective awareness. According to this hypothesis, Anaya's use of myth manifests a highly political objective, beneath the superficial stylistic marker of mystic aestheticism or, in Bourdieu's terms, the realization of a myth manifests Anaya's capacity to transcend "the antinomies of determinism and freedom, conditioning and creativity, consciousness and the unconscious, or the individual and society" (54).

The aim of this paper is to look into one of Anaya's mythographic stories, *The Legend of La Llorona* (1984), in order to explore the ways in which the specific narrative constructs a collective identity of the present, using a cultural reserve from the past. Although the short novel considered here has not received the same critical attention as *Bless Me, Ultima* or *Heart of Aztlan*, it is examined for its mystic plot pattern, which distances the contents of the novels from contemporary experience (unlike *Bless Me, Ultima* and *Heart of Aztlan*), but which also becomes a vibrant affirmation of present-day Chicano identity. More explicitly, *The Legend of La Llorona* creates an amalgam of indigenous religion, mythography and history against the background of *mestizo* genesis. The text refrains from any reference to contemporary *campesino* or barrio experience, yet it serves the premise that Anaya's use of myth supersedes the definition of an essentialist, nativistic "blithe celebration" (Pérez-Torres 9). Far from

---

[3] In an insightful discussion of Chicano poetry, *Movements in Chicano Poetry: Against Myths, Against Margins* (1995), Rafael Pérez-Torres comments on the citation of myths as a common technique among Chicano poets. Pérez -Torres considers the use of myth often illuminating in the process of self-affirmation, but he also warns that myths can induce artists and their readership to embrace escapism, what he terms "nativism." In Pérez-Torres's own words: "At one point there exists the need to distinguish oneself from the colonizing society. This involves the re-evaluation of traditional cultural forms, [...] an affirmation of the unique characters of the colonized culture. This can, when productive, empower an entire constituency. At worst, it can result in an unexamined nativism that values without scrutiny those things it takes to be precolonial. [...] At moments, the uncritical (and often reified) reclamation of the Aztec comes dangerously close to being a blithe and uninformed celebration of anything non-Western" (8-9). Pérez-Torres quite successfully points out the possible dangers in the use of myths. Nevertheless, Anaya's texts bypass the pitfall of appearing "blithe" because their writer employs myths with a critical eye, and with the will to adapt them to contemporary Chicano communal needs.

indulging in an obsolete gratification in mythic narratives, Anaya's version of an antique myth becomes an instrumental literary production and a symbol of social struggle in order to (re)construct the collective Chicano identity of the present. This paper shows that the cultural expression of La Llorona first retains the mythic memory of present-day Chicanos and second reassesses the rise of *mestizaje* in the Americas, through the lenses of epic insight.

Chicano Cultural Identity and Collective Awareness

In the short story *The Legend of La Llorona*, Anaya presents a fresh version of a classic Latino tale whose general story-line centers on the hardships of a female folk character. La Llorona is the betrayed, abandoned woman who kills her children in order to avenge her husband's indifference. From then on she turns into a ghost, haunting the earth with her shrieking cries in search of her children. The tale epitomizes the desperation of a neglected woman, the urge to react to desolation, and the eternal quest for emotional completion. The myth of La Llorona or the Wailing Woman, as the name translates into English, is probably the most popular tale in Latin America, and one passed on by word of mouth among *mestizos* across the Americas and throughout time.[4] Moreover, there is a plethora of La Llorona stories, and a few cultural theorists say they originate in Spain, while most locate their conception in the colonial Americas. The suggestion is that since the tale of La Llorona is a segment of the Latino cultural stock, and one that can be traced back to the pre or early colonization era of the Americas, then it is almost impossible to retain

---

[4]   The terms "myth" and "folktale" appear frequently in this paper. I admit that I have found great difficulty in grasping the similarities and differences between them. In fact, I have come to the conclusion that there are only rudimentary distinctions as to what the aforementioned terms signify. The most concise definition I have traced is the one proposed by Geza Roheim, who claims that "[i]n a myth the actors are mostly divine and sometimes human. In a folktale the *dramatis personae* are mostly human and especially the hero, frequently with supernatural beings as his opponents. In a myth we have definite locality; in a folktale the actors are nameless, the scene is just anywhere. A myth is part of a creed; it is believed by the narrator. The folktale is purely fiction, and not intended to be anything else" (34). Should we accept that the myth and the folktale "[h]ave a common origin, a type of narrative from which both have developed in the course of evolution," then they are both offspring of the same imaginative impetus. Thus, myth and folktale share basic elements in their plot structures (37). When I refer to the folktale of *The Legend of La Llorona* I signify the stock of a recurrent narrative within *mexicano* communities. On the other hand, the use of the term myth, points to Anaya's version of the story, which elevates the central female character to epic and godly stature and specifies the chronotope of the story. See Roheim, "Myth and Folktale."

its constituent parts unaltered throughout time. If culture is alive and always in flux and if myths are part of the cultural identity of a group of people, then each mythic reproduction reflects a contemporary social reality and fulfills a specific "social function" (Malinowski 117). In other words, a myth is likely to have as many versions as the story-tellers who undertake its narration or performance. Accordingly, the present-day reader or listener can merely identify the motif of the folktale in its numerous modifications by individual story-tellers, while amidst this bewildering variety, or what Arturo Ramírez calls the "diffusion" of the myth, there is always a structural core or a basic plot-pattern in every story of the myth (1992). This structural core or plot-axis is adapted to the needs of a group in order to mediate a social judgment, to enter the dynamics of an "ideologeme,"[5] or to convey the potential mythographer's apprehension of the mythic pattern (Jameson 87). Similarly, Anaya draws upon the basic story-line of the tale of the Wailing Woman, but at the same time he modifies the myth in order to convey a moral to his Chicano target audience. This point implies an inherent dualism: on the one hand, there is the general cultural reserve of La Llorona's tale, and on the other hand, there is Anaya's fresh version of the myth. The implication is that there is the general narrative of La Llorona as transmitted among *mestizos* throughout the race's history, but there is also Anaya's homomorphism in his reproduction and appropriation of a specific expression of the Chicano cultural legacy. Looked at on a temporal span, the tale of La Llorona is a diachronic cultural practice, whereas Anaya's *The Legend of La Llorona* is the synchronic realization of the myth's constituent parts and an instrumental production that serves a social function.

Anaya's adaptation of the tale departs from the familial crisis motif of most traditional Latino versions, and becomes deeply rooted in history. In fact, Anaya re-visions the tale as an allegory of the *mestizo* race's origin and La Llorona is personified as La Malinche, the Indian daughter of a village chief on the east coast of the Americas, and the female originator of Latino miscegenation in her union with a Spanish conqueror. Anaya's modification of the myth endows it with the validity of the true story of La Malinche.[6] And contrary to the pejorative labels against Malinche as *la*

---

[5]   Fredric Jameson's notion of the "ideologeme" signifies the mediation between "concepts of ideology as abstract opinion, class value, and the like, and the narrative materials" (87). Following the "ideologeme" in mythopoeisis, mythic texts do not escape the real but enter the world of politics and the discourse of class relations in subtle and yet effective ways.

[6]   From this point onwards, the Spanish article "La" will be omitted and references to the female protagonist of *The Legend of La Llorona* will be made as "Malinche" in accordance to Anaya's use of the name. There is certainly an intricate semiotic register in Anaya's omission of the Spanish article "La," which is also a political

chingada (the violated or the fucked one), which has circulated in the Chicano community from the militant 1960s to day, Anaya's story elevates his Indian protagonist and restores her dignity. Despite the fact that Malinche pledges her love to the Spanish Captain, throughout the story she remains true to her indigenous cultural identity and to the native people. Anaya presents Malinche as widely respected by the Indians because of her beauty and supernatural powers. She is an insightful, politicized female character, who attends meetings with the village council "when it discussed the social ceremonies of the village" and argues that "the village should not be dominated by the Aztec empire and tribute should not be sent to Moctezuma, the lord of the Aztecs" (14-5). When the first Spanish *conquistadores* arrive in the Americas, the Indians mistake them for the priests of the deity Quetzalcoatl. In awe, the local people welcome the Spaniards with the false belief that the prophecy of Quetzalcoatl's return from the East coast has been fulfilled. However, Malinche realizes that the newcomers "in the floating houses" were not priests or gods, but "pale men" (15). Because of her unique ability to learn "customs and the languages," she picks up the Castilian language immediately and helps the Captain of the shipwrecked Spanish soldiers to advance inland. To her unwary mind, the pale men can help the Indians of the provinces resist Moctezuma's harsh tax-collections. Soon, Malinche falls in love with the Captain and gives birth to his twin sons, Olin and Tizoc. In the meantime, the Captain manages to conquer most of the Aztec territory including the imperial city of Tenochtitlan. Malinche becomes the Captain's consort, and by having helped him advance inland, she unwittingly aids in the capture of her own people. Throughout this time she has undertaken to educate her sons in the Aztec ways. Thus, she instructs them in the local religious and cultural practices despite the Captain's strict prohibitions. When the Captain becomes the powerful ruler of the New World, he decides to return to Spain with the twins, governed by his utopian ambition that his sons will be granted royal honors in the Spanish court. At the prospect of parting with her children, Malinche kills the twins. She, in fact, follows the Medea-motif of tragic infanticide, and sacrifices her children to save them from a future of slavery and degradation among the colonizers. At the end of the story, in the midst of a storm, Malinche appears as a half-deity and accounts for her horrible deed:

> "Yes, I have been wronged" Malinche answered standing tall and noble before [the captain and the Spanish soldiers]. "My sons were to be made slaves, and I paid for their liberation dearly. Now they are dead [...], but other sons of Mexico

---

designation of both Malinche and his reading public as English-speaking peoples. However, the ongoing "functionalist" approach to myth in relation to identity-cognizance does not allow space for a comparative linguistic study of the names "Malinche" or "La Malinche."

will rise against you and avenge this deed. The future will not forgive any of us."
(89)

The denouement abridges the mythic aspect of La Llorona with the true story of Malinche. In other words, Malinche becomes La Llorona upon declaring: "I, Malinche, princess and mother of the Mexicans, will forever be known as the woman who cries for her sons" (89). Then she disappears into the darkness leaving behind "her grief, and penance, and her wailing cry" (89). Shocking though it is, the end of the story encapsulates the moral of Anaya's myth, which is a powerful statement against exploitation and disenfranchisement, even at the cost of self-sacrifice.

The Legend of La Llorona manifests a double-faceted literary production in its fusion of mythical elements with the historical dilemmas Malinche confronted. First, the story touches upon the legacy of the wailing woman, and second it endows the myth with historical dimensions. To some extent, Anaya correlates symbolic mythmaking with factual historiography, since the characters of the story are not mere figments of the author's imagination, but real-life personae that can be traced in the bulky pages of historiographic texts on *mestizaje*. Concomitantly, the folkloric essence of *The Legend of La Llorona* is deciphered on the one hand with Malinche's experience (the Native-American woman who has been accused of helping Cortez conquer the Americas and gave birth to the first Hispano-Indians), and on the other hand with the Captain's experience who personifies Cortez (the Spanish *conquistador*, who also embodies the colonizing aspect of Chicano identity). As the archetype of a father-figure, Cortez is not only the representative of the intruders' force, but also the one who engenders the half-breed race of Chicanos. The underlying doctrine in Malinche and the Captain's union is that the history of the Chicano race is not complete unless it takes into consideration the links with Castilians across the Atlantic.

Malinche and the Captain embody Anaya's designation of *mestizo* origin, and the individual Chicano reader of *The Legend of La Llorona* has a point of departure in his/her process to identity-cognition, once the progenitors of Chicanismo are specified. In fact, this is a crucial recognition and a point of reversal in the Mexican-American community's self-identification, considering the profound emphasis on the race's Indian-ness during the political rhetoric of *el movimiento*. Anaya's emphasis on the Spanish-European ancestry in the Chicano gene pool and racial residue is a reformation and a bold departure from the Native-American biological identity so fervently propagated during the Chicano Movement. Along these lines, *The Legend of La Llorona* treats Chicanismo as a fractured group and provides the ground for viewing "the formerly unified [sense of identity as] split into his or her constituent parts, in which a single

homogenous style is superseded by a number of heterogeneous fashions"
(Gutiérrez 61). This heterogeneous quality of *mestizo* identity is advocated
by Anaya with the claim that the present-day Chicano individual does
indeed avow a specific ethnic identity or practice certain poetics of
existence, but Malinche and the Captain's relationship provides the
historical and cultural refuge which presents the Chicano as a fragmented
cultural identity. The corollary is that *mestizos* cannot be either strictly
Indian or Hispanic, but a combination of the two. As products of
miscegenation, Chicanos view the world with a double-consciousness: on
the one hand, that of the colonizing father-figure, and on the other hand,
that of the colonized mother-figure. This double-consciousness means that
their presence in the Americas is likely to structure a contrasting feeling for
"apprehending and experiencing the world and [their] place or
placelessness in it" (Gutiérrez 61).

Malinche's character is central in Anaya's definition of *mestizaje* not
only for her role as the female originator of *la bronze raza*, but also for her
symbolic connection to the colonization era of the Americas. Malinche's
actions and the way she corresponds to other characters in the story depict
the new state of affairs between the indigenous peoples and the Spaniards.
As far as the Indians are concerned, they always think highly of her and
elevate her to the status of a demi-goddess. "Malintzin," which is her true
Indian name,

> was truly a gifted woman, a noble person, and full of kindness when she went to
> heal the old and the infirm. An aura of light seemed to glow around her. On her
> eleventh birthday when she became a woman and was given her name,
> Malintzin, was dressed in a cotton skirt of white, with a huipil of many colors
> [...]. The young men of the village admired her beauty and smiled at her when
> she passed by, but Malintzin remained aloof. (15-6)

Naming the central female character carries significant proportions in
the story. The Indians call her "Malintzin," but when the Captain meets her
for the first time he changes her name into "Malinche," thus symbolically
interfering with her true identity:

> A heathen who can speak the language of Castile, the Captain thought. What a
> beautiful creature. He took her hand and felt Malintzin's strength. Then he
> smiled. "What is your name?" he asked. "I am Malintzin," she replied.
> "Malinche," he repeated the name, changing the sound, assuring she would
> thereafter be known as Malinche. (18)

According to postcolonial theory, a hegemonic or ruling class holds
people in its grip "by a kind of perverted logic," which distorts and
disfigures the colonized identity (Fanon 170). Similarly, the Spanish
conquistador's logic distorts "Malintzin" into "Malinche" and ironically

wins the active consent of Chicanos, who henceforth use the name
"Malinche" instead of "Malintzin." Malintzin herself naively concedes to
the renaming process, and in so doing she symbolically succumbs to the
colonizer's force. After the first encounter with the Captain, she establishes
a new subjectivity defined by the colonizer's authority. Her new name
relates her identity-perception to the newcomers and the new era that all the
natives anticipate is precisely this change in self-awareness, which goes
hand-in-hand with the Spaniards. From now on, Spanish colonizers define
the Indians. Therefore, not only the initial union between Malinche and the
Captain, but also the colonizing power of naming becomes central in
defining the *mestizo* race.

As the story progresses, Spanish forces conquer most of the Aztec
territory including the imperial city of Mexico-Tenochtitlan, and Malinche
realizes the inhumane imperialism of the *conquistadores*. In fact, Malinche
comprehends that far from co-existing peacefully with the Spanish, the
colonizer's rule subordinates and marginalizes Indian socio-cultural life.
Playing the role of the chorus in this epic-like story, the Indians turn to the
female protagonist for help and call her by her heathen name "Malintzin."
In a symbolic and highly political fashion, they strike the chords of
Malinche's Indian identity. If we accept the assumption that "to signify the
self is to engage in practices of freedom" then the use of the name
"Malintzin" is part of a resistance mechanism against the presence of a
hegemonic regime (Watney 160). Thus, although the Castilians have
(re)defined her as "Malinche," the heathens cling to her indigenous name;
and in so doing, they (re)set the perimeters of their Indian-ness and refute
the power of the colonizing force. With the juxtaposition in the use of the
names "Malinche" and "Malintzin," Anaya draws a line between Chicanos
and Indians. "Malinche" is the only name employed by present-day
Chicanos, whereas "Malintzin" has fallen into complete oblivion. What
Anaya implies is that Chicanos have used and abused the name "Malinche"
in accordance with the Spanish conquerors' symbolic undertones. In
contrast, the Indians in *The Legend of La Llorona* retain the name
"Malintzin," thus reclaiming for the female protagonist her Indian identity.
For Anaya, the Chicano socio-cultural identity is different from the Indian
one, and the use of the names "Malinche" or "Malintzin" is the symbolic
site where that difference is played out.

Towards the end of the narrative, the Captain reveals his imperialist
intentions towards the natives. As the ultimate voice of authority, the
Captain carries on naming and setting new identities for the Native-
Americans, his twin sons and Malinche. He considers the New World as
"the land of savages" (52) and does not pursue a peaceful coexistence with
the heathens, but seeks to exploit and subordinate the colonized peoples of
the Americas. In vain, Malinche protests against the abuse of the Indians,

while the Captain exercises his power with the advancement of more "naming" instances against the twins and Malinche. He asserts that Malinche's "own people don't accept [the twins], because they are not pure Indians" (52). The Captain clearly designates Olin and Tizoc as mixed-blood subjectivities and stresses their difference from the locals. The Spanish colonizer forcefully names the boys and attempts to distance them from their Indian (half) self. By maintaining Olin and Tizoc's non-purity, the Captain wishes to draw the twins away from their heathen identity. As for Malinche, he accords her the identity of a traitor to her own race. The Captain maintains that she is as much to blame for the captivity of her people as he is:

> "You were my ally. You were at my side throughout the early days, during the march to Tlaxcala and Cholula, and here to Mexico where we met the great Moctezuma. You interpreted for me, so my words were yours. Don't you see, among your people there are already some who whisper your name, and to them Malinche means traitor!" (53)

The Captain openly speaks the words of those present-day activist Chicanos who embrace "the historical representation of Malinche as a treacherous whore who betrayed her own people" (Gutiérrez 52). Indeed, the Spanish *conquistador* is the one who defines the Indian woman as a *chingada*, "the passive, inert and open [female], who is defenseless against the exterior world" (Gutiérrez 52). In contrast to the Indian walk-ons, who people Anaya's story and turn to their native "Malintzin" for help, the Captain is the one who endows Malinche with the pejorative identity of a traitor to her own race.

After the climactic argument with the Captain over the boys' departure to imperial Spain, Malinche attempts to break free from Tenochtitlan along with her sons. Because she has been faced with the immediate danger of being parted from the boys, she decides to escape, but her effort is thwarted. Not only have orders been given not to let Malinche leave the city of Tenochtitlan, but she is also not allowed to pledge her faith to the heathen gods. Malinche is both physically and culturally in captivity. Her Indian identity is controlled and marginalized by the rule of the newcomers, and she realizes that "she was being backed into a corner from which there was no escape" (63). Malinche has to act accordingly in this new condition of enslavement. So, she tricks the Captain into granting her a little time alone with her sons. She takes the boys to the hidden temple of the Aztec gods, where she decides to offer them as sacrifice to the War God Huitziopochtli. At the heathen temple she prays to the war god, asking for strength to proceed with the sacrifice:

> She prayed and revealed her soul to the God of War, and the dark chamber grew suffocating with the sweet smoke of incense [...]. "Make me strong!" she cried.

"Blind my eyes to the blood I must shed! As I was once the first consort of the Spaniard, now make me a warrior against his enslavement! I pray, tell me what I must do! Mexico must be free! Must my own sons be the first warriors to die in this struggle? Must they lead the way for the future?" As before, she heard the god answer her prayers. Yes, the voice in the interior of the chamber seemed to say, the spirits of your sons will guide the warriors of the new struggle. A new breed of men born of this world will come behind them to free Mexico, to free the spirit of the people. Mexico will be free! And you, Malinche, will live forever in the legends of your people. Go on spill the blood of the warriors! The blood will cleanse you of the past, Mexico will enter a new age! Go! (77)

Unlike the basic plot-structure of most La Llorona tales, Malinche commits the sacrifice not to avenge the Captain's betrayal towards her, but as a token political action for the future generations. Malinche demystifies the illusion of a Hispanic-Indian co-existence and faces the present reality of the Indians' subjugation. So, "she puts away the past and thinks of her commitment to the freedom of her people" (78). And that commitment is synonymous with infanticide in order to protect her children from eternal enslavement. As a mother-figure to the whole race of *mestizos*, Malinche professes self-sacrifice as the ultimate defense against peregrination.

Conclusion

In *The Legend of La Llorona*, Rudolfo Alfonso Anaya undertakes the task of rehabilitating Malinche's archetype and suggests that *mexicanos* should take pride in her because she is the precursor of *la raza* and the one who sets the foundations for activism against racial exploitation. For Anaya, Malinche is neither a *chingada* nor a traitor. She rises to mythic stature because the whole race of present-day Latinos stem from her existence. And the way the mythic element of La Llorona's tale blends with the historical perspective attributes legendary qualities to Malinche. Infanticide may sound cruel and inhumane, yet Anaya justifies it as a brave deed, which allows room for a better *mestizo* future. Finally, in connection with the cultural trajectory of *The Legend of La Llorona*, one must consider the codes that Anaya employs to arouse *mestizo* communality. Anaya addresses his narrative to a specific group, which is peoples of *mestizo* origin, and expects to evoke an emotional response from them. The story of La Llorona, which has been recounted among *mexicanos* since time immemorial, applies both to the unconscious mind and to the "conscious co-ordination" of the members of the same group (Bourdieu 54). The legend of La Llorona is a popular story, identifiable to the majority of Chicanos. Popular tales have the power to root themselves in the subconscious mind because their audiences mystically internalize them.[7] And since popular tales may address vast groups of people, even whole nations, they bring about a sense of collective awareness. Indeed, folkloric tales have the impetus of "homogenizing"[8] a group, because they practice the conditions of bringing community members together through emotional attachment (Bourdieu 54). Tales accumulate in the storage of collective memories, and memory "is not merely something that we deliberately evoke, but it is also something that comes charged with emotion and is highly prized" (Warnock 14). In other words, the power of a popular story is in its capacity to "co-ordinate" people by means of a subconscious emotional arousal. Because "communication of consciousness presupposes community of unconsciousness," subtly, yet successfully, Anaya negotiates the homogeneity of *mestizos* (Bourdieu 58). A legend is a folk element which regenerates the past, thus becoming a major part of a given group's cultural identity. Thus, in a participatory mood the myth (in our case the myth of La Llorona) draws the people together to a communal experience. In short, the reading or listening public of the myth are urged to communicate, not literally, but in an emotional trajectory. In this light, the mythographer's intention is not truly innocent. More to the point, Anaya assumes the role of a social agent, seeking "collective mobilization," and *The Legend of La Llorona* is an instrumental narrative in the direction of social *praxis* (Bourdieu 59). [9]

---

[7]   For more on the importance of folklore in the construction of a collective identity, see Tomas Atencio's mode of social research in "Resolana."

[8]   The terms "conscious coordination" and "homogenization" are loans from Pierre Bourdieu's "Structures, Habitus and Practices" (1990), where the notion of the "habitus" is discussed in relation to collectivization. According to Bourdieu, the habitus is "a product of history [...] a system of dispositions--a present past that tends to perpetuate itself into the future by reactivation in similarly structured practices, an internal law [...]--the principle of the continuity and regularity which objectivism sees in social practices" (54). In this paper a cautious attempt has been made to describe myths as part of the Latino habitus, which is a shared cultural compatibility, running through time, but which is also constantly being modified to adapt a specific social and historical reality. In short, similar to Bourdieu's habitus, myths combine primordial and synchronic elements, or put differently the mystic and the pragmatic segments of self-cognizance.

[9]   The specific use of Bourdieu's term of the "collective mobilization" does not imply activism against a dominant group in the sense of marching the streets and forming picketing lines, but refers to a conscious reconsideration of the community's identity. My point is that Anaya inspires a new perception of *mestizo* identity and encourages his Latino reading public to explore their common history and culture. See Bourdieu "Structures, Habitus and Practices."

Works Cited

Adereth, Max. "What is 'Littérature Engagée'?" *Marxists on Literature: An Anthology.* Ed. David Craig. Harmondsworth: Penguin, 1975. 445-85.

Anaya, Rudolfo Alfonso. *Bless Me, Ultima.* Berkeley: Ouinto Sol, 1972.

---. *Heart of Aztlan.* Albuquerque: U of New Mexico P, 1988.

---. *The Legend of La Llorona.* Berkeley: Tonatiuh-Quinto Sol, 1984.

---. *The Silence of the Llano: Short Stories.* Berkeley: Tonatiuh-Quinto Sol, 1982.

----. *Tortuga.* Berkeley: Editorial Justa, 1979.

Atencio, Tomas. "Resolana: A Chicano Pathway to Knowledge." *Ernesto Galarza Commemorative Lecture: Third Annual Lecture.* Stanford Center for Chicano Research, SCCR, California (1988): 1-21.

Bourdieu, Pierre. "Structures, Habitus and Practices." *The Logic of Practice.* Trans. Richard Nice. Cambridge: Polity, 1990. 52-65.

Gutiérrez, Ramon A. "Community, Patriarchy and Individualism: The Politics of Chicano History and the Dream of Equality." *American Quarterly* 45. 1 (March 1993): 44-72.

Hall, Stuart. "Cultural Identity and Diaspora." *Identity, Community, Culture, Difference.* Ed. Jonathan Rutherford. London: Lawrence, 1990. 222-37.

Jameson, Fredrick. *The Political Unconscious: Narrative as a Socially Symbolic Act.* Ithaca: Cornell UP, 1981.

Malinowski, Bronislaw. *Magic, Science and Religion.* Westport: Greenwood, 1984.

Pérez-Torres, Raphael. *Movements in Chicano Poetry: Against Myths, Against Margins.* Cambridge: Cambridge UP, 1995.

Ramirez, Arturo. "La Llorona: Structure and Archetype." *Chicano Border Culture and Folklore.* Eds. José Villarino and Arturo Ramírez. San Diego: Marin, 1992. 19-26.

Roheim, Geza. "Myth and Folktale." *Myth and Literature.* Ed. John B. Vickery. Lincoln: U of Nebraska P, 1966. 33-45.

Saldivar, Ramon. "A Dialectic of Difference: Toward a Theory of the Chicano Novel." *Contemporary Chicano Fiction: A Critical Survey.* Ed. Vernon E. Lattin. Binghampton: Bilingual/Editorial Bilingüe, 1986. 13-31.

Sommers, Joseph. "Critical Approaches to Chicano Literature." *The Identification and Analysis of Chicano Literature.* Ed. Fransisco Jiménez. New York: Bilingual/Editorial Bilingüe, 1979. 143-52.

Warnock, Mary. *Memory.* London: Faber, 1987.

Watney, Simon. "Practices of Freedom: Citizenship and the Politics of Identity in the Age of AIDS." *Identity, Community, Culture, Difference.* Ed. Jonathan Rutherford. London: Lawrence, 1990. 157-87.

SIDONIE SMITH

Narrated Lives and the Contemporary Regime of Human Rights: Mobilizing Stories, Campaigns, Ethnicities

In our recent book, *Human Rights and Narrated Lives: The Ethics of Recognition*, Kay Schaffer and I explore the conjunction of life narration, broadly defined, and the contemporary regime of human rights. We are particularly interested in issues related to the production, circulation, and reception of life storytelling enlisted in campaigns for human rights, campaigns such as the struggle of former World War II sex prisoners (sometimes referred to as "comfort women") to witness to the degradation and exploitation they endured more than fifty-years ago, and the struggle on behalf of prisoner rights in the United States. In our study, we look expansively at the multiple sites of personal storytelling attached to human rights campaigns: published life narratives; fact-finding in the field; handbooks and websites; nationally-based human rights commissions; human rights commission reports; collections of testimonies; stories in the media; and the scattered everyday venues through which narratives circulate. We do so in order to assess the efficacies of life storytelling for tellers and for audiences and the institutional expectations and constraints that shape the kinds of stories that can be told and the way those stories are reproduced. Here, I want to extend the analyses developed in *Human Rights and Narrated Lives* by exploring one story of suffering ethnicity, its production in Eastern Europe and circulation in the United States. I do so in order to assay what we might learn about the mobilization and globalization of stories of ethnic suffering in a human rights regime that serves as one of the central "managers" of ethnicity today.[1]

The resurgence of ethnic nationalism attending the end of the Cold War and the reorganization of politics in Eastern Europe has set large numbers of people in motion–into refugee camps, resettlement programs, and diasporic communities in receiving nations such as the United States. Under violent assault, displaced, haunted by traumatic memories, members of ethnic communities turn to life storytelling to extend global recognition of the violence unleashed against people on the basis of their ethnic identification. Their acts of narration emerge out of local contexts of rights violations. But to the extent that local movements "go international" these witnesses participate through their storytelling in global processes that create a climate for the intelligibility, reception, and recognition of new

---

[1]   See Chow on the management of ethnicity (11).

stories about ethnicity under assault. Gillian Whitlock calls this breakthrough to public attention a "discursive threshold" (144). Since the language of human rights is the contemporary *lingua franca* for addressing the problem of suffering and injustice (Ignatieff 7), the attachment of personal storytelling to the discourse and the institutions of the human rights regime helps witnesses push attention to specific environments of suffering across a discursive threshold. The embeddedness of stories of ethnic suffering in the discourses, institutions, and practices of the human rights regime offers those who tell their stories a narrative framework, a context, an audience, and a subject position as the victim of human rights abuse.

Through their stories of ethnic suffering, witnesses expose the violence inflicted by those pursuing the project of ethnic nationalism as a goal of state formation. They also reveal the complexities and conundrums involved in telling stories of ethnic difference and grievance through frameworks and institutions founded on the concept of abstract universality. In order to circulate their stories within the global circuits of the human rights regime and bring crises of violence and suffering to a larger public, witnesses give their stories over to journalists, publishers, publicity agents, marketers, and rights activists whose framings of personal narratives participate in the commodification of suffering, the reification of the universalized subject position of innocent victim, and the displacement of historical complexity by the feel-good opportunities of empathetic identification.

In this essay, I cannot possibly do justice to the complexities of the conjunction of life storytelling and the contemporary regime of human rights as that conjunction captures and complicates transnational ethnic formations and the remembering of suffering at this historical moment. What I can do here is to comment briefly on debates that capture the tension between individual and group rights having to do with ethnicity under assault; locate one published narrative of besieged ethnicity in Eastern Europe that circulated in the United States, Zlata Filipovici *Zlata's Diary*; and elucidate some of the contradictory effects of the commodification of narratives of suffering ethnicity through a rights regime that attaches abstract universality to ethnic difference under assault.

The Rights Regime and Ethnic Suffering

"The allure of rights language in the post-cold War era," notes Richard A. Wilson, "is that it prescribes basic citizenship rights and constitutionalism as an antidote to ethnic nationalism" (3). The founding assumption informing human rights discourse and the practical politics of human rights institutions and mechanisms shifts the ethical locus of communal identification from the imagined community of the "nation" to the citizenship community of the "state," which seeks to "build legitimate and representative state institutions which respect fundamental human rights" (Wilson 5). In states respecting fundamental human rights, ethnic "difference" recedes as an organizing principle and symbolic site of identification; and the more universalized concept of citizenship rights is advanced. Ethno-nationalism, nationalism built around an "ethnic core" of identification, history, culture, language, and values, is expected to give way to constitutional democracy where inclusive citizenship rights are enshrined in law. This possible future, at least, is the "allure" of the human rights regime.

In the fifty years since the ratification of the Universal Declaration of Human Rights, however, the relationship of individual (or citizen) rights to group rights has been a vexed, often conflictual and contradictory one. Two decades of draft documents and energetic debates followed the signing of the Universal Declaration of Human Rights in 1948, as delegates struggled to flesh out the principles articulated in the UDHR through the International Covenants on Civil and Political Rights and on Economic, Social, and Cultural Rights (both of which were ratified in 1966). Debates revolved around the question of what rights were foundational to individuals. Enlightenment principles undergirding the rights of self-determination and of freedom and autonomy privilege individual over state interests. In fact, within this philosophical and legal framework, individual and state rights are presented as oppositional. Thus, a declaration of universal civil and political rights would delimit the power of the state over the individual, and protect individual against the brute power and subtle encroachments of the state.[2] Within international law, these rights bear *jus cogens* status; that is, they are rights perceived to be normative, universal, and binding for all people.

The idea that individual rights take precedence over the interests of the state has continued to spark arguments, both political and philosophical, about the status of individuals within human rights law and the implications of their communal affiliations for that law. This tension between individual rights and state aspirations played out in the drafting and final approval of the Covenant on Economic, Social, and Cultural Rights which affirmed the centrality of living conditions related to health, education, employment, and leisure. These goal-oriented rights stipulate a desirable future, one in which all peoples have achieved an enabling standard of living. With aspiration rights (sometimes called second generational rights), individual

---

[2]   Rights scholars describe these rights, among them the right to be free from genocide, torture, slavery, murder, arbitrary detention, and systematic racial discrimination, as "first generation" rights.

and state interests can be consonant with one another in that the state can play a significant role in fostering the goals of social and economic development, thereby improving conditions for all people. The common good established through state interest, however, can also conflict with individual rights, a situation that may lead to a curb on individual rights in the interests of state goals (such as civic harmony and economic development).

With the debates and struggles around a third generation of rights claimed by groups (minorities within member states, indigenous communities) additional tensions have emerged in the regime of human rights around the vexed relation of state-formation and ethnic nationalism. In May of 1917, Woodrow Wilson first articulated the principle of self-determination for culturally distinct groups in regard to political instability in the Balkans. "No right anywhere exists to hand peoples about from sovereignty to sovereignty as if they were property," proclaimed Wilson in an address to Congress during the First World War.[3] At that historical moment, the principle of self-determination of distinct groups "justified," according to Anaya, the reconfiguration of states within Eastern Europe along ethnic lines (76).[4] While absent from the UDHR, the notion of self-determination of peoples was subsequently included in the Covenant for Civil and Political Rights as Article 27, a statement of group self-determination that supplemented Article 1 as a statement of self-determination for individuals.[5] Contemporary articulations of the principle of self-determination of peoples have attended two kinds of political realignments since World War II: decolonizing processes that led to the emergence of new sovereign states and minority and indigenous rights movements within sovereign states.

Indigenous and minority groups have harnessed their aspirations to the founding principles of the United Nations. Group action and advocacy eventuated in new instruments, including the ILO Convention 169 on Indigenous and Tribal Peoples (1991), which replaced the earlier, and paternalistic Convention 107; the United Nations Declaration on the Rights of Persons Belonging to National or Ethnic, Religious and Linguistic Minorities (1992); and the Draft Declaration on the Rights of Indigenous People (1993). Together, these instruments acknowledge and support indigenous and minority claims to cultural integrity, identity, language, religion, and land rights. They also call into question the basic

---

[3]   See Umozurike (6-11). Anaya cites the Wilson quote (82).
[4]   The history of this principle of self-determination is a complex one, more thoroughly explored by Anaya and Robbins and Stamatopoulou.
[5]   "In those States in which ethnic, religious or linguistic minorities exist, persons belonging to such minorities shall not be denied the right, in community with other members of their group, to enjoy their own culture, to profess and practice their own religion, or to use their own language."

philosophies and politics underlying human rights principles and their implementation.

Third-generation rights demonstrate minority and indigenous peoples' success in forging transnational coalitions, making their concerns heard by a global public, and enlisting the support necessary to bring about an extension of human rights parameters. The politics of the advancement of group rights, however, remains complicated and sometimes problematic. As of now, there has been no ratification of a Declaration on the Rights of Indigenous Peoples. Vigorous and public campaigns for group rights can lead, as has happened in Australia, to a backlash within the larger community against the claims to specific group rights. Or vigorous pursuit of group rights by one group can prompt dissonant claims coming from different groups within the same nation (see Yamamoto).[6] Configured as the right of peoples to self-determination, the pursuit of group rights could potentially undermine the principle of state sovereignty upon which the United Nations and the human rights regime were founded. According to Bruce Robbins and Elsa Stamatopoulou, the effects of ratifying the principle of self-determination of peoples would involve affirming a definition of "people." It would involve "questioning the legitimacy of the states in which those peoples reside." It would involve an international commitment to aligning the territory of "states" with "a people" so recognized. It would involve international agreement on the "internationally acknowledged right to unilateral secession." It would involve "dismembering" many of those states that fought for self-determination through wars of decolonization (425).

The conundrum that Robbins and Stamatopoulou point to is that the principle of the self-determination of peoples can empower ethnic nationalism, thereby undoing the UN's emphasis on citizenship rights. The claim for self-determination sometimes attached to the calls for group rights could have the effect of spurring ethnic nationalism and emboldening those who would force their dream of ethnic purity upon a heterogeneous population. In other contexts, human rights discourse can be invoked and human rights politics pursued in the interests of ethnic nationalism, as Shih Chih-yu illuminates in his discussion of contemporary rights politics in Taiwan and the Kou Ming Tang construction and promotion of an "indigenous" Taiwanese identity distinct from any transnational "Chinese" identity. The pursuit of human rights can be framed as the pursuit of an ethnic national identity, and thus more about identity politics in particular

---

[6]   As a way of moving forward and more effectively adjudicating claims based on group rights, Robbins and Stamatopoulou call for the careful disentangling of invocations of the right of self-determination of peoples and more targeted invocations of cultural rights.

national contexts and less about "universal" concepts of human rights
(146).

Calls for group rights attend the material effects and the affective
energies associated with the politics of difference within the contemporary
nation-state. Claims on behalf of the group gain their moral force and
ethical charge through the stories told by victims and witnesses to ethnic
suffering. The voice of the witness becomes the voice of group memory.
And the authority of the voice derives from the claim to first-person
knowledge and experience of suffering. That is, the power of the claim
comes from the subject position of "the victim" as constituted by human
rights discourse and law. And here is yet another conundrum associated
with the pursuit of ethnic grievance through the circuits of the regime of
human rights. Victims of an assault on ethnic difference and particularity
make claims through recourse to the discourses of abstract universality.
Through the contemporary human rights regime, victims of violence
incited by ethnic nationalism and their advocates contest the power of the
nation-state to violate the "universal" rights of members of groups
identified through ethnicity.

Finally, the institutions and mechanisms of grievance, adjudication, and
redress are themselves implicated in this larger tension between the rights
of individuals and the rights of people in collectivities. To clarify this
tension, I invoke an exemplary situation of rights practice we cited in
Human Rights and Narrated Lives. When Japanese Americans sought
reparative justice through the U.S. Congress for their internment during
World War II, they sought to argue their case *as a group* on the grounds of
systemic and structural ethnic discrimination. At the Tribunal, lawyers for
the claimants tried to introduce social and systemic arguments concerning
long-term discrimination of one group (the Japanese American plaintiffs
who had been interned during the War) by another group (the American
government). Tribunal officials excluded these arguments, however; and
plaintiff lawyers had instead to present their plaintiffs in purely legal terms
as individuals seeking individual damages. In this process, individual
plaintiffs could not tell stories of differential war experiences, or claim
differential reparations. Paradoxically, then, those individuals making
claims before the Tribunal had to present themselves at once as individuals
and as "representatives" of the group, and mount a case that effaced the
differential experiences of individuals within the group. In other words,
only certain kinds of stories of injustice could be told and legitimated
within the Tribunal's terms of reference. On the one hand, Japanese
Americans won their case and gained reparations because, as Eric
Yamamoto contends, they were able to frame their case tightly within the
American law/Enlightenment paradigm of individual rights (493, 498). On
the other hand, rather than challenging universal principles that exclude

differences, these processes strengthened the political integrity and efficacy of a system of law that the claims themselves contested.

This case of personal storytelling in the regime of human rights suggests how it is that life narration reproduces, is animated by, and contributes to the paradoxes at the heart of human rights discourse and practice: the uneasy enfolding of the universal in the ethnic particular. Elicited, framed, produced, circulated, and received within the contemporary regime of human rights, the life story of ethnic suffering at once ennobles an authentic (and sentimentalized) voice of suffering and depersonalizes that voice, precisely because of the commodification of suffering in the global flows of the human rights regime. Emerging from a local site of ethnic struggle, the story enters the Western-dominated global circuits through which it can lose its local specificity. It can reach global audiences far from its point of origin, there to be interpreted and reproduced in ways that universalize suffering and elide difference.

The story of *Zlata's Diary* offers us a case in point for considering these irresolvable tensions.

Zlata's Diary and the Ethics of Ethnic Identities

Reflecting on the dynamic relay between the ethnic, the national, and the diasporic, Ien Ang notes that "the rise of militant, separatist neo-nationalisms in Eastern Europe and elsewhere in the world signals an intensification of the appeal of ethnic absolutism and exclusionism which underpin the homeland myth, and which is based on the fantasy of a complete juncture of 'where you're from' and 'where you're at'" (34). She notes, as have Robbins and Stamatopoulou, the power of "the principle of nationalist universalism," or what she describes as "the fantasmatic vision of a new world *order* consisting of hundreds of self-contained, self-identical nations" (Ang 34). The struggle to enforce this new world order was dramatically and traumatically witnessed in the events in the former Yugoslavia in the 1990s. In the midst of the "new Europe," the people of the former Yugoslavia found themselves the subjects of salient ethnicities.

In the wake of President Tito's death and the loss of Soviet hegemony in Eastern Europe, the former Yugoslavia fractured into ethnic and (tenuously) multi-ethnic states. Croatia and Slovenia declared independence in 1991. In early March of 1992, the government of Bosnia-Hercegovina held a referendum on independence from the Yugoslav federation (dominated by Serbia), which was boycotted by the Bosnian Serbs. The Bosnia parliament declared independence on April 5, 1992. Before official recognition of the decision by the European Community on

April 6th, however, wars for ethnic dominance and hegemony erupted in Bosnia. Successionist Serb paramilitaries armed and launched their bid to gain control of the new country for annexation to the Republic of Serbia. Immediately, the city of Sarajevo came under siege, one that would last until a cease-fire went into effect in late 1995. Inhabitants of the mountain-surrounded, multi-ethnic city of Sarajevo, which had gained the world's attention when it hosted the international athletes and spectators of the 1984 Olympic Games, found themselves trapped inside the blockaded city, forced to organize their everyday lives so as to evade sniper bullets and mortar attacks and to find scarce food and medical supplies. Bosnian Serb paramilitaries, supported by Slobadan Milosevic in the Republic of Serbia, pursued a policy of genocide ("ethnic cleansing") for which they are now being held accountable in the international war crimes trials at the Hague. By early 1994 the United Nations reported that some 10,000 people had lost their lives or gone missing, among them 1,500 children; another 56,000 had been wounded, including 15,000 children.[7] Eventually, the international community intervened, taking action against the besieging Serbs. As the Serbian paramilitaries lost ground, peace negotiations gained momentum. In October 1995, the United Nations brokered a cease-fire in Bosnia; in December the Dayton Accords were signed, establishing the blueprint for post-war stability, involving two autonomous governmental entities, the Federation of Bosnia and Herzegovina (or the Muslim-Croat Federation) and the Republika Srpska. In late February of 1996 the Bosnian government declared the siege of Sarajevo officially over.

Throughout the four-year siege, journalists assigned to Sarajevo reported on the realities of life lived under siege, the deaths of non-combatants, and devastation of the city and its infrastructure. They brought their stories of the siege to an international public. Yet foreign journalists were not the only ones to provide stories of ethnic cleansing and ethnicity under assault to the wider world. Slatko Dizdarevici's *Sarajevo: A War Journal* (1993) chronicled the early years of the siege. Then in late 1993 another personal story reached an international audience, this one the diary of a young girl.

For a two-year period from September 1991 to October 1993, the young Zlata Filipovici kept a diary in which she recorded her everyday life in an increasingly besieged Sarajevo. Through her diaristic record of that everyday life, the young Bosnian-Croat described, and sometimes reflected upon, the disintegration of a cosmopolitan way of life and the gradual disruption and degradation of middle class familiality through the war of

---

[7]   See the Final report of the United Nations Commission of Experts established pursuant to security council resolution 780 (1992) submitted May 27, 1994, on the UN report see website http://www.ess.uwe.ac.uk/comexpert/ANX/VI-01.htm#I.C Accessed August 15, 2004.

ethnic nationalisms and the genocidal assault of Bosnian Serb paramilitaries. In the summer of 1993, Zlata shared her diary with her teacher, who subsequently found a publisher in Sarajevo. Through the sponsorship of the International Centre for Peace, the diary was originally published in Croat by UNICEF. With the recognition of the diary in Bosnia, Zlata became a "celebrity" victim, labeled "the young Anne Frank" of Sarejevo. Recognizing the affective appeal and power of personalizing the story of the siege through its refraction in the eyes of the young girl, international journalists covering the war turned their attention to "Zlata's" story.

Several months after its publication in Sarajevo, a French photographer took a copy of Zlata's diary to Paris where Le Robert Laffont-Fixot made a successful bid to become its French publisher. Le Robert Laffont-Fixot also provided the money and means to fly Zlata and her family from Sarajevo to Paris just before Christmas of 1993. In early 1994 the French translation of the diary appeared as *Journal de Zlata*. In this instance, life writing functioned as a means of life saving. The material diary became a commodity through which a life's sheer survival and betterment could be exchanged. Zlata's diary writing gained her and her family escape from snipers and the bombs of the siege and enabled her to start a new life in Paris (and subsequently Ireland).

From Paris the diary traveled to New York City where it was auctioned off in a sale conducted by its French publisher. With a bid of $560,000, Viking Penguin (a subsidiary of Penguin Books) won the rights to publish *Zlata's Diary: A Child's Life* in-Sarajevo and did so in March of 1994. After publication in the U.S., the diary began to reach an ever-widening mass audience. Irene Webb of International Creative Management subsequently bought the rights to represent the book in any movie deal. As reported in the New York Times, January 19, 1994, Webb announced: "It's like the '*Diary of Anne Frank*,' but with a happy ending" (C20). Upon publication, the English language version of the diary circulated broadly within the United States, becoming "an extraordinary national best seller," according to the book cover. Eventually it moved into the social studies curricula in the nation's public schools. As one website announces: "Zlata's diary brings Sarajevo home as no news report ever could." (The Unsung Heroes of Dialogue).

In the years after the diary's publication, Zlata became a "spokeschild" for the conditions of ethnic genocide and displacement in the former Yugoslavia, appearing through the auspices of the United Nations as an ambassador speaking on behalf of the children of Bosnia. International attention brought increased interest in the conditions in the former Yugoslavia and, after the cessations of fighting, in the rights of the child internationally. In 1995 Zlata appeared as a special guest at the 1995

Children's World Peace Festival in San Francisco. The attention garnered by the diary and its circulation within the United States and Europe produced an aura-effect around Zlata herself, elevating her and legimating her as a "universal" voice of the child suffering from human rights abuses. Since those years, Zlata has continued as an activist on behalf of the human rights of children, helping to launch UNICEF reports on the impact of armed conflict on children. Her diary continues to be highlighted as suggested reading on websites mounted by activists working on behalf of the UN Convention on the Rights of the Child. During the summer of 2004, a stage version of *Zlata's Diary* produced by Communicado Productions toured Scotland. Though no longer a child, Zlata continues to speak on behalf of besieged childhood from her home in Dublin.

Reflections on this Story of Suffering Ethnicity:
Inter-ethnic appeals and the production of collective memory

Through the publication of the diary in the west, "Zlata" becomes a marketable archetype of the suffering victim of ethnic nationalism in extremis. The publication of her story of lost childhood, of innocence under assault, is meant to lend immediacy to calls for intervention on the part of the international community in the ethnic war in Bosnia and the organized acts of genocide enacted in service to nationalist myths and the nationalist "fantasy of a utopic space to be occupied by all those who suffered 'the same' violence at the hands of the enemy.[8] And yet, the case of *Zlata's Diary* suggests how interethnic the appeal to ethnicity under assault becomes.

Within Zlata's dairy and within its zones of circulation and reception, Jewish ethnicity comes to underwrite the aura of suffering of a largely unmarked Croatian ethnicity. Here is an instance in which one ethnicity gets attached to another ethnicity globalized in world memory through a particular mode of life writing, the child's diary. Zlata herself invokes the comparison to Anne Frank early in her *Diary*. Like Anne Frank she chooses a name for her diary. Writing on Monday, March 30, 1992, she opens her entry with "Hey, Diary! You know what I think? Since Anne Frank called her diary Kitty, maybe I could give you a name too" (27). In all subsequent entries she addresses the diary as "Mimmy," projecting an affectionate and interested interlocutor and keeper of Zlata's secrets. Moreover, already in 1993 in Sarajevo, Zlata at thirteen was called "the

---

[8]   Wilson here cites the work of Glenn Bowman and his discussion of the ways in which "the narrating of past mass violations plays a constitutive role in the formation of all nationalisms" (Wilson 16). Wilson does not give a reference for the Bowman paper.

young Anne Frank," (v of introduction). The identification of Zlata's story with the story of Anne Frank, its modeling upon the earlier text, its adoption of the earlier diarist's mode of address to an interlocutor; all these citations suggest the way in which the truth effects of this contemporary girl, this "Zlata," derive from the earlier editing and marketing of "Anne Frank" as a figure of universalized innocence and heroic suffering whose celebrity can be borrowed in making claims about the struggle against racial violence and ethnic cleansing.

In Zlata's self-positioning in her diary as a modern-day Anne Frank and in the marketing of "Zlata" as a new "Anne Frank," both narrator and marketer assume the global resonance of the iconic figure of Anne Frank, assume that "Anne Frank" will be collectively remembered as having been tragically lost in the Holocaust. The affective appeal of the Sarajevan girl's story of lost childhood becomes intelligible to a broad educated readership through the global aftereffects of collective world memory of another "ethnic" girl's narrative of lost girlhood and lost life. The haunting remains of "Anne Frank," and the aura of the Holocaust as paradigmatic event of 20th century genocide, attaches itself to this "child's" narrative as Zlata and her publishers attach her story to that of Anne Frank, who has through her widely read *Diary*, as the website for the Anne Frank Foundation puts it, "In this instance, Jewish ethnicity functions as an ethnicity of reference in the globalization of the human rights regime."

This aspect of the production and circulation of *Zlata's Diary* within the regime of human rights points to ethnic remembering and storytelling as an historical effect of trans-ethnic comparisons; an interethnic energy distributed across unevenly remembered events in world memory. The forces of globalization, Clifford Bob notes, offer victims and activists responding to ethnic violence "symbols of oppression and repertoires of contention" through which to organize and project their local grievances in an international arena (134). Brent Edwards argues that "the level of the international is accessed unevenly by subjects with different historical relations to the nation" (7). I would adapt his argument to make the point that the level of the transnational is assessed unevenly by ethnic subjects with different historical relations to the global circuits of world memory.

The depoliticization of a globalized ethnic suffering.

In her critique of the sentimentalization of suffering, Karyn Ball has called for the comparative study of traumatic histories, in order, she writes, "to forge links among traumatic histories that would raise Americans' historical consciousness and promote their sense of civic responsibility" (15). Ball's is a call for comparative studies of histories of suffering, necessary to complicating any one model of traumatic remembering, any one paradigm for understanding witness testimony, and any singular model of possibilities for recovery and recognition. In one sense we might read *Zlata's Diary* as pursuing, at once consciously and unwittingly, that "strategy of comparison in order to forge links among traumatic histories" by yoking "Zlata" and "Anne Frank." Here is a strategy of comparison in action. And yet, this strategy of comparison from the ground up as it were, and through the perspective of an adolescent immersed in a globalized popular culture dominated by the cultural hegemony of the United States, may not so much illuminate the incommensurable differences and the specificities of ethnic histories; but may have the effect of flattening history through an appeal to empathetic, de-politicized sentimentality.

As a text commanding response and responsible action, Zlata's diary is represented and marketed in ways that sentimentalize the suffering Bosnian-Croat subject by lifting that subject outside history and politics. The commodification of stories of ethnic suffering obscures the complex politics of historical events, stylizes the story to suit an educated international audience familiar with narratives of individual triumph over adversity, evokes emotive responses trained on the feel-good qualities of successful resolution, and often universalizes the story of suffering so as to erase incommensurable differences and the horror of violence. The commodification of the young girl's diary gives us a version of the story of "Anne Frank"--but with a happy ending.

Yet there is more to the relationship established between the contemporary Zlata and the 1940s Anne Frank. The forces of commodification have framed the earlier diary as well. In successive decades since its initial publication, *The Diary of Anne Frank* has been edited and interpreted, reedited and reinterpreted, marketed and circulated, to give some of its audiences an "Americanized" "Anne Frank" situated not in a determinative ethnicity but situated as an adolescent subject inspiring hope and promise "for everyone." As an early reviewer of the stage version of the *Diary* wrote in 1955, "Anne Frank is a Little Orphan Annie brought into vibrant life" (New York *Daily News* October 6, qtd in Rosenfeld). Alvin H. Rosenfeld suggests that the early version of the diary and the 1955 stage play based on the diary adapted by Goodrich and Hackett present "an image of Anne Frank that would be widely acceptable to large numbers of people in the postwar period. . . . one characterized by such irrepressible hope and tenacious optimism as to overcome any final sense of a cruel end" (251-2). He further elaborates how the play and its reviews erase the haunting marks of ethnic difference, eliding references to the Jewishness of the Frank family and playing up the figure of the "universal" teenager, struggling with her own adolescence and hopeful about the future. The Jewish particularities of the Anne Frank who lived in the attic and died in Bergen Belsen are suppressed in order to broadcast a story of universal inspiration. Made into a story that "speaks" to "everyone" about what Hanno Loewy points to as "the personalized world of family experience" (156), the diary of Anne Frank becomes a story that can no longer speak of ethnic difference. The iconic "Anne Frank" becomes an abstract universal "detached from her own vivid sense of herself as a Jew" (Rosenfeld 257). Rosenfeld defines Anne Frank as a "contemporary cultural icon" (244), whose name is so well-known that "[t]o the world at large" the 1.5 million children who perished in the Holocaust "all bear one name—that of Anne Frank" (243).[9] "Anne Frank" has become the child that died in the genocidal Holocaust.

The production, circulation, and reception of Zlata's story of ethnicity under assault as "the deepest truth about the Bosnia situation" has had the effect of "leech[ing]," according to David Rieff, "the Bosnian tragedy of its complexity" (32). Given that ethnicity (and the global visibility and saliency of particular ethnic identifications) are historical effects of modernity set in motion with the articulation of universal categories of abstract equality (see Kazanjian 4-27; Eller XX), then the trackings of ethnicities enfolded in one another at once create a superfluity of the particularities of difference and cancel differences through the abstract equality (universalism) of those who share suffering. The figure of the child commodified in the global flows of the rights regime and its management of ethnicity becomes the sentimental public face of ethnic trauma and the violence of ethnic nationalism, the essentialized figure of the community's "victim" and its victimization. To put it another way, "Zlata," with her invocation of "Anne Frank," becomes "ethnicity's besieged child."

The remains of ethnic suffering

The commodification of ethnic suffering also contributes to the ethnic as a site of sentimental attachment. For members of communities experiencing contemporary displacement, ethnicity can function as a trace of continuity across rupture; and stories of ethnic suffering can offer occasions for constituting the remembered past as a resource for understanding identities in the social present (Eller XX). When Zlata's Diary enters into circuits of consumption in the U.S. and western Europe–

---

9   As Rosenfeld makes clear, "Anne Frank" is remembered differently in different communities at different historical moments. After analyzing the Americanization of "Anne Frank," he goes on to explore the reception of the diary by Germans and by Jewish writers and intellectuals. "[I]n both Germany and Israel one finds a common history marked by a common symbol but shaped by very different motives and yielding diverse interpretations of the past" (277).

through the purchase of the rights to publish and the film rights --the narrative begins to circulate in venues where it can be invoked as a marker of Croatian ethnicity under assault, or a lost Bosnian cosmopolitanism, thereby sustaining nationalist narratives of suffering and loss so often central to the imagination of the ethnic as a site of sentimental attachment. Because reading narratives of suffering and loss is not only "a profoundly personal act, belonging to a psychological sphere, but . . . also the effect of inhabiting various cultural spaces" (Bennett and Kennedy 7), published narratives such as this diary produce an archive of memories of "ethnicity." The story might thereby set in motion new releases of affective energies (Guattari 36); and those energies can be put to use in the social struggles over competing rememberings of "Bosnia" and its wars of ethnic nationalisms. This story can become a part of the cultural stories, the reservoir of collective memory upon which ethnic nationalism is both founded and sustained.

For some, then, Zlata's Diary participates in the production and circulation of new collective memories (for members of the diasporan Croation community in the US, for instance), offering a future site of melancholy, what David Eng and David Kazanjian defines as the "psychic and material practices of loss and its remains" (5). It puts in play residual glimpses of the past as remembered tradition of interethnic community or ethnic grievance. Contributing to "a contemporary landscape of memory" (Bennett and Kennedy 8) through which future subjects may negotiate their ethnic attachments and pasts, it may underwrite future historical grievances. This narrative of loss told through the voice of the "innocent" child becomes a site of melancholy which "creates a realm of traces open to signification, a hermeneutic domain of what remains of loss" (Eng and Kazanjian 4). The child becomes the sentimental public figure of ethnic trauma.

The universalized innocence of ethnic appeals

The marketing of Zlata as a victim/commentator on suffering ethnicity presents the young girl in the subject position of unassailable innocent. As Kay Schaffer and I note in Human Rights and Narrated Lives, some victims of human rights abuses are more easily equated with victimage than others; and the child is, as Hughes D'aeth suggests in his discussion of the film Rabbit Proof Fence, the most accessible, least complicated and readily believable of victim identities. In the context of human rights campaigns, life narrators are expected to take up the subject position of "innocent" victims; and they are expected to be able to occupy that position with moral authority. And yet, the person whose rights are violated cannot always be assumed to occupy the subject position of innocent victim. The marketing of sentimental suffering, especially through a child's eye narrative viewpoint and the trope of childhood lost, obscures the permeability of the categories of victim and perpetrator, and obscures the relationship of perpetrator to beneficiary. Such stories reinforce the differentiated identities of ethnic victim and ethnic perpetrator, reinforce rather than confuse the moral alignment of innocence and victimization. Begging the question of innocence in childhood, we might say that in human rights discourse and campaigns "the child" is given to speak for the better part of "ourselves," the better part of human nature, the better part of our community. Rieff, in his critique of *Zlata's Diary*, assails the way in which the child is made to speak wisdom, to be positioned as the voice of knowledge (33).[10]

The "innocence" effect is produced through Zlata's self-conscious invocation of the trope of lost childhood and her shifting terms of reference. Within her diary, Zlata is self conscious about the importance of her narrative, its possible attraction to others. She even writes about becoming a "personality" after the initial publication of the diary. And once interest is expressed in her diary, she begins to reflect on the situation in Sarajevo in rather poignant ways. Zlata's self-consciousness about her celebrity and her recognition of her role as representative child of Sarajevo emphasizing the tragedy of "lost childhood" (a discourse that comes from the journalists and advocates who take up her story) undoes the truth effect of "innocent child" and the "child's eye view" otherwise produced through diary. Already, within the production of the diary, the politics of commodified sentimentality is evident.

The innocent effect is also reinforced through the packaging of *Zlata's Diary* and the paratextual use of photographs which visualize the young girls' story as a sentimentalized drama of lost childhood. One photograph in particular captures "innocence" and the "production of innocence" at the same time. There is a photo of Zlata in bed, framed by the caption: "Zlata, who loves books, reads by candlelight." To get the picture for mass distribution through global media, the candlelight has to be photographed; photographed, it is overwhelmed and rendered inauthentic by the light from the flash of the bulb. Through such visuals, the authenticity of sentimental childhood is at once produced and exposed as artificial, as the reviewer for *Newsweek* Magazine noted (27). My point here is not that the diary is "inauthentic" or "suspect" as witness testimony. It is, rather, to point to the

---

[10] Rieff also indicts the way she is made to speak as a commentator on behalf of Bosnia innocence. Comparing the versions of the diary published in Paris and in the United States and the interpolations added to the Viking Penguin edition, he notes the addition of references to political events and critiques of the leaders and their antics (33-4).

commercialization of the diary and its capture in what Lauren Berlant has described as sentimental politics, here a politics of the ethical (soliciting response and responsibility across social divides) that obscures the difficult politics of histories of difference and violence. We see here the modernist project of producing the authority of universalized innocence.

Saving whose child

The paratextual apparatus of the "introduction" to the diary enlists the reader in action in response to this child witness and her story. In her preface, journalist Janine di Giovanni orients the reader to the text to come, prompting the reader to adopt an activist stance. She writes: "Zlata kept a careful record of the chilling events-the deaths, the mutilations, the sufferings. When we read her diaries, we think of desperation, of confusion and of innocence lost, because a child should not be seeing, should not be living with this kind of horror. Her tragedy becomes our tragedy because we know what is happening in Sarajevo. And still, we do not act" (xii). Di Giovanni establishes a reading praxis that foregrounds the figure of the innocent child and the trope of innocence lost, orienting a global middle-class readership to the "representative" story of all the suffering children of Sarajevo.

Di Giovanni assumes an adult audience implicated, as surrogate parents, in this tragedy. The journalist can address these readers as passive bystanders to massive human suffering. For the journalist introducing the narrative to the western reader, the point is to prompt the affect of shame. Here, as elsewhere in the era of humanitarianism and human rights, images of children and lost childhoods are invoked to shame individuals, communities, nations, and that imagined "international community" into action. Those images become invitations to rescue. And the reader is addressed as the universal parent, called to respond as the parent of all children. The diary and its paratext shift the register of appeal from the particularity of the ethnic subject under duress to the universal abstraction of the child of human rights. But the appeal of "the child" in need of saving is that the child is everybody's child and thus nobody's specific child, living in a specific location.

There is yet another large audience for Zlata's Diary, other young people in classrooms in Europe and the United States. An "innocent" victim of and witness to ethnicity besieged, Zlata writes from her location within a middle-class family. And her diary is marketed to a broad middle-class readership educated about, familiar with, and prepared to respond to stories of childhood suffering. The published version includes a cast of family characters and a photo album, with images of the wholesome, open-faced, smiling Zlata, a figure of the innocent child tugging on the sympathies of the reader. The home is middle-class, the occasions of the photos birthday parties and family outings. The photo album appeals to western readers – both adults and children, presenting a home and a family the educated reader can imagine inhabiting.

Throughout the diary, Zlata's citation of global popular culture resonates in its references with the lives of young people in Western Europe and the United States. The constant citation of a global popular culture (a popular culture whose primary though by no means whole point of reference is the US) situates the subject of the diary in a non-differentiated space of consumer adolescence and global youth culture. In this, Zlata is "representative" of a commodified and "universal" adolescent subject knowledgeable about and attentive to the products, icons, celebrities, and self-descriptions of the global marketplace. As she interweaves comments on the common references of global youth culture and the trope of childhood lost, Zlata assumes the subject position of the universal middle-class child anxious about childhood itself.[11]

The international community looked on, watched the war in Bosnia on nightly news, and failed to take decisive action to intervene in the early years of the seige. *Zlata's Diary* made, and continues to make, good reading in the social studies courses of US and European classrooms. But as Thomas Keenan argues so persuasively in his exploration of the mutually constituting intersection of endless images of suffering and political inaction, "images, information, and knowledge will never guarantee any outcome, nor will they force or drive any action. They are, in that sense, like weapons or words: a condition, but not a sufficient one" (114). And yet, Zlata herself gained stature as a spokesperson for the UN's covenant on the rights of the child. She and her story continue to spur occasions for children from around the world to connect through organized and on-line activities. In this, Zlata and her diary have participated in and contributed to a new arena of human rights activism.

And yet, to turn the argument around once again: As Lisa Makman has observed, children themselves have now become the crusading upholders of the rights of the child to a childhood perceived by increasing numbers of people in industrialized democracies as under assault. Makman tracks recent UN discourse about "the world's children" and attributes this focus on childhood under assault to cultural anxieties, circulating in the mainstream media in the United States, about the "ero[sion]" of a

---

[11] Stuart Hall has cautioned that cultural formations may work in contradictory ways. There is at once the force of homogenization and universalization across national and ethnic differences through appeals to global mass culture. There is also the incorporation and reflection back through global mass culture of the specific context of ethnic difference and its histories of suffering (Hall 32). I recognize I am overstating the former case here.

"universal" innocent childhood due to the influences of new technologies and global media (289, 291)   Through the commodification of stories of ethnic suffering and the sentimentalized "channels of affective identification and empathy" (Berlant 53), ethnicity's besieged child is becoming the universally besieged child of a universally besieged childhood.

Conclusion

As a marker of identity and difference, ethnicity is an effect of modernity rather than a residue from the past prior to modernity. Ethnicity, Jack David Eller suggests, is "a radical appropriation and application of otherness to the practical domain" (XX). Thus, modernity involves what Rey Chow describes as "the systematic *codification and management of ethnicity*" (11). The contemporary regime of human rights is a primary site for this project of codification and management. In human rights campaigns targeted on ethnic rights in the midst of ethnic nationalism in extremis, ethnicity has to be "managed" as immobile difference through a modernist fiction of a totalizing ethnicity (a definitive inside to a collectivity) under assault from an outside (see Chow). Moreover, human rights discourse and campaigns are responses to, and in turn engage in, the production of salient ethnicities and ethnicities of reference.

This case study of *Zlata's Diary* and the problematics of ethnic suffering exposes the "logical contradictions" and "epistemic paradoxes" (Kader 14) enfolded within and enfolding the production, circulation, and reception of personal narratives in the regime of human rights. Abstract universality and ethnic difference are both "mythographic reductions" at once underwriting, energizing, and reconfiguring the human rights regime. Through the pathways and byways of global circuits localized and local circuits globalized, the tensions binding abstract universality and ethnic difference release energies that reconnect, diverge, and converge around the international community's struggle with injustice and suffering. I have used *Zlata's Diary* to reflect on the circuits of ethnicity as sentimental politics in the regime of human rights. And so let me conclude with some observations about the conjunction of the human rights regime and narrations of suffering ethnicity.

Narratives enlisted in and attached to human rights campaigns participate in the articulation of a history of suffering and loss attached to ethnic identity and the articulation of communal fictions of ethnicity (imaginings and grievances). Narratives of suffering and loss bind communities sharing some common "ethnic" past (or language, culture, defining events), across their local, national, and diasporic differences at the same time that they appeal to others who do not share that ethnic marker. They provide historical information, intergenerational communication, rallying cries, sites of healing. They offer a means to claim rights and demand redress, and also to claim a shared past and shared tradition. They ignite an affective charge attached to identity under assault, project a figure of victimage for political mobilization, and serve as a means of shaming the nation and the international community into acknowledging and redressing claims. Because they are so critical to the contemporary regime of human rights, stories such as that presented in *Zlata's Diary* become cultural capital, for individuals and for ethnic communities. Sometimes the publication and circulation of a specific narrative becomes a "focusing event" (Bob 136, citing Kingdon 99-100) that galvanizes international attention and action, as was the case with Rigoberta Menchú's *I Rigoberta Menchu: An Indian Woman in Guatemala* which gained recognition of the situation of Guatemala's indigenous community in their struggle against a repressive state.[12]

Emanating from local settings that are inflected by and inflect the global, life stories are taken up in a host of different, formal and informal, material and symbolic, sites and networks where they undergo further transformations. In effect, narratives of suffering such as *Zlata's Diary* are produced, circulated, and received within an intricate, uneven, and overlapping set of spheres: the local, the national, the regional, the global. They also travel within overlapping, uneven, and intersecting zones of ethnic identification and affiliation: the diasporic, the transethnic; the national ethnic, and the local ethnic–all heterogeneous zones of identification and historical tracings differently located, differently accessed. Moreover, such stories, as we have seen, unfold through and enfold overlapping, uneven, and contradictory appeals to ethnic singularity and abstract universality at once.

Finally, commodified narratives of suffering ethnicity enter a global field saturated with multiple modes of appeal and cues to interpretation. They reach for readers/viewers/the public, calling that public into definition (as a middle-class public of parents and children; as an ethnic public of dispersed Bosnia Croat refugees). As with all such appeals, suggests Thomas Keenan, "the public is the possibility of being a target and of being missed" (108).

---

[12] For an extended discussion of the publication and reception of Menchu's narrative, see Smith and Schaffer (29-31).

Note

I have adapted the discussion of the "three generations" of human rights from an early draft of a co-authored chapter (subsequently eliminated) for my recent book *Human Rights and Narrated Lives: The Ethics of Recognition*, co-authored with Kay Schaffer. I am also indebted to Kay for her comments on certain aspects of the framing and marketing of *Zlata's Diary*. I am also indebted to John Cords for his research assistance.

Works Cited

Anaya, S James. *Indigenous Peoples in International Law*. New York: Oxford University Press, 1996.

---. "Indigenous Peoples and Their Demands within the Modern Human Rights Movement." *The Universal Declaration*. Ed. Topoulou Elsa Stama Yael Danieli. Amityville: Baywood, 1999. 149-61.

Ang, Ien. *On Not Speaking Chinese: Living between Asia and the West*. London: Routledge, 2001.

Anne Frank Foundation. *Responsibilities of the Anne Frank-Fonds* webpage. Available: www.annefrank.ch/content/default.htm. Accessed September 15, 2004.

Ball, Karyn. "Trauma and Its Institutional Destinies." *Cultural Critique* 46.Fall (2000): 1-44.

Bennett, Jill, and Roseanne Kennedy. *World Memory: Personal Trajectories in Global Time*. London: Palgrave, 2003.

Berlant, Lauren. "The Subject of True Feeling: Pain, Privacy, and Politics." *Cultural Pluralism, Identity Politics, and the Law*. Eds. Austin Sasat and Thomas R. Kearns. Ann Arbor: University of Michigan Press, 1999. 49-84.

Bob, Clifford. "Globalization and the Social Construction of Human Rights Campaigns." *Globalization and Human Rights*. Ed. Alison Brysk. Berkeley: University of California Press, 2002. 133-47.

Chow, Rey. "Introduction: On Chineseness as a Theoretical Problem." *Boundary 2* 25.3 (1998): 1-24.

Dizdarevi, Slatko. *Sarajevo: A War Journal*. Trans. Anselm Hollo. Ney York: Fromm International, 1993.

Downey, John K. "Suffering as Common Ground." *Constructing Human Rights in the Age of Globalization*. Ed. Mahmood Monshipouri, et al. Armonk, NY: M. E. Sharpe, 2003. 308-27.

Edwards, Brent. *The Practice of Diaspora: Literature, Translation, and the Rise of*

Black Internationalism. Cambridge: Harvard UP, 2003.

Eller, Jack David. "Ethnicity, Culture, and "the Past"." *Michigan Quarterly Review* 36.4 (1997): 552-601.

Eng, David L. and David Kazanjian. *Loss: The Politics of Mourning.* Berkeley: University of California, 2003.

Filipovici, Zlata. *Zlata's Diary: A Child's Life in Sarajevo.* New York and London: Penguin, 1994.

Guattari, Félix. *The Three Ecologies.* Trans. Ian Pindar, and Paul Sutton. London: Athlone, 2000.

Hall, Stuart. "The Local and the Global: Globalization and Ethnicity." *Culture, Globalization, and the World-System: Contemporary Conditions for the Representation of Identity.* Ed. Anthony D. King. Minneapolis: University of Minnesota, 1997.

Hughes D'aeth, Tony. *Which Rabbit-Proof Fence? Empathy, Assimilation, Hollywood.* Sept. 2002. Australian Humanities Review. Available: http://www.lib.latrobe.edu.au/AHR/archive/Issue-September-2002/hughesdaeth.htm. 4 June 2003.

Ignatieff, Michael. *Human Rights as Politics and Idolatry.* Princeton: Princeton University Press, 2001.

Kadir, Djelal. "Introduction: America and Its Studies." <u>PMLA</u> 118.1 (2003): 9-24.

Kazanjian, David. *The Colonizing Trick: National Culture and Imperial Citizenship in Early America.* Minneapolis: U of Minnesota, 2003.

Keenan, Thomas. "Publicity and Indifference (Sarajevo on Television)." *PMLA* 117.1 (2002): 104-16.

Kingdon, John. *Agendas, Alternatives, and Public Policies.* New York: Harper-Collins, 1984, 2d ed.

Loewy, Hanno. "Saving the Child: The "Universalisation" of Anne Frank." Trans. Russell West. *Marginal Voices, Marginal Forms: Diaries in European Literature and History.* Ed. Rachael Langford, and Russell West. Amsterdam: Rodopi, 1999. 156-74.

Lyall, Sarah. "Auction of a War Diary." *New York Times* January 19 1994, sec. C: 20+.

Makman, Lisa Hermine. "Child Crusaders: The Literature of Global Childhood." *The Lion and the Unicorn* 26 (2002): 287-304.

Mench'u, Rigoberta. *I, Rigoberta Menchú: An Indian Woman in Guatemala.* London and New York: Verso, 1984.

New York Daily News October 6, 1955 1955.

Newsweek Magazine. "Child of War: The Diary of Zlata Filipovic." February 28 1994: 24-27.

Rieff, David. "Youth and Consequences: *Zlata's Diary*: A Child's Life in Sarajevo." *The New Republic* March 28 1994: 31-35.

Robbins, Bruce and Elsa Stamatopoulou. "Reflections on Culture and Cultural Rights." *The South Atlantic Quarterly* 103.2/3 (2004): 419-34.

Rosenfeld, Alvin H. "Popularization and Memory: The Case of Anne Frank." *Lessons and Legacies: The Meaning of the Holocaust in a Changing World*. Ed. Peter Hayes. Evanston: Northwestern UP, 1991. 243-78.

Schaffer, Kay and Sidonie Smith. *Human Rights and Narrated Lives: The Ethics of Recognition*. New York: Palgrave Macmillan, 2004.

Shih Chih-yu. "Human Rights as Identities: Difference and Discrimination in Taiwan's China Policy." *Debating Human Rights: Critical Essays from the United States and Asia*. Ed. Peter Van Ness. London: Routledge, 1999. 144-63.

Umozurike, A. *Self-Determination in International Law*. Hamden, CN: Archon Books, 1972.

United Nations. *Final Report of the United Nations Commission of Experts*. 1994. webpage. August 15 2004.

The Unsung Heroes of Dialogue. webpage. Available: www.un.org/Dialogue/heroes.htm. February 10 2004.

Whitlock, Gillian. *The Intimate Empire: Reading Women's Autobiography*. London: Cassell, 2000.

Wilson, Richard A. "The Sizwe Will Not Go Away: The Truth and Reconciliation Commission, Human Rights and Nation-Building in South Africa." *African Studies* 55.2 (1996): 1-20.

Yamamoto, Eric K. "Racial Reparations: Japanese American Redress and African American Claims." *Boston College Law Review* 40.1 (1998): 477-523.

PIRJO AHOKAS

Constructing a Transnational, Postmodern Female Identity in
Bharati Mukherjee's *Desirable Daughters* and Monica Ali's *Brick
Lane*

   The increasing volume of novels by diasporic South Asian women
writers living in Britain and the United States is a relatively new
phenomenon. These novels are written within a global context dominated
by the West and reflect the impact of massive postcolonial population
migration. Two examples of this trend are Bharati Mukherjee's Desirable
Daughters (2002) and Monica Ali's Brick Lane (2003). In Mukherjee's and
Ali's novels, the diasporic female protagonists try to utilize cultural
hybridity, the fusion of cultures and cross-cultural influences, in order to
challenge their gender and "race" oppression. In both cases, this is achieved
by creating a fictional space in which marginalized and displaced female
protagonists struggle to gain control over their lives.
   The Indian-born American author Bharati Mukherjee is part of a group
of female South Asian writers who began publishing their work in the
1970s and 1980s. Much of her previous fiction depicts the transformations
of alienated immigrant women in their isolated new environments. The
fictional protagonist of Desirable Daughters, Mukherjee's sixth novel, is
Tara Chatterjee, a divorced Bengali Brahmin1 woman living in the United
States. The second author to be discussed, the Oxbridge-educated Monica
Ali, was born in Bangladesh and raised in Britain. The protagonist of her
highly acclaimed debut novel Brick Lane is Nazneen, a young girl who
moves to London from a village in Bangladesh. Both Mukherjee's and Ali's
protagonists try to forge new and more viable identities in their respective
adopted countries by challenging the traditional, passive and docile notions
of female identity prevalent in their countries of origin. As diasporic
migrants who maintain various forms of contact with their home countries,
these protagonists are able to enact transnational identities. Ultimately,
these transnational identities challenge the initial binary of "home" and
"abroad" and prove conducive to the emergence of postmodern female
subjectivities characterized by fluidity, multiplicity and heterogeneity.
   In this essay, I will trace Tara and Nazneen's contrasting responses to
the process of constructing and enacting a transnational, postmodern
female identity. This will be done by examining how the intersecting

---

[1]   Indrani Mitra points out that "Brahmin" is Mukerjees novelistic code for the upper
   class or caste. Mitra 290, 296.

discourses of gender, "race," and class function in this process. In my reading of the novels, I will draw on anti-racist and critically transnational feminisms as well as on recent theories of performativity. While various kinds of identity politics which arose in the 1970s engendered a hierarchy of oppressions and often carried with them the promise of a unified, fully realized subjectivity (Grewal 232), today's critical approaches help question fixed identity constructions and can shed light on different aspects of identity as mutually constitutive.

In a variety of ways, Mukherjee's and Ali's novels correlate with the emerging postmodern discourse on difference which, according to black British feminists, has opened up the possibility of a new "feminism of difference" (Mirza 19). Instead of valorizing difference as oppression and asserting identity as an end in itself (Aziz 75), the new feminism of difference celebrates difference as enriching, and urges marginalized women "to incorporate both the deconstruction of subjectivity and the political necessity of asserting identity" (Aziz 77). While defying the constraints of identity politics, recent writings by American feminists of color-and those by proponents of transnational feminist practices alike-deconstruct totalizing forms of female subjectivity and emphasize the emergence of oppositional subject positions within a global context. In Mukherjee's and Ali's novels, the undermining of totalizing forms of female subjectivity is connected to cultural hybridity, which, even through conflict and at risk, is potentially transformative. Moreover, the ongoing process of self-definition is partly linked to continuous cultural hybridization, which is a historically nonfinalized process shaped not only by diasporic experiences, but also by the political mobilization of difference (Rassool 202-203, Shohat 10).

The new identities in Desirable Daughters and Brick Lane are also forged in the context of the genre of postcolonial fiction, which has recently undergone significant changes. Dominic Head has noted a new phase in postcolonial migrant literature in Britain, in which a sense of meaningful hybridity has replaced the sense of disabling failure (Head 107-108). Homi K. Bhabha's "hybrid" concept has also been adopted by a number of other scholars of the recent British and American postcolonial writing tradition in their articulation of an empowering notion of global boundary crossings and transnational linkages across time and space. Hence, for Mukherjee's and Ali's gendered and racialized protagonists, cultural hybridity serves as an enabling survival strategy which signifies change and agency.

Diaspora and Homing Desire

Literary critics typically point out Mukherjee's enthusiastic celebration of assimilation into the white American mainstream culture as well as her wish to be viewed "as an American writer in the tradition of other American writers whose parents and grandparents had passed through Ellis Island" (qtd. in Alessandrini 268). While several of Mukherjee's critics point out that her idea of America depends upon an almost constant enactment of hybridity based upon the freedom of a newcomer to maximise her or his opportunities while in the host country (Stoneham 83), many also argue that her portrayal of the development of migrant subjects is problematic because of the relative ease with which these subjects make their cultural transitions (Nyman 54). Brinda Bose's emphasis on the multi-layered construction of postcolonial female identity in the adopted country is useful, because it calls attention to what is glossed over in Mukherjee's fiction. Although Desirable Daughters differs from the author's previous novels in its portrayal of the contemporary process of globalization, one can still interpret the novel using Bose's viewpoint concerning the initial transformation of the earlier female protagonists. Bose writes: "I am assuming that there are two levels of marginality that we are dealing with here: the marginal protagonist, in terms of where she comes from, and the marginality of what she does not say, in terms of her covering up anxieties in order to fit more easily into the new life" (50). Referring to Gayatri Spivak's modified theory of the marginal as a place of argument and critical moment, Bose goes on to explain that both levels of marginality in Mukherjee's work need to be read not only as opposed to the center but also as an accomplice of the center (50). This notion of marginalization allows keen insight into the complexity and ambiguity of Tara's construction of a new identity in Desirable Daughters.

After the abolition of immigration quotas in 1965, Indian immigrants to the United States came to be viewed as urban, college-educated skilled professionals, who took advantage of the English colonial education system in the subcontinent (Katrak 194).2 In Desirable Daughters, Tara Chatterjee and Bish, her ex-husband, are fictional representatives of this so-called "second wave" of South Asian immigration to California. Postcolonial scholars tend to link the histories of modernity and colonialism, acknowledging the transnational effects of post modernity on the global economy. Not surprisingly, Mukherjee's Bish personifies the machinations of contemporary global capitalism: he has utilized the expansion of worldwide connections and transnational linkages to establish a computer network called CHATTY which enables him to become a Silicon Valley multi-millionaire.

On the surface, Tara and her ex-husband appear to be fully Americanized, but many of their attitudes have been molded by British

---

2 See also Bahri and Vasudeva 5.

colonialism. One of the effects of British colonial rule in the nineteenth century was the consolidation of a gendered public and private sphere among the Indian middle class (Mohanty 63), whereby women were pushed into the seclusion of the private space of home (Sangari and Vaid 11). This spatial and social segregation is still implicitly reflected in Bish's outlook in Desirable Daughters. Whilst Bish initially utilizes the skills of his educated wife in order to launch his company, he is subsequently revealed to be an Indian traditionalist. Thus, Tara is expected to be a docile and pliant housewife and mother. One of the reasons given for their divorce in the novel is that Tara suffers from loneliness inside the "private" sphere of marriage.

In this context, it is important that postcolonial scholars connect the distinctive postcolonial crisis of identity to a concern with developing an effective and identifiable relationship between self and place (Ashcroft et al. 8-9). For example, Chandra Talpade Mohanty explains the historical background of the struggle of Indian feminists by drawing on a bhadralok ("respectable" people) notion of middle class Indian womanhood-a notion derived from Victorian ideas of the pure and homebound nature of women (63). Tara may have been able to divorce, but her approving reference to metaphorical Victorian houses reveals the problematic nature of her more independent lifestyle in America. This new lifestyle is symbolized by her earthquake scarred house in San Francisco, in which she lives with her ex-hippie lover and teenage son who comes out as gay. Bose has astutely noted that in Mukherjee's fiction "a woman's sexual freedom often functions as a measure of her increasing detachment from traditional sexual mores and, correspondingly, of her assimilation" in the United States (60). Clearly, when Tara unfavorably juxtaposes her home-described as "a time bomb" (Mukherjee 260)-with the "proudly restored" three-storied Victorian houses in her street (Mukherjee 24, 25), this not only evokes an association between Victorian England and colonial India, but also shows that her seemingly liberated life in California rests uneasily with her colonial convent upbringing and elitist background.

In Cartographies of Diaspora, Avtar Brah links the process of diasporic identity formation to the concept of "homing desire," which is a concept Susheila Nasta applies to postcolonial literature. By drawing attention to the ambiguity of homing desire, Nasta argues that it is "a desire to reinvent and rewrite home as much as a desire to come to terms with an exile from it" (7). In the light of Nasta's observation, Tara still needs to establish a "home" in her diasporic location. Furthermore, "homing desire" is also an integral part of the strategy a postcolonial migrant follows in the process of identity formation. For Tara, the creation of a new female identity involves a series of symbolic journeys in which she struggles with the unresolved complexities of her diasporic life. The catalyst for Tara's homing desire in the novel is the arrival in her home of a young man from India who claims to be the "illegimate" son of her oldest sister, Padma, who is supposedly childless. This stirs Tara's investigation into her family and background. The relationship between place and self is also problematic for the fictional Bengali migrants in Ali's Brick Lane. The title of the novel refers to an area in East London which was once part of a Roman burial ground and, since the early 18th century, has received successive waves of refugees and immigrants.1 The title, therefore, alludes to a globalizing tendency set in motion in antiquity. Paradoxically, although Bengali immigrants are thought to be the most recent arrivals in the Brick Lane area, even they have been coming to the East End for over two hundred years (Sandhu 10). Similarly to Tara, Nazneen enters into an arranged marriage at the age of eighteen, and is brought to London in the mid-1980s by her considerably older husband, Chanu Ahmed. Moreover, mirroring the life story of Tara and her husband, Chanu has attended university and is studying for an Open University degree. Nazneen's father is the second wealthiest man in the village, whereas Nazneen has only received a basic education. This discrepancy between Nazneen's and Chanu's educational backgrounds conforms to a Bangladeshi custom, according to which the husband must always be better educated than his wife (Lindström 73).

In the narrative present, the family lives in a gloomy council estate crammed with other Bengali tenants. The seclusion of women in the Purdah2 region of South East Asia (which includes Bangladesh) is reflected in the strict spatial boundaries that divide the Muslim community in Brick Lane into two distinct and segregated worlds: those of men and women.3 The exclusion of women from public space is also observed in Chanu and Nazneen's home. Interestingly, even though Chanu has been in England for sixteen years and boasts of his education, he is in fact only superficially Westernized. Chanu's superficially Western attitude is reflected in his expectation that Nazneen should stay at home and his belief that there is no need for her to learn English.

While space plays an important part in identity formation, both novels demonstrate that performative identities are not always constantly fixed. According to Judith Butler, whose work concentrates on the performative aspects of the constitution of identity and subjectivity, gender identity is a sequence of acts which takes place in the context of the discourses by which it is formed.4 In Nazneen's home village, her enactment of a submissive female identity is constituted and maintained through the reproduction of the gendered norms of Islamic culture. Even in the context

---

1   See Sandhu passim.
2   For a definition, see, Mandelbaum 2.
3   See, for instance, Mandelbaum 2.
4   See, for instance, Butler, *Bodies* 7-8.

of an urban nuclear family, Nazneen follows the gendered norms of the Purdah region which require a wife to be respectful and self-effacing within her domestic household.5 Nazneen's nightly forays to the refrigerator are indicative of her following practices from the Purdah region where married women can only eat after the men have been served (Mandelbaum 13). In fact, although Chanu urges Nazneen to eat at mealtimes, she always refuses to do so. Butler has argued that whilst obedient subjects are constrained by the power structures within which they are located, a destabilizing process of resignification enables an individual to resist normalization (15). Considering Butler's critical arguments, Nazneen's midnight meals, made up of leftovers, do not only constitute a sign of her subordinate gender position but also include an element of her early resistance to patriarchal customs: "She showed her self-restraint like this. Her self-denial. She wanted to make it visible" (Ali 62). As a result, Nazneen's defiant thoughts mark the first step towards a process of reconstituting her identity.

Even if diasporic locations shape migrant identities, one should also be attentive to additional features of identity construction. Indeed, in discussing contemporary migration, Brah argues that "all diasporas are differentiated, heterogeneous, contested spaces, even as they are implicated in the construction of 'we'" (184). Whilst tradition-bound Muslim societies prohibit social mixing between genders and discourage any communication between unrelated men and women (Mernissi 489, 491), Muslim women have their own social networks. This gendered social segregation is displayed within Nazneen's block of council flats in Tower Hamlets, where she is quickly befriended by the local circle of Muslim women who visit each other in the afternoons. In Ali's novel, as in reality, ethnic and racial diversity characterizes communities such as Tower Hamlets, which also includes a significant number of white inhabitants (Hall 220). It is of crucial importance for Nazneen's process of resistance that she begins to question and challenge the dominant gender norms after carefully observing the lives of other women in her neighborhood. The changes taking place in the lives of the Bangladeshi women around her who have adjusted to the new conditions are particularly meaningful for Nazneen's subversive identity reconstruction. By meeting each other in the absence of men, those women secure a space within which they can discuss their personal concerns and reinterpret their female identities in ways they find empowering in their diasporic location. In the Muslim community, streets are seen as male spaces; yet, even at an early stage, Nazneen transgresses these codes by exploring the area around Brick Lane. In short, Nazneen's homing desire not only reinforces her critique of the confining norms of patriarchal authority, but also compels her to seek alternative diasporic

---

5   See, for instance, Mandelbaum 2.

locations as a means to reconstitute her female identity.

New Clothes, New Identities?

In Desirable Daughters and Brick Lane, the children of the protagonists internalize and emulate "Western" values and forms of behavior. In Brick Lane, Chanu and Nazneen's older daughter, Shahana, does everything to resist her father's attempts to immerse her in Bengali culture. However, contrary to the view that exposure to two different cultures provokes inter-generational conflict (Brah 40-43), the maternal figures in Mukherjee's and Ali's novels appear to be empowered by the fact that their children challenge the traditional patriarchal value system.

When addressing the issue of sexual segregation in Brick Lane, one can apply Fatima Mernissi's argument that, in spite of the ideal of female chastity, sexual segregation in the Muslim order paradoxically "heightens the sexual dimension of any interaction between men and women" (491). As in Desirable Daughters, Nazneen's sexual assimilation is measured by an extra-marital affair with Karim, who is a sweatshop middleman. Karim arrives in Nazneen's house after she has become a "home-worker," and he embodies a more self-reliant second-generation Bangladeshi youth. Proudly claiming England as his country, Karim is also a leader of the Bengal Tigers, an anti-racist and anti-imperialist Islamic group. By focusing on Karim, the novel highlights the worldwide politicization of Islam as well as the rise in hostile discrimination against Muslim communities.[6] Nazneen ultimately breaks off the passionate love affair because she realizes that Karim is no different to Chanu in seeing her as his ideal Bengali wife and mother. Nevertheless, the relationship has a great impact on politicizing her identity and results in her realizing that she needs to develop a basis for collective bonding with other diasporic women.

In the context of Mukherjee's and Ali's novels, Brah's definition of "diaspora" as multi-locationality within and across territorial, cultural, and psychic boundaries acquires additional significance (197). Trying to negotiate a course of action that would defy the contradictory discourses which surround her, Nazneen expresses her homing desire in two different ways: she keeps the transnational lines of communication open between her home country and London, but also looks for evidence of feminist resistance in the female diasporic community. On the one hand, stitching zips and buttons offers Nazneen a much-needed source of income after Chanu has resigned from his council job. On the other hand, it highlights the exploitation of female home workers, who have neither job security nor employment protection.

---

[6]   See Hall 224; Ahmad 45-47.

Asian women have a long tradition of struggling against oppressive practices, both in the sub-continent and in Britain, and Asian feminism has been praised as "one of the most creative and vigorous forces within contemporary black politics in Britain" (Brah 81, 83). Razia, a daring working class woman from Bangladesh, seems to epitomize many of the virtues attributed to Asian feminists in Britain. Even in the early sections of Brick Lane, Razia utilizes cultural hybridity as a survival strategy against both the dominant culture and the Muslim community. In a similar manner to Celie-the oppressed black protagonist in Alice Walker's controversial novel The Color Purple (1982) who progresses from victimhood to an assertion of self-defined subjectivity-the low-paid home workers set up a company, with Razia as the driving force. Interestingly, while Celie's firm concentrates on unisex pants, the diasporic women's co-operative designs and sells "Fusion Fashion" style clothing. Ultimately, Razia offers an empowering model for the emergence of Nazneen's new hybridized identity, one that is capable of fusing heterogeneous cultures.

Clothing has been regarded as one of the props for the enactment of ethnic identity. In an article tracing a trend running through Mukherjee's work in the period between 1975 and 1997, Helena Grice argues that the author "has latterly reached the point whereby identity can be figured as a performance, and a choice" (94). Clearly, choice of clothing plays an important role in the enactment of Tara's new ethnic identity. In California, she feels a great need to adjust to being a "California Girl" and to look like everybody else in the neighborhood: "I am not the only blue-jeaned woman with a pashmina shawl around my shoulders and broken-down running shoes on my feet" (Mukherjee 79). Even if the pashmina has been a status symbol in the East for centuries, Tara's choice to wear a pashmina shawl with her casual Western clothes should not be interpreted as a sign of her South Asianness. In actual fact, it seems to demonstrate her awareness of the recent trend for pashmina shawls in the West. Indeed, Tara's entire outfit works to reinforce the reader's perception of her as believing in assimilationist immigration. Furthermore, her masquerading as an all-American girl gives visual evidence of the fact that she is not only assertively trying to identify herself with the white mainstream culture, but also that ethnic and gender identities are repeatedly produced through performativity. As will be shown, Tara also enacts her South Asian identity by repeating conventions of "respectable" Indian femininity.

While many scholars reacted to Butler's work on performativity with great enthusiasm, some underestimated the complexity of her argument by simply understanding gender performativity as a matter of choice. In her preface to Bodies That Matter (1993), Butler explicitly refutes the idea that gender can be chosen in a way that resembles selecting an outfit from a wardrobe (x). Butler's cautionary note and her emphasis on the importance of the power structures within which gender is located also apply to "race" and ethnicity, both of which intersect with gender and are equally determined by surrounding discourses. Racializing interpellations are a reiterated practice which participates in the social regulation of "race" and are linked with the history of racism (Bodies 18).7

Turning to the issue of prosperous Third World immigrants to the United States, Ella Shohat points out that they have not suffered racial discrimination in their home countries. They arrive "after their psyches have been shaped" and, therefore, are not prepared for a painful racialization in their new host country (29). This phenomenon seems to be reflected in Mukherjee's characterization of Tara, who repeatedly stresses her inclusion in her multicultural neighborhood. At the same time, however, she is intensely aware of American racism towards her: "I am not the only Indian on the block. All the same, I stand out, I am convinced. I don't belong here [...]; worse I do not want to belong" (Mukherjee 79). Tara's statement reveals her deep ambivalence toward American society and its promise of equality for all.

Similarly to Nazneen, who exchanges letters with her sister Hasina, Tara maintains transnational contacts by regularly communicating with family members in her home country. Padma, her oldest sister, lives in New York where she runs a Bengali television show and designs expensive "Museum quality" silk saris (Mukherjee 196). She commodifies her Indianness by selling her designer saris and jewelry at parties, a commercial activity which is thought to be "a kind of home shopping service for upscale Indians" (Mukherjee 231). Padma takes Tara to one such party, where the eclectic tastes and commodified ethnicities of a group of wealthy diasporic Indian consumers-"la crème de la crème of Bengali New Jersey society" to Padma–surface (Mukherjee 187). Indeed, the house itself is "a faux-Tuscan villa" the grounds of which extend to a distant line of Japanese fruit trees, and where the dining room floors boast of "faces and figures copied from the excavation of Pompeii" (Mukherjee 240). With its amalgamation of styles, the house not only speaks of its owners' imperial taste, but it also reflects the exoticist discourse of the dominant culture. According to Graham Huggan, exoticist discourse is complicit with the essentialist labeling and attractive packaging of difference which relays it back again to the assimilating mainstream (22, 24). Small wonder, then, that Padma's customers also construct Indianness as a commodified, fixed essence.8

Padma uses Tara as a model at the party, thereby requiring her to abandon her American clothes. This episode can be interpreted in the context of recent research into class, linking it to the theory and politics of

---

7   See Butler,*Bodies* 18.
8   Cf. Nyman 63.

performativity.9 Dressed in one of Padma's most glamorous saris, "the last word in Calcutta elegance," and wearing expensive jewelry, Tara personifies desirable upper-class Bengali femininity to her sister's satisfaction and economic profit (Mukherjee 196). While recent theoretical discussions of identity argue that it is the effect of performance, Tara's temporary repetition of normalized "Indian" codes of gender, class, and ethnicity feels to her like an empty and one-sided process of imposition. Looking at her "ludicrously overdressed" (Mukherjee 196) image in the mirror, she wonders: "I had no sense of myself [...]. Ask who I was, and it might have taken me a second or two to remember" (Mukherjee 205). Crucially, Tara's homing desire is demonstrated by her acceptance of Padma's party invitation, but her ambivalent identification with Indianness leads her to question traditional gender roles. What Tara identifies as typically Indian during the house tour given by her hostess are signs of "the intense avoidance of gender confusion" (Mukherjee 243). Tellingly, she also cannot help noticing that the groups at the party "appeared rigidly segregated as to sex" (Mukherjee 249). Ultimately, as a gender-conscious Westernized woman, Tara seems to view the segregated female and male social groups as evidence of Indian women's unequal social position.

Diaspora and Class

It has been said that, on average, Bangladeshis are "four times more 'deprived' than any other identifiable group" in Britain (Hall 219), and together with Muslims of Pakistani origin they have been described as a "new underclass" (Ahmad 49). Brick Lane also shows that the formation of Asian-British identity is determined by class differences (Brah 48). Chanu is such a case in point. Having arrived in London in the late 1960s with a university degree from Dhaka, he appears to have been influenced by the liberal rhetoric of an era which favored integration "as equal opportunity, accompanied by cultural diversity, in an atmosphere of mutual trust" (Brah 25). Perhaps not surprisingly, as an ambitious young man, Chanu nurtures highly optimistic hopes about his future in England: "I thought there would be a red carpet laid out for me. I was going to join the Civil Service and become Private Secretary to the Prime Minister" (Ali 26). While Britain initially encouraged immigration from the former colonies, the passing of the 1971 Immigration Act virtually ended primary immigration. Furthermore, the emergence of the New Right and the onset of economic recession in the early Thatcherite 1980s instigated a new form of cultural

---

9   See Fraser 107-108, 119-125.

racism with roots extending back to Britain's exclusive, racialized past. Indeed, the New Right went as far as to construct "the essence of being British to be white, without explicitly proclaiming to do so" (Brah 165). When experiencing the racialized "glass ceiling" of blocked promotion, Chanu defensively exhibits an attitude of superiority not only to his family and other members of the Bangladeshi community in Tower Hamlets-whom he labels as lower-class villagers-but also to some of his British colleagues whom he sees as having the mindset of "the white under-class" (Ali 29). As an urban, westernized, British-educated immigrant, Chanu identifies strongly with members of the British middle and upper classes who used to form the colonial élite.

In her study of colonial masculinity, Mrinalini Sinha analyzes the emergence and effects of two stereotypical constructs in India in the late nineteenth century: the "manly Englishman" and the "effeminate Bengali babu." Initially, the most typical representatives of "effeminate babus" were Western-educated middle-class Bengali Hindus, but, over time, the stereotype was greatly expanded to include the educated Indian middle class who challenged the privileges of the British colonial élite (16). Importantly, Sinha argues that the construction of both "national" British and "colonial" Indian politics of masculinity "must be understood in relation to one another, and as constitutive of each other" (7). In many ways, Chanu's attitude towards the British seems to echo historically the two categories Sinha sees as constitutive of Bengali masculinity.

It is commonly accepted that British literature played an important role in colonization. Lacking a "manly" physique which would associate him with an Englishman, Nazneen's husband is devoted to the study of English literature, commonly regarded as a pivotal medium for the colonial civilizing mission. Small wonder, therefore, that Chanu—the quintessential "mimic man" of colonial discourse—blames his British colleagues for knowing "nothing of the Brontës and Thackerays" (Ali 29). As with English literature, English soap advertising has also served as an exemplary form of mediation for the imperial civilizing mission. Anne McClintock writes: "Soap offered the promise of spiritual salvation and regeneration through commodity consumption, a regime of domestic hygiene that could restore the threatened potency of the imperial body politic and the race" (211). With this in mind, it is only fitting that when Chanu moves back to Bangladesh he plans to sell and manufacture English soap. Indeed, Chanu's mission to sell an "imperial" commodity can be seen as an attempt to purify his fellow countrymen and countrywomen in order for them to become acceptable neocolonial subjects.

While still in London, Chanu's intense preoccupation with class makes him deem Mrs. Islam, the usurer, one of the few "respectable" people in Tower Hamlets, whereas class affiliations do not seem to play any role in Nazneen's choice of friends. In contrast, Mukherjee's Tara is not only interested in observing signs of gendered class differentiation, but also shows great interest in the performative constitution of classed subjects. Her first meeting with the man who claims to be Padma's son is only one instance of many: "No middle-class Bengali man would smoke in front of his elders" (Mukherjee 38). Moreover, in spite of her racialized subject position in the United States, Tara's grossly condescending opinions about American street-crowds reveal her sense of class superiority. Hence, if the faces on the streets of Queens look to her like "not quite India's underclass, but its hungering classes" (Mukherjee 201), the street people in San Francisco resemble "a small army of America's untouchables, a mockery of everything immigrant behavior stands for" (Mukherjee 79). Considering the claim of one of Mukherjee's critics, mainly, that her "narrative method is best described as social satire" (Pati 198), parts of the novel can indeed be read as a mocking exposé of Tara's inability to reflect upon her contradictory views as a westernized Indian woman in the United States.

Tara's homing desire leads her to an encounter with a group of well-to-do Indians in New York. The narrator's satirical intent is evident, however, in her portrayal of Tara's inability to identify with them. In the novel, the group of materialistic and socially arrogant Indians serves as a satirical representation of the dominant culture's racist stereotype of Asian Americans as a "model minority." In addition to involving a trip to the East coast, Tara's homing desire makes her reminisce about her former life in India. It is obvious that she idealizes her childhood in the "nineteenth-century Raj-style fortress of a home [...] set behind a wall topped with glass shards" (Mukherjee 32, 33). The history of the family is traced back to the last quarter of the nineteenth century. At that time, the erosion of hierarchical ties between the older aristocratic élite and the newly formed social groups led to the rise of two distinct groups within the Bengali bhadralok (Sinha 6). Although the family's desirable address in those years "practically shouted 'old money'" (Mukherjee 33), Tara admits that her parents were not born into Calcutta's old upper class. It is for this reason that Tara's reminiscing about her overly protected childhood in Calcutta demonstrates how her parents maintained their superior caste as a position of absolute privilege. This was achieved by "othering" members of the same community who did not have a similar background: "Any community whose roots were not in Bengal, preferably in the eastern half of Bengal; anything like the Marwari, Parsi, or Sindhi community, was seen as alien and money-grubbing, worthy of disrespect, if not outright contempt" (Mukherjee 214). In hindsight, Tara realizes the damaging effect of her parents' hypocritical exclusions. Nevertheless, only fleetingly does she pause to question the justification of her caste and class privileges. Ultimately, Tara's journey of self-discovery involves a trip to India. And, while this trip offers her a belated view of her old self, it also opens up the possibility of learning to know the other through learning to know the self.

Transnational, Postmodern Female Identity: An Open-ended Search

The debate surrounding the controversial "Parekh Report" (The Future of Multi-Ethnic Britain) from October 2000 is evidence of the widely accepted notion that contemporary Britain is a multicultural society (Fortier 2). In response to the report, the lifestyles of Asians were celebrated as "intensely hybrid" (Fortier 15), and ethnic communities were regarded as "signifiers of the urban postmodern experience" (Hall 221). Moreover, areas like Brick Lane were conceived as trendy places where white middle-class Britons could sample ethnic products and express their approval of the decentering of Englishness (Fortier 14-16). This pleasure-seeking phenomenon of sampling commodified foreign cultures which has emerged in the last few years is described by Anne-Mari Fortier as a "chic notion of hybridity." The critic claims that such a notion of hybridity hides the power relations between the dominant white groups and the migrant communities (12).

In Brick Lane, the new identities of migrant women-like Razia and Nazneen-bear the imprint of a different kind of postmodern hybridity. Razia not only holds a British passport but also signals her hybridized identity by wearing a Union Jack top over a pair of traditional salwaar pants. Stuart Hall regards hybridity as a process of cultural translation, which he describes as "agonistic because it is never completed but rests with its undecidability" (226). Thus, even if Razia and Nazneen personally experience their fluid and hybridized identities as liberating, it is important to recognize that they still have to contest and negotiate their new identities in a racist society. Predicated on openness, the official multicultural discourse of the dominant British culture defines its own terms of inclusion (Fortier 6). White people are largely invisible in Mukherjee's and Ali's novels. Nevertheless, Nazneen's casual encounter with a white woman in the aftermath of September 11, when British Muslims were repeatedly required to declare their allegiance to Britain (Fortier 6), is indicative of her awareness of the terms and conditions of cultural inclusion:

"She looked at Nazneen with a ready kindness, a half-smile on her lips but in her eyes there was nothing. It was the way she might look at a familiar object, [...] a blankness reserved for known quantities like pieces of furniture or brown women in saris who cooked rice and raised their children and obeyed their husbands" (Ali 325). In spite of the widely accepted notion that Britain is a multicultural nation, this instance reveals what Hall has referred to as the costs of hybridity, as a process of cultural translation (226): the white woman automatically projects the stereotypical image of a downtrodden, victimized South Asian woman onto Nazneen.

Throughout Brick Lane, Nazneen's yearning for a fluid and mobile identity is associated with her fascination with the weightless movements of ice-skaters. This conforms to Inderpal Grewal's description of postmodern, transnational identities which reject "the modernist binaries that construct the 'Western subject'" and are "always revised, always in the process of becoming" (251). While the identities of the ice skaters Nazneen fantasizes about keep fluctuating and follow her own process of inner change, the book concludes with a comically exaggerated ice-skating scene in which Razia and Nazneen's daughters take Nazneen to skate. The scene is reminiscent of a similar episode in Toni Morrison's Beloved (1987) in that both skating scenes figure a liminal female space which emphasizes female group solidarity. Of equal importance is the fact that the ice-skating scene in Brick Lane highlights the significance of female bonding in the process of Nazneen's identity transformation. Ali has been compared to Zadie Smith, and, indeed, the utopian ending of Smith's book is suggestive of the vision of the intergenerational gathering of marginalized women on the Caribbean islands at the end of White Teeth (2000). When Nazneen wonders if she can skate in a sari, Razia jokingly answers: "This is England [...]. You can do whatever you like" (Ali 413). By concluding the novel with these joyously affirmative words, the narrator of Ali's novel suggests that diasporic women can finally claim England as their home.

Mukherjee's narrator does not posit as neat a conclusion as Ali's. In the process of reconciling with her aged parents, the migrant protagonist, when visiting the family home with her son, continues to negotiate the relationship between her past in India and her diasporic present in the United States. Tara is ill at ease whilst in her country of birth and, despite the increasing divorce rate in India, she conceals the breakdown of her marriage as well as her son's homosexuality-both of which are openly discussed in California. Furthermore, while Tara is in Bombay, the immense social chasms in contemporary India are symbolized by the spacious fifteen-floor luxury apartment that is owned by Tara's middle sister and her husband that overlooks rocks where crowds of seemingly threatening poor people gather.

Significantly, although neither the narrator nor the protagonist comments on the hierarchical social structure in India, the siblings' conversation about the Tree-Bride, Tara Lata, whose story opens the novel, indicates Tara's interest in the history of Indian women's active political participation. The Tree-Bride is not only Tara's namesake but also a distant relative, who, in 1879, at the age of five was literally married to a tree after the sudden death of her prospective groom. She went on to be a heroine of the Independence Movement in the 1940s. This figure has a deep impact on Tara, who admires her single, independent, and socially meaningful life.

Contemporary postcolonial feminists criticize the anti-colonial resistance movement because its struggle against British colonialism did not lead to the political emancipation of women in India. In the late nineteenth century, the construction of the modern "new woman" was linked to concepts of "mother" and "femininity" (Thapar 82), and the sanctified mother/wife, empowered by the same spiritual realm as the glorified wives of Hindu gods, became an icon of India (Sen 468, Thapar 84). Subsequently, the prototypical female construct was modified according to the changing political atmosphere, and a number of women belonging to the revolutionary movement transgressed traditional gender roles (Sen 477). Tara Lata is a revolutionary freedom fighter who, nevertheless, never leaves her palace-house: "It's said that she's not ventured beyond the walls of her compound in over sixty years" (Mukherjee 309). In keeping with the spiritual role of the new woman, Tara Lata, also known as Tara Ma, is a strong mother figure who nurses the wounded and dying participants in the East Bengal insurrection in her house. Yet, she is not associated with the emergence of nationalist women in the public sphere.

Although Tara Lata did not enter the public arena until she was dragged out of her home to face death by colonial authorities in the early 1940s, this is not the case with most contemporary postcolonial feminists. They have criticized the rhetoric of independent India, which they find alienating because of its dissociation from the everyday lives of subaltern women and from any other marginalized or exploited group. Critical self-reflection plays an essential role in the construction of transnational, postmodern female identities, but, unlike postcolonial feminists, Mukherjee's Tara does not attempt to identify with the plight of the oppressed and disadvantaged groups in contemporary India. Whilst it is clear that Tara has a personal use for the heroic narrative of female individualism that is commonly associated with white Western feminism, it remains troublingly unclear how the social activism of the Tree-Bride can relate to her own future.

In its own way, each novel probes deeply into the performative construction of diasporic female identities. Each female protagonist uses homing desire as a strategy of creating a new identity and employs the hybridity generated by her displaced location to question and challenge prescribed patriarchal conceptions of gender. In Brick Lane, Nazneen undergoes a strenuous deconstruction and reconstruction of her traditional identity, ultimately achieving the possibility of agency with the aid of a small community of resistant South Asian women. While Nazneen maintains close connections with Bangladesh, Mukherjee's Tara wavers between the United States and India. Holding on tenuously to her class and caste privileges, she tries to reconnect to her past and is consequently caught between a number of conflicting discourses. Nonetheless, in spite of the different political implications of their narrative solutions, Desirable Daughters and Brick Lane represent the complex search for a transnational postmodern female identity as an open-ended and ongoing process of becoming.

Works Cited

Ahmad, Fauzia. "Dilemmas in Theorizing South Asian Muslim Women." *South Asian Women in Diaspora*. Ed. Nirmal Puwar and Parvati Raghuram. Oxford: Berg, 2004. 43-65.

Alessandrini, Anthony. "Reading Bharati Mukherjee, Reading Globalization." *World Bank Literature*. Ed. Amitava Kumar. Minneapolis: U of Minnesota P, 2003. 265-279.

Ali, Monica. *Brick Lane*. London: Doubleday, 2003.

Ashcroft, Bill, Gareth Griffiths, and Helen Tiffin. *The Empire Writes Back: Theory and Practice in Post-Colonial Literatures*. London: Routledge, 1989.

Aziz, Razia. "Feminism and the Challenge of Racism: Deviance or Difference?" *Black British Feminism: A Reader*. Ed. Heidi Safia Mirza. London: Routledge, 1998. 70-77.

Bahri, Deepika and Mary Vasudeva. "Introduction." *Between the Lines: South Asians and Postcoloniality*. Ed. Deepika Bahri and Mary Vasudeva. Philadelphia: Temple UP, 1996. 1-32.

Bose, Brinda. "A Question of Identity: Where Gender, Race, and America Meet in Bharati Mukherjee." *Bharati Mukherjee: Critical Perspectives*. Ed. Emmanuel S. Nelson. New York: Garland, 1993. 47-63.

Brah, Avtar. *Cartographies of Diaspora: Contesting Identities*. London: Routledge, 2002.

Butler, Judith. *Bodies That Matter: On the Discursive Limits of "Sex."* New York: Routledge, 1993.

Fortier, Anne-Marie. "Multiculturalism and the New Face of Britain." 28 Nov. 2003.
    Date Accessed: 24 June 2004 Available at: http//www.comp.lancs.ac.uk/sociology/ papers/Fortier-Multiculturalism.pdf>.

Fraser, Mariam. "Classing Queer: Politics of Competition." *Performativity & Belonging*. Ed. Vikki Bell. London: SAGE, 1999. 107-131.

Grewal, Inderpal. "Autobiographic Subjects and Diasporic Locations: Meatless Days and Borderlands." *Scattered Hegemonies: Postmodernity and Transnational Feminist Practices*. Ed. Inderpal Grewal and Caren Kaplan. Minneapolis: U of Minnesota P, 1997. 231-254.

Grice, Helena. " 'Who speaks for us?': Bharati Mukherjee and the politics of immigration." *Comparative American Studies: An International Journal* 1. 1 (2000): 81-86.

Hall, Stuart. "Conclusion: the Multi-cultural Question." *Un/settled Multiculturalisms: Diasporas, Entanglements, Transruptions.* Ed. Barnor Hesse. London: Zed Books, 2000. 209-41.

Head, Dominic. "Zadie Smith's *White Teeth.*" *Contemporary British Fiction.* Ed. Richard W. Lane, Rod Megham, and Philip Thew. Cambridge: Polity, 2003. 106-119.

Huggan, Graham. *The Postcolonial Exotic: Marketing the Margins.* London: Routledge, 2001.

Katrak, Ketu K. "South Asian American Literature." *An Interethnic Companion to Asian American Literature.* Ed. King-Kok Cheung. Cambridge: Cambridge UP, 1997. 192-218.

Lindström, Ritva. "Naisen asema Bangladeshissä. Selvitys naisen asemasta terveyden, koulutuksen ja työllisyyden näkökulmista vuosina 1980-1994." M.A. Thesis, U of Turku, 1996.

Mandelbaum, David G. *Women's Seclusion in North India, Bangladesh, and Pakistan.* Tucson: The U of Arizona P, 1993.

McClintock, Anne. *Imperial Leather: Race, Gender and Sexuality in the Colonial Context.* New York: Routledge, 1995.

Mernissi, Fatima. "The Meaning of Spatial Boundaries." *Feminist Postcolonial Theory: A Reader.* Ed. Reina Lewis and Sara Mills. Edinburgh: Edinburgh UP, 2003. 489-501.

Mirza, Heidi Safia. "Introduction: Mapping a Genealogy of Black British Feminism." *Black British Feminism: A Reader.* Ed. Heidi Safia Mirza. London: Routledge, 1998. 1-28.

Mitra, Indrani. "'Luminous Brahmin Children Must Be Saved': Imperialist Ideologies, 'Postcolonial' Histories in Bharati Mukherjee's *The Tiger's Daughter.*" *Between the Lines: South Asians and Postcoloniality.* Ed. Deepika Bahri and Mary Vasudeva. Philadelphia: Temple UP, 1996. 284-97.

Mohanty, Chandra Talpade. *Feminism Without Borders: Decolonizing Theory, Practicing Solidarity.* Durham: Duke UP, 2003.

Mukherjee, Bharati. *Desirable Daughters.* New York: Hyperion, 2002.

Nasta, Shusheila. *Home Truths: Fictions of the South Asian Diaspora in Britain.* Houndmills: Palgrave, 2002.

Nyman, Jopi. "Transnational Travel in Bharati Mukherjee's *Desirable Daughters.*" *The Atlantic Literary Review* 3. 4 (2002): 53-66.

Pati, Mitali R. "Love and the Indian Immigrant in Bharati Mukherjee's Short Fiction." *Bharati Mukherjee: Critical Perspectives.* Ed. Emmanuel S. Nelson. New York: Garland, 1993. 197-211.

Rassool, Naz . "Fractured or flexible identities? Life histories of 'black' diasporic women in Britain." *Black British Feminism.* Ed. Heidi Safia Mirza. London: Routledge, 1997. 187-204.

Sandhu, Sukhdev. "Come hungry, leave edgy." *London Review of Books* 9 Oct. 2003: 10-13.

Sangari, Kumkum and Sudesh Vaid. "Recasting Women: An Introduction." *Recasting Women: Essays in Indian Colonial History*. Ed. Kumkum Sangari and Sudesh Vaid. New Brunswick, New Jersey: Rutgers UP, 1999. 1-26.

Sen, Samita. "Towards a Feminist Politics? The Indian Women's Movement in Historical Perspective." *The Violence of Development: The Politics of Identity, Gender and Social Inequalities in India*. Ed. Karin Kapadia. London: Zed Books, 2002. 459-524.

Shohat, Ella. "Introduction." *Talking Visions: Multicultural Feminism in a Transnational Age*. Ed. Ella Shohat. New York: New Museum of Contemporary Art, n.d. 2-62.

Sinha, Mrinalini. *Colonial Masculinity: The 'Manly' Englishman' and the 'Effeminate Bengali' in the Late Nineteenth Century*. Manchester: Manchester UP, 1995.

Stoneham, Geraldine. "' 'It's a Free Country': Visions of Hybridity in the Metropolis." *Comparing Postcolonial Literatures: Dislocations*. Ed. Berry Ashok and Patricia Murray. London: Macmillan, 2000. 81-92.

Thapar, Suruchi. "Women as Activists; Women as Symbols: A Study of the Indian Nationalist Movement." *Feminist Review* 44 (1993): 81-96.

ANJOOM MUKADAM & SHARMINA MAWANI

Nizari Ismailis in the West: Negotiating National, Religious and Ethnic Identities

Introduction

There is "nothing peculiarly modern about the problem of identity" (Smith 129) as individuals have always differentiated themselves from others. The process of forming identities and defining oneself involves identifying what one is as well as what one is not; it is an expression of similarities as well as differences. The construction of identities is based on oppositions, primarily between "us" and "them" (Pilkington; Woodward), and while the issue of identity is a fundamental concern of individuals during their lives, it becomes more of a concern "when something assumed to be fixed, coherent and stable is displaced by the experience of doubt and uncertainty" (Mercer 43).

The notion of self that arises from a post-structuralist perspective is one that is pluraralist, emergent, dialogic, fluid, shifting and culturally shaped. However, cultural difference has dominated the discourse relating to those whose heritage is from minority ethnic communities and the mobilization of persons around a particular expression of identity is seen by some as a threat to the desire for a broad framework of common belonging. Terms such as "immigrant" and "diaspora" continue to be used when referring to second-generation individuals. However, there is an urgent need to focus on commonality, equality, respect, and inclusion in today's multi-ethnic nations that celebrate and cherish cultural diversity without using these cultural differences as an excuse for exclusion and discrimination. For many second-generation Ismailis of Gujarati descent, the combined pursuit of exclusion and assimilation resulted in discrimination, cultural displacement, marginalisation, as well as a loss of identity and self-esteem. They were commonly referred to in essentialist terms as being "between two cultures" or "the half-way generation".

This paper will examine the ways in which this generation are confronting issues and finding their rightful place in the multicultural societies in which they live. Considering the results of our study, it appears that second-generation Ismailis are asserting a positive ethnic identity. In addition, they are selecting an acculturative strategy with regard to cultural adaptation-one which reflects essential commonalities in terms of cultural preferences to food, dress, music, etc., while maintaining integral aspects of their Indian culture, such as religion and language.

Theoretical Background

While culture was formerly seen as largely homogeneous, bounded and tightly connected to clearly delineated social groups, it is now increasingly conceptualized as an unbounded flow of signification with an uncertain and contestable foundation in social groups. Terms like "hybridization" have thus been proposed in order to see culture in a more processual, dynamic light. There are some very good reasons for this reconceptualization, notably the fact that ethnographic evidence shows much less clear-cut boundaries and less internal homogeneity in social groups than was formerly believed to be the case. More specifically, it could be pointed out that the intensified globalization processes of recent decades-encompassing the flow of ideas as well as people and commodities-entails an accelerated pace of cultural change as well as an unprecedented degree of cultural complexity in many places. On the one hand, cultural universes are increasingly unbounded, mixed and changing. On the other hand, boundaries are being strengthened and recreated through identity politics-be it ethnic, nationalist or religious. Although cultural differences between groups sharing the same space diminish, the social boundaries may indeed be strengthened.

Post-structuralism is marked by a rejection of totalizing and essentialist concepts and subjects are seen to be culturally and discursively structured. Post-structuralism reasserts the importance of process, change, and circumstance, and sees human beings as active creators of culture. Hence, it takes culture beyond the limitations of the structuralists, through the realization of heterogeneity, fragmentation and discontinuity, and the multiple, conflicting and contesting meanings and values (Moya and Hames-Garcia). Within a poststructuralist framework, the discussion of ethnicities and identities has shifted beyond the notion that these concepts are fixed and constructed in isolation. Post-structuralism has made gains in recent years because of its allowance of cultural pluralism which challenges the fixed status of established categories like sex, class, "race" and ethnicity (Foster and Froman; Bhabha). Liberalism, tolerance, and pluralism lead us to embrace the idea of multiplicity. One of the central tenets of contemporary Euro-American thought is that the pursuit of personal freedom and, by association, individual autonomy is seen as a fundamental right that should not be affected by the demands of others, including one's immediate family (Ballard). Naturally, to those from differing cultural traditions these expectations are unrealistic and undermine the reciprocities and obligations set about by kinship ties.

These two faces of liberalism are naturally incommensurable. Gray argues that there is no single ideal cultural system on which all humanity can be agreed: "If liberalism has a future, it is in giving up a search for a rational consensus on the best way of life [...] the good life comes in many varieties"(1-3). Gray also extrapolates this argument: "the span of good lives of which humans are capable cannot be contained in any one community or tradition. The good for humans is too beset by conflict for that to be possible. For the same reason, the good life cannot be contained in any one regime" (6). He supports the view that the object of toleration is not about laying down the foundations for consensus, rather to promote mutual coexistence in arenas of diversity:

> A theory of *modus vivendi* is not the search for an ideal regime, liberal or otherwise. It has no truck with the notion of an ideal regime. It aims to find terms on which different ways of life can live well together. *Modus vivendi* is liberal toleration adapted to the historical fact of pluralism. The ethical theory underpinning *modus vivendi* is value-pluralism. The most fundamental value-pluralist claim is that there are many kinds of human flourishing, some of which cannot be compared in value. Among the many kinds of good lives that humans can live there are some that are neither better nor worse than one another, nor the same in worth, but incommensurably-that is to say, differently-valuable. (6)

Parekh agrees with the views of Gray:

> Britain needs a broadly agreed body of shared values. These include such procedural values as respect for civil authority, tolerance, mutual respect, freedom of expression and commitment to the democratic resolution of differences, as well as such basic ethical norms as respect for human dignity, belief in the equal worth of all human beings and the equality of races and sexes and respect for privacy. Although these and related values do not eliminate deep differences about the content of the good life and are not by themselves enough to foster a sense of common belonging, they provide a basic framework for social co-operation, for resolving such differences as remain for developing common bonds of citizenship. (22)

These views relate to all societies that aim to promote cultural diversity without using cultural differences as an excuse for exclusion and discrimination. Ballard stresses the fact that most human societies are culturally plural and that cultural pluralism is a regular feature of human social organization and that exposure to and familiarity with a range of cultural codes is a normal human experience. The Parekh Report questions fixed boundaries that are implied when referring to members of so-called communities:

> Post-migration communities are distinct cultural formations, but they are not cut off from the rest of British society. It is true that maintaining tradition is critical to their self-identities, but their sense of community owes as much to how they are treated as to where they came from. These communities are not, and have never aspired to be, separate enclaves. They are not permanently locked into unchanging traditions, but interact at every level with mainstream social life, constantly adapting and diversifying their inherited beliefs and values in the light of the migration experience. (27)

Likewise, Brah echoes the sentiments of The Parekh Report and shows clearly how the everyday lives of South Asians in Britain are lived through multiple modalities:

> Asian-British cultures are not simply a carry-over from the sub-continent but are now "native" to different regions and localities of Britain. Asian cultures of London, for example, may be distinguished from those of Birmingham. Similarly, East London cultural life has its own distinctive features compared with the local cultures of West London. There are some commonalities, of course, dependent on which particular modality-religion, region, language, class, etc.-is singled out. For example, Panjabi cultures have their own specificities compared with Gujerati or Bengali cultures. On the other hand, all Muslim groups, be they Panjabi, Gujerati or Bengali, share certain cultural specificities. But each case is simultaneously a dimension of region and locality-of "Englishness", "Scottishness", "Welshness", "Irishness", and so on...They can not be disaggregated into "Asian" and "British" components. They are fusions such that "Asian-British" is a new ensemble created and played out in the everyday life world. (137, 138)

It is this changing view of culture as fluid and multiple that is the essence of the second-generation trajectory. These individuals were born and brought up in the West; they are not outsiders and have a sense of loyalty to their country of birth. This is a generation that has struggled to gain acceptance and which now celebrates its multiple identities, its plurality, and its difference in societies that are more accepting of their global status as multi-ethnic nations. Hybrid identities are celebrated as progressive and Bhabha defines hybridity as the "third space": "This third space displaces the histories that constitute it, and sets up new structures of authority, new political initiatives, which are inadequately understood through received wisdom. The process of cultural hybridity gives rise to something different, something new and unrecognizable, a new arena of meaning and representation" (211). Moving away from the commonly used terminology "British Asian," Mukadam coined the term Indobrit® in 2003 to describe individuals with a specifically Indian cultural background and British nationality. She stresses that "this term is merely a means of identifying individuals who have a common trajectory and should not be viewed as being a fixed category that is imposed on individuals" (45). In Canada, the term Indo-Canadian is gaining popularity when making reference to post-diasporic Indians.

Context of the Study

The Nizari Ismaili Muslims constitute a minority amongst the Shia Muslims and primarily reside in Syria, Pakistan, India, Afghanistan, Tajikistan, Russia, China, Eastern Africa, Britain, Canada and the United States. They acknowledge Aga Khan IV as their present *Imam* (spiritual leader). The ethnic origin of the majority of the Nizari Ismailis[1] in the West is the Indian subcontinent, predominantly Sind, Punjab, Gujarat and Kacch (Mamiya).

The presence of minority ethnic communities in the West can be traced back over generations and this history has created the diversity that forms the mosaic of today's multicultural societies. The majority of the Ismailis in India, primarily residents of Gujarat, were subsistence farmers, farm workers, petty traders and merchants, though a few were engaged in business, construction and transportation. The famine of 1876 resulted in the deterioration of living and working conditions in Gujarat and upon the advice of the Imam the Ismailis began leaving India for more prosperous plains. It has been suggested that from as early as the *Imamat* (time in office) of Aga Khan I (1817-1881), Ismailis in Kacch and Gujarat were advised to migrate to East Africa. The economic opportunity awaiting the migrants in East Africa inspired the Gujarati slogan "Bas Chalo Afrika" ("Let us go to Africa") (Walji). Many traveled straight to the mainland, while others went to Zanzibar. It is important to note that not all Gujaratis migrated from India to East Africa (Gregory). Others moved to bigger Indian cities such as Pune, Bombay or Karachi and subsequently to the West as "once migrants." At its height in the 1960s, the Ismaili community in East Africa is estimated to have numbered over 50,000. However, rapid decline followed as voluntary and forced migration began during the process of Africanization (Clarke). Disaster was to strike in the most

---

[1] The term "Ismaili" will henceforth be used to refer to Nizari Ismailis of Gujarati descent.

unimaginable manner, and in August 1972 Idi Amin expelled approximately 50,000 Ugandan Asians from the country regardless of their nationality. Exodus had begun and resulted in the second phase of migration-this time to Britain, Canada, Austria, Italy, Malta, Spain, Belgium and South Asia. The United Nations office in Geneva (1973) estimates that the vast majority affected held British passports and that over 28,000 entered the United Kingdom. Due to racism, unfavorable economic conditions and strict immigration laws in Britain, many South Asians fled instead to Canada (Thakkar). These groups are commonly referred to as "twice migrants" (Bhachu). The "twice migrants" had entered the second phase in their journey from India to East Africa and then on to the United Kingdom and Canada.

The arrival of the East African Asians was to have a profound effect on the lives of both the white community and the "once migrants" already settled in Britain. Unlike the migrants who had arrived from India, many East African Asians had transferred funds from Africa to Britain before nationalization, and their subsequent expulsion (Brah; Hinnells). This gave many the advantage of being able to move into the leafy suburbs as opposed to deprived inner cities. The first-generation came to Britain as immigrants and were treated as such, their country of origin being India or East Africa. Rushdie, in his book "Imaginary Homelands," writes about his own position in Britain as a first-generation Indian: "Our identity is at once plural and partial. Sometimes we feel that we straddle two cultures; at other times, that we fall between two stools" (15). It is these very phrases that have been used-in our opinion, wrongly-to describe the second-generation. They have been categorized as being "neither one thing nor another" (Gidoomal 172), "between two cultures" (Watson; Anwar) and, more inappropriately, as "the half-way generation" (Taylor) which subscribes to the "melting pot" ideal of assimilation formulated by Glazer and Moynihan in the United States-an ideal that assumed that the third generation would be completely assimilated.

We argue that this is not the case; there, in fact, appears to be a fusion of East and West which supports the view of Nielsen that "young people who are living in and with both cultures [...] are beginning to create a functional synthesis of both" (116) and that of Khan that "the new generation is different in certain crucial respects from its elders but the strength of the home family and culture coupled with lack of equal treatment in wider society will probably ensure the maintenance of a distinctive identity and lifestyle" (87). Unlike Britain-where hostility was rife-Canada was more welcoming and this is evident in an address made by Aga Khan IV to the Ismaili community in 1978 in which he encouraged the newly settled Ismaili community to relinquish the "myth of return" and make Canada their permanent home (Anwar, 1979). Aga Khan IV also highlighted the tolerant and open-minded attitude of Canada:

[...] you are living in a country which welcomes people of different faiths, of different backgrounds, of different cultures, and therefore, we are fortunate in living in a country where our traditions, our faith, our community institutions, not only can survive, but are welcomed, and I consider that this is extremely important. There is no reason, there are no pressures, there are no attempts to have my Canadian jamaat change its traditions, the practice of its faith or other matters which affect or are part of our everyday lives. (*Kalam*, Vol. 1 29)

South Asian communities in the West are commonly referred to as a "diaspora," a population that is considered "deterritorialised" or "transnational," whose cultural origins are in another land (Vertovec). Mukadam questions the use of terminology that is commonly used in discourse related to the South Asian community in Britain:

It appears that the word "diaspora", like the word "immigrant", is no longer being used to refer to the first generation and continues to be used when making reference to the second generation and beyond. If the word "diaspora" refers to those whose cultural origins are in a different land, then how far back do these communities have to go before they are recognized as belonging to the new homeland or will academics and others always refer to them in relation to a past with which many, at best, have symbolic links? (96)

Rex argues that the term "diaspora" is misleading and prefers to use the term "transnational." We shall use the term post-diasporic to refer to second generation Indians as they have not themselves participated in any form of migration and are the offspring of those who made the journey. The term "diaspora" is another term that focuses on difference as opposed to commonality. Beverley McLachlin, Chief Justice of Canada, asked in the fourth annual LaFontaine-Baldwin lecture in March 2003: "Why, despite our manifest commonality, do our differences, real and perceived, tend to define our world and dominate our discourse and our conduct?" The majority of second generation Indians were born in the West and are therefore not strictly members of a "diaspora" or a "transnational" community.

Methodology

This study follows the work of Saeed et al. working on post-British identities among Glasgow Pakistani teenagers. As Anwar (1998, 192) indicates in his conclusion, "young Asians are adopting a new culture which is a synthesis of the 'old' and the 'new'," and the aim of this study is to investigate that fusion. Saeed et al carried out a study on the identity and ethnic orientation of Pakistani teenagers in Glasgow using the research methodology of McPartland and Kuhn, Hutnik, and Phinney. The main research questions in the present study are:

1. What labels do second-generation Nizari Ismailis of Gujarati descent in the West use to identify their ethnic identity?
2. To what degree have these individuals integrated into mainstream society?
3. Is there a difference between the ethnic self-identification strategy and cultural adaptation strategy employed by these participants?

The study was carried out in two stages using quantitative research analysis in the form of a questionnaire as well as qualitative research in the form of semi-structured interviews to "illuminate" the results found in the quantitative analysis. The participants selected for this study were second generation Ismailis of Gujarati descent born in London or Toronto from Gujarati/Kachchi-speaking family backgrounds, aged between 18 and 45. Blaxter, Hughes and Tight (79) explain the types of sampling used in this study as quota sampling-convenience sampling within groups in the population; purposive sampling-hand-picking supposedly typical or interesting cases; and snowball sampling-building up a sample through informants. A question that is often asked regarding ethnography is whether a few informants are capable of providing adequate information about a culture. Bernard is of the opinion that the answer to that question is "yes", but that it depends on two factors: a) choosing good informants, by which he means those who are selected for their competence as well as their representativeness; b) asking respondents questions about things they know about (165).

The questionnaire was formulated using Mukadam's quantitative research tool, as well as incorporating the work of Phinney and Saeed et al. The statement "[i]n terms of ethnic group, I consider myself to be...." was included in the questionnaire so as to ascertain what terms respondents chose when asked specifically about their ethnicity. Mukadam and Mawani further developed the questionnaire to include more specific questions related to Ismailism. Section 2 of the questionnaire asked the respondents questions about their likes and dislikes in terms of food, clothes, music, films, celebrations, etc. This was then used in conjunction with their response regarding their religious affiliation as well as their ability to speak and/or comprehend Gujarati. The questionnaire went through many stages of refinement both pre- and post-pilot study. The overall aim was to keep the questionnaire simple and easy to follow as a hypothesis driven instrument that included questions about the individuals' identity, culture and language. Questionnaires were submitted to individuals using various means, such as hand delivery, postal delivery, internet attachment, via a friend, and through the internet site http://www.communities.msn.co.uk/Indobrits. As is usually the case, obtaining the completed questionnaires was the grueling aspect of this task; excuses made for not completing the forms, incomplete forms and lost questionnaires were all part of the data collection process. However, with perseverance and a large dose of patience all the questionnaires were obtained, but at a much slower rate than had been anticipated. The snowballing procedure was not as effective as we had expected it to be and gentle persuasion was called for to encourage individuals to contact their friends and pass on the questionnaire. Another surprise for us was the fact that the internet was not chosen as the most effective means of completing the forms for those in London. However, the participants in Toronto preferred completing the questionnaire online.

The semi-structured interviews lasted approximately 45 minutes to an hour and the main difficulty encountered during this phase of the research was actually getting hold of the respondents; appointments were made and then cancelled, rescheduled and cancelled until finally we managed to complete the task. Many of the interviews were held at respondents' places of work, at their homes, by telephone, or over dinner at restaurants-all areas in which the individual(s) concerned would be in a relaxed frame of mind. For many, the interview was an emotional experience bringing back memories of an exodus from Africa, racism upon their arrival, and the scars of a life in a new land. For others, it was a time of reflection, one of achievement and pride embodied within an evolving plural society. As interviewers from within the community, we were privileged to be allowed access to the most private thoughts of those who had been kind enough to share their experiences with us. The respondents' honesty and tenacity was moving and it would appear that our position as "insiders" had positioned us so that we were trusted with information that is normally kept within the individual's private sphere. This is the qualitative dimension of the study that focuses on lives lived through a period of uncertainty, a time of conflict and racism, a time of change leading to a new vision of pluralism, diversity, and acceptance. These are their stories, and their comments do matter because they helped shape and bring about changes to the societies in which they reside.

Many of Mukadam's respondents are now successful business people who fled East Africa with their families and utilized the education pursued in British schools to achieve the kind of status that they have in today's society. Many of the working respondents are professionals: dentists, lawyers, I.T. specialists, doctors, entrepreneurs and teachers. This is not an unlikely set of second generation Ismailis in today's society, in which parents who ran corner shops sent their children to the "best" schools (for many parents private education was perceived as being superior) and urged them to pursue further education. It must be remembered at this stage that the Ismaili community is upwardly mobile and predominantly professional or business oriented.

Bernard (363) cites the work of Lofland in which it is stated that the two great sins of qualitative analysis are excessive analysis and avoiding analysis. We deduce from this that simplicity as well as illustration by quotation and analysis of respondents' statements is the key to the presentation of qualitative data. Charmaz and Mitchell indicate the importance of the respondents over methods implemented in a study:

> Methods are only a means, not an end. Our subjects" worlds and our rendering of them take precedence over methods and measures. A keen eye, receptive mind, discerning ear and steady hand bring us close to the studied phenomena and are more important than developing methodological tools. (161)

Results

Individuals lack one fixed identity; rather, identities are multiple and constantly shifting. Specific aspects of an individual's identity are salient in varying contexts and no one today is purely *one* thing. Labels, like Indian, woman, Muslim, or American, are no more than starting points" (Said 407). Mukadam developed the Diasporic and Post-Diasporic Identity Model (DPIM) to provide a clearer understanding of the overlapping and intersecting identities of the post-diasporic Indian community based on the results of her study. In Figure 1, DPIM has been applied to post-diasporic Nizari Ismailis of Gujarati descent living in Britain and Canada. It should be noted here that identity is fluid and that individuals may select one or more of these options depending on the environment in which they find themselves.

<u>Figure 1</u> The Diasporic and Post-Diasporic Identity Model (DPIM) as Applied to Post-Diasporic Nizari Ismailis of Gujarati Descent in the West

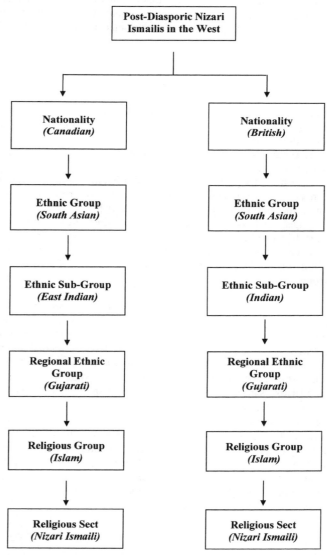

<u>Source</u>: Adapted from Mukadam (2003: 234)

In order to examine the results systematically, firstly there will be an examination of ethnic self-identification (the label chosen by an individual to express their individual ethnic identity) followed by an analysis of cultural adaptation strategies (the lifestyle choices made by an individual who is living in the West, but who belongs to a minority ethnic community).

Ethnic Self-Identification

The results from this study are shown using Hutnik's (1991) quadri-polar model (Figures 2 and 3) in which there are four options open to an individual from an ethnic community:

           1. Acculturative—e.g., those with hyphenated identities such as Indian-British.

           2. Assimilative—an individual who chooses this option sees himself or herself with respect to the majority group label, which for an Indian born in Britain would be British.

           3. Dissociative—an individual choosing this option sees himself/herself as a member of the ethnic minority group.

           4. Marginal—an individual choosing this option is indifferent to ethnic group identifications or *chooses* to identify with neither group.

From Figure 2 it is clear that an acculturative strategy is prevalent amongst post-diasporic Ismailis in London, with 59 percent of the respondents selecting this form of ethnic identity strategy.[2] Interestingly, the term British Asian (a term commonly used to describe second and third generation South Asians in Britain) was chosen by 41 percent of the respondents. The results from the Canadian sample were very similar to those of the British sample, with the majority of respondents (51%) opting for an acculturative strategy in cases where their ethnic self-identification was concerned. In Canada, there is no generally recognized term for second and third generation South Asians, although it appears that the term Indo-Canadian is gaining popularity. 24 percent of the Canadian sample identified themselves as Canadian Indian. A striking feature amongst this sample is the range of terms used by the individuals to describe their ethnic identity, incorporating aspects that reflect the trajectory of their parents; they are at once Canadian, Indian and East African.

---

2   These findings are in agreement with Modood et al (1997:331) who found the majority of Indians (65%) in their survey employed an acculturative strategy.

Figure 2: A Quadri-Polar Model of Ethnic Identity Strategy Amongst Post-Diasporic Ismailis in London

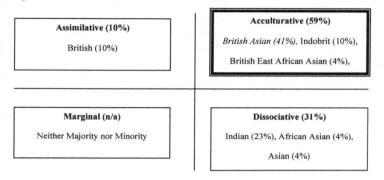

Figure 3: A Quadri-Polar Model of Ethnic Identity Strategy Amongst Post-Diasporic Ismailis in Toronto

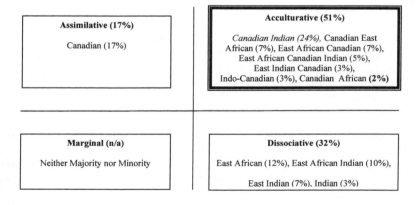

Cultural Adaptation Strategy

Hutnik states that historically there has been an implicit assumption that social behavior corresponds with labels of self-categorization, "if a person much prefers aspects of British culture (films, music, food, clothes, etc.) to Indian culture then that person will categorize him/herself in terms of the majority group dimension of his/her identity and will reject the ethnic minority label" (135). Although Hutnik suggested that the relationship between ethnic self-identification and cultural adaptation strategies should be examined, it is our understanding that no studies to date have looked at this issue. Mukadam and Mawani's current study examines the relationship between cultural adaptation and self-categorization. Respondents were placed into one of five cultural adaptation types based on their responses to questions relating to favorite food, favorite movie, favorite clothes, favorite music, celebrations, religious affiliation and minority ethnic language skill (oral or aural). The only section that provided two answers by many respondents was "celebrations" in which they wrote down a Muslim festival as well as a Western celebration, such as Christmas or New Year. Mukadam (237) formulated five cultural adaptation types:

a) Western-an individual who shows a preference for Western culture

b) Symbolic *Desi*[3]-*an* individual who predominantly shows a preference for Western culture, but shows an affinity to a few elements of Indian culture

c) Balanced—an individual who shows no clear preference for Western or Indian culture

d) Symbolic Western-an individual who predominantly shows a preference for Indian culture, but shows an affinity to a few elements of Western culture

e) *Desi*-an individual who shows a preference for Indian culture

The responses were then inserted into a bar graph to show the cultural adaptation strategy employed by Ismaili Indobrits and Indo-Canadians (see Figures 4 and 5). Figures 4 and 5 clearly show that the majority of post-diasporic Ismailis in Britain and Canada selected an acculturative cultural adaptation strategy. There appears to be a wide spectrum of acculturation, ranging from those who have integrated to a greater degree down to those who have maintained a greater affinity with the culture of the "homeland." Interestingly, *all* respondents included two aspects of Indian culture as part of their overall acculturative strategy: religious affiliation and their ability to speak/understand Gujarati/Kacchi. It should be pointed out here that there were significant age differences between the London and Toronto groups: those in London ranged between the ages of 22 and 45, and those in Toronto ranged between the ages of 18 and 25. Both groups were second generation, however there was a generational gap between these two sets of respondents. Figure 4 shows the similarity in cultural adaptation strategy amongst both male and female respondents, with the exception of the *Desi* category, which only constituted female respondents.

---

[3]   The term "*Desi*" is a Hindi word meaning "of the homeland."

Figure 4

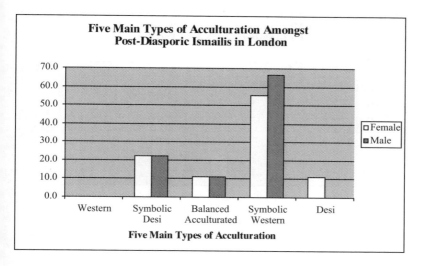

Unlike the London group, those in Toronto, who are in a younger age bracket, showed marked gender differences where cultural adaptation strategy was concerned. The Symbolic *Desi* category constituted mainly of male respondents, a fact which shows a greater move towards Western culture and integration. The female respondents exhibited a much more varied cultural adaptation strategy, which was fairly evenly distributed amongst four of the five main types of acculturation, none being present in the Western category. From these results it appears that the younger male respondents in Toronto are acculturating at a faster rate than females of the same age group. However, among the older group of second generation respondents in London, there was a more equal distribution based on gender, with the majority of both male and female respondents in the Symbolic Western category. Against our expectations, very few respondents from both the London and the Toronto groups were found in the Balanced Acculturated category: they were predominantly found on either side of this category, showing either an affinity towards Indian culture or a move towards greater integration and Western culture.

Figure 5

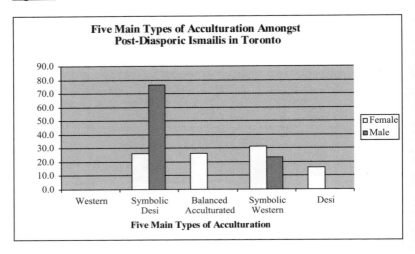

Conclusions

The aim of this study was to investigate the multiple identities of post-diasporic Ismailis in London and Toronto. Second generation identity is an arena that is often simplistically conceptualized and individuals have been carelessly placed in a situation in which they have had to choose one identity over another. Dominant conceptions of "between two cultures" and "the half-way generation" have been replaced by a more realistic picture, which encompasses the fluidity and complexity of two cultures co-existing in an evolving environment. The view that a choice had to be made between maintaining an Indian or a Western lifestyle has been replaced by one in which the respondents are given greater freedom for creativity and innovation. Ethnic identity is far from fixed and singular; it is complex, as this research has shown. Hutnik suggested that theories and research related to ethnic identity have tended to confuse two different aspects of ethnic minority identity; namely, that ethnic minority identity has two distinct, yet not necessarily related, components: 1. a consciously articulated stance or strategy of self-categorization; 2. an underlying system or body of beliefs, attitudes, values and behavior—or a style of cultural adaptation. Both of these aspects are developed in relation to the ethnic minority group and ethnic majority group in conjunction with each other. From the results of this study it appears that post-diasporic Ismailis are selecting an acculturative strategy in terms of both their ethnic self-identification and their cultural adaptation. This illustrates a positive image and reflects a sense of integrated ethnic and national identity. In addition, they have selected an acculturative strategy with regard to cultural adaptation, which reflects essential commonalities in terms of cultural preferences regarding food, dress, music, etc., while maintaining integral aspects of their Indian culture, such as religion and language. There is a clear indication that these two factors will play an increasingly important role in the lives of post-diasporic Ismailis living in the West.

Post-diasporic Ismailis are the fortunate ones who live in multi-ethnic Western societies that are more interested in their inclusion than exclusion. However, one aspect that cannot be ignored is the strong cultural, linguistic, and religious links that tie these individuals to the land of their ancestors. They may appear Western and speak in perfect English, they may acculturate and find a niche for themselves in Western societies, they may even consider the West to be home. Nonetheless, no matter how strong these ties are, these individuals remain inextricably linked to their cultural ancestry.

Works Cited

Anwar, M. *Between Two Cultures*. London: Community Relations Commission, 1975.

_____ *The Myth of Return*. London: Heinemann, 1979.

_____ *Between Cultures: Continuity and Change in the Lives of Young Asians*. London: Routledge, 1998.

Ballard, R. "Race, Ethnicity and Culture" in *New Directions in Sociology*. Ed. M. Holborn Ormskirk: Causeway, Accessed 09.01.03 <http://www.art.man.ac.uk/CASAS/pdfpapers/racecult.pdf>.

Bernard, H.R. *Research Methods in Anthropology*. London: Altamira, 1995.

Bhabha, H. "The Third Space" in *Identity; Community, Culture, Difference*. Ed. J. Rutherford London: Lawrence and Wishart, 1990. 207-21

_____ *The Location of Culture*. London: Routledge, 1994.

Bhachu, P. *Twice Migrants: East African Settlers in Britain*. London: Tavistock, 1985.

Blaxter, L., C. Hughes, and M. Tight. *How to Research*. Buckingham: Open U P, 1996.

Brah, A. *Cartographies of Diaspora*. London: Routledge, 1996.

Charmaz, K., and R. G. Mitchell. "Grounded Theory in Ethnography" in *Handbook of Ethnography*. Eds. P. Atkinson, et.al. London: Sage, 2001. 160-174

Clarke, P.B. "The Ismaili Sect in London." *Religion* 8.1 (1978): 68-84.

Foster, J.B. and Froman, W.J. *Thresholds of Western Culture: Identity, Postcoloniality, Transnationalism*. London: Continuum, 2002.

Gidoomal, R. *The UK Maharajahs: Inside the South Asian Success Story*. London: Nicholas Brealey, 1997.

Glazer, N. and Moynihan, D.*Beyond the Melting Pot*. Cambridge, MA: MIT P, 1970.

Gray, J *Two Faces of Liberalism*. Cambridge: Polity, 2000.

Gregory, R.G. *South Asians in East Africa: An Economic and Social History, 1890-1980*. Boulder: Westview, 1993.

Hinnells, J.R., ed. *The South Asian Religious Diaspora in Britain, Canada, and the United States*. New York: State U of New York P, 2000.

Hutnik, N. *Ethnic Minority Identity: The Case of Second Generation South Asians in Britain*. Unpublished PhD Thesis, Wolfson College, 1985.

_____ *Ethnic Minority Identity: A Social Psychological Perspective*. Oxford: Oxford Science Publications, 1991.

Kalam-e Imam-e-Zaman: Farmans to the Western World (1957-1991), Volume 1.

Khan, V.S. "The Mother Tongue of Linguistic Minorities in Multicultural England" *The Journal of Multilingual and Multicultural Development* 1(1) (1980): 71-88.

McLachlin, B. "The Civilization of Difference." *The Globe and Mail* March 7 2003, Accessed: 07.03.03 <http://www.globeandmail.com>.

McPartland, T. and Kuhn, M. "An Empirical Investigation of Self-Attitudes." *American Sociological Review* 19(1) (1954): 68-76

Mamiya, L. H. "Islam in the Americas." in *The Muslim Almanac: A Reference Work on the History, Faith, Culture, and Peoples of Islam*. Ed. A.A. Nanji. New York: Gale Research, 1996. 141-57.

Mercer, K. "Welcome to the Jungle: Identity and Diversity in Postmodern Politics" in *Identity: Community, Culture and Difference*. Ed. J. Rutherford. London: Lawrence & Wishart, 1990. 43-71.

Modood, T., R. Berthoud, J. Lakey, J. Nazroo, P. Smith, S. Virdee, and S. Reishon. *Ethnic Minorities in Britain: Diversity and Disadvantage: The Fourth National Survey of Ethnic Minorities*. London: Policy Studies Institute, 1997.

Moya, P.M.L. and Hames-Garcia, M.R. "Introduction" in *Reclaiming Identity: Realist Theory and Predicament of Postmodernism*. Eds. P.M.L. Moya and M.R. Hames-Garcia. Berkeley: U of California P, 2000. 1-28.

Mukadam, A. "*Until Death Do Us Part*'", Language as a Factor of Group Identity: Gujaratis*. Unpublished MA Dissertation, University of Reading, 1994.

_____ *Gujarati Speakers in London: Age, Gender and Religion in the Construction of Identity*. Unpublished PhD Thesis, University of Reading, 2003.

Nielsen, J.S. "Muslims in Britain: Ethnic Minorities, Community, or Ummah?" in *The South Asian Religious Diaspora in Britain, Canada, and the United States*. Ed. J.R. Hinnells. New York: State U of New York P, 2000. 106-125.

Parekh, B. *Integrating Minorities*. London: Institute of Contemporary Arts, 2001.

Phinney, J. "The Multigroup Ethnic Identity Measure: A New Scale for Use with Adolescents and Young Adults." *Journal of Adolescent Research* 7 (1992):156-76.

Pilkington, A. *Racial Disadvantage and Ethnic Diversity in Britain.* New York: Palgrave Macmillan, 2003.

Rex, J. "Communities, Diasporas, and Multiculturalism." *Migration* 33/34/35 (2002): 51-67.

The Runnymede Trust. *The Future of Multi-Ethnic Britain: The Parekh Report.* London: Profile Books, 2000.

Rushdie, S. *Imaginary Homelands.* London: Penguin, 1992.

Saeed, A., N. Blain, and D. Forbes. "New Ethnic and National Questions in Scotland: Post-British Identities." *Ethnic and Racial Studies* 22.5 (1999): 821-44.

Said, E. *Culture and Imperialism.* London: Vintage, 1993.

Smith, A. "The Formation of National Identity" in *Identity.* Ed. H. Harris. Oxford: Oxford U P, 1995. 129-153.

Taylor, P.H. *The Half-Way Generation.* Windsor: NFER, 1976.

Thakkar, R. "Gujaratis" in *Encyclopaedia of Canada's Peoples.* Ed. P.R. Magocsi. Toronto: U of Toronto P, 1999.

United Nations "Asians from Uganda in European Transit Camps." *New Community.* 2.3 (1973): 23-4.

Vertovec, S. *The Hindu Diaspora: Comparative Patterns.* London: Routledge, 2000.

Walji, S. R. *A History of the Ismaili Community in Tanzania.* Unpublished PhD Thesis, University of Wisconsin, 1974.

Watson, J.L., ed. *Between Two Cultures.* Oxford: Basil Blackwell, 1977.

Woodward, K. *Identity and Difference.* London: Sage, 1997.

ILANA XINOS

Narrating Captivity and Identity:
Christophorus Castanis' *The Greek Exile*
and the Genesis of the Greek-American

Christophorus Plato Castanis, a native of Greece, was a prolific writer who published a number of texts in America between 1844 and 1851.[1] During his lifetime, Castanis traveled back and forth between America and Greece. Interestingly, although Castanis considered America his "second motherland," he never immigrated to the United States (211). Moving both geographically and culturally between America and Greece, during a historical period in which nation-states began to emerge in the aftermath of revolutions in Europe, Castanis occupied a controversial subject position and remained preoccupied with his own identity. This preoccupation is realized in one of his most interesting texts, *The Greek Exile, or a Narrative of the Captivity and Escape of Christophorus Plato Castanis during the Massacre on the Island of Scio, by the Turks, together with Various Adventures in Greece and America. Written by Himself.* Published in 1851, *The Greek Exile* explores Castanis' captivity and enslavement by the Turks during the Greek Revolution (1821-1852).[2] The text is modeled after the captivity narrative, but borrows from several other popular

---

[1] Castanis' other publications include *An Essay on the Ancient and Modern Greek Languages Containing Remarks on the Accents, Pronunciation and Versification of the Greek Languages, with Historical Notes, etc. To which is Added Extracts from Modern Greek Authors; Christopoulos on Versification; an Oration Delivered before the New York Legislature; and a Guide to Acquire a Knowledge of the Modern Greek* (1844); *Interpretations of the Attributes of the Principal Fabulous Deities, with an Essay on the History of Mythology* (1844); *The Greek Boy and the Sunday-School: Comprising Ceremonies of the Greek Church, Mode of Baptism, Communion, Picture-Worship, etc.* (1847); *Oriental Amusing, Instructive, and Moral Dialogues; or Love and Disappointment of a Turk in the City of Washington: Comprised in Two Dialogues* (1849). Castanis possibly published another work entitled, *The Jewish Maiden of Scio's Citidel*, which is listed on *The Greek Exile*'s title page, but no other record of this work is extant.

[2] An earlier edition of *The Greek Exile* was published by Henry Howland, Printer, in 1845 under the title, *The Greek Captive: A Narrative of the Captivity and Escape of C.P. Castanis, during the Massacre on the Island of Scio by the Turks*. Castanis mentions this edition in *The Greek Exile*'s "Introductory Remarks," commenting, "The pressing demand for a second edition of 'The Greek Captive,' has aroused him to a task still greater; it is the present work of which the other is only a very small portion" (2).

American genres as well, including the Franklinian autobiography. The intertwining of American genres into his account highlights the fact that Castanis' subjectivity is complicated. He identifies culturally with America, American people, and American culture, as well as Greece, Greek people, and Greek culture, and therefore his identity is characterized by and bound to both cultures.

Because Castanis was a Greek who wrote in English and published texts in America, it might be tempting for us to call Castanis a Greek-American and to conceptualize his identity in terms of hybridity. According to postcolonial theorist Homi Bhabha, cultural identifiers like "Greek-American" are "hybrid hyphenations," which "emphasize the incommensurable elements-the stubborn chunks-as the basis for cultural identifications" (219). From a postcolonial perspective, these hyphenated identities suggest liminality, and the hyphen that connects the "incommensurable elements" or the "stubborn chunks" of cultural identity points to the creation of something new-a hybrid identity.[3] We could categorize Castanis as a hybrid hyphenation by first identifying instances in which American culture influenced his ideological consciousness, and then by pointing out the ways in which the text unconsciously reveals that American culture and Greek culture are incommensurable.[4]

However, to conceptualize Castanis' identity in terms of hybridity would be ahistorical: not only does Castanis not have a postcolonial lens with which to view his identity, but he is not concerned with creating a hybrid identity either. Instead, by focusing on the ideological similarities between America and Greece, Castanis advances the idea that identities should be based on shared ideological systems, not territorialization. Castanis' approach inverts the concept of hybridity because instead of forming a new identity-one that equals "the sum of the 'parts' of difference"-as hybridity does, Castanis attempts to emphasize similarities between the two nations and tries to alter the concept of nation formation to one that would include both Greece and America (Bhabha 2). Thus, Castanis attempts to make the incommensurable elements of his identity (or the cultures of both Greece and America) commensurable by linking

---

[3] In contradistinction to identity construction via hybridity, Castanis' approach is similar to that of early Greek immigrants to America. Anagnostou observes that in the early 20th century, hyphenated identities, i.e., Greek-American, were stigmatized because "the term 'Greek' signified a non-voluntary ascription (since it was granted at birth), ethnic nationalism, and a set of traditional cultural practices incompatible with American modernity" (38). This is exemplified in his essay which examines members of a Greek civic organization called AHEPA (American Hellenic Educational Progressive Association), who instead of the ethnic "Greek-American identity," opted for a non-ethnic "American Hellenic" identity.

[4] The clearest instance of cultural incommensurability is religion, which I discuss in detail in the penultimate section of this essay.

American and Greek ideological systems to those of ancient Greece. In doing so, Castanis explicitly connects Greek and American political ideologies, linking the institutions of ancient Greece to the American Republic. This linkage is consistent with nineteenth-century American ideology. As David Roessel points out, "[in the United States] [t]he American and Greek revolutions were regarded as kindred events; indeed the Greek rebellion was sometimes seen as a validation and extension of the American experiment as well as a return of the classical past" (93). Part of Castanis' purpose in writing his multi-generic text is to illustrate this ideology symbolically through his own life story.

The *Greek Exile*'s generic mélange is centered around the most formative event of Castanis' life-his captivity. Castanis devotes a relatively short portion of the text to his two-month enslavement, but his captivity permeates the text. Castanis' enslavement by the Turks took place during the Massacre of Chios in 1822, when he was eight-years-old. After his escape, Castanis was forced to flee Chios by stowing away on a merchant ship *en route* to the island Syra. Penniless and alone, young Castanis became a peddler until he left Syra bound for Nauplion where he encountered American philhellenes and relief agents. At Nauplion, a prominent American philhellene, Dr. Samuel Gridley Howe, hired Castanis as his servant. In 1827, Dr. Howe brought thirteen-year-old Castanis to America, where Howe and other benevolent philhellenes financed Castanis' education, and where Castanis became one of about forty war orphans brought to America by philhellenes and missionaries.[5]

Most scholars agree that these war orphans either returned to Greece or stayed in America. George Kourvetaris lists Castanis as a war orphan who returned to Greece (Appendix I). But the information Castanis provides in *The Greek Exile* complicates this picture because he returned to America for at least one lengthy stay. He returned to the States in 1837, ten years after his initial visit, and within two years began lecturing at Harvard "upon the modern dialect, manners, customs, and character of his countrymen" (190). In 1839, Castanis journeyed to universities and colleges across the Eastern seaboard giving lectures.

Castanis' journeys between Greece and America seem to qualify him as one of the "Greek wanderers" who, according to Thomas Burgess, "may be found, Odysseus-like, in every nook and cranny of the world" (13).

---

[5] Some scholars credit Howe alone for bringing these orphans to America, while others attribute other philhellenes and missionaries as well. For more information about these war orphans, see Scourby's *The Greek Americans*; Saloutos' *They Remember America: The Story of the Repatriated Greek-Americans*; Fenton and Hecker's *The Greeks in America 1528-1977*; Moskos' *The Greek Americans: Struggle and Success*.

However, the "Greek wanderers" Burgess refers to are actually early twentieth-century Greek immigrants, and Castanis does not fit neatly within the immigrant paradigm. Because he arrived in America approximately forty-years prior to the first wave of Greek immigration, Castanis has no social group with which to identify because "as yet there was no Greek ethnic community in America" (Kourvetaris 312). This key difference between nineteenth-century Greeks in America and their twentieth-century immigrant counterparts leaves Castanis no choice but to consider his identity in transnational terms.

Since *The Greek Exile* is largely concerned with creating a symbolic connection between America and Greece, Castanis is given to long classical digressions-mythological, philosophical, and historical-which are weaved into the text's patchwork structure. He also digresses about contemporary events in Greece, giving outlines of some of the major events of the Greek War for Independence (1821-1832), ethnographic accounts of Greeks and Turks, as well as a short chronicle of the Greek diaspora. Following the narrative proper, Castanis includes an essay on the pronunciation of modern Greek, a short diatribe on the arrival of a Turkish envoy to the U.S., an excerpt of modern Greek philosophy, several Greek folk songs, and a section entitled "A New Alphabet for the English Language," which describes elocutionist Andrew Comstock's phonetic alphabet (259).[6]

These selections work together to illustrate similarities between America and Greece, with the most explicit of these being the Comstock alphabet. Castanis writes that the Comstock alphabet is "a Cadmian invention by an American," drawing a parallel between Comstock and Cadmus, the classical figure who Herodotus credits for creating the Greek alphabet. Castanis observes that Comstock's alphabet "contains several Greek letters," and writes: "I was agreeably surprised to meet in Philadelphia such tokens of the past, such relics of my nation's glory, in the very type, prepared by an uncompromising hero of letters for this gigantic republic" (259). Interestingly, Comstock himself drew similar parallels between his activities and those of the classical Greeks. Lester Thonssen notes that, in addition to teaching practical elocution in Philadelphia, Comstock "operated a 'Vocal Gymnasium and Lyceum for Elocution,'" both institutions born in Greek antiquity (105). Castanis' political rhetoric is not unlike Comstock's, who, in the preface to his *Phonetic Speaker*, writes, "We hope that the new era in the republic of letters, which has been

---

[6]   Information about Comstock's phonetic alphabet is scarce, but Lester W. Thonssen writes "according to the testimony of many individuals whose recommendations appear both at the beginning and at the end of the book [Comstock's *A System of Elocution* (1844)]." Virgil L. Baker has noted that Comstock's phonetic alphabet appeared in his *Phonetic Speaker* (1846-7).

so long looked for has at length commenced. We trust that a brighter day has dawned upon the world. Instead of the old and imperfect Roman alphabet, we now have a new and perfect American alphabet of the English language" (qtd. in Thonssen 108). Hence, both Castanis and Comstock attribute the perfections of America to the institutions of classical Greece.

Comstock's alphabet and other "relics" of ancient Greece found in America serve as a substitute Greek ethnic community in America. By finding such outgrowths of ancient Greece and seeing them embraced as distinctly American, Castanis can imagine a community in the Andersonian sense. But while Benedict Anderson defines the nation as "an imagined political community," Castanis imagines the transnational entity of America and Greece as one community (6). In doing so, Castanis engages in an ongoing process of identity construction that Stuart Hall terms identification. Hall writes: "[I]dentification is constructed on the back of a recognition of some common origin or shared characteristics with another person or group, or with an ideal, and with the natural closure of solidarity and allegiance established on this foundation" (2). Castanis' attempts to link the ideologies of Greece and America via the foundation of ancient Greece establish the foundation for "solidarity" and "allegiance" that Hall describes. A key factor for Hall and one that is apt to Castanis' case is that identification "does not obliterate difference," but merges it in "a fantasy of incorporation" (3). By engaging in this process of identification, Castanis attempts to create an imagined community between himself, Greece, and America that glosses over the differences between the two cultures instead of joining them with a hyphen.

Itinerancy and Transnationality

Castanis employs classical models to construct his itinerant identity. He acknowledges the itinerant nature of his identity when he classifies himself as an "Odysseus-like" wanderer. In fact, *the Odyssey* becomes one of the text's controlling metaphors, and Castanis repeatedly refers to himself as a wanderer. When Castanis contemplates his first return to America after having lived in Greece for several years, he explains his wandering impulses and self-proclaimed transnationality:

> His desire of revisiting the friends of suffering humanity,[7] awakened a determination to re-embark upon a second tour. [...] The wanderer had tortured

---

[7] Castanis' text is marked by narrative discontinuity. The autobiographical narrator uses different pronouns to refer to himself, becoming the "I," "we," and "he" in the narrative. The autobiographical narrator also refers to himself by various names and titles, such as Christopher (Castanis' first name), Mustapha (the name given to him

his destiny to a roaming course, and when it was ready to start nothing could restrain it. [...] New York came to mind; the shade of Boston hovered near; and the very atmosphere of transatlantic nature filled his heart, and wafted every affection to the rock-bound coast of the Pilgrim's wintry flight. (177-8)

Castanis' friends and family try to dissuade him from returning to America, but Castanis is "an habitual wanderer" who cannot "desist from his eternal round of careering from shore to mount, and from the peak to the main again" (178). Castanis writes:

From his boyhood, he had been lionizing, from necessity, foreign shores, beyond Scio, and [...] who could by force of reason or feeling dissuade him from launching anew into the billowy deep? Just as well might you descend to Hades and endeavor to persuade Sisyphus to let the rock rest on the summit, as to ask the Chian Exile to hinder the rolling stones of his adventures from taking another revolution. Its habit of roving forbids the supposition. (178)

Here, Castanis constructs himself as captive and exile, accentuating the fact that, like Sisyphus, he has been forced into a cycle of perpetual motion. Castanis' situation as runaway slave and exile from both his birthplace and family has prompted his "lionizing" and "roving." Castanis does not perceive his itinerancy as voluntary, but as a part of his make-up that was set in motion by powers beyond his control.

Instead of focusing on just his own itinerancy, Castanis also continually looks for fellow itinerants to use as models for his own identity construction. Most notably, he evokes the idea of Lord Byron as a fellow transnational itinerant. He cites Byron's poetry throughout his text, and when he discusses Byron's role in the Greek war for independence, he describes Byron as "the English bard who was enrolled as a citizen of Greece," calling him "the Greek-spirited Byron" (151). According to Castanis, because Byron's spirit is Greek, Byron has two simultaneous identities: he is at once English and Greek, much as Castanis who is simultaneously American and Greek. Identity construction becomes voluntary and pluralistic according to Castanis: instead of being trapped in a continual cycle of wandering, Castanis here suggests that it is possible to choose his own identity. He is captive and exile insofar as his identity was ruptured or taken away at the point of captivity and exile, but Byron offers Castanis a model of transnationality that creates a metaphorical end to his

---

when he was a Turkish slave), "the Chian exile," "the poor pedlar," and "the boy of Scio" (44, 93, 95, 97, 107). This narrative disjuncture reflects Castanis' complex subjectivity, his fragmented sense of self and his inability to define himself or enact a specific identity. He is all of the names, titles, and pronouns that he calls himself, and yet none in particular. Indeed, using the novelistic convention of third person narration suggests a distance between the autobiographical narrator and his retrospective subject.

exile status. Following this model, if a person is by nature or necessity an itinerant, the person can have an identity. Yet, this identity has to be a transnational one. In other words, Castanis cannot be just Greek and Byron cannot be just English anymore. As Hall asserts, identities "arise from the narrativization of the self," and are "constituted within, not outside representation" (4). Through the written act of identifying Byron as both English and Greek, Castanis opens up a space with which to construct this type of transnational identity, "not the so-called return to roots but a coming-to-terms-with our 'routes'" (Hall 4). Hence, by establishing a connection with Byron, who is presented as an itinerant and a transnational subject, Castanis authenticates his own identity in turn.

Identity and a Founding Text

As a transnational itinerant, Castanis' experience may differ from that of early Greek immigrants to the United States, but even so, his text shares a characteristic of conventional immigrant autobiographies observed by William Boelhower. Throughout *The Greek Exile*, Castanis exhibits what Boelhower calls "the need to locate a founding text" (120). Boelhower explains: "As a text-type immigrant autobiography is architectonically a narrative of constitutional allegoresis. This means that its very attempt at coherence-its desire to *be* a text and achieve closure-actually depends on its success in verifying its own beginnings, having as it does the Constitution as its ultimate object" (119).

In order for immigrant autobiographers to verify their beginnings, Boelhower reasons that they must find an "ordering text of American identity and nationality" (121). This "ordering text" to which Boelhower refers is not a text, but rather a concept, or "the sort of constitutional universalism that made the actual Constitution possible" (133-34). Because America and modern Greece share the foundational principles of ancient Greece, Castanis is able to conceptualize a universal beginning for both nations and both cultures. Creating this universal beginning is vital for Castanis, who moves geographically between Greece and America and whose identity is both characterized by and bound to aspects of both cultures.

Castanis locates his founding text in the ideological systems of classical Greece and looks to classical Greece as the foundation of a cultural identity that accounts for his American cultural traits and ideologies. Castanis writes that "[d]uring his ten years' wanderings in his second motherland, he has found traces of his ancestral spirit and fresh mementoes of the indissoluble *connexion*, he might almost say *identity*, of the Greek and American character" (211). Castanis discovers the "character" of ancient Greece in America, a country he calls his "second motherland" and "adopted home" (210). Unlike early Greek immigrants who, as Yiorgos Kalogeras puts it, "narrated a community by building bridges between the past and the present of the Greeks in the U.S. and Greece," Castanis is not interested in enacting a Greek ethnic identity in America because that would separate him ethnically from Americans (16). Contrarily, Castanis "narrates" past and present Greeks *and* Americans to create a non-essentialist cultural category that includes both Greece and America, writing: "who can read without emotion Plato, Xenophon, and the other philosophical statesmen who analyzed both tyranny and democracy, and who reveal the springs of many political phenomena which America seems to have been reserved to exemplify" (253-4, 210). Castanis' discourse posits America as the symbolic rebirth of ancient Greece because America's ideological foundations reincarnate the political philosophies of the ancient Greek republic.[8] Discursively, Castanis uses the rhetoric of fulfillment to rework the Protestant vision of America as a "city on a hill" into a secular promised land, or the political fulfillment of ancient Greece.[9]

The fact that Castanis envisions America as the secular fulfillment of ancient Greece becomes apparent upon his initial arrival in America when he observes: "We had been banished, by want, to a home equivalent to that which we had lost by Turkish invasion" (134). Castanis' claim that the home he fled is "equivalent" to the one in which he has arrived is based on these two places' shared classical associations. As the autobiographical narrator suggests, American "architecture is classic," but, more importantly, American dominant ideologies can be traced back to the ideological systems of ancient Greece: "A Greek here beholds home-like objects, crowding about his path; the government is democratic; [...] the people are inquisitive; the society unprejudiced; and the literature of the country, even some of the highest models of oratory and poetry, are

---

[8]   Castanis' rationale prefigures that of early Greek immigrants. Yiorgos Anagnostou explains that these immigrants considered themselves "direct racial descendents of the ancient Greeks" because "the American ideals of republic citizenship were traced [by Greek immigrants] to ancient Greece," and that these immigrants felt that they "did not merely represent natural Americanness, they embodied 'ur-Americanness'" (46).

[9]   Castanis' secular vision is supported by Timothy Smith, who argues that Protestant typology is an apt description for the American ethnic experience, as well as for Protestants. Smith writes, "[f]rom its colonial beginnings, the migration of bonded groups or the formation of such groups in the new land made the biblical imagery of the Exodus seem a metaphor for the American experience, not only for English Puritans and Russian Jews, but for Christian villagers of Catholic, Protestant, and Orthodox persuasions from all parts of Europe" (1176).

grounded on Greek subjects" (211). For Castanis, these similarities erase the differences between the two cultures. Classical Greek ideological systems serve as the origin for both cultures, thus legitimizing Castanis' implicit claim that he is both Greek and American.

Castanis' ideological underpinnings tend not simply toward cultural inclusion, but also toward cosmopolitanism. Perry Anderson explains that enlightenment cosmopolitanism was characterized by universalism, and that "typically, it assumed a basic harmony between the interests of civilized nations [...] all potentially united in a common struggle against tyranny and superstition" (8). Anderson describes the Enlightenment as being marked by a "spirit of regional fraternity" (8). This spirit of fraternity abounds in Castanis' prose: «Would to God that nationality should continue to base itself upon community of sentiment and intellect, and no longer upon the natural boundaries which jealousy or hatred may interpose to separate the human race into hostile armies! The events of this date show that the epoch of universal union between nations is advancing» (117-8).

For Castanis, cosmopolitanism is a viable possibility for the future, but his present objective is to solidify the fraternal spirit between America and Greece for the sake of his personal identity. Therefore, even enlightenment thought cannot be separated from its classical roots: "Thy protégé, or son, Homer, whose genius was elicited and patronized by thee, thy son of the present century, Coray, and thy godlike forbearance under ancient tyrants, all thy genius and action afford nourishment to the world!" (87). Here, Castanis emphasizes the ideological and ancestral ties between Adamantios Korais, a leading Greek nationalist and enlightenment figure, and his classical predecessor, Homer, by incorporating enlightenment thinking into his founding text-an idea which, not surprisingly, echoes the writings of Korais.[10]

Castanis' bent toward cosmopolitanism is not unusual because, as a product of modernity,[11] Castanis was influenced by the concepts of enlightened Greek intellectuals like Korais, "the brightest gem of Grecian

---

[10] Korais writes, "From the 24th May I have been in the illustrious city of Paris, the home of all the arts and sciences, the new Athens. [...] All this would amaze anyone, but for a Greek, who knows that two thousand years ago in Athens his ancestors achieved a similar (perhaps a higher) level of wisdom, this amazement must be mingled with melancholy, when he reflects that such virtues are not only absent from the Greece of today, but they have been replaced by a thousand evils" (in Clogg 118).

[11] I find Anthony Giddens' definition of modernity particularly useful here. For Giddens, modernity "refer[s] to the institutions and modes of behaviour established first of all in post-feudal Europe" and "can be understood as roughly equivalent to 'the industrialised world', so long as it be recognized that industrialism is not its only institutional dimension" (15). Giddens also believes that the nation-state is one of modernity's key social forms.

talent adorning the present century" (22). By disseminating Enlightenment ideas, these intellectuals helped to create an "ideological transformation," which eventually ushered modern institutions into Greece, such as a national army, an educational system, a judiciary, and a national language. In pursuing those reforms, those enlightened intellectuals were attempting to model Greece after modern Western nations who they thought exemplified the fruition of ancient Greek institutions, inventions, insights, and intellectuals. Crucial to their project of modernization was the ideological gesture of linking modern Greece to ancient Greece and weakening the connection between modern Greece and its Byzantine past.[12] One thing Korais thought was necessary for the new Greek nation was to create a secular state and an autocephalous church, disconnecting the Orthodox church in Greece from the control of Constantinople and ridding it of its own Ottoman captivity. However, the idea of an independent church was looked upon as too Protestant by Korais' critics (Kitromilides 152, 162-66).

Castanis follows Korais' lead by drawing explicit connections between modern Greeks and ancient Greeks, but he also solidifies America's relationship to his founding text by drawing explicit connections between America's founding fathers and those of ancient Greece. For instance, when Castanis visits Mt. Vernon, he is reminded of Themistocles' tomb, and he has an unusual dream-like vision:

> Washington and Themistocles then appeared to my fancy. The trees assumed the appearance of Persian ships; and the Potomac that of the purple wave of the Salaminian straights. Washington stood as a spectator of the victory of Themistocles. Anon, Hellenic glory greeted my vision; anon barbaric darkness loomed terribly around. The clash of ancient armor was exchanged for the thunder of modern artillery, and the bloody Mars hovered in the midst of the sulphur smoke of destructive explosions, like volcanic eruptions hurling nations [...]. The spirit of liberty fled in distress from her native land and roamed westward, and soon the trackless wilderness became her domain. There the spirit of Washington acted, while that of Themistocles beheld the revival of popular

---

[12] According to Roudometof, Korais believed that "[b]y adopting the knowledge of the ancients that was preserved in the West, the modern Greeks could rise again and regain their proper position in the world. Of fundamental importance to such a program was the assumption of continuity between the 'ancients' and the 'moderns'. In Koraïs' writings, this continuity was strategically employed in order to establish the necessity for modernizing the Hellenic world. In order to become worthy of the sacred name they bore, modern Greeks needed to be 'enlightened,' an argument justifying Koraïs' modernist orientation without directly questioning the traditional ecclesiastical discourse. But even if cultural continuity with Orthodox philosophical tradition was to be preserved in principle, most of the Balkan Enlightenment emphasized Western scientific achievements in order to defeat Orthodox religious conservatism" (26).

sway and gave the Greek name of Democracy to the American form of
government. (209)

In his vision, Castanis projects Greece onto America, transforming the
American landscape into Greece and suggesting that America becomes
Greek in a similar way as the "spirit of liberty" that "fled" from Greece and
came to America to transform the American mental landscape. The
enlightenment concept of liberty here becomes the fraternal link between
the two countries. This is why Castanis writes:

> The name of Washington should be ever associated with that of the hero of
> Salamis; for America's warrior was not unassociated in intellect with the
> glorious past. He knew Themistocles in spirit, and acted as the Grecian would
> have acted under the same circumstances to support the cause of freedom and
> give a lesson of terror to ambitious and merciless tyrants. (209-10)

Castanis adeptly suggests that Washington's actions were actions of the
Greek founding father. The spirit of liberty which both Washington and
Themistocles share makes them compatriots in the same struggle against
"merciless tyrants".

Nonetheless, Washington is not the only example of an American with
innate characteristics of Greekness. Castanis provides examples among his
contemporaries as well: "Dr. Howe and Col. Miller, of Washington's
country went shoulder to shoulder with the Greek, and taught them that the
children of Democracy are one and indivisible wherever they go" (109).
Castanis links both of these philhellenes first to Washington and then to
ancient Greece, because, as "children of Democracy," Howe, Miller, and
Washington are considered descendants of ancient Greece. Through the
creation of a founding text, Castanis is able to make Greece and America
commensurable. Castanis' text elides cultural difference and posits the
claim that, as Democracy's children, both Greeks and Americans can be
identified as one group and are therefore equal and the same.

From Founding Text to Founding Father

Besides pairing the heroic figures of Washington and Themistocles,
Castanis pairs himself with the American figure with whom he most
identifies-Benjamin Franklin. Castanis attempts to build an American
identity that is also Greek by identifying himself with Franklin, a
cosmopolitan intellectual and an enlightenment figure. Like Castanis, who
spent his life moving between Greece and America, Franklin spent his life
moving between England, France, and America. Franklin's years in France
are most comparable to Castanis' years in America, and Franklin

considered France his second home just as Castanis considered America his second home. In some ways, the French even thought of Franklin as a "French" American (Isaacson 327). Castanis consciously constructs his identity in the image of Franklin, demonstrating the connection between himself, America's founding fathers, and a culturally inclusive founding text.

Franklin, too, self-consciously creates a persona in his *Autobiography*. The image of Franklin adopted by Americans in the nineteenth century is modeled after this persona, which Amy Apfel Kass calls "Franklin's Franklin" (58). Kass believes "Franklin's Franklin is centrally informed by a spirit of liberty" (58). This spirit of liberty, which Castanis sees as an outgrowth of classical Greek ideologies, is like Franklin in that both are "self-made" (58). Castanis seizes upon this image of Franklin and models himself after "America's incomparable sage, who snatched the lightning from heaven and the sceptre from tyrants" (142). Castanis makes several explicit references to Franklin throughout his text and models certain anecdotes after Franklin's *Autobiography*. He even draws on important parallels between himself and Franklin in framing his narrative around the central motif of captivity because, as a youth, Franklin experienced a type of bondage. Franklin was indentured to his brother against his will, but like Castanis, who escaped from the Turks, escaped indenture.

Carla Mulford argues that nineteenth-century Americans invoked the figure of Franklin "as a means of mediating the 'national image' of the United States as a hard working, benevolent, tolerant, Christian nation" (18). Castanis' Franklinian value system is most vivid in his stories of economic enterprise. Because Castanis' enslavement, escape, youthful independence, and success are some of his American traits, he is similar to Benjamin Franklin who left home as a teenager with little more than the clothes on his back but rose to become one of America's founding fathers. In his *Autobiography*, Franklin writes, "I found myself in New York near 300 miles from home, a Boy of 17, without the least Recommendation to or Knowledge of any Person in the Place, and with very little Money in my Pocket" (1326). Likewise, when Castanis escapes slavery and must flee from Chios, he is young, homeless, alone and "leveled to complete destitution" (95). He arrives on the island Syra and must earn a living. He writes, "[f]or the first time, I had launched forth upon life with nothing from my parents but their blessing; [...] I really felt that I had been thrown upon my own resources" (93). Unlike Franklin who "ha[d] a trade," Castanis does not, but, because of his practicality and ingenuity, he becomes a water peddler, selling his water with Franklinian zeal (1326).

Looking for a way to increase water sales, Castanis creates a jingle: "The echo of this couplet awakened the attention of the whole community, and [...] gave the market quite a start. Competition was alive in the water business, but who could rival the Chian exile aided by the swan-like notes of the dying innocence of his motherland" (97). Castanis' marketing technique is such a success that he puts other water peddlers out of business, placing him in a similar position as Franklin, whose printing shop is the most lucrative in town. Subsequently, Castanis learns something about the bitter world of business when the other peddlers conspire against him:

> On going to the fountain one day, not suspecting any ambush, he filled his jar [with water], and jogged along in fond anticipation of profit, counting his paras before they were paid. The jar was resting on his shoulder in short-lived tranquility, for on entering the suburbs, an opponent in disguise drew a sling with unerring precision, and darted a stone which dashed his poor jar in pieces, poured water down his neck, and left nothing but the handle adhering to his fingers. This made the poetic adventurer change his tone, hush his music, and [...] lay himself to dry in the sun. (97-8)

Castanis' experience, however, ends with a Franklinian twist. When seventeen-year-old Franklin was without money or friends, he met a kind old man named Dr. Brown. In an interesting parallel, when Castanis truly seems down and out, he meets a kind old man named Zygomalas.

Zygomalas is a fish merchant who takes Castanis under his wing and gives him a job selling fish after his jar is smashed by the angry water peddlers. Again, Castanis models himself after young Franklin, writing: «I ran from house to house, winging the fame of our assortment, and turning a penny or para in every method imaginable, putting in practice the precepts of Franklin, and demonstrating that 'time is money.' Disregarding all luxury, I was taught by experience, that a "penny saved is a penny gained." (99).

Castanis adheres to Franklin's model of industry, foreshadowing his rise in social and economic status. From water peddler to scholar and author, Castanis illustrates his ability to rise through hard work in the image of Franklin-the American self-made man. Castanis not only models his stories after Franklin's tales of industry, experience, and success, but he also deliberately sprinkles them with Franklin's "Poor Richard" adages, drawing an explicit parallel between himself and Franklin. Thus, through Castanis' attempt to construct his identity in the image of Franklin, we see how, once Castanis creates a founding text based on ancient Greece ideological systems, he attempts to self-consciously construct an identity based on that of a proto-typical American, moving from founding text to founding father.

Orthodoxy, Protestantism, and Modernization through Conversion

Although Castanis' Franklinian value system posits American ideologies that illustrate how Castanis situates himself within the American social imaginary, there are instances in the narrative that implicitly reveal the ways in which the autobiographical narrator does not fit within the American social imaginary.[13] A case in point is when Castanis explains his problematic religious opinions. These opinions throw into relief Castanis' complex subjectivity and problematize his attempt at identity construction.

When Castanis returns to Greece after his first voyage to America, his religious views have undergone a transformation: «The change wrought upon the Chian exile's mind, will appear in the succeeding narration, and show the beneficial influence of American society to dispel superstition. The friends of Greece can perceive the effect of their institutions upon a nation which looks to America as the Elysium of its hopes and prayers» (136).

Castanis describes his religious transformation in what Julio Ortega terms "the discourse of abundance." Ortega observes that this discourse is typical of texts of discovery and travel, and traces it back to Columbus's diaries:

> Columbus reproduces and intensifies the classical *locus amoenus*, but he inscribes it within another topos that gives life to a place of plenty: the topos of abundance. While the first topos invokes a classical discourse, the second (drawn from itinerant literature and the repertoire of Cocagne) infects the first with disquieting excess. The first topos names; the second overnames. The first reconfigures experience, and the second turns it into hyperbole. (373)

Castanis' discourse of abundance emphasizes that his personal transformation is critically linked to his disavowal of what he terms superstition. By evoking the *locus amoenus* of Elysium, and connecting it back to American Protestantism, Castanis "reconfigures experience" and "turns it into hyperbole." However, even though Castanis engages in the discourse of abundance, he is unable to reconcile his changing beliefs about religion. Hence, he does not renounce the Greek church, and describes himself in terms of having a split religious identity.

Castanis says that he was born in "the house of a distinguished Bishop, whom [his] mother was visiting" (18). Being born "in such a hallowed place" he writes, "was regarded by the superstitious as a favorable omen" (18). Castanis is like his enlightenment predecessor Korais, who sought to

---

[13] Here I am relying on Mulford's concept of the social imaginary, which she explains in the following terms: "a nation can be said to consist of a group of persons relating together. They imagine themselves in that they invent for themselves a political relationship which is socially determinable as a community. In other words, they imagine themselves together in such a way as to erase-or at least lessen the impact of-difference" (19).

modernize Greek institutions by emphasizing Greece's classical past while attempting to disconnect it from its Byzantine past-in particular the associations of Greek Orthodoxy with dark age Christianity (Runciman 393). So, while Castanis is careful not to criticize the Orthodox church directly, he, nevertheless, explicitly criticizes certain community members, "the superstitious," for the way in which they interpret the church's dogma. The important point here is that Castanis defines members of what he hopes will be his imagined community as excluded from that community.

According to Kourvetaris, many of the Greek war orphans were schooled in Protestant theology by missionaries and encouraged to return to Greece as missionaries themselves (311). Although Castanis never claims to have acted as a missionary, he tells us that he attended American missionary schools in Greece. And while he never officially converts to Protestantism, he admits that he unofficially converts during his first trip to America. In a way, Castanis' unofficial religious conversion is similar to what Anagnostou calls "the narrative of cultural assimilation," which is "perceived as a deeply felt conversion experience, a liberating rebirth." Anagnostou adds that "there is a productivity in reconfiguring the self, associated with the pleasures felt anew in the experience of 'disembedding' from traditional structures and participating in modernity" (28). While Castanis' conversion remains unofficial, illustrating a complication in his identity that he cannot work through, it also illustrates his participation in the projects of modernity and modernization: "began to change my ideas of religion, and was almost persuaded to be a Protestant; yet the generous, mild and indulgent character of that sect looks more to opinion than to formality, and desires not to convert the body but the soul. Such liberty allowed me to remain as I was, a Greek in church, but a Protestant in feeling" (135).

Castanis, who has been educated and enlightened, now internalizes a sense of Protestantism. Although he does not completely renounce Greek Orthodoxy, he, nonetheless, seems to hold that Protestantism can fulfill Greece religiously in a similar manner to that in which America can fulfill Greece politically.

When he returns to Greece after his first visit to America, Castanis reunites with his mother, a devout member of the Greek Orthodox Church. According to the rituals of her religion, she "rushed to the picture [of the Virgin Mary], and kissed it fervently," piously giving thanks for her son's safe return. Castanis, however, "neglected even making the sign of the cross, and after some days [...] blew out the taper [that she had lit], and assured [his] mother that [he] had transferred the light to [his] heart" (160-61). During this episode, Castanis describes his mother as being "completely astounded," claiming, "I cannot and shall not attempt to describe the mingled emotions, depicted on her brow, nor the expressions which I uttered to display my American ideas on religion. She allowed me to believe as my American friends had taught me, but begged me to let her die in her father's religion" (161). In this unresolved standoff with his mother, Castanis gives voice to opposing views about religion and to his own religious ambivalence. He internalizes religious beliefs by choosing that his soul be Protestant, but also recognizes that *his* beliefs will always be stained with the oil of the Greek Orthodox baptism. He also allows his mother's voice to oppose the text's dominant religious ideologies, give voice to Greek religious ideologies, and expose the complications in his subjectivity. This leaves him unable to formulate an American religious identity because Greek Orthodoxy and Protestantism are incommensurable.

Conclusion

By comparing America and modern Greece to ancient Greece, Castanis attempts to align his birth country with his adopted home. He does not simply hail America, but calls forth an America that hearkens back to his ancient Greek ancestors. Instead of calling attention to America's otherness, he calls attention to its similarity to Greece, while at the same time suggesting that ancient Greece is the reason for America's success as a nation: "As the city of Minerva, by the cultivation of free principles, reached the height of refinement, so may America yet arrive at greater celebrity, by imbibing their virtue, and rejecting their faults" (187). Because America has emulated the virtuous traits of ancient Greece, Castanis sees America as the incarnation of his classical heritage.

Although modern Greece lost its connection with ancient Greece during the years of the Turkish Occupation, it regained its independence with the help of America. Hence, Castanis places equal emphasis on the two nations' ideological systems because they were both born from a particular founding text: ancient Greece. When Castanis walks around Boston with several Greek sailors, they stop to hear a speech given by Daniel Webster. He notes: "a great concourse of citizens were thronging, to listen to a speech from Daniel Webster, the friend of the Greek cause. The sight of that champion of democracy impressed our minds, as with a vision of some ancestral personage of our own nation" (187). Castanis feels a sense of pride in aligning himself and Greece with the strength and benevolence of the American people because the foundation of America is the "spirit of liberty"-an ideology born in ancient Greece.

Ancient Greece is the ideological foundation within which Castanis places the cultures of modern Greece and America on equal footing. In this type of identity construction, there is no need for a hyphenated identity; for Castanis to say he is Greek is tantamount to saying he is American. While the unique method by which Castanis attempts to negotiate his identity distinguishes his self-understanding from present-day postcolonial theories and positions, it also reveals underlying conflicts that Castanis is unable to work through and perhaps even unable to acknowledge-a fact which is mostly evident in his religious transformation. Castanis' position is complex, because he is interested in constructing a type of identity that conforms to his itinerancy and must therefore include the cultural components of both Greece and America. By drawing on the ideas of enlightenment cosmopolitanism, Castanis tries to solidify the fraternal spirit between America and Greece, and, in doing so, to solidify his identity. Thus, instead of conceptualizing a multicultural identity which, like hybridity, is based on the articulation of cultural difference, Castanis conceptualizes a multicultural identity based on the articulation of cultural sameness. Ultimately, the value of Castanis' book should not be underestimated, for it allows us keen insight into the rare multicultural perspective of a nineteenth-century itinerant subject.

Works Cited

Anagnostou, Yiorgos. "Forget the Past, Remember the Ancestors! Modernity,'Whiteness,"American Hellenism, and the Politics of Memory in Early Greek America." *Journal of Modern Greek Studies* 22 (2004): 25-71.

Anderson, Perry. "Internationalism: A Breviary." *New Left Review* 14 (2002): 5-25.

Bhabha, Homi K. *The Location of Culture*. London: Routledge, 1994.

Boelhower, William. "The Beginning Text: Immigrant Autobiographies and Constitutional Allegoresis (Or, All's Well that Begins Well)." *The U.S. Constitution after 200 Years*. Editor? Amsterdam: Free UP, 1988.

Burgess, Thomas. *Greeks in America: An Account of their Coming, Progress, Customs, Living, and Aspirations. With an Historical Introduction and the Stories of Some Famous American-Greeks*. Boston: Sherman, French & Co., 1913.

Castanis, Christophorus Plato. *The Greek Exile, or a Narrative of the Captivity and Escape of Christophorus Plato Castanis during the Massacre on the Island of Scio, by the Turks, together with Various Adventures in Greece and America. Written by Himself*. Philadelphia: Lippincott, Grambo, & Co., 1851.

Clogg, Richard. *The Movement for Greek Independence 1770-1821: A Collection of Documents*. New York: Barnes & Noble, 1976.

Fenton, Heike and Melvin Hecker. *The Greeks in America 1528-1977*. Dobbs Ferry: Oceana Publications, 1978.

Franklin, Benjamin. *Benjamin Franklin Writings*. Notes J.A. Leo Lamay. New York: The Library of America, 1987.

Giddens, Anthony. *Modernity and Self-Identity: Self and Society in the Late Modern Age*. Stanford: Stanford UP, 1991.

Hall, Stuart. "Introduction: Who Needs 'Identity'?" Introduction. *Questions of Cultural Identity*. Ed. Paul du Gay and Stuart Hall. London: Sage, 1996. 1-17.

Isaacson, Walter. *Benjamin Franklin: An American Life*. New York: Simon & Schuster, 2003.

Kass, Amy Apfel. "Autobiography and American Identity: Another Look at Benjamin Franklin." *Cultural Visions: Essays in the History of Culture*. Eds. Benjamin C. Sax and Penny Schine. Amsterdam: Rodopi, 2000. 41-61.

Kalogeras, Yiorgos. "Narrating an Ethnic Group." *Journal of the Hellenic Diaspora* 18.2 (1992): 13-34.

Kitromilides, Paschalis M. "'Imagined Communities' and the Origins of the National Question in the Balkans." *European History Quarterly* 19 (1989): 149-94.

Kourvetaris, George A. "Greek-American Professionals: 1820's-1970's." *Balkan Studies* 18.2 (1977): 285-317.

Moskos, Charles C., Jr. *Greek Americans: Struggle and Success*. Englewood Cliffs: Prentice Hall, 1980.

Mulford, Carla. "Benjamin Franklin and the Myths of Nationhood." *Making America/Making American Literature: Franklin to Cooper*. Eds. A. Robert Lee and W.M. Verhoeven. Amsterdam: Rodopi, 1996.

Ortega, Julio. "The Discourse of Abundance." Trans. Nicolás Wey Gómez. *American LiteraryHistory* 4.3 (1992): 369-85.

Roessel, David. *In Byron's Shadow: Modern Greece in the English & American Imagination*. Oxford: Oxford UP, 2002.

Roudometof, Victor. "From Rum Millet to Greek Nation: Enlightenment, Secularization, and National Identity in Ottoman Balkan Society, 1453-1821." *Journal of Modern Greek Studies* 16 (1998): 11-48.

Runciman, Steven. *The Great Church in Captivity: A Study of the Patriarchate of Constantinople from the Eve of the Turkish Conquest to the Greek War of Independence*. 1968. Cambridge: Cambridge UP, 1985.

Saloutos, Theodore. *They Remember America: The Story of the Repatriated Greek-Americans*.Berkeley: U of California P, 1956.

Scourby, Alice. *The Greek Americans*. Boston: Twayne, 1984.

Thonssen, Lester W. "*A System of Elocution* (Book)." *Quarterly Journal of Speech* 19.1 (1933): 105-108. *Communication and Mass Media Complete*. EBSCO. Louisiana State U, Middleton Lib. 28 August 2005 <http://80-web11.epnet.com.libezp.lib.lsu.eduhttp://80-wweb11. epnet. com.libezp. lib. lsu.edu>.

STEFANO LUCONI

Italian-American Historiography and the Search for a Usable Past

Introduction

This essay is a case study of public history; namely, it focuses on the implications of historical analysis for the broader society within which a particular reconstruction of the past has been attempted. Nicola Gallerano has suggested-and it is somehow self-evident as well-that, regardless of scholars' intentions, historical interpretations are not necessarily confined to the ivory tower of academia, but have social consequences that can contribute to influencing public opinion and to shaping public policies. The *Schuldfrage*-that is, the debate about the German responsibilities in the outbreak of the world wars-is, perhaps, the best known example of that phenomenon (Habermas). Yet, even the interpretations of less devastating historical events can have a social impact. Thus, Italian-American studies, too, have lent themselves to public use. For instance, in her recent essay "La scoperta dell'America," Bénédicte Deschamps has examined how Italian Americans reconstructed the discovery of the New World, purportedly overemphasizing Christopher Columbus' Italian extraction, in order to legitimize the accommodation of their own minority group within U.S. society (416-28). Similarly, Guido Tintori has shown that Italian Americans tend to overlook the pre-war pro-Fascist feelings of their communities when they research the mistreatment of unnaturalized Italian immigrants in the United States at wartime (100-2).

Against this backdrop, this essay outlines Italian Americans' struggle for inclusion in affirmative action programs in the United States and points out that such efforts have relied on a selective interpretation of the Italian-American experience that stresses the condition of Italian Americans as a minority group whose plight has been shaped by ethnic prejudice and discrimination on the part of the U.S. establishment. It also argues that such endeavors have, on the one hand, helped the development of Italian-American studies as an academic discipline, while on the other they have eventually missed their main target following the current tendency to discontinue affirmative action programs in the United States and the recent improvement of Italian Americans' social and economic conditions. Therefore, the conclusion is that such a selective use of the past has not significantly contributed to the empowering of Italian Americans.

A clarification that needs to be made at this point is that the expression affirmative action refers to U.S. policies that aimed at remedying past social discrimination by allocating jobs and resources to socially disadvantaged groups (Swain). Implementing the 1964 Civil Rights Act, affirmative action was conceived primarily for African Americans and has been also extended to women since the mid 1960s. However, lack of a clear-cut definition of what an unprivileged group is has potentially made other minority groups eligible for the benefits of that legislation (Sindler). Hence, Italian Americans have been among the minorities that have endeavored to profit by affirmative action.

Italian Americans' Struggles for Inclusion in Affirmative Action Programs

In 1978, Philip Di Leo, an Italian-American medical student, appealed to the U.S. Supreme Court for admission to the University of Colorado under a special assistance program that granted underrepresented groups special enrolment opportunities. The program was intended for African Americans, Mexican Americans, and native Americans. Still, Di Leo contended that he was entitled to the benefits of the university's affirmative action policy on the grounds that he, too, was a member of an ethnic minority needing special attention because he had grown up in poverty in New York City's "Little Italy" (Hilliard). Ten years later, the counselors for Italian-American Congressman Mario Biaggi asked the federal court for the eastern district of New York to categorize Italian Americans as a "cognizable racial group" and to set aside a verdict of guilt passed on their client because the prosecution had discriminatorily used its peremptory challenges to exclude Biaggi's fellow ethnics from the jury that had convicted him of racketeering (Massaro 51-54). In 1992, as he has subsequently recalled in his account "The 80th Street Mafia," Joseph V. Scelsa appealed to the provisions of title VII of the 1964 Civil Rights Act to prevent the City University of New York (CUNY) from removing him from the position of director of the John D. Calandra Italian American Institute. As an individual of Italian descent, he claimed discrimination in the field of employment on the basis of national origin and also argued that Italian Americans were entitled to affirmative action protection (Helvesi).

The Supreme Court declined to review Di Leo's case (Greenhouse). In 1989, however, a federal court ruled that Italian Americans were definable as a racial group, even if the court limited its own holding to the eastern district of New York and denied the motion to quash Biaggi's guilty verdict (United States v. Biaggi, 673 F. Supp. 96, E.D.N.Y., 1989). Likewise, in

1992, a federal court ordered CUNY to retain Scelsa ("Civil Rights"). Such rulings were based primarily on the verdicts of previous legal cases. Nonetheless, starting with Rudolph J. Vecoli's path-breaking article "*Contadini* in Chicago," a few scholars studying the Italian experience in the United States have also contributed to the identification of Italian Americans as an ethnic minority in its own right. In the pursuit of such a goal, these scholars have marked a countertrend to the redefinition of American history in racial terms in the years that saw the rise of multiculturalism and the establishment of affirmative action programs (Pozzetta).

Ethnic Studies, Italian-American Identity, and Affirmative Action

As Nathan I. Huggins has pointed out, the elaboration of alternatives to a WASP master narrative in American ethnic history has tended to reflect the growing polarization of the United States along racial lines. In 1980, historian Richard Polenberg argued that class, ethnicity, and race were the three main categories that caused divisions within U.S. society. By the end of the century however, only race retained such a role in the wake of more than three decades of continuing deindustrialization and assimilation of white groups of European ancestry. Indeed, even before Polenberg's study came out, in his essay "Symbolic Ethnicity," sociologist Herbert J. Gans had already suggested that the various minorities of European extraction had become almost indistinguishable from one another and retained only a symbolic ethnic identity generally confined to leisure time activities. Similarly, in his 1990 *Ethnic Identity*, another sociologist, Richard Alba, stressed the successful emergence of a new type of American—the white European—who had been forged out of previously separated nationality groups. Against this backdrop, the relations between the two major racial groups in the country and the acquisition of a white ethnic identity by the members of the immigrant groups of European descent have become one of the most lively issues in ethnic studies in the last few years as the impact of research by Noel Ignatief, Karen Brodkin, and David R. Roediger has demonstrated.

It could be argued that such an outcome was a foregone conclusion. The ethnic revival of the late 1960s and 1970s coincided with the outburst of African Americans' claims and their ensuing conflicts with the white population. Furthermore, the emergence of a full-fledged ethnic consciousness among some nationality groups of European ancestry in those years often took the shape of a shared white backlash at the alleged encroachments of African Americans (Weed). Michael Novak provided a case in point for this attitude. In his 1972 best-seller, *The Rise of*

Unmeltable Ethnics, Novak conceived of an alliance among minorities of eastern- and southern-European descent that would forge a common white identity in their mutual efforts to curb the demands of both the politicized inner-city blacks and the "limousine liberals" of WASP extraction who supported African-American claims. Italian Americans bulked large among Novak's "unmeltable ethnics."

However, the fact that Italian Americans became a cohort of white Europeans-one that could not be distinguished from the other immigrant groups of European background-was hardly a social accomplishment for the members of an immigration minority who had long endured intolerance and discrimination because of their national origin, as shown by Bénédicte Deschamps in her essay "Le Racisme Anti-Italien." Rather, whiteness was a potential threat to Italian Americans' recently-achieved standing in U.S. society.

The allotment of benefits on the basis of racial and ethnic identities underlying affirmative action programs brought about a major transformation in the tradition of distributive politics in the United States. As Milton Gordon has contended, affirmative action marked the shift from color-blind liberal pluralism-which gave no formal recognition to categories of people on the basis of race and ethnicity-to corporate pluralism-which granted economic, political, and social rewards to organized racial and ethnic minorities, rather than to deserving individuals as such. The rationale behind affirmative action policies was to help members of identifiable groups overcome the consequences of previous discrimination by ensuring them preferential treatment in college admission, employment, representation in Congress through the redrawing of districts, and other sectors. Still, the implementation of these measures has generally proved to be counterproductive for Italian Americans. In the face of the growing polarization of American society along racial lines, civil-rights legislation has ensured equal-opportunities protection for non-white minorities. It has, therefore, normally ended up excluding Italian Americans from the beneficiaries of such provisions. Affirmative action has also empowered members of other ethnic groups to compete more effectively with Italian Americans in the field of education and the job market.

Italian-American Scholars and the Construction of an Italian-American Identity

Filopietistic interests commonly characterized the studies of the Italian experience in the United States published before the late 1960s, such as Giovanni Ermenegildo Schiavo's *Four Centuries of Italian-American*

History. Up to the 1960s, scholarship engaged itself mainly in a hagiographic defense of the contributions of Italian immigrants and their children to the cultural, political, economic, and social development of the United States in the attempt to counter stereotypes portraying Italian Americans as strangers who could not be assimilated. This approach not only became outdated in the face of the following and more sophisticated developments of social history that distanced research from the simplistic celebration of the immigrants' achievements (Tirabassi), but also proved unable to defend the ethnic interests of Italian Americans, as filopietism itself had intended to do. White-versus-black conflicts affected the 1960s and 1970s. In this perspective, stressing Italian Americans' accommodation within U.S. mainstream society and their contributions to the growth of American western-style civilization would have placed the offsprings of the turn-of-the-century Italian newcomers next to the Mayflower descendants in the ranks of white Americans. It would have also made Italian Americans part of the dominant racial group in U.S. history.

Such a characterization would have been most detrimental to Italian Americans. As J. Harvie Wilkinson has argued, "in the end, affirmative action rests on the perception of America as an oppressor nation. The list of beneficiaries in an affirmative action program is meant to read like a litany of victims" (146). Consequently, inclusion among the organized groups that were officially recognized as the targets of discrimination was instrumental in accessing several forms of social assistance.

This must have been clear to Di Leo. Actually, unlike Glazer and Gross-the advocates of the thesis that reverse discrimination underlay affirmative action-Di Leo did not challenge the constitutionality of such measures. Instead, he tried to have his own ethnic group added to the minorities that profited by those provisions. His stand mirrored the position of Jeno F. Paulucci, the chairperson of the National Italian American Foundation (NIAF), which was a powerful Italian-American lobby. In a 1977 op-ed, Paulucci pointed out that "we [Italian Americans] are more in favor of affirmative action than blacks are—because we are yet to benefit from it, and we need it badly. The fact is that Americans of Eastern and Southern European stock—Italians, Poles, Slavs, Lithuanians, Hungarians and others—are about as underrepresented in higher education as are blacks". Other Italian-American leaders followed suit. For instance, the proceedings of a 1979 conference sponsored by NIAF quoted the remarks of William Marcolino, who contended that affirmative action "could be used to the advantage of Italian-American students" (National Italian American Foundation 19).

However, in the late 1970s, Italian Americans had yet to prove that they qualified for such benefits. The reinterpretation of the Italian experience in the United States within the framework of multiculturalism has been used to advance the ethnic claims of Italian Americans to date. As the following paragraphs will show, this is especially true for studies that, in the attempt to highlight the agency of Italian Americans, have concluded that this immigrant group has had a specific history of its own and that the peculiarities of such an ordeal have insulated Italian Americans from the mainstream and have placed them among the minorities that have suffered from intolerance and discrimination in their adoptive country.

The conventional association of Italian immigrants and their offsprings with organized crime in the eyes of the broader U.S. society and the internment of a handful of suspected pro-Fascist sympathizers of Italian descent after the United States entered World War II have been instrumental in the representation of Italian Americans as victims of ethnic bigotry and prejudice (Albini, DiStasi). In addition, in his essay "The Italian Immigrants in the United States Labor Movement," Rudolph J. Vecoli has identified the alleged radicalism of many members of this nationality group as an additional factor pointing both to the detachment of Italian Americans from the establishment and to their discrimination as, in his opinion, the "Red Scare" and the ensuing Sacco-Vanzetti case seem to demonstrate.

Radicalism was obviously an overt challenge to the establishment of White Anglo-Saxon Protestants and has contributed to the U.S. society reacting against people of Italian extraction. Donna R. Gabaccia, Fraser M. Ottanelli, as well as Michael Miller Topp have further emphasized the Italianness of subversive political cultures. In the view of these scholars, the radicalism of Italian Americans supposedly drew on the pre-emigration experience of the newcomers of Italian origin and was nourished by a trans-national exchange of radical ideas between Italy and the United States. Conversely, one could easily argue that clientelism and political apathy, too, were part of the lives of prospective immigrants before they left their native country (Luconi, "Family Values" 51-52, 59-60). After all, strikebreaking, nonvoting, or subservience to corrupt party machines, all were widespread among Italian Americans (Luconi, "Italian Americans" 127-36; Garroni 34-49). Moreover, Vincent M. Lombardi and Matteo Pretelli have demonstrated that pro-Fascist feelings were expressed by a vast majority of Italian Americans even within the working class. In particular, many Italian Americans enjoyed the glory of the alleged achievements of the Fascist regime out of a sense of ethnic redress. They had endured ethnic intolerance for decades on the grounds of the supposed inferiority of the Italian people with respect to WASP standards. Thus, they supported dictator Benito Mussolini out of gratitude—because the *Duce* turned Italy into a great power that inspired awe worldwide—and, as a result, in the eyes of the American public, Italian Americans could no longer be considered an "inferior race" because of their national origin (Salvemini 110).

Such nationalistic sentiments were also clearly at odds with the claim that a large majority of Italian Americans were fierce internationalist radicals. Moreover, as John P. Diggins has shown, adherence to fascism aligned many Italian Americans with the favorable portrait of Mussolini as a modernizer and a benign dictator who prevailed within the U.S. establishment before Italy's entry into World War II.

As for voting behavior, the electorate of Italian ancestry voted overwhelmingly for Democratic presidential candidate Franklin D. Roosevelt in the 1930s. Still, Italian-American voters were attracted less by the New Deal labor and social legislation than by access to Democratic patronage and accommodation into their host society through the political recognition that the Democratic party granted them (Luconi, "La partecipazione" 491-97). Notwithstanding the prevailing expediency of Italian-American progressivism, labor militancy and radicalism have been the focuses of research into the Italian experience in the United States, such as in the collection *The Lost World of Italian American Radicalism* recently edited by Philip V. Cannistraro and Gerald Meyer. Considering this context, Salvatore J. LaGumina has even turned such a notorious gangster as Paolo Antonio Vaccarelli (alias Paul Kelly) into a champion of organized labour.

A remarkable instance of the emphasis placed on the presence of leftists among Italian Americans is the disproportionate attention devoted to Congressman Vito Marcantonio, who served in the House of Representatives from 1935 to 1939 and again between 1941 and 1951. For example, Gerald Meyer and Gil Fagiani have presented him as an outstanding example of Italian-American radicalism. Marcantonio did lean toward communism. However, as Peter Jackson has revealed, he was primarily the operator of one of the most effective political machines in the United States. It is also questionable to what extent Marcantonio's career was representative of the Italian-American experience. Most Italian Americans lobbied Congress for Italy's inclusion among the beneficiaries of the Marshall Plan and also intervened in the country's domestic politics to prevent the Communist Party from winning the 1948 parliamentary elections in their ancestral country (Wall). Yet, as his own speeches demonstrated, Marcantonio opposed U.S. involvement in Italy's internal affairs during the post-war years (251-56).

The misrepresentation of Marcantonio as the embodiment of the average Italian American continued in the late 1990s. At its annual meeting in November 1998, the American Italian Historical Association organized a thematic panel with the explicit purpose of putting the figure of Marcantonio forward as a model that could "counter the detrimental stereotypes and promote a positive image" of Italian Americans, as the introduction to the panel read ("More about"). According to this source, Marcantonio was chosen to perform such a role, not only because of his radical militancy but also on the grounds that, in the 1940s, he somehow foreran the civil rights legislation of the mid 1960s by advocating the repeal of the poll tax in order to enforce the enfranchisement of African-American voters in the South.

The focus on this latter feature of Marcantonio's activity in Congress was hardly casual. One of the major obstacles to the characterization of Italian Americans as victims of prejudice because of their minority status and to the demands for the benefits of affirmative action has been their inclusion among the groups of the American population who have, over time, developed a white self-perception and who have on occasion exhibited racist attitudes toward African Americans (Alba, *Italian Americans*; Guglielmo). Contrary to this interpretation, some historians of Italian ancestry, such as Rudolph J. Vecoli in his article "Are Italian Americans Just White Folks?" and Richard Gambino in his essay "Italian Americans," have made a point of showing that their fellow ethnics have retained an identity based on national ancestry and have not been subsumed by the larger group of white Europeans. Such an argument implies that Italian Americans hardly played a role in the reaction of whites against the black movement for civil and political rights and, therefore, cannot be associated with the dominant ethnic groups of European extraction that have been excluded from the rewards of corporate pluralism.

Dino Cinel and John Santucci have even contended that, at least in the early stages of the Italian immigration, common discriminatory assumptions often aligned Italian Americans with blacks. Indeed, there has been a tendency to emphasize the slight similarities between the African-American and Italian-American experiences. For instance, the lynching of at least thirty-four people of Italian ancestry between the mid 1880s and the outbreak of World War I has helped affiliate Italian Americans with African Americans as victims of white homicidal anger (Gambino, *Vendetta*; Salvetti). However, this scholarship seems to ignore another dimension of Italian-black relations. Studies by Arnold Shankman, Nadia Venturini, and Jonathan Reider have pointed out that anti-black feelings were voiced in the "Little Italies" not only in the 1960s and 1970s or at the time of the Italo-Ethiopian War, but also as early as following the 1896 defeat of the Italian army by Ethiopians at Aduwa.

Misrepresentation has affected the examination of the relations between Irish Americans and Italian Americans as well. Rudolph J. Vecoli in his article "Prelates and Peasants" and Richard A. Varbero in his essay "Philadelphia's South Italians and the Irish Church" have suggested that the Irish were traditionally the harshest competitors of Italian Americans at the workplace, or in politics, crime, and especially religious life. While both these immigrant groups were the targets of religious intolerance because of their common Catholic faith (D'Agostino 13-14, 32-52, 93-94,

105, 113, 126, 162, 309-11, 313-14), emphasis on such conflicts has contributed to stressing the strife of Italian Americans with a nationality group of European descent and, therefore, their resistance to the acquisition of a white ethnic identity. Focus on the rivalry between Irish Americans and Italian Americans has helped divert attention from the antipathy between Italian Americans and African Americans as well. In particular, few scholars have endeavored to reassess the role of Italian Americans in the reaction of whites against African-American militancy. Vecoli, in his essay "Ethnicity: A Neglected Dimension of American History," has contended that, although the rise of black power in the 1960s helped revitalize the ethnic self-consciousness of the European immigration minorities, each nationality group rediscovered an identity of its own (70). Frank Barbaro has also emphasized that the surge in affiliation with Italian-American organizations in the wake of the civil rights legislation enactment did not result from racist attitudes. Conversely, in his opinion, the growing membership of these associations demonstrates that affirmative action marked a revival of the self-perception of Italian Americans as Italians rather than their mere absorption into the broader ranks of white ethnics. Such an Italian-American identity, as Alfred Aversa has held, did not cause hostility toward African Americans. Instead, as Aversa has also maintained, black militancy provided, above all, a model for Italian-American activism that turned against the ethnic defamation and discrimination that the minority group still had to face in the late 1960s and early 1970s.

A similar attitude has affected the examination of Italian-American prejudice against African Americans. Italian-American scholars have generally overlooked political figures of Italian ancestry who championed the white reaction against African Americans or have tended to minimize their racist attitudes. Remarkably, Frank L. Rizzo has become a sort of pariah in Italian-American history because his racial conservatism and taste for black-baiting are obviously at odds with present-day political correctness (Luconi, "Frank L. Rizzo"). His hostility toward African Americans could undermine the hypothesis that the relations between Italian Americans and blacks have been friendly. It could also question the idea that Italian Americans have been discriminated against, and have not acted as discriminators. Therefore, for instance, although Rizzo was a two-term mayor of Philadelphia, one of the largest U.S. cities, Salvatore J. LaGumina et al. have concluded that, unlike rather obscure figures such as Admiral Bancroft Gherardi or meteorologist Salvatore Pagliuca, Rizzo does not deserve an entry in their *The Italian American Experience*, which is now a standard reference work on Italian Americans.

The most authoritative advocates of the characterization of Italian Americans as a discriminated ethnic group whose members still enact an identity based on national ancestry are scholars of Italian descent themselves. Moreover, personal concerns about the future of Italian Americans as an ethnic group influence these scholars' interest in Italian-American ethnicity. This has been the claim of a number of studies—such as Rudolph J. Vecoli's "Born Italian," Richard Gambino's *Blood of My Blood*, and Raymond A. Belliotti's *Seeking Identity*—which amalgamate research and autobiographical accounts.

A brief overview of the history of the American Italian Historical Association (AIHA) offers an insightful case in point for the increasing role of ethnic militancy in Italian-American studies in the United States. As Vecoli's "Proposal for an Italian-American Historical Society" argues, the AIHA was established as "an undertaking of objective scholarship the purpose of which would be to contribute to our understanding of the Italian experience in America" (2). However, the AIHA has progressively defended the thesis that an ethnic identity based on national ancestry, instead of racial affiliation, has indeed survived among Italian Americans. As former AIHA president Richard Juliani has complained, "the work of its members" has become "to defend the persistence of ethnicity among Italian Americans. And when another message is delivered, such as Alba's conclusions on assimilation, even some scholars and intellectuals are ready to shoot the messenger" (55).

In 1979, Francesco Cordasco used the podium of the twelfth conference of the AIHA to urge the Italian-American community to demand affirmative action for its members. Likewise, in the late 1990s, a growing number of Italian-American activists and militant groups took part in the annual symposia of the AIHA. Consequently, these meetings turned into an opportunity for attendees not only to stage scholarly debates, but also to voice ethnic claims. For instance, an official announcement for the 27th annual conference called on Italian-American activists to attend the meeting as well ("27th Annual Conference"). Furthermore, Frank J. Cavaioli, a former president of the AIHA, clearly outlined this sense of purpose. He listed the AIHA among the ethnic organizations that "contend for the benefits available [to ethnic groups] in society" and pointed out that "the formation of the American Italian Historical Association represented another achievement" for Italian Americans because, in his opinion, it contributed to "legitimat[ing] their past" and to giving them "a respectability so necessary in contemporary society" (70-71).

The connection between scholarship and ethnic militancy is even more obvious in the establishment of another academic institution that promotes research into Italian-American history. The John D. Calandra Italian American Institute at CUNY was created in 1978 following the revelation by New York State Senator Calandra regarding the discrimination against students of Italian extraction at CUNY and the ensuing designation of Italian Americans as an affirmative action category by Chancellor Robert J.

Kibbee in 1976. Indeed, the Institute's objectives—as stated in a memorandum that New York State's Italian-American legislators signed along with chancellor Kibbee—include such research topics as "the Italian American student and his concept of self" ("Italian Americans at CUNY" 3). Following in the footsteps of militant ethnic Italian-American organizations like CIAO (Casalena 10-11, 61-22), the documenting of the discrimination that Italian Americans faced in the field of education has also constituted a major topic for fellows of the Calandra Institute, as Joseph V. Scelsa and Vincenzo Milione have shown in their essay "Statistical Profile of Educational Attainment."

Conclusion

While calling for the consolidation of research into the Italian-American experience in the United States, Richard Gambino has pointed out that "we [Italian Americans] have an uncertain future largely because we do not know our past" ("The Future" ii). In theory, as Michael Frisch and Virginia Yans-McLaughlin have maintained, historians can effectively use the past to make minorities conscious of their identity and empower them. Furthermore, as Michael Kammen has remarked, "manipulating the past in order to mold the present" often underlies the practice of history (3). This does not necessarily mean that Italian-American scholars have had a political agenda in pursuing the study of their own ethnic group, although we cannot deny that stressing a communal identity based "on the sentimental solidarity of remembered victimhood" may in fact result in "historical myopia" (Buruma 23). Rather, it can be reasonably suggested that the findings of those scholars can be used to corroborate Italian Americans' claims for minority status and ensuing benefits. For example, after coordinating research into Italian-American internees during World War II, historian Lawrence DiStasi participated in the lobbying efforts of Italian-American ethnic organizations, such as the Order Sons of Italy in America to have Congress pass the 2000 Wartime Violation of Italian American Civil Liberties Act ("OSIA Supports H.R. 2442").

This essay has shown how a few Italian-American scholars who have been researching the experience of their own fellow ethnics have resorted to a selective use of the history of this immigration group in order to argue for the characterization of Italian Americans as a minority group in its own right—a group whose members deserve special protection in redress for past discrimination. Such scholars have undeniably legitimized Italian-American studies as an academic field. In the last few years, for instance, a number of universities, including Queens College of CUNY, have

established chairs in Italian-American Studies at the same time that Italian
and Modern Language Departments have introduced courses on the Italian-
American experience ("National Search"; Gioseffi 123-24; Gardaphe 109;
"Future"). Conversely, the extent to which such scholarship has managed
to effect any kind of empowerment for Italian Americans is at least
arguable. The United States have begun to back away from affirmative
action policies in the last few years (Chavez). At the same time, Italian
Americans have consolidated their standing in executive as well as
professional positions. For instance, William Egelman has shown that, in
2000, the percentage of New Yorkers of Italian ancestry in these
occupational categories was 38.8 percent as opposed to the 33.8 percent
that corresponded to the totality of people who lived in this city (3).
Attaining social prestige and opportunities, Italian Americans have today
become less concerned about affirmative action and other anti-
discrimination programs than about ethnic-blind policies like tax benefits
for the American middle class as a whole (O'Neill 99-101). Preferential
quotas for access to both education and the job market have eventually
become less appealing to those individuals who have achieved upward
social mobility on their own. Likewise, the search for a usable past to
support claims for inclusion in affirmative action programs has proved
outdated not only with respect to current neo-liberalism, but also
considering the prevailing orientation of the expanding Italian-American
middle class.

Works Cited

"27th Annual Conference." *AIHA Newsletter* 27.3-4 (1994): 6.

Alba, Richard D. *Ethnic Identity: The Transformation of White America*. New Haven:
Yale UP, 1990.

---. *Italian Americans: Into the Twilight of Ethnicity*. Englewood Cliffs: Prentice Hall,
1985.

Albini, Joseph L. *The American Mafia: Genesis of a Legend*. New York: Meredith,
1971.

Aversa, Alfred. "Italian Neo-Ethnicity: The Search for Self-Identity." *Journal of Ethnic
Studies* 6 (1978): 49-56.

Barbaro, Frank. "Ethnic Affirmation, Affirmative Action, and the Italian Americans."
Italian Americana 1 (1974): 41-58.

Belliotti, Raymond A. *Seeking Identity: Individualism versus Community in an Ethnic
Context*. Lawrence: UP of Kansas, 1995.

Brodkin, Karen. *How Jews Became White Folks and What That Says About Race in America*. New Brunswick: Rutgers UP, 1998.

Buruma, Ian. "The Joys and Perils of Victimhood." *The Best American Essays*. Ed. Alan Lightman. Boston: Houghton Mifflin, 2000. 20-31.

Calandra, John D. *A History of Italian-American Development at CUNY*. Albany: New York State Senate, 1978.

Cannistraro, Philip V., and Gerald Meyer, eds. *The Lost World of Italian American Radicalism*. Westport: Praeger, 2003.

Casalena, Josephine. "A Portrait of the Italian-American Community in New York City," 1975. Uunpublished typescript, Myron B. Kuropas Files, box 4, folder "Italian Ethnic Groups, 3," Gerald R. Ford Library, Ann Arbor, MI.

Cavaioli, Frank J. "Group Politics, Ethnicity, and Italian-Americans." *Immigration and Ethnicity: American Society—"Melting Pot" or "Salad Bowl."* Ed. Michael D'Innocenzo and Josef P. Sirefman. Westport: Greenwood, 1992. 61-74.

Chavez, Lydia. *The Color Bind: California's Battle to End Affirmative Action*. Berkeley: U of California P, 1998.

Cinel, Dino. "Sicilians in the Deep South: The Ironic Outcome of Isolation." *Studi Emigrazione* 27 (1990): 55-86.

"Civil Rights for Italian Americans." *John D. Calandra Italian American Institute* 9.2 (1994): 1.

Cordasco, Francesco. "Italian Americans and Affirmative Action: Admission to and Progress in the Academic Professions." *Italians in the United States*. Ed. Francesco Cordasco and Michael Vaughn Cordasco. Fairview: Junius, 1981. 195-204.

D'Agostino, Peter R. *Rome in America: Transnational Catholic Ideology from the Risorgimento to Fascism*. Chapel Hill: U of North Carolina P, 2004.

Deschamps, Bénédicte. "Le Racisme Anti-Italien aux Etats-Unis (1880-1940)." *Exclure au Nom de la Race (Etats-Unis, Irlande, Grande-Bretagne)*. Ed. Michel Prum. Paris: Syllepse, 2000. 59-81.

---. "La Scoperta dell'America Narrata dai Giornali Italo-Americani, 1880-1992." *Comunicare il Passato: Cinema, Giornali e Libri di Testo nella Narrazione Storica*. Ed. Simone Cinotto and Marco Mariano. Turin: L'Harmattan Italia, 2004. 409-38.

Diggins, John P. *Mussolini and Fascism: The View from America*. Princeton: Princeton UP, 1972.

DiStasi, Lawrence, ed. *Una Storia Segreta: The Secret History of Italian American Evacuation and Internment during World War II*. Berkeley: Heyday, 2001.

Egelman, William. "Italian Americans in New York City: The 2000 Census." Paper presented at 36th Conference of the American Italian Historical Association. Boca Raton. 6-8 Nov. 2003.

Fagiani, Gil. "East Harlem and Vito Marcantonio: My Search for a Progressive Italian-American Identity." *Voices in Italian Americana* 5 (1994): 23-42.

Frisch, Michael H. *A Shared Authority: Essays on the Craft and Meaning of Oral and Public History*. Albany: State U of New York P, 1990.

"Future of Italian-American Studies at U.S. Universities." *AIHA Newsletter* 37.1-2 (2004): 11-22.

Gabaccia Donna R., and Fraser M. Ottanelli, eds. *Italian Workers of the World: Labor Migration and the Formation of Multiethnic States*. Urbana: U of Illinois P, 2001.

Gallerano, Nicola. "History and the Public Use of History." *The Social Responsibility of the Historian*. Ed. François Bédarida. Oxford: Berghahn, 1994. 85-102.

Gambino, Richard. *Blood of My Blood: The Dilemma of the Italian Americans*. Garden City: Doubleday, 1974.

---. "The Future of Italian American Studies: A Specific Agenda." *Italian American Review* 5 (1996): i-iv.

---. "Italian Americans, Today's Immigrants, Multiculturalism, and the Mark of Cain." *The Italian American Heritage: A Companion to Literature and Arts*. Ed. Pellegrino D'Acierno. New York: Garland, 1999. 69-74.

---. *Vendetta*. Garden City: Doubleday, 1977.

Gans, Herbert J. "Symbolic Ethnicity: The Future of Ethnic Groups and Cultures in America." Herbert J. Gans et al., eds. *On the Making of Americans: Essays in Honor of David Riesman*. Philadelphia: U of Pennsylvania P, 1979. 193-220.

Gardaphe, Fred L. "Identical Difference: Notes on Italian and Italian-American Identities." *The Essence of Italian Culture and the Challenge of a Global Age*. Ed. Paolo Janni and George F. McLean. Washington: Council for Research in Values and Philosophy, 2003. 93-111.

Garroni, Maria Susanna. "Immigrati e Cittadini: L'essere 'Americani' degli Italoamericani tra Otto e Novecento." *Contemporanea* 5 (2002): 32-49.

Gioseffi, Daniela. "Is There a Renaissance in Italian-American Literature? *Sì, Sì* and We're All in It Together." *Italian American Review* 5 (1996-97): 21-32.

Glazer, Nathan. *Affirmative Discrimination: Ethnic Inequality and Public Policy*. New York: Basic Books, 1975.

Gordon, Milton. "Liberal vs. Corporate Pluralism." *Society* 33 (1996): 37-40.

Greenhouse, Linda. "Justices to Review a Village Rule Curbing Solicitations for Charity." *New York Times* 24 Apr. 1978, late ed.: D17.

Gross, Barry R. *Reverse Discrimination*. Buffalo: Prometheus, 1977.

Guglielmo, Thomas A. *White on Arrival: Italians, Race, Color, and Power in Chicago, 1890-1945*. New York: Oxford UP, 2003.

Habermas, Jürgen. "Concerning the Public Use of History." *New German Critique* 44 (1988): 40-50.

Helvesi, Dennis. "Federal Inquiry into Bias Charges against CUNY." *New York Times* 6 May 1992, late ed.: B9.

Hilliard, Carl. "The Colorado Supreme Court." *New York Times* News Service and the Associated Press. 29 Aug. 1978: 55-56.

Huggins, Nathan I. "The Deforming Mirror of Truth: Slavery and the Master Narrative of American History." *Radical History Review* 49 (1991): 25-46.

Ignatiev, Noel. *How the Irish Became White*. New York: Routledge, 1995.

"Italian Americans at CUNY, 1960-1991." *John D. Calandra Italian American Institute* 9.2 (1994): 2-4.

Jackson, Peter. "Vito Marcantonio and Ethnic Politics in New York." *Ethnic and Racial Studies* 6 (1983): 50-71.

Juliani, Richard N. "Identity and Ethnicity: The Italian Case." *The Columbus People: Perspectives in Italian Immigration to the Americas and Australia*. Ed. Lydio F. Tomasi, Piero Gastaldo, and Thomas Row. Staten Island: Center for Migration Studies, 1994. 54-57.

Kammen, Michael. *Mystic Chords of Memory: The Transformation of Tradition in American Culture*. New York: Knopf, 1991.

LaGumina, Salvatore J. "Paul Vaccarelli: The Lightning Change Artist of Organized Labor." *Italian Americana* 14 (1996): 24-45.

---, et al., eds. *The Italian American Experience: An Encyclopedia*. New York: Garland, 2000.

Lombardi, Vincent M. "Italian American Workers and the Response to Fascism." *Pane e Lavoro: The Italian American Working Class*. Ed. George E. Pozzetta. Toronto: Multicultural History Society of Ontario, 1980. 141-57.

Luconi, Stefano. "Family Values, Labor Militancy, and Voting Behavior in a Working-Class Italian-American Community." *Industry, Technology, Labor, and the Italian-American Communities*. Ed. Mario Aste et al. Staten Island, NY: American Italian Historical Association, 1997. 50-61.

---. "Frank L. Rizzo and the Whitening of Italian Americans in Philadelphia." *Are Italians White? How Race Is Made in America*. Ed. Jennifer Guglielmo and Salvatore Salerno. New York: Routledge, 2003. 177-91.

---. "Italian Americans and Machine Politics: A Case Study Reassessment from the Bottom Up." *Italian Americana* 15 (1997): 123-42.

---. "La Partecipazione Politica in America del Nord." *Storia dell'Emigrazione Italiana: Arrivi*. Ed. Piero Bevilacqua, Andreina De Clementi, and Emilio Franzina. Rome: Donzelli, 2002. 489-506.

Marcantonio, Vito. *I Vote My Conscience: Debates, Speeches, and Writings of Vito Marcantonio*. Ed. Annette T. Rubinstein. New York: Vito Marcantonio Memorial Fund, 1956.

Massaro, Dominic R. "Italian Americans as a Cognizable Racial Group." *Italian Americans in a Multicultural Society*. Ed. Jerome Krase and Judith N. DeSena. Stony Brook: Forum Italicum, 1994. 44-55.

Meyer, Gerald. *Vito Marcantonio: Radical Politician, 1902-1954*. Albany: State U of New York P, 1989.

"More about the 1998 AIHA conference." *AIHA Newsletter* 31.1-2 (1998): 4.

National Italian American Foundation. *The Role of Americans of Italian Heritage in the 1980s*. Washington: National Italian American Foundation, 1979.

"National Search for Distinguished Professor." *John D. Calandra Italian American Institute* 10.1 (1994-95): 6.

Novak, Michael. *The Rise of Unmeltable Ethnics: Politics and Culture in the Seventies*. New York: Macmillan, 1972.

O'Neill, Timothy J. *Bakke & the Politics of Equality: Friends and Foes in the Classroom of Litigation*. Middletown: Wesleyan UP, 1985.

"OSIA Supports H.R. 2442." Press Release. 26 Oct. 1999. 12 Apr. 2004 <http://www.osia.org/public/legislative/hr2442pressrelease.asp>.

Paulucci, Jeno F. "For Affirmative Action for Some Whites." *New York Times* 26 Nov. 1977, late ed.: A17.

Polenberg, Richard. *One Nation Divisible: Class, Race, and Ethnicity in the United States since 1938*. New York: Viking, 1980.

Pozzetta, George E. "Immigrants and Ethnics: The State of Italian-American Historiography." *Journal of American Ethnic History* 9 (1989): 67-95.

Pretelli, Matteo. "Tra Estremismo e Moderazione: Il Ruolo dei Circoli Fascisti Italo-Americani nella Politica Estera Italiana degli anni Trenta." *Studi Emigrazione* 40 (2003): 315-27.

Reider, Jonathan. *Canarsie: The Jews and Italians against Liberalism*. Cambridge: Harvard UP, 1985.

Roediger, David R. *Colored White: Transcending the Racial Past*. Berkeley: U of California P, 2002.

Salvemini, Gaetano. *Memorie di un Fuoruscito*. Milan: Feltrinelli, 1960.

Salvetti, Patrizia. *Corda e Sapone*. Rome: Donzelli, 2003.

Santucci, John. "Early 20th Century Inter-Ethnic Relations: A Case Study in North Carolina." *Italian Americans in Transition*. Ed. Joseph V. Scelsa, Salvatore J. LaGumina, and Lydio F. Tomasi. Staten Island: American Italian Historical Association, 1990. 127-35.

Scelsa, Joseph V. "The 80th Street Mafia." *Beyond the Godfather: Italian American Writers on the Real Italian American Experience*. Ed. A. Kenneth Cingoli and Jay Parini. Hanover: UP of New England, 1997. 289-306.

---, and Vincenzo Milione. "Statistical Profile of Educational Attainment Including High School Dropout Rate Indicators for Italian American and Other Race/Ethnic Population: United States, New York State, and New York City." *To See the Past More Clearly: The Enrichment of the Italian Heritage, 1890-1990*. Ed. Harral E. Landry. Austin: Nortex, 1994. 1-18.

Schiavo, Giovanni Ermenegildo. *Four Centuries of Italian-American History*. New York: Vigo, 1952.

Shankman, Arnold. "The Image of the Italian in the Afro-American Press, 1886-1936." *Italian Americana* 4 (1978): 30-49.

Sindler, Allan P. *Bakke, Defunis, and Minority Admissions: The Quest for Equal Opportunity*. New York: Longman, 1978.

Swain, Carol M. "Affirmative Action: Legislative History, Judicial Interpretations, Public Consensus." *America Becoming: Racial Trends and Their Consequences*. Ed. Neil J. Smeiser, William Julius Wilson, and Faith Mitchell. Washington: National

Academy, 2001. 318-47.

Tintori, Guido. "Italiani *Enemy Aliens*: I Civili Residenti negli Stati Uniti d'America durante la Seconda Guerra Mondiale." *Altreitalie* 28 (2004): 83-109.

Tirabassi, Maddalena. "Un Decennio di Storiografia Statunitense sull'Immigrazione Italiana." *Movimento Operaio e Socialista* 2 (1981): 145-60.

Topp, Michael Miller. *Those without a Country: The Political Culture of Italian American Syndicalists*. Minneapolis: U of Minnesota P, 2001.

Varbero, Richard A. "Philadelphia's South Italians and the Irish Church: A History of Cultural Conflict." *The Religious Experience of Italian Americans*. Ed. Silvano M. Tomasi. Staten Island: American Italian Historical Association, 1975. 31-52.

Vecoli, Rudolph J. "Are Italian Americans Just White Folks?" *Italian Americana* 13 (1995): 149-61.

---. "Contadini in Chicago: A Critique of the Uprooted." *Journal of American History* 51 (1964): 404-17.

---. "Born Italian: Color Me Red, White, and Green." *Soundings* 61 (1973): 117-23.

---. "Ethnicity: A Neglected Dimension of American History." *The State of American History*. Ed. Herbert Jacob Bass. New York: Quadrangle, 1970. 70-88.

---. "The Italian Immigrants in the United States Labor Movement from 1880 to 1929." *Gli Italiani fuori d'Italia: Gli Emigrati Italiani nei Movimenti Operai dei Paesi d'Adozione (1880-1940)*. Ed. Bruno Bezza. Milan: Angeli, 1983. 257-306.

---. "Prelates and Peasants: Italian Immigrants and the Catholic Church." *Journal of Social History* 2 (1969): 217-68.

---. "A Proposal for an Italian-American Historical Society," 27 Dec. 1966. Paper presented at the organizational meeting of the Italian American Historical Association, Leonard Covello Papers, box 81, folder 29, Balch Institute for Ethnic Studies, Philadelphia.

Venturini, Nadia. *Neri e Italiani a Harlem: Gli Anni Trenta e la Guerra d'Etiopia*. Rome: Edizioni Lavoro, 1990.

Wall, Wendy L. "America's 'Best Propagandist': Italian Americans and the 1948 'Letters to Italy' Campaign." *Cold War Constructions: The Political Culture of United States Imperialism, 1945-1966*. Ed. Christian G. Appy. Amherst: U of Massachusetts P, 2000. 89-109.

Weed, Perry L. *The White Ethnic Movement and Ethnic Politics*. New York: Preager, 1973.

Wilkinson, J. Harvie. *One Nation Indivisible: How Ethnic Separatism Threatens America*. Reading: Addison-Wesley, 1997.

Yans-McLaughlin, Virginia, ed. *Immigration Reconsidered: History, Sociology, and Politics*. New York: Oxford UP, 1990.

STEPANKA KORYTOVA-MAGSTADT

The Elite, the Peasants, and Woodrow Wilson: American Slovaks and Their Homeland, 1914-1918

> "A human lifetime is 80 years long on average. A person imagines and organizes his life with that span in mind[. . .] the very notion of homeland, with all its emotional power, is bound up with the relative brevity of our life, which allows us too little time to become attached to some other country, to other countries, to other languages.
> Milan Kunderta

On October 29, 1918, Czechs and Slovaks were united in an independent Czechoslovakia. The independence was a result of combined diplomatic efforts of elites. T. G. Masaryk played the key role together with other Czech and Slovak leaders in Europe and in the United States, supported by the general Czech and Slovak public. A host of other factors contributed to the effort, including Czechs and Slovaks living in the United States and the Czech and Slovak army volunteers on the side of the Allies. Most historians customarily attribute the positive outcome of the struggle for an independent Czechoslovakia to Woodrow Wilson, thus, for the most part, ignoring historical sources.[1] They also neglect to examine all the major forces behind that effort.

The role played by the Czech and Slovak immigrants in the United States was significant; however, only a few authors have peeled the "glossy cover" off that effort. The accounts either fail to mention all the key players, or they rarely go underneath the "packaging" of cooperation. Customarily, these accounts give little more than a cursory nod toward such Slovak figures as Milan Getting and Albert Mamatej, and their willingness (or not) to cooperate with the Czechs. The fragmentation of the elite leaders' opinions and the complexity of the concept of national identity among the masses contributed to a divided movement—a fact that is not commonly known.

James Olson, one the few authors who have dealt with the ethnic dimension in American history, thought that East European peasants "had little sense of nationalism," but that the educated leaders and refugees, many of them coming to the United States after the 1848 revolution, had

---

[1] Mark Stolarik, *The Slovak Americans,* Otto Urban, *Ceska spolecnost, 1848-1918* [Czech Society, 1848-1918], Josef Polisensky, History of Czechoslovakia in Outline, Karel Pichlik, Victor Mamatej-see below.

"well-developed national loyalties" (126). This, mostly middle-class, elite founded the proto-national organizations on which the East European peasants—a term used throughout this paper to refer to people other than elites; in fact, working class immigrants in the U.S.-built their fraternal and mutual support organizations. "If ethnic politics based on an independent Poland or Bohemia or Hungary seemed remote to the peasant majority, it was real and immediate to the literate, politically conscious minority," wrote Olson (126). In the case of the Czech and Slovak elite the situation was more complex than Olson realized. Although ethnic politics were real and immediate, opinions ranged along a spectrum of Catholic, Protestant and freethinking points of view, often resulting in seemingly insurmountable barriers between the various groups. Besides religion, there were also culture, education, a missing sense of national identity (in the case of some Slovaks), and diverse experiences in the United States, to mention just a few factors (other than class) which affected national self-consciousness.

Both Czechs and Slovaks, in New York City, Chicago, Pittsburgh, Cleveland, or Milwaukee, were heterogeneous groups with different ideas and approaches to the future organization of their homeland. For example, the Czech Freethinkers in Chicago, the Czech Catholic conservatives in St. Louis, and the Slovak leaders in Pittsburgh could not find a common political platform: the freethinkers supported an independent Czechoslovakia, the Slovak Catholics generally preferred the status quo, i.e., the Hapsburg Empire, and the Protestant Slovaks in Pittsburgh longed for autonomy for Slovakia. Thus, we must question how united the ethnic elite were in their visions of the future organization of their homelands-whether these evoked a united Czechoslovakia or two separate countries. The effort of elite leaders towards the liberation of their homeland may have been the last stand against their own and their "peasant majority's" assimilation. However, what was the role of the peasant majority, so "remote"-to use Olson's terminology-from the elite's decision-making? Could emigrants, who left under various circumstances and at various times, understand their brothers' and sisters' wishes in the homeland? Finally, what was the role played by Woodrow Wilson in facilitating the independence of the central and south-central European countries?

Olson assumed that "more conscious of politics and ethnicity than ever before, the eastern European immigrants gradually acquired a strong sense of ethnic nationalism. By 1914 they were deeply concerned with events in Europe [and], through their national organizations, [Czech and Slovak Americans] played a critical role in persuading President Wilson to insist on the creation of an independent Czechoslovakia in 1918" (137). This paper re-examines the role and the relative importance of the three components of the effort to create an independent Czechoslovakia as these relate to the Slovak experience in particular: the role of the peasant majority, the role of the Czech and Slovak elite, and the influence the Slovaks had on Woodrow Wilson's foreign policy. The thought process by which the immigrant elite came to national consciousness in the "colonies"-the term T. G. Masaryk used to refer to the Czech and Slovak settlements abroad-was complex. If the Slovak compatriots in the U.S. went through stages during which they could not agree on one coherent program for the future administration and organization of their nation, the cause may have been the mixed signals from the homeland. Many people in the Czech lands believed that their destiny was forever bound with Austria, but, on the other hand, the Czech and Slovak leaders living in temporary exile were most adamant about the need for Czech and Slovak self-determination (Pichlik 179-181). The main questions in the European homeland were: was it necessary to dismantle the Empire? And, if so, should the newly created country look for allies in the East-the Russophile and Slavonic kingdom faction supported this idea—or should it look towards allies in the West?

Opinions on the future of the Empire changed over time. When the government in Vienna approved universal suffrage in 1907, the Austrian system began to develop towards democracy. The Habsburg Emperor Charles I, however, was unable to understand that a reorganization of the Empire into a federation was the only option available if the Empire were to be kept intact. When he declared federalism on October 18, 1918, it was too late (Kohak 134).

While the "Czech sentiment for complete independence began to crystallize during the last year of the war, thinking about Slovakia's future position in the state was far from crystalline" (Skalnik Leff 39). However, if the Slovaks in Slovakia were unsure about their national aspirations, how could the Slovak-Americans decide on an appropriate course of action?

The Czechs and Slovaks in America were unable to speak in one voice: political and social stratification, lack of leadership, physical distance between the individual settlements, and the European war atmosphere all contributed to this lack of unity (Vojta Benes 271). Any concerted effort was further retarded by opposition to revolutionary activity from the pacifists and from some Catholics. Some people feared that any activity not sanctioned by the U.S. government would make them even more unpopular with the generally anti-immigrant public and ironically undermine their assimilation into American culture.[2]

---

[2] Dr. Iska, editor Jan Jelinek from Chicago, editor Svagrovsky from Cleveland, citizen Cejka from St. Louis, *Hlasatel*, Catholic *Narod*, Pittsburgh Christian newspapers, the *American Sokol* and the *American* from Baltimore.

The majority of Slovaks arrived in the U.S. shortly before the war broke out, and their concerns thus centered on day-to-day existence. Although Slovaks arrived in large numbers between the 1890s and 1900s (700,000 by the end of WWI), they were too "new" to the country and too poor to reflect on how they were to act politically.[3] Moreover, only a few people knew who the Slovaks were, let alone what their political goals might have been (Mamatey, *The United States* 130). These Slovaks were in no position to think about or take action for the benefit of their native land. Some individuals may have offered some help, but the overwhelming majority simply struggled to survive in a new country where living constituted a challenge in itself. There was no money or energy left to be spent on issues concerning the future of their homeland. This was probably true of most Slovaks in America.

The absence of a sense of national identity was another issue. Slovaks immigrated as either Magyars or as people oppressed by Magyars. There was also a group of Slovaks who were linguistically and otherwise assimilated-"Magyarones" (Kopanic 274). The Slovaks-both the leaders and the peasant majority-had to first develop a national identity in the United States in order to think of themselves as Slovaks. Only then could they accept the idea of a common state with the Czechs. Even in the homeland, a clearly defined national identity on the level of the masses was absent among Slovaks in northern Hungary (modern Slovakia was, in fact, northern Hungary during the Austro-Hungarian Empire). A historian found that in areas inhabited by Slovaks in the Austro-Hungarian Empire "the base for national consciousness had broadened somewhat since the earliest nationalist impulse; census respondents in 1920 were still prone to offer regionally or religiously defined self-identifications to the census-takers, or even such politically unappetizing national monstrosities as 'Magyar-Slovak'" (Skalnik Leff 19). Furthermore, while Slovaks used their mother tongue at home, there were cases of people who were not able to write in Slovak (Skalnik Leff 18). Magyarization and "its elitist ethos had a profound effect on the potential for leadership of a Slovak movement" (Skalnik Leff 18). Hungarian effort to change Slovaks into Magyars had eroded Slovaks' feeling of national belonging leaving a "mass of individuals, differentiated by class" (Skalnik Leff 19).

Victor Mamatey, a son of the Slovak Protestant leader Albert Mamatej, thought that the Protestant Slovaks, a minority in Slovakia, were the main bearers of Slovak culture and speakers of the language with a strong Slavic sentiment, in contrast to the Slovaks from eastern Slovakia who were "illiterate and possessed no clear-cut national consciousness" ("Slovaks"

---

[3] Mamatey, "The Slovaks" 227. Mamatey describes the Slovaks as "underdeveloped," most of them peasants making their living by cultivating land. Intelligentsia formed a very small proportion, both among the immigrants and in the homeland.

229). The Protestant Slovaks were usually Russophiles, a fact which inhibited their partnership with the pro-western Masaryk. It was hard for the Slovaks to accept predominantly western-oriented Czechs, especially when these were of the radical freethinking persuasion. Vojta Benes, Masaryk's emissary in the United States, considered the core of problematic relations a result of the fact that most leaders left Slovakia before the idea of Czechoslovakia became concrete. "They brought the idea of Slovak separatism [to America] and an unrealistic Pan-Slavism, and by upholding these ideas they were doing great disservice to the Slovak cause" (Benes 285). In 1917 and even in the first half of 1918, a major Slovak-American Protestant organization, *Narodny Slovensky Spolok* (N.S.S.) [the National Slovak Association], still thought in terms of a Slavonic union. This was after Albert Mamatej had signed the Cleveland Pact with the Czechs in 1915 about working together for a union of the two nations. Support for a Czechoslovak independence began only when the Slovak-Americans accepted that an independent Slovakia was not viable, a realization that came at the end of the war.

Czech attitude toward Slovaks further complicated any cooperation between the two groups for an independent Czechoslovakia. Throughout the war, Czech-Americans often displayed a degree of superiority and a patronizing attitude toward the Slovaks who wanted to be treated as equals and not as ignorant Slovaks. Many Catholic Slovaks expressed this sentiment, and so, given a choice between two evils, they were inclined to choose the lesser of the two: the Hungarians who they knew better, rather than the largely freethinking Czechs who they regarded domineering (287).

The Slovak elite's political views often determined their approaches to the reorganization of Central Europe. When the European war broke out, only the Slovak socialists were eager to cooperate with the Czechs. The editor of the *Rovnost' Ludu* wrote, in early October 1915, that it was

> a waste of time to write where we, the Slovaks should belong when the war is over. The clerics in Pittsburgh (together with the Slovak League) are for an independent Slovakia. They fear that Czech freethinking and socialist ideas would contaminate the Slovak nation if they lived together in one country. We do not expect miracles from this war but since it is here we wish the Slovaks and the Czechs to live in one state with two languages, because they belong with each other historically and in the interests of their own survival. (Pichlik 154)

The Slovak socialists' view did not represent the point of view of the Slovak majority. Albert Mamatej's and the Slovak League's reaction was significantly more cautious. Having discussed the issue of the future of Slovakia at several conferences during the summer of 1914, the Slovak League of America, whose members came mainly from a Protestant educated class, drafted the *Memorandum of the Slovak League of America*.

The draftees of the memorandum expected Slovaks to become a culturally and administratively autonomous entity (Mamatey "Slovaks" 232).[4] Published in September 1914 in various international languages and printed "in a handsome brochure," the Memorandum was sent to the belligerent governments and to the U.S. State Department. Thus, the Slovak elite's political activity in the U.S. on behalf of the Slovaks in their homeland began (Mamatey "Slovaks" 232).

While the leaders of *Ceské narodni sdruzeni* (the Bohemian National Alliance) discussed the Czechoslovak idea as early as September 1914, Mamatej, adhering to pragmatic solutions, thought that the Slovaks should work for either autonomy or something resembling the United States of Czechoslovakia.[5] In March 1915, however, he still warned that many Slovaks sensed a danger in coexisting with the Czechs in one country, for they feared that the pressure to assimilate was exercised on the part of the Czechs rather than the Hungarians. Mamatej's rather *naive* view was that the Slovaks were more likely to force the Hungarians to assimilate than the other way around (Benes 291).

Mamatej's influence was paramount. Besides being the head of the Slovak League, a Slovak umbrella organization, he also presided over the *Narodny Slovensky Spolok* founded in Pittsburgh in 1890.[6] This organization was Slavophile and anti-Hungarian, an attitude expressed in the articles that appeared in the *Narodny Kalendar* [National Almanac], a mouthpiece of the organization.

The Slovak-American elite fought on several fronts. They wanted to show patriotic loyalty to the United States, but also to excite patriotic feelings for Slovakia among the peasant majority. If they wanted to win public support for their cause, whatever that might have been, the Slovak elite, acting on behalf of the peasant majority, also wanted to project the image of loyal immigrants when reactions against immigration and a hysteria about "hyphenated Americans" prevailed in the U.S. Mamatej stressed: "The U.S. has been very patient with the people who were disloyal in this conflict. We expect our loyalties to be under scrutiny. Last year we organized patriotic festivities, collections for the American Red Cross. Officers and individual brothers understand what is expected from us" (qtd. in Narodny calendar 25: 49). The N.S.S. also organized a number

---

[4] This position was prompted by Count Michael Karolyi's visit to the United States in the spring of 1914. Karolyi, a Hungarian nationalist, came to the U. S. to address Hungarian organizations to inspire them for the Hungarian independence movement. The Slovaks organized counter-meetings in which they denounced him and expressed anti-Hungarian sentiments.

[5] This idea became the basis for the Pittsburgh Agreement of 1918.

[6] This was the oldest Slovak national mutual support organization open to all male and female regardless of faith. It offered a life insurance, and it had lodges in most Slovak settlements.

of fund-raising activities to support schools in Slovakia, and donated clothes, bandages and medication to the widows and orphans of Slovak veterans and to the Slovak POWs in Serbia (qtd. in Narodny calendar 25: 41).

The Slovak leaders in the N.S.S. welcomed the entrance of the U.S. into the war, because Wilson promised to fight for ideas such as "democracy, the rights of the oppressed, the rights of the small nations. The rights will be achieved by the collaboration of the free nations that will bring about peace and security to all the nations and the whole world will be liberated" (qtd. in Narodny calendar 26: 48). At that time, however, fighting for the ideas of the small nations in Central Europe was a rhetorical exercise, since any dismembering of the Hapsburg Empire-a "dualist monster" as seen by Czech and Slovak propaganda-was not on Wilson's foreign policy agenda in 1917 (Pergler, *Heart* 14).

The members of small nations, such as Bohemia and Slovakia, who decided to emigrate were not all welcome in the U.S. The American public, intellectuals at American universities, and some members of the government were all prejudiced against the peoples from Eastern Europe. For example, John W. Burgess of Columbia University in *Political Science and Comparative Constitutional Law* classified the Teutonic peoples as political nations par excellence, while he stressed that the Slavs "lacked political capacity" (Pergler, *Czechoslovak* 8). The Czech and Slovak cultural elite's reaction to such statements was designed to change American public opinion *and* to unite the Slovaks and the Czechs behind the cause of Czech and Slovak nationhood, reminding them of their cultures. This, the Czech and Slovak elites hoped, would delay the Americanization process.

If Mamatej employed his rhetoric, on the one hand, to appeal to the aspirations of the heterogeneous groups of Slovaks, while on the other, to endear Slovaks to the U.S. public, Milan Getting-an activist for the Czechoslovak cause—represented those Slovaks closest to the Czech pro-Masaryk elite. A member of the Slovak cultural elite, Getting was educated in Slovakia and pursued further education in the United States. He was involved in the *Sokol* organization in Pittsburgh prior to his departure for New York City where he became an editor of the *Slovensky Sokol* [The Slovak Falcon] (Benes 286). Getting was an ambitious man and felt excluded from the important decision-making processes since the Slovak power center was in Pittsburgh. In fact, he was particularly impatient with Mamatej. In cosmopolitan New York City, where ideologies could be freely embraced, Getting failed to understand the situation in which Mamatej must have found himself because of having to address conflicting fractions within the Slovak League and the conservative Pittsburgh community of Slovaks.

Another influence on Getting was his international contacts. He corresponded with the Czechs at home who informed him about the situation in pre-1914 Slovakia and Bohemia. Based on the information he received and the contacts he had, he concluded that the Hungarians would not recognize an independent Slovakia. He wanted Slovakia to join the Czech lands as a new political entity and opposed any other alternative. He, and many Slovak *Sokol* members, feared that the Czechs would wither away under the Germans and that the same would happen to Slovaks under Hungarian rule. To discuss the future of Slovaks and lobby institutions of power, Getting founded an organization called *Sdruzeni Americkych Slovakov* [The Alliance of American Slovaks] (Benes 283).

In 1915, the year of the Cleveland conference during which the Czechs met with the Slovaks, Getting described the Slovak question as tragic:

> For the last 100 years the Slovaks have fought the Hungarians, we cannot get far on our own but we need to unite. What do we want? A Slovak kingdom? Not even Mamatey, Daxner, etc believe in this, what then? A republic? That can be done only if the nation is large and mature. With Hungarians? We don't want that. What do we want – the Slav idea? That means a unification of small nations with larger ones. The Czecho-Slovak idea is the only solution out of the darkness, but here we disagree with no hope to agree (Getting family papers Box 3, Folder 2).

Getting grew impatient with the apathy of most Slovaks, including the Slovak League leaders as well as Slovak immigrants.

> Katolicka jednota [The Catholic Union] had one good politician: Furdek, but he is no longer here, Narodny Slovensky Spolok [N.S.S.] has their leaders well entrenched and they will not let good characters lead the organization. These organizations could do more that they know. The editorial board is not very intelligent and they are completely under the influence of the Jew[7] [probably Orbach, a member of the League's board-ed.]. They are not interested in the Slovak cause, they want to be left alone and they would rather sacrifice the Slovak idea. It is funny that they see in Getting [speaking of himself in 3rd person] a competition in NY, but how does he harm anybody in Pittsburgh, Cleveland, and Chicago? Is he that powerful? (Getting family papers Box 3, Folder 2).

Thus, he gave up trying to influence the Slovak League leaders, because, as he said, "[a]t the Congress [of the Slovak League] they [the leaders of the Slovak League-ed.] appointed whomever they wanted to have in the

---

[7]   Another factor adding to the complexity of the issues involved was the anti-Semitism of some Slovaks here felt by Milan Getting, otherwise a freethinking liberal.

committee, they fixed the bylaws, and they will take and not take whomever they like" (Getting family papers Box 3, Folder 2). Subsequently, frustrated with the Slovak League, Getting decided to found other branches of the *Politické Sdruzenie* [Political Alliance].

Getting and other Czech and Slovak leaders thought that the Slovaks feared assimilation to the Czech culture and that, if offered a choice, they would rather be assimilated by an entity they knew, by Hungarians for example, rather than by Czechs (Benes 291). The Slovak elite knew that Hungarians would not agree to Slovak autonomy, while they expected that Czechs would agree to it. Therefore, Getting thought that if both sides-the Czech and the Slovak elite-could accept the concept of a federation of two autonomous states, they could then agree on a common state. He concluded that autonomy was not negotiable for the Slovak elite. Any negotiations with the Czechs ought to begin on the premise of autonomy. More specifically, the negotiating principles should include the Slovak's own Diet and administration-in terms of education, economy, political, legal, and religious affairs. In 1915, the year he outlined the principles, he feared that Czechoslovakia would be insignificant without a protector, so he recommended that Russia-at that time he still looked to the East-should be approached via a prince from the Romanoff Tsar family(Benes 291). Vojta Benes, representing the Czech point of view, agreed in principle and hoped that, given this wide spectrum of ideas and guarantees, the options for autonomy within Czechoslovakia would be acceptable to most (Benes 291).

The activist Getting and the cautious Mamatej represented only two major views of the elite on the future of the Slovaks in Europe. If Pittsburgh were the bastion of the Slovak League and of the people Getting criticized, in New York and Chicago the freethinking and *Sokol* elements prevailed and were more open to new ideas. There, the divisions were smaller. In Chicago, the Slovaks read Czech newspapers-for there were none in Slovak—and were influenced by them. However, in Cleveland and in Pittsburgh where there was a high concentration of Slovaks, the opposition to the Czechoslovak idea was stronger and less open to voices outside the Slovak community.

By 1918, war developments showed that any political union with the Hungarians would mean the "kiss of death." Therefore, in spite of the differences, cooperation between all the main parties of the Czech and Slovak propaganda and the proto-government of Czechoslovakia-including the executive Masaryk-"was very close" (Mamatey "Slovaks" 233). Their work climaxed with the signing of the Pittsburgh Agreement on May 31, 1918, following which fragmented groups of Czechs and Slovaks came together. Getting and Mamatej-both satisfied with the prospect of a Slovak autonomy within a newly created state-signed the Agreement together with the representatives of the Bohemian National Alliance, the Federation of Czech Catholics, and the Slovak League of America and T. G. Masaryk.

The Pittsburgh Agreement was intended to placate the remnants of the Russophile faction among the Slovaks, who were given a set of specific guarantees-their own administration, courts and the language-as protection against "Czechofization" in the new state. Albert Mamatej insisted on insertion of a Slovak "Diet" (Mamatey "Slovaks" 237). Mamatej concluded: "The Czechs and Slovaks lived to see something we had not dreamt about a year or several years ago–the recognition of an independent country of Czechoslovakia by all the Allies. This name has been accepted recently. Together with our soldiers we became members of Wilson's Legion of Honor" (*Narodny kalendar* 26: 52).

Historians today are skeptical about the Czech intention to implement the Agreement in the independent Czechoslovakia following World War I. The document was signed during the wartime negotiations with the purpose of gaining international support, and the intention was to consolidate the Slovak community behind it (Skalnik Leff 152). T. G. Masaryk wrote in his memoirs that the Pittsburgh Convention was not a *treaty* between Czechs and Slovaks of America: "It was concluded in order to appease a small Slovak faction which was dreaming of God knows what sort of independence for Slovakia, since the ideas of some Russian Slavophiles, and of Ludovit Stur and Svatozar Hurban-Vajansky, Slovak nationalists, had taken root even among the American Slovaks" (Masaryk 209). Masaryk deemed the Convention to be a "local understanding between American Czechs and Slovaks" (Masaryk 209). In 1918, he addressed the various designs for Slovakia's future: he regarded Slovak autonomy within Hungary as "politically impractical under the circumstances and [argued that] the idea of Slovakia's independence should not be taken seriously since the political world does not know Slovakia and would not support such an effort" (Masaryk 209). Slovak wishes were unknown in the West and, after the breakup of the Hapsburg Empire, this "[W]estern ignorance of Slovak goals enabled the Allies to bypass the Slovaks when redrawing the map of Europe" (Kirschbaum 3). A Slovak-American historian admitted that the American people were "virtually unaware of their [Slovak] existence until the spring 1918" (Mamatey "Slovaks" 242), therefore, the propaganda on behalf of the Slovaks was not effective.

Masaryk was savvy and anticipated problems between the Slovaks and the Czechs in the U.S. He recognized that many issues remained unresolved; a fact illustrated by his telegraph message to E. Benes, the Czechoslovak minister of foreign affairs. Reporting to him about the creation of a network of Czechoslovak consulates in New York City, Chicago, and Pittsburgh, Masaryk wrote: "[T]he Pittsburgh Consulate will be in charge of Slovaks and administered in Slovak. That will give Slovaks opportunity to solve the question of official language and *its relation to Czech*."[8]

The continuing Czech-Slovak fragmentation was only one of the many problems that the elite leaders had to solve. The most difficult problem for the Czecho-Slovak leaders was the unwillingness of the U. S. executive branch to support their political goals. Throughout the war, the immigrant cultural leaders from Central European nations tried to gain the support of the U.S. government for the recognition of their nation's right to independence—a fruitless effort that lasted until the end of the war. The Allied policy was to keep the Austro-Hungarian Empire intact, but to exclude it from the German sphere of influence. The Empire would, thus, be a counterweight to Berlin. Creation of numerous national independent countries-Masaryk's goal-was only one of the options.

Slovak and Czech contacts in both Chambers of the U.S. Congress – Senators William S. Kenyon and William H. King, Republicans from Iowa, and Adolph J. Sabath, congressional Democrat from Illinois and a native of Bohemia had agreed to sponsor a resolution that would advocate a "Bohemian-Slovak State," but the resolution never came to vote (O'Grady, "Introduction" 10). Representatives of the Czech- and Slovak-Americans met with the Secretary of State Robert Lansing in June 1917. Having expressed their loyalty to the United States, they told Lansing that Czechs and Slovaks wanted to unite in an independent country. Lansing reacted positively to their declaration of loyalty, but did not respond to their demand for independence (Mamatey, *The United States* 131).

The fate of the Empire was only decided when the Allies realized that they would not reach a separate peaceful agreement with Vienna. Only then could the Empire be dissolved and independent countries created (Mamatey, *The United States* 300). The war revealed that Vienna could not dislodge itself from German dominance. Thus, the breaking up of the Empire seemed more acceptable to the Allies, particularly following the "wave of revolution" that spread throughout Europe towards the end of the war. Nationalism would soon become the buffer against revolution, since nations seeking the liberation of their homelands were less prone to the post-war atmosphere in Europe than socialist revolutionaries (Belina 142-143).

---

[8] 22th October 1918, Washington. Telegraph message from T. G. Masaryk, the Chair of the Provisional Czechoslovak Government to E. Benes, the minister of Foreign Affairs. AUTGM, MA, France, VIII-15 f, k. 4. In *Vznik Ceskoslovenska, 1918: Dokumenty ceskoslovenské zahranicni politiky* Praha: Ústav mezinárodních vztahů, 1994, 324.

Wilson and Masaryk are considered to be the founding fathers of Czechoslovakia. A statue of Wilson was erected in Prague immediately following WWI as a token of gratitude, and American Slovaks named their capital *Wilsonovo město* [Wilson's city-ed.], before they resolved to call it Bratislava in 1918-1919 (Klimek 130). There is no historical evidence, however, to suggest that Wilson was remotely interested in creating an independent Czechoslovakia. In late 1917, the American president was still negotiating a separate peace with Austria, which would mean leaving the Empire intact. The negotiations were not successful, and so, on January 8, 1918, Woodrow Wilson called for "the freest opportunity of autonomous development" for the peoples of Austria-Hungary, but did not mention the word *independence* in his Fourteen Points speech (Mamatey "Slovaks" 225). He made it clear that Austria should not be destroyed and that individual nationalities could expect *only* autonomy (O'Grady "Introduction" 15).

T. G. Masaryk arrived in Chicago on May 5, 1918, but Wilson saw him on June 19 for only forty-five minutes. The main topic was not the independence of European Czechs and Slovaks, but the Russian Civil War (Odlozilik 215). Wilson gave no answer to Masaryk regarding the future of Central Europe, for, in his June and July political analysis for the Allies, Masaryk called for the dismemberment of Austria-Hungary and asked America "to be one of the *decisive* political and strategic [al] leader[s]" (Klimek 149).

Wilson recognized the Czechoslovak National Council—a government in exile-in Paris in September 1918, only after the other Allies had done so (O'Grady "Introduction" 17), and only then was the U.S. government "prepared to enter formally into relations with the *de facto* government thus recognized" (Mamatey "Slovaks" 236). On October 18—ten days prior to the declaration of an independent Czechoslovakia—Wilson decided that autonomous development for the nations within the empire was not possible, and sent a note to that effect to Austria (Klimek 159). The day after the declaration of independence, October 29th, Masaryk, frustrated with the U.S. administration, wrote a letter to Lansing asking him not to continue negotiations with the Austrians regarding matters concerning Czechoslovakia, as it was up to the Czechoslovak government to do that (Klimek 340, 341). This note concluded conversations with the U.S. Administration over the matter of Czechoslovak sovereignty in the U.S.

Thus, Wilson's agreeing to the dismemberment of the Empire had nothing to do with the Czech and Slovak elite representatives, including T. G. Masaryk, or with the Czechoslovak Legion in Siberia, or with the Czech and Slovak Americans. The wartime activities of the elites had no obvious impact on the U.S Executive. Ultimately, Olson did not look under the "glossy-cover."

Wilson's role in creating an independent Czechoslovakia was close to none. The Czechs and Slovaks evidently were not high on Wilson's list of priorities with respect to Central Europeans since "except for the Poles, Wilson granted the Central Europeans nothing until he had made the decision to break up the empire [...] [and only then] did he permit, and publicly encourage, the immigrants to organize efforts to control events in Central Europe." (O'Grady, "Introduction" 21). Walter Lippman summed up the U.S. strategy during WWI when he wrote: "Our fundamental interest in this crisis is not a complicated system of rights but a definite and practical, tangible end"—the defense of the Atlantic world" (Lippman xi). Thus, regardless of the leaders' wartime activity, or conflicting beliefs and disagreements about the destiny of their mother country, Slovakia became part of Czechoslovakia. The United States government recognized it by default, and not as a result of a patriotic peasant majority's efforts or of the work of ethnic elites.

Olson concludes his book saying that, thanks to the WWI, "the eastern European peasants in America rediscovered their links to the fortunes of the Old World" (138), and that these fortunes "bound the immigrants into self-conscious communities" (Olson, 224). In my opinion, some peasants did discover these links, but many Slovaks grew disillusioned with the way in which their homeland was dealt in 1918. Generally, the elite continued to be involved in the politics of Slovakia, but the peasants strengthened their ties with their families in Slovakia on a communal level and, as a result, developed their own American-Slovak identity.

Works Cited

Belina, Pavel, Jiří Rak, Jiri Pokorny et al. *Dejiny zemi koruny ceské, II*. Praha: Paseka, 1992.

Benes, Vojta. *Ceskoslovenski Amerika v Odboji*. Praha: Nakladatestvy Pokrok, 1931.

Getting Family Papers. HSMP Archives MSS# 186. John Heinz Western Pennsylvania History Research Center.

Hammack, David, C., Diane L. Grabowski, and John J. Grabowski, eds. *Identity, Conflict, and Cooperation: Central Europeans in Cleveland, 1850-1930*. Cleveland, Ohio: The Western Reserve Historical Society, 2002.

Kirschbaum, Stanislav J. *A History of Slovakia: The Struggle for Survival*. New York: St. Martin's Griffin, 1995.

Klimek Antonin. *Rijen 1918: Vznik Ceskoslovenska*. Praha: Paseka, 1998.

Kohak, Erazim, *Narod v nas*. Toronto: Sixty-Eight Publishers, 1978.

Kopanic, Michael. "The Slovaks in Cleveland." in *Identity, conflict, and cooperation: Central Europeans in Cleveland, 1850-1930*. Ed. David C. Hammack, Diane L.

Grabowski, and John J. Grabowski. Cleveland, Ohio: The Western Reserve Historical Society, 2002. 249-306.

Kundera, Milan. *Ignorance: A Novel.* New York: Harper Collins Publishers, 2000.

Lippman, Walter. *Early Writings.* New York: Liveright, 1970.

Mamatey, Victor S. "The Slovaks and Carpatho-Ruthenians." in *The Immigrants' Influence on Wilson's Peace Policies.* Ed. Joseph P. O'Grady. Lexington, KY: U of Kentucky P, 1967. 224-249.

---. The United States and East Central Europe, 1914-1918: A study of Wilsonian Diplomacy and Propaganda. Princeton, NJ: Princeton U P, 1957.

Masaryk, Tomas G. *The Making of a State: Memoirs and Observations, 1914-1918.* Transl. Henry Wickham Steed. London: George Allen & Unwin Ltd., 1927.

Narodny kalendar vols. xxv, xxvi.

O'Grady, Joseph, P., ed. *The Immigrants' Influence on Wilson's Peace Policies.* Lexington, KY: U of Kentucky P, 1967.Odložilík, Otakar. "The Czechs" in *The Immigrants' Influence on Wilson's Peace Policies.* Ed. Joseph O'Grady. Lexington, KY: U of Kentucky P, 1967. 204-223.

Olson, James S. *The Ethnic Dimensions in American History.* 2nd ed. New York: St. Martin's, 1994.

Pichlik, Karel. *Zahranicni odboj 1914-1918 bez legend.* Praha: Svoboda, 1968.

Pergler, Charles. *The Czechoslovak State.* New York: Czechoslovak Arts Club, 1919. ---. *The Heart of Europe.* Chicago: The Bohemian National Alliance, 1917.

Skalnik Leff, Carol. *National Conflict in Czechoslovakia: The Making and Remaking of a State, 1918-1987.* Princeton, NJ: Princeton U P, 1988.

Vznik Ceskoslovenska, 1918: Dokumenty Ceskoslovenské zahranicni politiky. Praha: Ústav   mezinarodnych vztahů, 1994.

HALE YILMAZ

Construction of a New Laz Identity in Turkey and its Future Prospects

People living in the eastern Black Sea region of Turkey are popularly known as Laz regardless of their ethnolinguistic affiliations. The Eastern Black Sea region does not have fixed geographical borders. It may loosely be defined as east of Samsun, but for people living in the region, east is defined not by where they are, but by the town next to their east, until one hits the town of Pazar where a zone begins in which the majority of the inhabitants belong to an ethnolinguistic group called the Laz.[1] This paper aims at understanding the Laz cultural movement that has been evolving in Turkey and in the diaspora community in Germany since the 1980s. The first two sections provide the relevant demographic and historical context. Section three analyzes the emergence of the movement in response to perceived threats to the existence of Laz language and culture. Section four argues and demonstrates that the movement that emerged with a desire to preserve and revitalize the Laz culture has, in fact, been defining and re-defining Laz culture and identity by drawing on sources in language, history and folklore. The final section discusses the sociopolitical implications and the future of the movement in the larger context of questions pertaining to nationalism, the democratization of Turkey, and its inclusion in the European Union.

Background demographic information

The Laz are Muslims by religion, and are of South Caucasian origin linguistically. The Laz language, or Lazuri as the speakers of the language call it, is closely related to the Mingrelian language spoken by the Mingrelians in Georgia, and to a lesser extent to Georgian. Historically, the Laz have lived in the eastern Black Sea area that consituted the *Lazistan*

---

[1] This paper deals not with the Laz in its popular sense, but with the Laz ethnolinguistic community, focusing on the recent Laz cultural movement. The confusion regarding the term Laz cannot be dealt with in detail in this paper, but it has been extensively discussed, for instance, in Meeker's "The Black Sea Turks" 318-45. Some scholars now use the term 'Laz' when they refer to it in its popular sense and the term 'Lazi' when they refer to the linguistic group. In this paper I use the term 'Laz' exclusively and the group to which I refer is clear given the context.

sub-province in Ottoman times. Today, the Ottoman Lazistan roughly corresponds to the provinces of Rize and Artvin in northeastern Turkey.[2] In much of Rize and parts of Artvin, the Laz constitute the majority of the population, but the region is not ethnically and linguistically homogenous. Other groups-mainly Turks, *Hemshinlis*, smaller numbers of Muslim Georgians, and Muslim Greeks-also live in this region.[3] Currently, both in terms of demography and in terms of the ongoing Laz cultural movement, it is appropriate to talk about the Laz in three different geographical areas. In addition to the Rize-Artvin area, or the historical *Lazistan*, one must consider the Laz in Western Turkey, especially in the Istanbul-Izmit area, as well as the small Laz diaspora communities in Western Europe, especially in Germany.

The size of the Laz population in Turkey cannot be established with certainty since Turkish census categories do not specify the ethnic origin of respondents. Some liberal estimates estimate the total number of the Laz population in Turkey between one and one-and-a-half million.[4] The size of the small Laz community in Germany is somewhere between 1.000 and 1.500 people. The number of actual Lazuri speakers is estimated to be much smaller. According to Wolfgang Feurstein, there are 250.000 Lazuri speakers in Turkey. More recently, Chris Hann and Ildiko Bellér-Hann

---

[2] For information on the Laz under the Ottoman Empire, see Meeker's *Nation of Empire: The Ottoman Legacy of Turkish Modernity*, Meeker's "Note on 'The Last Laz Risings and the Downfall of the Pontic Derebeys' by A. Bryer," Bryer's "The Last Laz Risings and the Downfall of the Pontic Derebeys, 1812-1840," Bryer's "Some Notes on the Laz and Tzan" (Part 1) and (Part 2).

[3] For further background on the Laz in Turkey including questions of Laz ethnicity and ethnicity in the eastern Black Sea provinces of Turkey see Alexandre Toumarkine, *Les Lazes en Turquie (XIXe-XXe siècles)*; Rüdiger Benninghaus, "The Laz: An Example of Multiple Identification" in Peter Alford Andrews, ed., 497-502; and Meeker, "The Black Sea Turks." On the Armenian speaking Muslim Hemshinli neighbours of the Laz, see Benninghaus, "Zur Herkunft und Identitat der Hemsinli", 475-97.

[4] "Laz Vakfi Girisim Komitesi'nden Yüksel Yilmaz ile Görüsme," 7. Ildiko Bellér-Hann and Chris Hann estimated the permanent population of Lazistan to be appoximately 400,000. Their calculations were based on 1997 figures and included the whole Rize province and Arhavi, Hopa and Borçka counties of Artvin. Consider also Bellér-Hann and Hann, (*Turkish Region: State, Market & Social Identities on the East Black Sea Coast*, 4, esp. footnote 4.) For an approximate estimation of the total number of ethnically Laz persons living in Turkey one should subtract from the above 400,000 estimation the number of individuals from other ethnic groups in the region and add to the result the number of ethnic Laz people living in the Western provinces, such as Kocaeli, Sakarya, Istanbul and Bolu. This constitutes a rather challenging, if not impossible, task that is complicated by factors such as mixed settlement patterns in the Western cities and the status of children of marriages with non-Laz individuals.

have argued that there are no more than 100.000 Lazuri speakers in the Rize-Artvin region (11).

Assimilationist tendencies of the Laz in Turkey

The Turkish state recognizes the Turkish nation as the only legitimate collective identification for its citizens. One fundamental goal of the state in early Republican Turkey was to build a modern, secular nation out of the ethnically diverse Muslim Anatolian population.[5] Ethnic, religious, tribal and other group identities were seen by the state as barriers against the cultivation of a unified national culture. Therefore, the Turkish state never recognized group identities and often repressed them when they constituted a challenge to the official national identity.[6]

Scholars and other observers have often referred to Turkey as a fairly successful case of nation-building. Within the Turkish experiment, the Laz have been referred to as a particularly successful case of integration into the larger national culture. For example, Rüdiger Benninghaus has observed that the Laz in Turkey do not have a strong ethnic consciousness and that they do not take pride in their Laz ethnicity and language ("The Laz" 497-502). More recently, after long periods of anthropological field research in Rize, Ildiko Bellér-Hann and Chris Hann have argued that the people of Lazistan have not defined themselves in ethnic terms (222). They maintain that no single ideology-Kemalist, ethnic Laz, or other-has become the dominant element of the culture in this region. They have observed that the culture in the Lazistan region contains elements from diverse sources— including Islamic, traditional Ottoman, Turkish nationalist, global, and local and socio-economic. Moreover, it has been suggested that rather than adopt singular exclusive identities, people of Lazistan have been "muddling through" a number of identities.[7]

Emergence of the movement to protect Laz language and culture

---

[5] There were still non-Muslim minorities, mainly Jews, Greeks/Rum and Armenians. However, religious diversity had been greatly reduced through wars, expulsion, population exchange, and voluntary exits by the early years of the Republic.

[6] On the Turkish nationalist ideology and practice of the early republican state, consider Çağgaptay; Kadioglu; Yildiz; and Üstel.

[7] Bellér-Hann and Hann borrow the term "muddling through" (a term attributed originally to Charles Lindblom) from anthropologist Steven Sampson to refer to individuals' ability to adapt to and compromise with the complexity and multiplicity of identities rather than settle with the dominance of a singular identity, such as Kemalist or Turkish. (*Turkish Region*, Chapter 8 "Ethnicity," esp. p. 198).

Unlike the situation in Rize and Artvin, since the 1980s a new Laz cultural movement has emerged in Cologne, Germany and in Istanbul among a number of self-appointed Laz intellectual leaders and activists.[8] These activists have compared the Laz to an "endangered species" and campaigned for its protection. They have argued that the very existence of Laz culture and identity is being threatened and that something needs to be done to preserve and enhance that culture.[9]

I have found the theoretical framework developed by David Lake and Donald Rothchild very helpful in conceptualizing and understanding the recent Laz ethno-cultural movement. According to Lake and Rothchild, ethnic conflicts often emerge when a group feels that its social, political, economic, or cultural rights are being challenged or taken away by another group and that the state cannot or does not want to protect those rights. They note that the threats might emanate from the state itself, especially when the state does not recognize a group's rights or challenges them. Initially, the feeling of fear does not need to be shared by the majority of the group. Once intellectuals, political activists or other leaders within the group recognize a threat to the group, they can take the initiative to mobilize the rest of the community. They can define the threat for the rest of the group and suggest strategies to deal with it. This recognition on the part of intellectuals stirs a process that can lead not only to a struggle for

---

[8] I use the term "Laz activists" as a general category to refer to those individuals who have been actively involved in the ongoing Laz cultural movement. The term does not necessarily imply formal membership in a Laz organization in Turkey or in the diaspora. Activists tend to be relatively well educated men and women most of whom are Laz ethnics themselves. They tend to be middle-class professionals, including, but not limited to, lawyers, engineers, musicians, writers, and retired civil service professionals. With the proliferation of Internet sites and online forums devoted to Laz cultural issues, it becomes increasingly more difficult to distinguish between activists and their target audiences as the Internet makes active participation possible for all persons interested in the movement. Activists themselves, however, may disagree with my choice of the term.

[9] In the second issue of the journal *OGNI*, there is a fascinating illustration entitled "Hayvanlar, Insanlar ve Haklari" [Animals, Humans and Their Rights] that reveals what is at the heart of this process. On the top left side of the page, there is a picture of a rare bird whose habitat is Southeast Turkey. The caption reads: "'Kelaynak': A bird... An endangered species... It is under protection." Juxtaposed is the picture of a young Laz man in his traditional costume. The caption reads: "Kulaberi Sedat: A Laz man. An endangered species... Not under protection..." In the lower part of the page the following remarks are found: "Both of them have the right to preserve and develop their existence ... Because each one of them is an element of the universal culture ..." (42). This illustration illustrates both the central cultural concerns as well as the essentializing tendencies of the movement. See the illustration in Appendix 1.

the protection of what is being threatened, but potentially to a transformation and redefinitions of the rights and the threats involved.[10]

In the case of the recent Laz movement, the activists have perceived a threat to the very existence of Laz culture and identity. In their publications in periodicals such as *Ogni* and *Mjora* and on their Internet sites, the Laz activists have discussed extensively the reasons for and the sources of the threats faced by the Laz. Many of them have argued that the Turkish state is to blame, because it has followed a policy of denial and assimilation since the beginning of the Republic in 1923.[11] They note that the state did not recognize the existence of Lazuri as a distinct language, claiming it was a dialect of Turkish spoken in the eastern Black Sea region. The state also placed prohibitions on the use of Lazuri in speaking, writing, and in publications—it prohibited the use of the Laz language in schools, and it replaced place names in Lazuri and other local languages by Turkish place names.[12]

Laz activists refer to specific examples of the limitations placed on the Laz language ("Yerel Diller 13-16). One such case concerns a Laz newspaper (written in a Laz alphabet based on Latin characters) that began publication in Soviet Georgia in 1929. The cabinet in Ankara passed a ruling in February 1930 (no. 8927) that prohibited the newspaper Mqita Muruzxi from circulating in Turkey.[13] There is essentially no information on the circulation of this newspaper in Turkey, yet the cabinet decision suggests that it was either brought into the country or that the government was afraid that it would be. This case is relevant to the *Mjora* authors not

---

[10] For a discussion of the Kurdish ethnic revival and conflict in Turkey that employs a similar conceptual framework, see Içduygu, Romano and Sirkeci. The authors argue that the environment of both material and nonmaterial insecurity contributes to politicization of ethnic identity and ethnic mobilization. Their main departure from the Lake and Rothchild approach followed in this paper is that they see insecurity as a structural factor, whereas Lake and Rothchild stress the perception of fear and the ensuing processes.

[11] See, for instance, Besli, "Kendinde/Kendin Olman Bilinci Üzerine Düsünceler" 3, 4. Regarding activists' focus on assimilationist policies of the Turkish state, Bellér-Hann makes the point that the adoption of Turkish and Islamic cultural elements by the Laz cannot be explained simply as a result of a few decades of state policies. She argues that such cultural change came as a result of processes that were centuries long and that cannot be reversed ("Dogu Karadeniz Kiyisinda" 45,46).

[12] For such statements see, for instance, Ismail A. Bucaklisi, "Laz Dili/Lazuri Nena" 46-51. On the Turkification of place names, see the list of place names with both the old Laz and the new Turkish names in Ali Ihsan Aksamaz's *Kafkasya'dan Karadeniz'e Lazlarin Tarihsel Yolculugu*, 27-29.

[13] *Mjora* 1, no.1 (Spring 2000): 17-18. Decision number is 8927, not 8924 as given in *Mjora*. For the text of the cabinet decision, see Basbakanlik Cumhuriyet Arsivi (Prime Minister's Republic Archive) 030.18.1.2.8.10.18. In an appendix/ek to this file (8927: 86-101), there is a sample issue of the newspaper *Muruzxi*, including a translated version of it in Turkish.

so much because of how widely the Laz language newspaper may have been read but in terms of the attitude exhibited by the Turkish government toward the Laz.

Activists have been recording their personal experiences of linguistic assimilation. A specific example of this kind of experience related by *Mjora* is the story of the late Recai Özgün. In an interview with *Mjora*, Özgün tells that, in the fourth and fifth years of his elementary school education in the 1930s, he was a member of his school "Committee for the Prevention of the Speaking of the Laz Language."[14] Özgün, himself of Laz origin, states that neither the students and their parents nor the teachers in the school regarded the situation as a policy of assimilation. He explains that the school policy had a practical purpose, not an assimilationist one, since it aimed at improving the students' Turkish language abilities which were necessary for the students' success at school and work. Özgün's childhood experience has often been referred to as a perfect example of the assimilationist state policies in the activists' effort to document the sources of the threat faced by the Laz (Aksamaz "Yerel Diller" 14).

Another major source of the threat addressed by the Laz intellectuals and activists is also associated with the state, and concerns the way the discussion of the Kurdish language, and of cultural, educational, and political rights have evolved in Turkey over the last two decades. These intellectuals express their concern that the issue of cultural and identity rights in Turkey has largely been reduced to an issue of Kurdish rights, further marginalizing other smaller ethnic groups such as the Laz.[15]

The Laz activists have referred to a number of other factors that contribute to the larger threat, such as modernization, urbanization and migration. They have also extended the responsibility to the Laz people themselves. They argue that both the masses and the traditional Laz intellectuals are to blame: many Laz families did not teach their own language and culture to their children under the assumption that their success depended on their fluency in the Turkish language and their full participation in Turkish culture. They also blame the Laz intellectuals of the earlier decades for having dismissed the Laz language and culture as backward and peasant-like in their commitment to modernization and

---

[14] M. Recai Özgün, "Lazca Ile Mücadele Kolu," 59. Özgün died in July 2004 at age eighty following a sudden illness. Özgün saw the common Ottoman past and participation in the war of liberation as important elements of Laz identity that united the Laz with the larger nation. This point is clearly emphasized in his last novel, *Laz Muhammed*.

[15] See, for instance, Ismail Avci Bucaklisi "Diller Tartismasi ve Lazca" and Sarigina Besli, ""Kendinde/Kendin Olman Bilinci Üzerine Düğünceler." For a discussion of the domination of Kurdish within the linguistic rights debate, regarding the Arabic speaking communities in Hatay specifically, see Joan Smith/Kocamahlul, 45-47.

Turkish national unity.[16] Despite the recognition of such factors, the state remains for the activists the principal source of the threat to the Laz identity and culture.

For the Laz intellectuals and activists, it is fundamental first to establish that the Laz culture is being threatened. Within this process, the issue that is more critical than the threat itself is identifying and defining the distinct Laz culture. As Lake and Rothchild argue, this process involves not only preservation and defense of the existing culture, but also the potential of a creative re-interpretation and redefinition of that culture. Activists work with historical sources, yet they render new meaning to the past, as well as to the present, through a selective and imaginative reading of it. As Bellér-Hann and Hann have noted, the Laz culture that the activists have been promoting is one that the Laz women and men have to learn anew, quite similar to the way the Turks had to learn their newly constructed national culture in the early Republican period (214-224).

Priorities of the Laz cultural activists

In the process of constructing and defining the Laz culture, the activists focus on Laz language, history, customs and traditions. Lazuri, or the Laz language, is the main pillar of the Laz culture and identity for the activists. Language is what distinguishes the Laz from other groups,[17] and it is through Lazuri that individual members can eventually imagine and identify with a Laz community (Anderson). Language efforts of the activists have first focused on establishing that Lazuri is not a dialect of Turkish, Georgian, or Pontic Greek, but a distinct language. They have also focused on the development of the Laz language as a written language. Even though there were a few experiments with different alphabets in the late nineteenth and early twentieth centuries, Lazuri has survived mainly as an oral language. In their language efforts, especially in the writing of an alphabet for Lazuri, the activists have benefited greatly from a number of linguists and folklorists who themselves are not Laz—most importantly from Wolfgang Feurstein, who has committed himself to the survival of Laz language and culture.[18] Feurstein organized a cultural center (Albeitskreislazebura) in Germany in 1984 for the promotion of Laz culture and led the efforts for the creation of an alphabet and a dictionary for Lazuri. The same year, Feurstein published a Laz alphabet based on the

---

[16] See, for example, Ismail A. Bucaklisi, "Lazuri Nena" *Mjora*, 50,51.
[17] This point is discussed in detail in Chris Hann, "Ethnicity, Language and Politics in North-east Turkey," 121-156.
[18] For Feurstein's views on the threats faced by the Laz language and culture and possible course of action, see his "Mingrelisch, Lazisch, Swanisch."

Turkish alphabet with some modifications.[19] Since the Laz are already literate in Turkish, a modified Turkish alphabet would facilitate Lazuri literacy—an important consideration, especially since Lazuri literacy would have to be gained on a voluntary basis and through informal channels.

Since then, the activists have been promoting the rejuvenation of the Laz language and literature based on the new alphabet. This process also involves the crucial task of standardizing Lazuri. On the one hand, the activists have been publishing articles that discuss various aspects of the Laz language and emphasize the significance of the mother tongue in the formation of an individual's cultural identity. On the other hand, they have introduced the new Laz alphabet via the Turkish alphabet and published a few Turkish-Lazuri Lazuri-Turkish dictionaries and Lazuri grammars.[20] The activists have also been including mini dictionaries and language lessons in their periodicals and on their Internet sites. Their aim has been not only to make the young generations of the Laz people literate in the Laz language, but also to transform the Laz oral culture and record it in writing. They have paid particular attention to the incorporation in the Laz language of Laz place names and terms about different topics, such as plants and animals. They have been collecting and publishing Laz poems, stories, proverbs and riddles, often in both the original and in Turkish translation. *Mjora* has also experimented with a small newspaper section in the Laz language. The Lazebura group based in Cologne has been offering Laz language classes. It has also created the Laz alphabet and a Laz language font as well as made a number of articles and other information on the Laz language and culture freely available on its Internet site that is accessible in three languages: Turkish, English, and German. The use of new information technologies by the new Laz movement has so far been quite limited, but the Internet is probably one of its most promising avenues for the dissemination and sharing of information in the coming years. The activists have also been debating various options to make Laz language classes more easily accessible both in Turkey and Germany.

---

[19] Feurstein, *Lazuri Alfabe*. A second volume was added in the form of a reading/school book. Feurstein, *Nananena Lazca ders kitabi*. I have not had access to these two volumes. The author's name may appear as Fahri Lazoglu or Fahri Kahraman on the cover. I have followed the citation in Ildiko Bellér Hann, "Myth and history on the Eastern Black Sea Coast," 507.

[20] Among these dictionaries and grammars are Ismail Avci Bucaklisi and Hasan Uzunhasanoglu, *Lazuri-Turkuli Nanapuna. Lazca-Turkce Sozluk*; Metin Erten, *Lazca-Turkce Turkce-Lazca Sozluk. Lazuri-Turkuli Turkuli-Lazuri Nenapuna*; Yilmaz Avci, *Lazuri Nenaçkina Lazca Dilbilgisi*; and an example of cooperative work between Laz intellectuals and outside scholars: Goichi Kojima and Ismail Avci Bucaklisi, *Lazuri Grameri. Lazca Gramer/Laz Grammar*.

Another key aspect of defining the Laz culture and identity is through the activists' reading of history.[21] Putting history in the service of a group requires imagining a distinct and undisrupted past for that group, a past that extends back to ancient times. With regard to the Laz community, a key element of this reinterpretation is the emphasis on the Laz as one of the ancient cultures of Anatolia. An editorial in *Mjora* wrote that the Laz people lived in northeast Anatolia a thousand years before the battle of Manzikert, referring to the first major battle in eastern Anatolia between the Selcuk Turks and the Byzantines in 1071 (Neden Mjora 9). This statement not only intends to remind the readers that the Laz and the Turks are two distinct groups coming from different origins, but also that the Laz are the native people of the land whereas the Turks are newcomers. Such "myths of antiquity" can provide self-esteem and self-legitimation, but such myths may also be utilized to provide historical legitimacy to a group's claims over others (Schöpflin 96, 97)

In a similar case, a contributor to the *Lazebura Bulletin* claimed that, 150 years ago, the Laz had a different language, a different religion, and a different alphabet than they do today.[22] Such arguments not only re-interpret history, but, more importantly, distort it in the name of documenting the group's distinct culture in the past. Contrary to Köksal's claim, the Laz had converted from Christianity to Islam by the seventeenth century; therefore, they did not have a different religion in the nineteenth century.[23] While it is true that more people spoke Lazuri in the nineteenth century, the claim that they had a different alphabet has no credibility since Lazuri was not yet a written language at that time.

Another aspect of the reinterpretation of the Laz history is the creation of Laz heros. One such case is Faik Efendi of Hopa under the reign of Sultan Abdülhamit II. There are several contradictory versions of Faik Efendi's story, but the point is not which is the version closest to historical reality. Faik Efendi is best remembered for his efforts to initiate a Laz alphabet. Whether he was arrested and sent to exile or was actually shot and killed by "the enemies of the Laz people" does not matter much. He is commemorated for his efforts to develop the Laz language and for the persecution he faced from the Ottoman authorities because of those efforts.[24]

---

[21] For a discussion of ideological readings of Laz history by Turkish, Laz and Georgian nationalist historians, see Ildiko Beller Hann's "Dogu Karadeniz Kiyisinda Efsane ve Tarih," 17-50.

[22] Serpil Köksal, "Azinliklar Üzerine."

[23] See, for instance, Toumarkine, *Les Lazes en Turquie*, 2, and Ildiko Beller Hann, "Dogu Karadeniz Kiyisinda Efsane ve Tarih," p. 21.

[24] Mehmedali Baris Besli, "Tarihe Karsi Kisa Bir Tarih," pp. 16, 17; Ali Ihsan Aksamaz, *Dil-Tarih-Kültür-Gelenekleriyle Lazlar*, p. 191.

Another personality now commemorated by the Laz intellectuals as a Laz hero is Helimişi Xasani from the town of Hopa. Xasani went to the Soviet Union in 1932 and lived there until his death in 1976. Much of that time he spent in Georgia, but there were also years of exile in Siberia. He left behind a number of works, including recordings of Laz songs and poetry, children's stories, a novel entitled "A Laz girl in Korea," and a number of paintings. Now he is celebrated as a writer, poet, and painter of the Laz people.[25] Xasani also happened to be a member of the Turkish Communist Party and that was probably why he ended up in the Soviet Union in the first place, but personalities as well as events are often appropriated in the name of a group's distinct identity.

A central aspect of this process of identity construction is the search for the (or an) authentic Laz culture that involves discovery, recovery and invention of Laz customs and traditions.[26] Activists have again benefited from the scholarly works and interests of folklorists and linguists in the preservation of Laz cultural authenticity. Journalist N. Ascherson has related the story of Feurstein's commitment to the survival of the authentic Laz culture:

> It was in the 1960s that Feurstein first went to the Lazi country, travelling among their villages and learning their language. What happened to this mild, fair-bearded man was something like a religious revelation. It dawned on him that the Lazi were what Germans call a Volk--an authentic national group with a rich folk identity, which was about to be lost forever. He resolved to save it. [27]

Declaring a culture dead or dying, as Regina Bendix notes, "promotes the search for not yet discovered and hence authentic folklore" (9). While Feurstein's determination to preserve what he saw as an authentic culture would be applauded in the name of linguistic and cultural diversity,[28]

---

[25] See, for instance, Ismail A. Bucaklisi, "Romantik Bir Laz Sürgün Helimisi Xasani" pp. 30-33. As with many of the contributions to *Ogni* and *Mjora*, this piece is also accessible to readers on the Internet (www.karalahana.com/helimisi.htm). Hence, both traditional and electronic forms of media are utilized to access target audiences.

[26] See Eric Hobsbawm and Terence Ranger, eds., *The Invention of Tradition*.

[27] Neal Ascherson, 'Journey to the end of an alphabet,' *The Independent on Sunday*, 7 November 1993, quoted in Bellér Hann, "Myth and history" pp. 497, 98.

[28] See the essays in *Endangered Languages: Current issues and future prospects*, eds. Lenore A. Grenoble and Lindsay J. Whaley for discussions of the role of the linguist in the preservation of linguistic diversity. See also, George Hewitt, "Yet a third consideration of *Völker, Sprachen und Kulturen des südlichen Kaukasus,*" on the linguists' role in the preservation of southern Caucasian languages in Georgia. Hewitt's essay focuses on Mingrelian, and discusses how nationalist cultural, educational and language policies of the twentieth century brought Mingreliean and others such as Svan to the edge of extinction. The essay also makes recommendations that can help ensure the viability of these languages. Hewitt calls

Bendix questions the value of the whole concept of authenticity "in the age of transculturation" and warns of the potential linkage between folklore and politics. Folklore's quest for the discovery of authentic cultures serves the interests of nationalist ideologies as authenticity helps to legitimize essentialist nationalist claims to uniqueness and particularism (7, 8).

For the Laz activists, the authentic Laz culture is to be found among the Laz folk in the homeland, or Lazona. Homeland and its folk, especially the elderly, are romanticized as the bearers of the true Laz culture. Travel to the homeland acquires a special meaning for the activists in the diaspora. By traveling to Lazona the activists hope to discover, document and experience the true culture of the Laz folk. Paradoxically, it is also the same folk whose consciousness may have to be awakened by the traveling activists. Once the activists arrive, Lazona might prove a mixed blessing, even somewhat of a disappointment. Selma Koçiva, one of the leading figures of the movement in the German diaspora, expresses this point forcefully in her book *Lazona*.[29] When Koçiva makes an effort to start a conversation in Lazuri in a store in Ardesen, the elderly shopkeeper responds positively to Koçiva, while the young clerk responds only in Turkish ("Bir Laz" 75, 76). In a local wedding the activist notes the *tulum* (bagpipe) music and the *horon* dances, yet complains that the atmosphere was still not authentic ("2000 Yilinda" 1).

For the activists, the borders of Lazona stretch eastward into Georgia, into Batum and Sarp, as expressed by an activist in "We the Laz are a big family divided between Turkey and Georgia" Koçiva "Sarpi" In fact, it may be to the east of the Georgian border that the activist hopes to find Laz authenticity, in the ancestral lands and amongst the Mingrelian brethren. Selma Koçiva, one of the leading figures of the movement in Germany, expresses her longing for those lands in her *Lazona*:

> I must take Teona with me and just go. I must search for my roots in the Caucasus. I must go to *Zugdidi*, to the country of the Mingrelians. I must converse with them concerning our common destiny. I must open up the past. I must cross beyond the borders of this Anatolia and go to the true homeland. (Koçiva "Düslerimin")

Once the border has been crossed at Sarp, the travelers report encounters with the Laz authenticity: hearing children speak Lazuri, drinking Laz

---

for active participation by linguists in the preservation of endangered languages, distinguishing between two distinct processes: language and cultural preservation on the one hand, and political independence on the other.

[29] Koçiva's *Lazona*, a collection of her essays on Laz folklore and culture, was first published in Germany in 1999. It was reprinted in Turkey by Tümzamanlar Yayincilik. Certain sections of the book were deemed too sensitive and left out of the Turkish edition by the publisher.

wine, visiting museums, centuries old Laz churches, and castles from the time of the Kingdom of Lazika.[30] Travel to certain sites acquires a holy dimension and almost becomes a secular pilgrimage. Relating his visit to the tomb of Helimisi Xasani, an activist wrote that "in commemoration of this great man every Laz should visit Hasani's tomb at least once" (Arkaburi). This call initiates a commemoration practice that, if successful, could enhance Xasani's mythification as a Laz hero.

In the search for the authentic Laz culture, music has played a central role. The rhetorical interest expressed by intellectuals and activists in the preservation and promotion of authentic Laz music has been coupled with the making of actual musical productions. Since the early 1990s, a small number of artists, whose membership overlaps with that of the activists, have dedicated themselves to the promotion of Laz music. Efforts have focused on the revival of instruments such as the *tulum* (bagpipe) and the *kemençe* (fiddle) as authentic Laz musical instruments, promotion of *horon* as the traditional Laz folkdance, revival of authentic forms such as the *destan*, and collection of folk songs from Laz villages. While there has been a general concern about preserving the authenticity of the music, there has been some discrepancy about merging the "authentic" with the "modern." For example, the group Zugasi Berepe (Children of the Sea) made the first ethnic Laz/rock album *Va Miskunan* (We Don't Know) in 1995 combining traditional melodies and instruments with elements of rock music. The group split after another album, yet group member Kazim Koyuncu has continued to produce music mixing traditional Laz and modern elements.

Another musician, Birol Topaloglu, an engineer by training who went back to his village to preserve Laz music, has focused more on the question of authenticity. His declared goal is to make Laz culture eternal by making authentic Laz music.[31] To that end he has been visiting villages, discovering and recording old ballads, epics, *horon*s, lullabies and other forms of songs that are dying. His sources are often old women in the villages since women are considered the real bearers and transmitters of a tradition because their contact with other cultures and languages tends to be minimal. In a 2001 album entitled "Lazeburi: Documentary of Authentic Laz Music," Topaloglu brought together some of his own compilations as well as a number of earlier recordings, including several pieces by Helimisi Xasani to whom the album was dedicated.

---

[30] See Kutay Arkaburi, "Lazona'ya ziyaret." See also Koçiva, "Sarpi ve Samegrelo Izlenimlerim."

[31] See Nicolas Cheviron, "Preserving the Music of the Laz"; Birol Topaloğlu, "Öze Yolculuk" pp. 41-45; and Mehmet Akgül, "Say 'best thing' he can do is sing in the Laz language."

When put in the larger context of the Laz cultural movement, these well-intentioned efforts to preserve one's musical heritage may involve the risk of contributing to the building of an essentialist and static group identity and to establishing boundaries by making exclusive claims to otherwise shared cultural practises.[32] For instance, the emphasis on *tulum* as an authentic Laz musical instrument does not seem to take note of the fact that *tulum* is as much a part of the Hemshinli musical culture as of the "hybrid" culture emerging upon the contact of the two groups.[33] Similarly, *kemençe*/fiddle, the other instrument claimed to be an authentic Laz instrument, is not only played by very few Laz these days (note 12 p. 153), but is also shared and even claimed by other cultures, such as Iranian ("Musical Tradition 31).

Activists have often referred to hawking, or falconry, as a specifically Laz tradition, even though it has been practiced by other groups as well.[34] Activists' interest in hawking can be seen as the re-discovery and revival of a dying tradition. The first detailed account of this tradition that I have encountered is in M. Recai Özgün's *Atmaca* (Hawk). In this work, a biographical narrative incorporates notes on folklore, including a section on the hawking tradition. In addition to providing lengthy discussions of the practice and the culture of hawking, Özgün relates Orhan's (who appears to be the author himself) stories of hawking from his childhood and youth years in Arhavi back in the 1930s and 1940s. Subsequent narratives about and celebration of hawking as a Laz tradition seem to be based on this single source,[35] which suggests that current practice of hawking may actually be hard to encounter.

A Laz activist has recently discovered a Laz tradition called "pagara," which is a celebration of the coming of the spring (Aksyolu). What is described as "pagara" sounds very much like the spring celebrations in many parts of the Middle East region that originated in the Zoroastrian culture. In the 1980s, Kurdish nationalists in Turkey called it "Nawrouz" and successfully raised it to the status of a symbol of Kurdish culture and nationalism. The state responded in the early 1990s by incorporating "Nevruz" to the calendar of national holidays as an ancient Turkish

---

[32] The following remarks by Bendix are worth quoting: "Textualized expressive culture such as songs and tales can, with the aid of the rhetoric of authenticity, be transformed from an experience of individual transcendence to a symbol of the inevitability of national unity" (*In Search of Authenticity*, 20).

[33] Chris Hann speaks of a festival, where he observed Laz Hemshinli hybridity in music, dance, and clothing. See his "Ethnicity" 131 and n.12 on 153.

[34] Özgün, *Atmaca*; Özgün, "Atmaca (Siftheri)" pp. 24-27. For later narratives and claims on hawking based on this work, see, for instance, "Lazlarda Kültürel Yapı."

[35] An exception that defies reliance on Özgün's account may be Cemil Telci, "Atmaca Üzerine," pp. 8,9. But, here too, the author remembers hawking in his village in Findikli, during his childhood years in the 1960s.

celebration. The Laz activists wish to appropriate "Nevruz" as a specifically Laz tradition, even though this is a celebration that has already been claimed and contested by Kurdish and Turkish nationalists. An important factor that is curiously missing from the activists' construction of Laz identity is Islam. This can only in part be explained by the secularism of the movement. At least equally important a reason might be that, as Islam has been an important aspect of the culture throughout Anatolia and is often associated with Turkishness, it does not help establish Laz cultural distinction. On the contrary, it highlights cultural continuities, a fact which does not assist the Laz activists who are competing for the primacy of the ethnic identities of Laz individuals over other identifications, such as Ottoman, Islamic, Turkish, regional or local.

Sociopolitical implications and future prospects of the Laz cultural movement

Once the activists have begun defining the group and the threats faced by the group, a rather critical question emerges: what are the political implications of this process, and how do those implications affect the future of the movement? The activists in the German diaspora community and, to some extent, those in Istanbul tend to agree that there is a political dimension to the Laz cultural movement. There is no established consensus on what the political implications are, yet the activists have been voicing a number of demands that cross the boundaries of the political. The most fundamental demands are the official recognition of the Laz ethnic minority and the Laz language by the state of Turkey. Demands for full language and cultural rights include: the right to learn Lazuri in public schools as a native language, the right to pursue education in Lazuri, and the restoration of Laz place names.[36] There are also less openly and less frequently stated implied demands, such as autonomy or other regional arrangements.[37]

---

[36] Such demands have constantly been expressed in a number of books by Laz intellectuals such as Aksamaz, *Kafkasya'dan Karadeniz'e Lazlarin Tarihsel Yolculugu*; Aksamaz, *Dil-Tarih-Kültür-Gelenekleriyle Lazlar*; Özgün, *Lazlar*; in journals *Ogni* and *Mjora*; as well as on Internet sites devoted to the Laz culture, such as lazebura.com and karalahana.com. See, for instance, the public proclamation by the Lazebura group "Türkiyede Lazlarda [*sic*] var" and Koçiva's "Demokratik Taleplerimiz".

[37] For statements having such implications see, for example, Koçiva, *Lazona: Laz Halk Gerçekligi Üzerine*. The book was reprinted in Turkey by Tümzamanlar Yayincilik. Certain sections of the book were deemed too sensitive and left out of the Turkish edition by the publisher.

The Laz cultural movement, especially given its political dimension, has the potential to evolve into an open conflict with the state. In the long term, the worst-case scenario would be a conflict between attempts at suppression by the state and armed resistance by the group. This would mean something similar to the PKK era in the Kurdish case, but on a smaller scale. The best-case scenario would be a smooth, peaceful resolution that satisfies both the state and the Laz movement through further democratization and acceptance by the state of some form of multiculturalism.

Fortunately, the worst-case scenario is unlikely to happen for a number of reasons. Both the Laz activists and the state have witnessed the PKK experience and they do not wish to live through a similar conflict. Many of the Laz activists denounce the use of violence for political ends. The radical activists tend to be members of the Laz diaspora in Germany, and not committed nationalists in the homeland. The Laz have too small and fragmented a geographical and population basis for an effective armed struggle. Many members of the Laz community in Turkey live in the Western provinces mixed with or surrounded by other groups. Population is ethnically mixed even in the Rize and Artvin provinces. More importantly, there is no popular support for the activists' cause in "Lazona/the homeland," that is, the Rize and Artvin provinces. There is also no external support base adjacent to the region, at least for the time being.

The best-case scenario for a quick and smooth resolution is also unlikely. Activists, especially those based in Europe, will not easily give up their demands, just as the Turkish state ideology-based on a unified Turkish nation and a unitary state-will not change radically in the foreseeable future. The outcome will probably be somewhere between the two extreme scenarios and it will probably be closer to the best-case than the worst. A number of key factors will shape the future prospects of the Laz cultural movement. One key factor is the response of the Turkish state. So far, the state has not been very tolerant towards the expression of Laz ethnic identity, perceiving it as a threat to the national unity and territorial integrity of Turkey. The state has intervened with the Laz intellectuals' and activists' activities that it deemed threatening. For example, in 1993 the first issue of the Laz cultural journal *Ogni* was withdrawn from circulation and the editor was brought before the National Security Court in Istanbul on the grounds of separatism. The court acquitted the editor and allowed for the continuation of the publication.[38] In another instance, following a

---

[38] For the text of the Court's decision on *Ogni* dated 5 April 1994 see "Karar: Ogni Beraat Etti..." pp. 45, 46. *Ogni* discontinued after its sixth issue. In 2000, Civi Yazilari began publishing *Mjora*, a series dedicated to Laz history, culture, and art. The judiciary intervened after two issues, closing down *Mjora* on procedural grounds in July 2000.

radio program in Ardesen, Rize, in 1999, musician Birol Topaloglu was taken before the court by the public prosecutor on the grounds of inciting the public to hatred and enmity on the basis of race. Topaloglu defended himself arguing he did not have any separatist goals and that his aim was only to help preserve Laz culture, especially its language and music. The National Security Court decided to quash the indictment brought against Topaloglu.[39] In a similar case, Koçiva's book *Lazona*, quoted above, was confiscated in January 2002 and charges were pressed against both the author and the publisher, again under Article 312 of the Turkish Penal Code, on the grounds of incitement to hatred and enmity on the basis of race. The case closed with *Lazona*'s acquittal in 2003.[40]

Further democratization, or the move away from democracy, will have an impact on recognition of group rights. Continuation and actual implementation of such democratizing measures will also depend on the process of Turkey's inclusion in the European Union. The state is willing to make concessions in order to fulfill the requirements for EU membership, including the "Copenhagen political criteria" of 1993 that ask for full recognition of minority rights. Closer integration within the EU would moderate the position of the state vis-a-vis groups demanding group-specific rights. The debate about the recognition of specific group rights has mainly revolved around the Kurdish issue. However, developments regarding Kurdish cultural rights-for instance, the outcome of the debate on Kurdish language rights, including the question of education in Kurdish-will influence the way the state views similar demands by smaller ethnic groups.

Recently there have been some important developments concerning language rights. The latest political reform package that was implemented in 2003 recognizes the right to teach languages traditionally spoken by Turkish citizens in private classes. More recently, a new statute on broadcasting introduced in January 2004 recognizes the right to broadcast in languages traditionally spoken by Turkish citizens, albeit following very strict rules. On 7 June 2004, the public television and radio TRT started broadcasting in five such languages including Arabic, Bosnian, Circassian, Kirmanchi (Kurdish) and Zaza (Kurdish). Even though the Laz language was not included among the five, prospects for its inclusion in the future are high. A group of Laz intellectuals and activists have petitioned the TRT for the inclusion of Lazuri under the new regulation and the Lazebura group has started a petition campaign on their Internet site.[41] Reactions from the media and the public to the new broadcasting policy have been rather diverse. While some have criticized the policy for excluding certain

---

[39] www.lazebura.com/lazebura.V/cibarisi1.htm.
[40] "Lazona Beraat Etti."
[41] "TRT'den Lazca yayin talebi."

languages or rejected it as a superficial act denying any substantive broadcasting rights in those languages, others, for instance some Bosnian associations, have criticized the inclusion of Bosnian, arguing that, as Turkish citizens, they don't consider themselves a minority and that they have not asked for broadcasting in Bosnian.[42]

At the heart of the political debate is how to recognize group rights and still maintain peace and unity. While some see the new broadcasting policy as a step in the direction of full recognition of minority rights, others warn that it may lead to fragmentation and conflict. A key concern in this debate is how to reconcile Turkishness and Turkish nationalism with the rising identity claims that would be strengthened with the recognition of language rights. In other words, if Turkish nationalism can no longer provide the ideological means for unity, can it be redefined or replaced by other tools or mechanisms so as to accommodate change? In this context, constitutional citizenship has been suggested as an alternative model that requires allegiance not to the nation but to a political community, based on a constitutional system that recognizes diversity.[43] This model has found symbolic expression in the appropriation of Kemal Atatürk's famous aphorism "How happy is the one who says I am a Turk" into "How happy is the one who says I am a citizen of the Republic of Turkey." While such a model requires the tremendous task of the gradual disassociation of state and citizenship from Turkish nationalism, the simultaneous building of new group identities with essentialist claims would not help that process of transformation.

Prospects for conflict and peace will also depend on how the Laz movement itself will evolve. Whether the Laz movement in the diaspora community will become more moderate or more radical, and whether it will stay unified or split into smaller groups will be critical. How the activists in Germany and Istanbul relate to other groups and institutions in Turkey with an interest in the Laz culture will also be important. Relevant in this context is the position of the SIMA in Izmit that combines cultural interests with regional and economic concerns. SIMA Dogu Karadenizliler Vakfi was founded in 1996 in Izmit. Even though it is sometimes referred to as the Laz Foundation, neither the Foundation's name nor its charter contain the word Laz. According to the SIMA Charter,[44] the Foundation aims at promoting economic and social solidarity, preserving the common culture, and promoting education, health, sports, and tourism among a group of citizens carefully defined as: a. "Those living in the counties of Borçka, Hopa, Arhavi, Findikli, Ardesen and Pazar." b. Those originally

---

[42] "Bosnaklar sitemkâr."
[43] See, for instance, Içduygu, Romano and Sirkeci.
[44] Full text of "Dogu Karadenizliler Hizmet Vakfi Vakif Senedi" is available in M. Recai Özgün's *Kurtulusumuzun Öyküsü*, pp. 107-130.

from those regions currently residing in other parts of the country. c. Individuals who have been settled in the country following wars or immigration originating from territories with similar cultures that have been lost to Turkey. d. Individuals who fit one of the above criteria and are currently living abroad. Based on this article, it is obvious that even if there may be a regional dimension to SIMA, one that is similar to the homeland/*hemsehri* associations in the big cities, SIMA is mainly interested in cooperation among the Laz. The towns specified in the Charter are the towns in the Rize and Artvin provinces that form a contiguous zone of Lazuri speakers. The careful wording of the charter may have been an act of caution to prevent any potential state sanctions; it may also have been a compromise in language to satisfy different opinions among the SIMA founders.

SIMA's officials acknowledge the foundation's interest in promoting Laz language and culture, but are careful to note that their interests are not limited to Laz cultural issues. Asked about the Foundation's goals, SIMA president defined the foundation's mission as "to live and to promote Laz culture and language" within the territorial integrity of the Turkish Republic and led by the principles of Atatürk. He was also quick to add that SIMA is open to all from the Black Sea region east of Samsun. Concerning SIMA's view on Laz cultural activities in Germany, he rejected any SIMA association with such groups and emphasized that SIMA is against ethnic nationalism.[45] While SIMA views the diaspora group in Germany as too radical and even dangerous, the diaspora movement considers SIMA too conservative and coopted by Turkish nationalism (Koçiva "Laz Vakfi 200-203). Looking at the foundation's periodical publication *SIMA* and based on my visit to SIMA, it appears that the majority of SIMA officials and members are individuals who have successfully integrated into the larger Turkish society socially and economically. These people want to maintain and develop their regional and cultural heritage, yet they also want to keep enjoying full benefits of Turkish citizenship as contractors, engineers, businessmen, or civil servants, regardless of their more intimate cultural associations. This position was well illustrated by Recai Özgün's identification of himself as "a constitutional citizen of the Republic of Turkey of Laz origin,"(59) a formulation made with reference to the ongoing debates regarding Turkish nationalism and citizenship. The SIMA group are more pragmatic and more moderate in their claims, yet it must also be noted there may be some generational divide within the foundation, with the younger people being more focused on cultural production and closer to the diaspora position. It does not seem likely that the SIMA, Istanbul, and diaspora groups will merge in the near future; yet, the

---

[45] Güngör Sahinkaya, interview by author, 21 August 2003.

boundaries between these groups are not fixed and some activists may be affiliated with two, or even all three, of these groups.

Perhaps the most important factor for the future of the Laz cultural movement will be the success or failure of the intellectuals and activists in mobilizing the Laz population-both in the Eastern Black Sea region and in Western Turkey. If they can persuade a significant segment of the Laz population in Turkey that their culture is in danger and that what the intellectuals tell them is in their culture's interest, this could turn into a mass movement. Their success in communicating that message partly depends on how the message is presented as well as on the effective utilization of all available means, such as print media, the Internet, music, and possibly broadcasting. Increased Lazuri literacy and the group's interest in social and environmental causes could play an important role in mobilizing public support.

Scholars and other observers will find it interesting to see how the Laz cultural movement continues to evolve as a case of language revival and identity construction in the early twenty-first century. The future of the movement will depend on a complex interplay of factors, ranging from the conscious choices of the Laz activists and the Turkish state to the developments regarding Kurdish nationalism and Turkey's inclusion in the European Union. It may be too early to state if the progress made towards the preservation and revitalization of Lazuri has reached an irreversible point. Activists will continue their efforts to revive and develop the Laz language. The Laz identity is also still in the making. Activists will continue to debate and define what constitutes Lazness. Perhaps the greatest challenge the activists will face is to avoid defining Lazness as an exclusive and essentialist identity in direct opposition to Turkishness. Hence, it remains to be seen if the movement can build a Laz identity that recognizes the multiplicity of identities of Laz individuals.

Works Cited

Akgül, Mehmet. "Say 'best thing' he can do is sing in the Laz language." Accessed 28 July 2004. <http://www.kalan.com/scripts/Dergi.asp?t=3&yid=9256>.

Aksamaz, Ali Ihsan. *Dil-Tarih-Kültür-Gelenekleriyle Lazlar.* [The Laz People with their Language, History, Culture and Traditions] Istanbul: Sorun Yayinlari, 2000.

---. *Kafkasya'dan Karadeniz'e Lazlarin Tarihsel Yolculugu.* [Historical Journey of the Laz from Caucasia to the Black Sea] Istanbul: Civiyazilari, 1997.

---. "Yerel Diller: Ana Dilleri Yasatmak Mi? Öldürmek Mi?." [Local Languages: Preserve or Kill Mother Tongues?] *SIMA Dogu Karadenizliler Hizmet Vakfi Üç Aylik Kültür, Sanat, Edebiyat Dergisi* no.5 (2003): 13-16.

Aksoylu, Kamil. "Lazona'da Bahar." [Spring in Lazona] *Laz Forum* 14 April 2002. Online.<http://www.network54.com/Hide/Forum/message?forumid=57404&mesage id=1018813298>.

Anderson, Benedict. *Imagined Communities: Reflections on the Origin and Spread of Nationalism.* London, New York: Verso, 1991.

Andrews, Peter Alford, ed. (with the assistance of Rüdiger Benninghaus) *Ethnic Groups in the Republic of Turkey.* Wiesbaden: Dr. Ludwig Reichert Verlag, 1989.

Arkaburi, Kutay. "Lazona'ya ziyaret ve Birol Topaloglu Portekiz Festival Konseri ve Laz Sergisi." [Visit to Lazona, Birol Topaloglu Festival Concert and Laz Exhibit in Portugal]   Accessed   24   July   2004 <http://www.lazebura.net/09_arsiv/lazonaya_ziyaret.htm>.

Avci, Yilmaz. *Lazuri Nenaçkina Lazca Dilbilgisi.* [Laz Grammar] Istanbul: Etno-Kültür Kitaplari, 2002.

Basbakanlik   Cumhuriyet   Arsivi   (Prime   Minister's   Republic   Archive) 030.18.1.2.8.10.18. Appendix/*ek* (8927: 86-101).

Bellér-Hann, Ildiko, and Chris Hann. *Turkish Region: State, Market & Social Identities on the East Black Sea Coast.* Oxford: James Currey; Santa Fe, NM: School of American Research Press, 2001.

Bendix, Regina. *In Search of Authenticity: The Formation of Folklore Studies.* Madison: U of Wisconsin P, 1997.

Benninghaus, Rüdiger. "The Laz: An Example of Multiple Identification." in Andrews. 497-502.

---. "Zur Herkunft und Identitat der Hemşinli" in Andrews, *Ethnic Groups.* 475-97.

Besli, Mehmedali Baris. "Tarihe Karsi Kisa Bir Tarih" [A Short History Against History] *Mjora. Lazlarin Tarih Edebiyat Kültür ve Sanat Dosyasi,* no.1 (Winter 2000): 16, 17.

Besli, Sarigina. "Kendinde/Kendin Olman Bilinci Üzerine Düsünceler. Lazlik Bilincinin Uyanmasina Içten Bir Bakis" [Thoughts on knowing oneself/being oneself. A candid look at the awakening of Laz consciousness] *Ogni,* no.1 (November 1993): 3, 4.

"Bosnaklar sitemkâr." [Bosnians are reproachful] *Radikal* (Istanbul) 14 June 2004.

Bryer, Anthony. "The Last Laz Risings and the Downfall of the Pontic Derebeys, 1812-1840." *Bedi Kartlisa* 26 (1969): 191-210.

---. "Some Notes on the Laz and Tzan" *Bedi Kartlisa* 21/22 (1966): 174-195 (Part 1) and 23/24 (1967):161-168 (Part 2).

Bucaklisi, Ismail Avci. "Diller Tartismasi ve Lazca." [The Debate on Languages and Laz Language] Accessed 14 July 2004. Available at http://www.lazebura.com/ Dil/dillertartismasi.htm.

---. "Laz Dili/Lazuri Nena." [Laz Language] *Mjora* no.1 (Winter 2000): 46-51.

---. "Romantik Bir Laz Sürgün Helimisi Xasani." [Helimisi Hasani. A Romantic Laz Exile] *Mjora. Lazlarin Tarih Edebiyat Kültür ve Sanat Dosyasi* no.1 (Winter 2000): 30-33. Also available at www.karalahana.com/helimisi.htm.

Bucaklisi, Ismail Avci and Hasan Uzunhasanoglu. *Lazuri-Turkuli Nanapuna. Lazca-Türkçe Sözlük.* [Laz-Turkish Dictionary] Istanbul: Akyüz, 1999.

Cheviron, Nicolas. "Preserving the Music of the Laz." *Le Monde* (Paris) 26 June 2001 reprinted in *World Press Review* (September 2001): 37.

Cagaptay, Soner. "Crafting the Turkish Nation: Kemalism and Turkish Nationalism in the 1930s." Ph.D. Dissertation, Yale University, 2003.

Erten, Metin. *Lazca-Türkçe Türkçe-Lazca Sözlük. Lazuri-Turkuli Turkuli-Lazuri Nenapuna.* [Laz-Turkish Turkish-Laz Dictionary] Istanbul: Anahtar Kitaplar, 2000.

Feurstein, Wolfgang. *Lazuri Alfabe; lazca alfabe; entwurf eines lazischen alphabetes* (Parpali 1) Gundelfingen, Lazebura, 1984.

---. "Mingrelisch, Lazisch, Swanisch: alte Sprachen und Kulturen der Kolchis vor dem baldigen Untergang." *Caucasian Perspectives.* Ed. George Hewitt. München: Lincom Europa, 1992. 285-328.

---. *Nananena Lazca ders kitabi, Lasisches Schulbuch* (Parpali 2) Freundenstadt: Kaukasus Verlag, 1991.

Grenoble, Lenore A. and Lindsay J. Whaley, eds. *Endangered Languages: Current issues and future prospects.* Cambridge: Cambridge U P, 1998.

Hann, Ildiko Beller. "Dogu Karadeniz Kiyisinda Efsane ve Tarih." in Ildiko Beller Hann, *Dogu Karadenizde Efsane Tarih ve Kültür,* trans. and ed. Ali Ihsan Aksamaz from Ildiko Beller Hann "Myth and history on the Eastern Black Sea Coast." Istanbul: Civiyazilari, 1999. 17-50.

---. "Myth and history on the Eastern Black Sea Coast" *Central Asian Survey* 14.4 (1995): 497, 98.

Hann, Chris. "Ethnicity, Language and Politics in North-east Turkey." *The Politics of Ethnic Consciousness.* eds. Cora Govers and Hans Vermeulen. London: Macmillan Press, 1997; New York, NY: St. Martin's Press, 1997. 121-156.

"Hayvanlar, Insanlar ve Haklari." [Animals, Humans and Their Rights] *Ogni* no.2 (Jan. 1994): 42.

Hewitt, George. "Yet a third consideration of *Völker, Sprachen und Kulturen des südlichen Kaukasus.*" *Central Asian Survey* 14.2 (1995): 285-310.

Hobsbawm, Eric, and Terence Ranger, eds. *The Invention of Tradition.* Cambridge: Cambridge U P, 1983.

Içduygu, Ahmet, David Romano and Ibrahim Sirkeci. "The Ethnic Question in an Environment of Insecurity: The Kurds in Turkey." *Ethnic and Racial Studies* 22.6 (November 1999): pages 991-1010.

Kadioglu, Ayse. "The Paradox of Turkish Nationalism and the Construction of Official Identity." *Middle Eastern Studies* 32. 2 (April 1996): 177-193.

"Karar: Ogni Beraat Etti..." [Decision: Ogni Acquitted] *Ogni* no. 5 (July-August 1994): 45, 46.

Koçiva, Selma. "Bir Laz Kentine Yolculuk." [Journey to a Laz City] *Lazona: 69-76.* (pagination refers to the Istanbul edition).

---. "Demokratik Taleplerimiz." [Our Democratic Demands] 18 July 2001. Online. Available at www.lazebura.com/arsiv/taleplerimiz.htm.

---. "Düslerimin Kenti Tiflis." [T'bilisi the City of my Dreams] *Lazona*. (Istanbul edition) 267-69 (pagination refers to the Istanbul edition).

---. "2000 Yilinda Lazona'daydim (1)" [I was in Lazona in 2000] *Lazebura* no. 4. Accessed on April 5, 2002. 5 April 2002. Available at http://www.lazebura.com/dergi2/lazonadaydim.htm.

---. *Lazona: Laz Halk Gerçekligi Üzerine.* [Lazona: On the Reality of Laz Folk] Frankfurt: BDE, 1999.

---. *Lazona: Laz Halk Gerçekligi Üzerine.* [Lazona: On the Reality of Laz Folk] Istanbul: Tümzamanlar, 2000.

---. "Laz Vakfi Netlesmeli." [Laz Foundation should clarify itself] *Lazona* 200-2003 (pagination refers to the Istanbul edition) 200-203.

---. "Sarpi ve Samegrelo Izlenimlerim" [My impressions of Sarpi and Samegrelo] 17 October 2001. Accessed on 5 April 2002. Available at http://www.lazebura.com/arsiv/index.htm?cid=15.

Kojima, Goichi and Ismail Avci Bucaklisi. *Lazuri Grameri. Lazca Gramer/Laz Grammar.* Istanbul: Civiyazilari, 2003.

Köksal, Serpil. "Azinliklar Üzerine." [On Minorities] *Lazebura* No. 4 (March 2001) Online. 5 April 2002. Available at http://www.lazebura.com/dergi2/azinliklar.htm.

Lake, David A., and Donald Rothchild. "Containing Fear: The Origins and Management of Ethnic Conflict." *International Security* 21.2 (Fall 1996): 41-75.

"Laz Vakfi Girisim Komitesi'nden Yüksel Yılmaz ile Görüşme." [Interview with Yüksel Yilmaz from the Committee for the Establishment of a Laz Foundation] *Ogni* no.1 (November 1993): 7.

"Lazlarda Kültürel Yapi." [Cultural Structure of the Laz] *Lazebura*. Online. 5 April 2002. Available at www.lazebura.com/kultur/kulturelyapi.htm.

"Lazona Beraat Etti." [Lazona acquitted] *Ozgur Politika*. Online. Accessed May 2, 2004 Available at http://www.ozgurpolitika.org/2003/12/22/allkul.html.

Meeker, Michael. "The Black Sea Turks: Some Aspects of Their Ethnic and Cultural Background" *International Journal of Middle East Studies* 2 (1971): 318-45.

---. *Nation of Empire: The Ottoman Legacy of Turkish Modernity.* Berkeley: U of California P, 2002.

---. "Note on 'The Last Laz Risings and the Downfall of the Pontic Derebeys' by A. Bryer." *Bedi Kartlisa* 26 (1969): 250-252.

"The Musical Tradition." *Persian Heritage* 9.34 (Summer 2004): 31.

"Neden Mjora." [Why Mjora] *Mjora* no.1 (Winter 2000): 9.

Özgün, M. Recai. *Atmaca*. [Hawk] Istanbul: n.p., 1993?.

---. "Atmaca (Siftheri)" [Hawk] *Fırtınanın Sesi* 1.1 (December 2000): 24-27.

---. *Kurtulusumuzun Öyküsü (Büyük Nutuk Penceresinden)* [The Story of our Liberation (Through the Window of the Great Speech)] İzmit: SİMA, 1998.

---. *Laz Muhammed*. Istanbul: Chiviyazıları, 2004.

---. "Lazca Ile Mücadele Kolu Baskanligindan Laz Kültürünün Arastirilmasina Uzanan Bir Yol: M. Recai Özgün." [A road stretching from the Presidency of the Committee for the Prevention of the Speaking of Laz Language to Research on Laz Culture] Interview by Melahat Bul, *Mjora* 1.1 (Spring 2000): 59.

---. *Lazlar*. [The Laz] Istanbul: Civiyazilari,1996.

Schöpflin, George. *Nations Identity Power*. NewYork: New York U P, 2000.

Smith/Kocamahlul, Joan. "In the Shadow of Kurdish: The Silence of Other Ethnolinguistic Minorities in Turkey." *Middle East Report* no. 219 (Summer 2001): 45-47.

Sahinkaya, Güngör. Personal interview. Izmit, Turkey, 21 August 2003.

Telci, Cemil. "Atmaca Üzerine." [On Hawks] *SIMA* 2, no. 4: 8,9.

Topaloglu, Birol. "Öze Yolculuk." [Journey to the Essence] *Mjora* no.1 (2000): 41-45.

Toumarkine, Alexandre. *Les Lazes en Turquie (XIXe-XXe siècles)*. İstanbul: ISIS, 1995.

"TRT'den Lazca yayin talebi." [Request from TRT for broadcasting in Lazca] 30 June 2004. Accessed 14 July 2004. Available at http://www.lazebura.net/09_arsiv/haber/ fullnews/php?id=71.

"Türkiyede Lazlarda [*sic*] var." [In Turkey there are Lazes as well] *Lazebura* No. 4. March 2001. Internet. Accessed 5 April 2002. Available at http://www.lazebura.com/ dergi2/bildiri.htm.

Üstel, Füsun. *Imparatorluktan Ulus Devlete Türk Milliyetçiligi: Türk Ocaklari (1912-1931)*.[Turkish Nationalism from Empire to Nation State: Turkish Hearths (1912-1931)] Istanbul: Iletisim, 1997.

Yildiz, Ahmet. *"Ne Mutlu Türküm Diyebilene" Türk Ulusal Kimliğinin Etno-Seküler Sınırları(1919-1938)*. ["How Happy is the one who can say I am a Turk" Ethno-Secular Boundaries of Turkish National Identity] Istanbul: Iletisim, 2001.

Appendix 1. "Animals, Humans and their Rights"

AӠULUTİ BӠİӠAT

HAYVANLAR, İNSANLAR VE HAKLARI

Kelaynak: Bir Kuş
Nesli tükeniyor........
Koruma altında......

Ǩulaberi Sedat: Bir Laz
Nesli tükeniyor.........
Korunma altında değil..........

HER İKİSİNİN DE VARLIKLARINI KORUMA VE GELİŞTİRMEYE HAKLARI VAR...
ÇÜNKÜ ONLAR EVRENSEL KÜLTÜRÜN BİRER UNSURU.....

AMA.....
S.O.S.

42　kelaynak : Gerontrous eremita

OGNİ
Ocak 1994

Contributors and Editors

PIRJO AHOKAS is a Professor of Comparative Literature at the University of Turku, Finland. She is the author of *Forging a New Self*, a monograph on Bernard Malamud's novels, and co-editor of *Reclaiming Memory: American Representations of the Holocaust*. She has published essays on ethnic writing and is currently working on a book on contemporary American women's literature.

ELEFTHERIA ARAPOGLOU teaches at the department of American Literature and Culture of Aristotle University in Thessaloniki, Greece. She has received several fellowships and scholarships, from the Fulbright foundation, the Center of Mark Twain Studies in Elmira New York, the European Association of American Studies, the Princeton University Library, and the Greek State Scholarship Foundation. Dr Arapoglou has presented numerous papers at international conferences, some of which have appeared at selected conference proceedings, in *The Journal of Modern Hellenism*, and in *MELUS*. Her research interests include the cultural production of space in the modernist tradition, literary sociology, and cultural studies. Currently, Dr. Arapoglou is working on a book project on Women's Imperial Positionings at the Turn of the Century and Demetra Vaka Brown.

MITA BANERJEE is Professor of American Studies at the University of Mainz, Germany. She is the author of *The Churneyfication of History: Salman Rushdie, Michael Ondaatje, Bharati Mukherjee and the Postcolonial Debate*.

SOPHIA EMMANOUILIDOU holds a PhD in Chicano Studies from Aristotle University of Thessaloniki, Greece and teaches in the History and Anthropology Department of the University of Peloponnese, Kalamata, Greece.

PIN-CHIA FENG is Dean of Academic Affairs and Professor of the Department of Foreign Languages and Literatures and the Institute of Foreign Literatures and Linguistics, National Chiao Tung University, Taiwan, R.O.C. Currently she also serves as President of the Comparative Literature Association of ROC. She received her Ph.D. in English from the University of Wisconsin-Madison (1994). Feng writes on issues of gender, race, and representation in films as well as in Asian American, African American and Afro-Caribbean literatures. Her publications include *The Female Bildungsroman by Toni Morrison and Maxine Hong Kingston*

(1998) and *En-Gendering Chinese Americas: Reading Chinese American Women Writers* (2001). She is also the Chinese translator of Toni Morrison's *Love* (2005).

YIORGOS KALOGERAS is Professor of American Ethnic and Minority Studies, Aristotle University, Thessaloniki, Greece. He specializes in Greek immigration to the USA. His most recent publications include the new editions of Demetra Vaka Brown's narratives about the Ottoman harems, *Haremlik: Some Pages from the Life of Turkish Women* (2004) [originally published in 1909] and *The Unveiled Ladies of Stamboul* (2005) [originally published in 1923].

STEPANKA KORYTOVA-MAGSTADT has lived in the Czech Republic, and was educated in the UK, and US. She holds a Ph.D. in History from Charles University, Prague and she currently teaches American Studies there as well as at the University of West Bohemia at Pilsen. She has published a book on Czech emigration, *To Reap a Bountiful Harvest: Czech Migration Beyond the Mississippi River, 1860-1900* and articles on migration and ethnicity. She is interested in ethnic women's clubs in Chicago, and works on a manuscript on diaspora and its ties to the Homeland.

CHRIS LALONDE is the author of *Grave Concerns, Trickster Turns: The Novels of Louis Owens, William Faulkner and the Rites of Passage*, and numerous articles on Native American literatures and modern American literature. He is an Associate Professor of English and Native American Studies at the State University of New York, College at Oswego.

STEFANO LUCONI (Ph.D. in American Studies) teaches History of North America at the University of Florence, Italy, and specializes in Italian immigration to the United States. His publications in this field include *Little Italies e New Deal: Lacoalizione rooseveltiana e il voto italo-americano a Filadelfia e Pittsburg* (Milan: Angeli, 2002).

LINDA J. MANNEY is a trained cognitive linguist and completed a M.A. and Ph.D. in Linguistics at the University of California, San Diego, U.S.A. Her research interests include critical discourse analysis, cognitive anthropology and sociocultural models of language acquisiton. She has published a number of articles in *Studies in Language, Functions of Language, Journal of Modern Greek Studies*, and the *Journal of the Hellenic Diaspora*, and a monograph *Middle Voice in Modern Greek* published by John Benjamins (2000).

SHARMINA MAWANI is a final year PhD student in the Department for the Study of Religions at School of Oriental and African Studies (SOAS) University of London, UK. She completed her Masters degree in Social Anthropology from the London School of Economics. Her Masters dissertation is entitled *Devotional Songs of the South Asian Nizari Ismailis in Toronto: The Attitudes of the Older Generation*. Currently she is investigating the centrality of the *ginans* (devotional songs) in the formation of the ethno-linguistic and religious identities of the Nizari Ismaili Muslims of Gujarati ancestry in Toronto and Mumbai. She is particularly interested in the manner in which traditional religious practices are evolving in contemporary western society.

KAEKO MOCHIZUKI graduated from Tsuda College, Tokyo. She finished graduate school at Tsuda College in 1975 and in 1976 she graduated from Smith College, Northampton. Since 1977, she is a Professor at Ehime University.

ANJOOM MUKADAM is Co-Director of the Evaluation Unit at the Centre for Excellence in Leadership, Lancaster University. She received her doctorate in Sociolinguistics from the University of Reading in December 2003. Her thesis is entitled *Gujarati Speakers in London: Age, Gender and Religion in the Construction of Identity*.

GARY Y. OKIHIRO is professor of international and public affairs and director of the Center for the Study of Ethnicity and Race at Columbia University in the City of New York.

JOHN LLOYD PURDY is Professor of English at Western Washington University. His works include *Word Ways: The Novels of D'Arcy McNickle* (1990), and *The Legacy of D'Arcy McNickle: Writer, Historian, Activist* (1996), which he edited. He has published poetry and fiction in national journals and numerous articles and interviews on/with Native American authors, including James Welch, Leslie Marmon Silko, N. Scott Momaday, Louis Owens, Simon Ortiz, Sherman Alexie, Gerald Vizenor and Elizabeth Cook Lynn. He won the Writer of the Year award from the Wordcraft Circle of Native American Writers and Storytellers for his anthology, *Nothing But the Truth: An Anthology of Native American Literatures*.

SIDONIE SMITH is Martha Guernsey Colby Collegiate Professor of English and Women's Studies and Chair of the English Department at the University of Michigan. Her fields of interest include human rights and personal narrative, women's autobiography, women's travel narrative and memory, women's studies in literature more generally, feminist theory, and postcolonial literatures. Prof. Smith's publications include: *A Poetics of Women's Autobiography: Marginality and the Fictions of Self-Representation* (Indiana University Press, 1987); *Subjectivity, Identity, and the Body: Women's Autobiographical Practices in the Twentieth Century* (Indiana University Press, 1993); *Getting a Life: Everyday Uses of Autobiography* (co-edited with Julia Watson, University of Minnesota Press, 1996); *Writing New Identities: Gender, Nation, and Immigration in Contemporary Europe* (co-edited with Gisela Brinker-Gabler, University of Minnesota Press, 1997); *Women, Autobiography, Theory: A Reader* (co-edited with Julia Watson, University of Wisconsin Press, 1998); *Reading Autobiography: A Guide for Interpreting Life Narratives* (with Julia Watson, University of Minnesota, 2001); *Moving Lives: Women's Twentieth Century Travel Narratives* (University of Minnesota, 2001); *Interfaces: Women's Visual and Performance Autobiography* (co-edited with Julia Watson, University of Michigan Press, 2002); *Human Rights and Narrated Lives: The Ethics of Recognition* (with Kay Schaffer, Palgrave Macmillan, 2004); and numerous articles.

ELKE STURM TRIGONAKIS was born in Germany, studied Latin, English, French and Russian at school and finished her basic studies in Romanic Philology in Heidelberg in 1986 receiving an M.A in Spanish Literature, Portuguese Linguistics and General Linguistics. In 1993, she completed her Ph.D. thesis, a comparative study of the city novel which was eventually published in German and Catalan. After two years as lecturer in Spanish Literature at the University of Paderborn/Germany, she was appointed lecturer in Comparative Literature at the Department of German Language of the Aristotle University Thessaloniki. Her research interests include urban literature, the picaresque novel, world literature, hybridity and multilingualism.

ILANA XINOS received her BA in English from the College of William and Mary and is currently a Ph.D. candidate at Louisiana State University.

HALE YILMAZ has recently defended her dissertation entitled "Reform, Social Change and State-Society Encounters in early Republican Turkey" at the University of Utah. She is currently a Visiting Assistant Professor at the University of Montana, where she teaches Middle Eastern history.